W9-BIE-596

The Rhetoric of Humor

A BEDFORD SPOTLIGHT READER

The Rhetoric of Humor

A BEDFORD SPOTLIGHT READER

Kirk Boyle
University of North Carolina Asheville

bedford/st.martin's
Macmillan Learning
Boston | New York

For Bedford/St. Martin's
Vice President, Editorial, Macmillan Learning Humanities: Edwin Hill
Editorial Director, English: Karen S. Henry
Senior Publisher for Composition, Business and Technical Writing,
Developmental Writing: Leasa Burton
Executive Editor: John E. Sullivan III
Developmental Editor: Jonathan Douglas
Publishing Services Manager: Andrea Cava
Production Supervisor: Carolyn Quimby
Marketing Manager: Joy Fisher Williams
Project Management: Jouve
Photo Research Manager: Martha Friedman
Photo Researcher: Sheri Blaney
Permissions Researcher: Barbara Hernandez/Bookworm
Senior Art Director: Anna Palchik
Text Design: Castle Design; Janis Owens, Books By Design, Inc.
Cover Design: William Boardman
Cover Photo: FourOaks / Getty Images
Composition: Jouve
Printing and Binding: RR Donnelley and Sons

Copyright © 2017 by Bedford/St. Martin's.

Manufactured in the United States of America.

1   0   9   8   7   6
f   e   d   c   b   a

For information, write: Bedford/St. Martin's, 75 Arlington Street, Boston,
MA 02116   (617-399-4000)

ISBN 978-1-319-02013-2

Acknowledgments

*Text acknowledgments and copyrights appear at the back of the book on pages
333-335, which constitute an extension of the copyright page. Art acknowledgments and copyrights appear on the same page as the art selections they cover.*

The Bedford Spotlight Reader Series is a growing line of single-theme readers, each featuring Bedford's trademark care and quality. The readers in the series collect thoughtfully chosen readings sufficient for an entire writing course—about 35 selections—to allow instructors to provide carefully developed, high-quality instruction at an affordable price. Bedford Spotlight Readers are designed to help students make inquiries from multiple perspectives, opening up topics such as borders, food, gender, happiness, humor, money, monsters, and sustainability to critical analysis. An editorial board of a dozen compositionists whose programs focus on specific themes have assisted in the development of the series.

Bedford Spotlight Readers offer plenty of material for a composition course while keeping the price low. Each volume in the series offers multiple perspectives on the topic and its effects on individuals and society. Chapters are built around central questions such as "What takes place when we laugh?" and "What determines what we eat?" and so offer numerous entry points for inquiry and discussion. High-interest readings, chosen for their suitability in the classroom, represent a mix of genres and disciplines as well as a choice of accessible and challenging selections to allow instructors to tailor their approach. Each chapter thus brings to light related—even surprising—questions and ideas.

A rich editorial apparatus provides a sound pedagogical foundation. A general introduction, chapter introductions, and headnotes provide context. Following each selection, writing prompts provide avenues of inquiry tuned to different levels of engagement, from reading comprehension ("Understanding the Text") to critical analysis ("Reflection and Response"), to the kind of integrative analysis appropriate to research papers ("Making Connections"). A web site for the series offers support for teaching, with a sample syllabus, additional readings, video links, and more; visit **macmillanlearning.com/spotlight**.

The comedian Mel Brooks once said that "tragedy is when I cut my finger; comedy is when you fall into an open sewer and die." We laugh at Brooks's definition of comedy, but why? We intuitively recognize humor when we hear and see it, but we frequently struggle to explain why we "make the spasmodic inarticulate sounds, the movements of the facial muscles, shaking of the sides, etc., which are the instinctive expressions of lively amusement, scorn, exultation, etc." (the definition of the verb *laugh* from the *Shorter Oxford English Dictionary*). Indeed, genuine laughter is involuntary, an unconscious physical reaction to a humorous stimulus that can be so pleasurable it hurts. All of us can fondly remember a time when we laughed so hard that tears streamed down our faces and we convulsed until our bellies ached. Listening to someone explain why something is funny can often be just as painful, however. Author E. B. White compared studying humor to dissecting a frog: "Humor can be dissected," quipped White, "but the thing dies in the process." We may initially laugh at the idea of someone falling into an open sewer and dying, but the laughs soon fade when we painstakingly review each step in the person's demise and strive to explain why we found it funny in the first place.

White's observation, then, certainly has its merit. A joke requiring explanation is often a failed joke, and a recounted humorous incident can lose its comic luster. Nevertheless, the intellectual satisfactions derived from examining humor as a cultural phenomenon outlast the fleeting pleasures of mindless consumption or uncritical veneration of comedians and comedic texts. This book wagers that students can improve their academic writing skills by honing their sense of humor and that their enjoyment of the latter will make the former less difficult. It presupposes that educators need not choose between teaching and delighting. Pedagogy can, to borrow Horace's maxim about poetry, entertain as it instructs. Professors can design first-year writing courses that combine laughing with learning so that students obtain *and* retain rhetorical knowledge that facilitates their becoming better critical readers and academic writers. To learn about laughing is to learn while laughing.

The ubiquity of humor makes it not only a powerful teaching tool but also a topic with a solid chance of piquing students' interest. All humans laugh, and we laugh at many of the same things for strikingly similar reasons regardless of our different cultural identities or particular senses of humor. Even when we serve as the butt of a joke or as an outsider not privy to a laugh, difference-dependent comedy enlightens us about our humanity—or inhumanity, as the case may be. In short, what we laugh at reveals who we are.

Like the issues of borders, food, happiness, money, monsters, gender, and sustainability in the other Bedford Spotlight Readers, humor has the kind of universal relevance requisite for general education courses. However, most American institutions of higher education do not bear out the verity of British-educated psychologist Edward de Bono's claim that "[h]umor is by far the most significant behavior of the human mind."[1] Although literature departments and film programs teach comedy as a genre from time to time, humor and laughter remain understudied in the academy. This curricular oversight is understandable, considering that humor lacks a home discipline. However, the same interdisciplinary nature of humor that limits its appearance on university syllabi makes it the perfect topic to use in general education courses that introduce students to academic writing and inquiry across the disciplines. Comedic texts and performers question societal assumptions and up-end our commonsense perceptions of reality, which is precisely the purpose of the critical thinking skills we instill in our first-year writing, humanities, liberal arts, and cultural studies students.

Thus far, I have made a case explaining why humor, as a pedagogical device, interdisciplinary subject, and form of critical thinking itself, belongs in the university's core curriculum. I now turn to why humor works as a theme for a first-year writing course. I designed *The Rhetoric of Humor* to avoid three traps common to theme-based composition courses: *thematic creep,* which adversely affects a course's structure; *thematic polemic,* which adversely affects its content; and *thematic fatigue,* which adversely affects its audience. Thematic creep refers to the widespread concern among instructors about adopting a theme for a course that they feel is already overburdened with material to cover and learning outcomes to meet. Themes threaten to overrun first-year writing courses with class discussions on sociological content that crowds out coverage of academic argumentation; rhetorical concerns about persuasion, structure, and style; and the conventions of grammar, punctuation, and mechanics. In the past, when I developed writing courses on labor studies, an election season, or college itself, for example, my students and I would inevitably get caught up exploring the topic at the expense of focusing on writing. Because comedy is not only an issue worthy of

---

[1]Quoted in Angela Balakrishnan, "Edward de Bono: 'Iraq? They just need to think it through,'" *The Guardian*, April 23, 2007.

critical examination but also a discursive style and genre, instructors who teach a humor-themed writing course need not fret over competing course content. Analyses of comedic language never veer far from questions about writing and argumentation.

To highlight the connection between humor and rhetoric, I have structured this book's five chapters according to the elements of Kenneth Burke's dramatistic pentad: act, scene, agent, purpose, and agency. Burke developed his theatrical model of symbolic action in *A Grammar of Motives* (1945) to answer the question, "What is involved when we say what people are doing and why they are doing it?"[2] With this model as a foundation, *The Rhetoric of Humor* invites students to investigate what people are doing in humorous rhetorical situations and why. It asks them to explore and communicate their understanding of the following:

- What takes place during a comic **act**
- How **scene** influences whether or not an act is humorous
- Who or what is a comic **agent** or comedian
- What is the **purpose** of political satire
- How one composes (**agency**) an effective comic argument

The readings focus on the rhetorical element of their respective chapters. In addition, introductory headnotes and follow-up questions accompany each reading and emphasize other concepts essential to rhetorical analysis, such as audience, author, mode, genre, forum, context, style, stasis, thesis, ethos, logos, pathos, evidence, assumptions, fallacies, ideology, and so on. Of course, no thematic reader can replace the rigor of a handbook on rhetoric, and I would advise instructors to visit **macmillanlearning.com /spotlight** for supplemental materials that will reinforce rhetorical instruction, such as a sample syllabus and additional readings and video links that you may find useful. You can also learn more about Jeff Ousborne's concise book on reading, writing, and research processes, *Critical Reading and Writing: A Bedford Spotlight Rhetoric*, which you can package with this book for free. Together with *The Rhetoric of Humor*, these resources will familiarize your students with the key components of a rhetorical situation as they study the *what, when, where, who, why,* and *how* of humor.

While thematic creep jeopardizes the structure of a first-year writing course, thematic polemic dissuades student buy-in to course content. For

---

[2]Kenneth Burke, *A Grammar of Motives*, Berkeley: University of California Press, 1969/1945, xv.

the most part, students understand that humans are political animals for whom everything is an argument, but they often resist composition courses that appear more interested in promoting a political agenda than in delivering writing instruction. I have not shied away from politics in choosing selections that address offensive humor, joke about diversity and identity issues, and rebuke the privileged and powerful, not to mention the creation of an entire chapter devoted to the role of satire in a democratic society. Humor is certainly as political as any other course theme, perhaps more so, but it is a political issue of form rather than content. The theme of humor gets students to analyze the rhetoric as much as the substance of arguments concerning social class, gender, race, ethnicity, disability, age, and sexuality, and it permits your writing class to be political in general as opposed to being committed to a particular political issue or partisan cause.

A course focused on the rhetoric of humor enables students to interrogate their world without indoctrinating them in a particular ideology. Because humor often works to defuse tension and get people of different political stripes talking about difficult issues, writing instructors can use comic rhetoric to mediate civil discourse in the classroom and on the page. A humor-themed writing course empowers students to think and write critically about political issues and cultural productions that matter to them. Such a course puts into practice Russel Durst's pragmatic theory for overcoming the schism between functional and critical pedagogies of composition: *reflective instrumentalism*.[3] Students learn the basic moves of academic writing that they will need to succeed in their collegiate and professional careers by reading comic arguments and writing arguments about humor, and vice versa (reading arguments about humor and writing their own comic arguments). At the same time, they strike their own balance between accommodating the status quo and challenging its dictates.

I have already mentioned reasons why teaching the rhetoric of humor should help you avoid the third pitfall of a required general education course: thematic fatigue. Over the course of a ten- to sixteen-week semester, the motivation of students to read and write about a single cultural studies theme is likely to wane. In my experience, cultivating students' comic sensibilities by raising their rhetorical awareness increases and maintains their morale with regard to writing, especially with a mix of assignments that provide them leeway on choosing topics. Prompt your

---

[3]See Durst's book *Collision Course: Conflict, Negotiation, and Learning in College Composition* (NCTE, 1999).

students to write essays that theorize how a comedic text creates humor; that analyze the rhetoric of their favorite comedian; that use research-based evidence to argue about the social, political, and/or historical significance of a comedic genre; and that persuade an audience while making them laugh.

Humor is pleasurable by its very nature: it aims to amuse. By contrast, writing well is difficult and frequently distressing for amateurs in general and for first-year writing students in particular. Most students arrive on campus intimidated by the prospect of learning how to become a college-level writer. Successful courses — like persuasive essays — are designed with their audience in mind, and students respond positively to a certain amount of levity in the first-year writing classroom. A humor-themed course can help you deliver writing instruction while teaching students to welcome the hazards of learning. Education can be painful at times, but it is not joyless, especially when coupled with intellectual humility, courage, and perseverance . . . to say nothing of a sense of humor. It is my hope that this book can help you teach your students to embrace and overcome these challenges, and maybe even have some fun while doing so.

Acknowledgments

I have taught composition courses since 2001, and have desired to edit a single-themed reader for at least half that tenure. I wish first to thank the executive editor of The Bedford Spotlight Reader Series, John E. Sullivan III, for giving me the opportunity to fulfill this professional goal and for overseeing the project in its early stages of development. I am also grateful that he put this book into the hands of Jonathan Douglas, who has proven to be a most astute and amiable editor. It was a pleasure to work with Jonathan through myriad drafts of the manuscript, which improved significantly with his guidance. Thanks also to John Shannon, Andrea Cava, and Marianne L'Abbate for their work in preparing the final manuscript.

The reviewers who commented on the proposal provided invaluable feedback on shaping the individual chapters and maintaining a focus on rhetoric. Jonathan Alexander (University of California, Irvine) has long been a mentor, and I thank him for his recommendation to include more readings about genre. My good friend Abby Dubisar (Iowa State University) sent me articles on humor and rhetoric for months after commenting on the proposal. Thank you also to Jessica Cooke (University of North Georgia), Jared Hegwood (Georgia Regents University), Matthew Horton (University of North Georgia), and Jason Palmeri (Miami University).

This book would not have been possible without Lorena Russell, the director of the University of North Carolina Asheville's (UNCA) quality enhancement plan on critical thinking. The courses I developed while participating in this program allowed me to test my hypothesis that comedy can promote critical thinking in the classroom, and I thank Lorena for her generous support, professional guidance, and friendship.

I am grateful to many folks who have informed my writing pedagogy over the years and who provided advice that helped shape this particular book. My colleagues at UNCA who teach first-year writing are an incredible bunch. It's a pleasure to work with Deborah James, Erica Abrams-Locklear, Cynthia Chadwick, Eileen Crowe, Brian Graves, Evan Gurney, Anne Jansen, Leslee Johnson, Katherine Min, Tamiko Murray, Jessica Pisano, Deaver Traywick, and Amanda Wray. My department chair, Merritt Moseley, shared his insights on humor and has been a superb mentor, as have been Patrick Bahls, Gary Ettari, Michael Gillum, David Hopes, Lori Horvitz, and Holly Iglesias. I owe UNCA alum Jesse Rice-Evans a debt of gratitude for drawing my attention to Julia Drake's "The Boy from *Jurassic Park*'s College Application Essay." I am obliged to everyone in the Department of English at Francis Marion University, where I spent a memorable year teaching first-year writing courses. Special thanks goes to Amy Lea Clemons for keeping Kenneth Burke on my mind. From my formative decade at the University of Cincinnati (UC), I would like to thank Kristin Carlson, Kristin Czarnecki, Russell Durst, Michele Griegel-Mccord, Alli Hammond, Margaret Lindgren, Molly McCaffery, Laura Micciche, Robert Murdock, and Lucy Schultz. The friends I made as a teaching assistant and then adjunct professor at UC are too numerous to list—you know who you are. From the bottom of my heart, thank you for making me a better pedagogue and person. Thanks also to Michael Griffith for recommending Chris Bachelder's essay "The Dead Chipmunk," and to Lisa Beckelhimer for sharing her experience with editing a composition reader. I would be remiss if I did not acknowledge my writing students from the past fifteen years at the University of Cincinnati, Northern Kentucky University, Thomas More College, Francis Marion University, and the University of North Carolina Asheville. I especially thank those who wrote essays and contributed to class discussions about the rhetoric of humor.

I owe my sense of humor to my friends and family. As with all that I do, this book would not have been possible without their love and support. Thank you, thank you, thank you.

Finally, I dedicate this book to my partner in crime, Amber. Without her making me laugh every day, I don't know what I would do.

— Kirk Boyle

Bedford/St. Martin's offers resources and format choices that help you and your students get even more out of your book and course. To learn more about or to order any of the following products, contact your Bedford/St. Martin's sales representative, e-mail sales support (**sales_support@bfwpub.com**), or visit the web site at **macmillanlearning.com/spotlight**.

Select Value Packages

Add value to your text by packaging one of the following resources with *The Rhetoric of Humor*. To learn more about package options for any of the following products, contact your Bedford/St. Martin's sales representative or visit **macmillanlearning.com/spotlight**.

Writer's Help 2.0 is a powerful online writing resource that helps students find answers whether they are searching for writing advice on their own or as part of an assignment.

- **Smart search**
  Built on research with more than 1,600 student writers, the smart search in Writer's Help 2.0 provides reliable results even when students use novice terms, such as *flow* and *unstuck*.

- **Trusted content from our best-selling handbooks**
  Choose *Writer's Help 2.0, Hacker Version*, or *Writer's Help 2.0, Lunsford Version*, and ensure that students have clear advice and examples for all of their writing questions.

- **Adaptive exercises that engage students**
  Writer's Help 2.0 includes LearningCurve, game-like online quizzing that adapts to what students already know and helps them focus on what they need to learn.

Student access can be packaged with *The Rhetoric of Humor* at a significant discount. Order package ISBN 978-1-319-10691-1 for *Writer's Help 2.0, Hacker Version*, or package ISBN 978-1-319-10688-1 for *Writer's Help 2.0, Lunsford Version*, to ensure that your students have easy access to online writing support. Students who rent a book or buy a used book can purchase access to Writer's Help 2.0 at **macmillanlearning.com/writershelp2**.

Instructors may request free access by registering as an instructor at **macmillanlearning.com/writershelp2**. For technical support, visit **macmillanlearning.com/getsupport**.

LaunchPad Solo for Readers and Writers allows students to work on whatever they need help with the most. At home or in class, students learn at their own pace, with instruction tailored to each student's unique needs. *LaunchPad Solo for Readers and Writers* features:

- **Prebuilt units that support a learning arc**
  Each easy-to-assign unit is comprised of a pretest check, multimedia instruction and assessment, and a posttest that assesses what students have learned about critical reading, the writing process, using sources, grammar, style, and mechanics help for multilingual writers.

- **Video introductions to many topics**
  Introductions offer an overview of the unit's topic, and many include a brief, accessible video to illustrate the concepts at hand.

- **Adaptive quizzing for targeted learning**
  Most units include LearningCurve, game-like adaptive quizzing that focuses on the areas in which each student needs the most help.

- **The ability to monitor student progress**
  Use our Gradebook to see which students are on track and which need additional help with specific topics.

LaunchPad Solo for Readers and Writers can be **packaged at a significant discount**. Order package ISBN 978-1-319-10693-5 to ensure that your students can take full advantage. Visit **macmillanlearning.com/catalog /readwrite** for more information.

Critical Reading and Writing: A Bedford Spotlight Rhetoric, **by Jeff Ousborne**, is a brief supplement that provides coverage of critical reading, thinking, writing, and research. It is designed to work with any of the books in The Bedford Spotlight Reader Series. *Critical Reading and Writing: A Bedford Spotlight Rhetoric* (a $10 value!) can be packaged for **free** with your book. Contact your sales representative for a package ISBN.

Portfolio Keeping, **Third Edition, by Nedra Reynolds and Elizabeth Davis**, provides all the information that students need to use the portfolio method successfully in a writing course. *Portfolio Teaching*, a companion guide for instructors, provides the practical information that instructors and writing program administrators need to use the portfolio method successfully in a writing course. To order *Portfolio Keeping* packaged with this text, contact your local sales representative for a package ISBN.

Package with *any* brief rhetoric at a significant discount. Visit **macmillanlearning.com/rhetorics** to see the many books available, and contact your sales representative for a package ISBN.

Instructor Resources

You have a lot to do in your course. Bedford/St. Martin's wants to make it easy for you to find the support you need—and to get it quickly.

The additional instructor's resources for *The Rhetoric of Humor* are available as downloadable files from the Bedford/St. Martin's online catalog at **macmillanlearning.com/spotlight**. In addition to a sample syllabus, the instructor's resources include a list of additional readings, web sites, videos, and other resources on the rhetoric of humor to assign with the book.

Teaching Central offers the entire list of Bedford/St. Martin's print and online professional resources in one place. You'll find landmark reference works, sourcebooks on pedagogical issues, award-winning collections, and practical advice for the classroom—all free for instructors. Visit **macmillanlearning.com/teachingcentral**.

Join our community! The Macmillan English Community is now Bedford/St. Martin's home for professional resources, featuring *Bedford Bits*, our popular blog site offering new ideas for the composition classroom and composition teachers. Connect and converse with a growing team of Bedford authors and top scholars who blog on *Bits*: Andrea Lunsford, Nancy Sommers, Steve Bernhardt, Traci Gardner, Barclay Barrios, Jack Solomon, Susan Bernstein, Elizabeth Wardle, Doug Downs, Liz Losh, Jonathan Alexander, and Donna Winchell.

In addition, you'll find an expanding collection of additional resources that support your teaching.

- Sign up for webinars.
- Download resources from our professional resource series that support your teaching.
- Start a discussion.
- Ask a question.
- Follow your favorite members.
- Review projects in the pipeline.

Visit **community.macmillan.com** to join the conversation with your fellow teachers.

Contents

Introduction for Students   1

Chapter 1   Act: What Takes Place When We Laugh?   9

Chapter 2   Scene: When and Where Does Humor Occur?   67

Chapter 3   Agent: Who (or What) Is a Comedian?   127

Chapter 4 Purpose: What Is the Function of Satire in a Democratic Society? 203

Chapter 5 Agency: How Do You Write a Comic Argument? 271

Contents by Discipline

Gender and Sexuality Studies

Journalism

Literature

Philosophy

Political Science

Contents by Theme

Film and Television

Gender and Women's Experiences

The Politics of Humor

Social Media and the Internet

Theories of Humor

The Rhetoric of Humor

A BEDFORD SPOTLIGHT READER

Introduction for Students

The comic frame should enable people to be observers of themselves, while acting. Its ultimate [goal] would not be passiveness, but maximum consciousness. One would 'transcend' [one]self by noting [one's] own foibles.

—Kenneth Burke[1]

What Is Rhetoric?

Rhetoric is the art of persuasion, the effective use of language to achieve a goal like convincing someone to go to a party, become vegan, or join the armed services. We study rhetoric to assess the quality of arguments, and we practice rhetoric to improve our advocacy skills. If you want to lower your chances of being duped while increasing your odds at being influential, you study and practice rhetoric. In many respects, you are already a student of rhetoric, but you may not fully realize it. You deliver hundreds of messages each day with how you dress, consume, move about, text, and socialize, and you interpret the subtle rhetorical cues of others in order to determine if you identify with them or not. More explicitly, you converse with your family, friends, classmates, and coworkers, and you decode the appeals made by advertisers for your dollar and by politicians for your vote. Learning about rhetoric in college will not only strengthen your skills as a writer, orator, reader, and listener, reader and listener but will also make you a better student of life.

University writing instructors have long used the work of Kenneth Burke (1897–1993) to teach rhetorical appeals and analysis. Many textbooks on academic writing, for example, cite Burke's famous parlor passage to introduce the concept of argument:

> Imagine that you enter a parlor. You come late. When you arrive, others have long preceded you, and they are engaged in a heated discussion, a discussion too heated for them to pause and tell you exactly what it is about. In fact, the discussion had already begun long before any of them

---

[1] Kenneth Burke, *Attitudes Toward History*. Boston: Beacon Press, 1961/1937, 171.

got there, so that no one present is qualified to retrace for you all the steps that had gone before. You listen for a while, until you decide that you have caught the tenor of the argument; then you put in your oar. Someone answers; you answer him; another comes to your defense; another aligns himself against you, to either the embarrassment or gratification of your opponent, depending upon the quality of your ally's assistance. However, the discussion is interminable. The hour grows late, you must depart. And you do depart, with the discussion still vigorously in progress.[2]

Burke uses the parlor as a metaphor of the rhetorical situation. To make a persuasive case, you must first listen to what others have said. Only after reading to become informed about a controversial issue or disputable question — a *stasis*, in rhetorical terms — can you arrive at a defensible *thesis*, or position on the issue. While composing your main argument, you qualify your claims based on the objections of naysayers and the evidence you gather from research. You receive feedback from your peers and professor. You revise. You eventually submit a polished product, but it will not be the final word in this heated debate.

Why Should I Study the Rhetoric of Humor?

Extending beyond academic argument, Burke's parlor metaphor intimates that human life is fundamentally rhetorical. Many questions we tackle long precede and survive us because they cannot ultimately be answered, only pragmatically debated. We are familiar with such questions being posed by philosophers, politicians, and art critics; however, scientists who devote themselves to examining the cosmos objectively also engage in debates over problems that they confront at the limits of empirical knowledge. Even when they can accurately describe the harmful effects of the Western diet on our health or the impact of greenhouse gases on global climate change, for example, they must rely on rhetoric to frame their findings in a significant way that spurs political action and secures further research funding.

Rhetoricians interpret the symbolic world to understand and alter that which is socially constructed. Human beings are biological animals, of

---

[2]Kenneth Burke, *The Philosophy of Literary Form: Studies in Symbolic Action.* Berkeley: University of California, 1973/1941, 110–111.

course, but we are also, in the words of Burke, "symbol-using animals." Our difference from other fauna is perhaps nowhere more evident than in our laughter at animals acting like humans and humans acting like animals. Think of internet memes and comic strips that translate the thoughts of cats and dogs, or a time when your friend made an involuntary noise in public. We get a kick out of these texts and moments because they reveal the human condition as one caught between a world that we inherited from natural evolution and one that we co-create everyday through our society's cultural practices. For rhetoricians like Burke, it is language that makes and marks the difference between natural and human history.

Becoming an adept rhetorician and rhetorical analyzer requires you to grow closely attuned to language, which in turn should make you a more socially aware person — a critical thinker, in other words — and that should come in handy inside and outside your school's walls. It certainly does for comedians. Some of the best critical thinkers in society are humorists. Humor defamiliarizes the world by prompting us to look awry at what we have come to ignore because we have been staring at it for so long. Burke argued that a "perspective by incongruity" could offer a "comic corrective" to thoughtless beliefs and behaviors. Comic perceptions can heighten our self-awareness. Comic writers who produce comedic texts — stand-up routines, sketches, essays, films, television programs, cartoon strips, podcasts, web content, and so on — question what we take for granted, render common sense absurd, and challenge the status quo. In essence, good comedians are master rhetoricians. They use humor to persuade an audience to agree with their worldview, and the laughter they elicit is a form of consensus.

Dramatism and Burke's Pentad

So while this book aims to make you a more competent writer and critical thinker, it also intends to cultivate your sense of humor by increasing your awareness of comic rhetoric. Burke once again proves useful in this endeavor. Recall that Burke had an expansive view of rhetoric. He understood the actions and interactions of us "symbol-using animals" in theatrical terms. For Burke, as Shakespeare famously penned, "All the

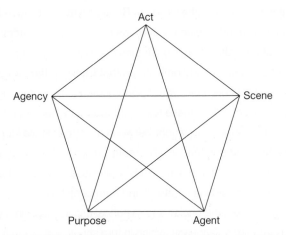

Act

Agency

Scene

Purpose

Agent

Figure 1.1 **This model with the five interconnected elements of dramatism shows one way to visualize Burke's theory.**

world's a stage, / And all the men and women merely players." To understand the motives underlying our actions, Burke devised a heuristic, or learning device, that he called the "dramatistic pentad" (Figure 1.1). As the name suggests, the dramatistic pentad includes five theatrical elements: act, scene, agent, purpose, and agency. Identifying these five elements will help you "map" a *rhetorical situation*. As Burke writes, "any complete statement about motives will offer some kind of answer to these five questions: what was done (act), when or where it was done (scene), who did it (agent), how he did it (agency), and why (purpose)."[3]

Take the comedian Louis C.K.'s (agent) performance of "Everything's Amazing and Nobody's Happy" (act) on Conan O'Brien's late-night show in 2009 (scene). In this comedic bit, which you can view on YouTube, Louis C.K. claims that twenty-first-century technologies have created an "amazing, amazing world" that is "wasted on the crappiest generation of just spoiled idiots that don't care." He creates a perspective by incongruity when he contrasts today's technology with the inconveniences (or sheer absence) of technologies in previous eras (agency). As comic rhetoric, "Everything's Amazing and Nobody's Happy" makes us laugh in recognition

[3]Kenneth Burke, *A Grammar of Motives*. Berkeley: University of California, 1969/1945, xv.

of such entitled behavior. Because we ourselves are most likely guilty of complaining about what we should recognize as privileges, the bit also serves to remind us to remain in awe of our technology and not take it for granted (purpose). In framing our foible comically, Louis C.K. enables us to become more self-aware and able to transcend our limited purview.

By identifying the elements of the dramatistic pentad, we are able to arrive at an interpretation of this particular piece of comic rhetoric. We can acquire further understanding of the rhetoric of humor by analyzing the interrelationships between the elements (what Burke called "ratios"). Focusing on the relationship between scene and agent, for example, we discover that Conan's show provides Louis C.K. with a platform to - promote his ethical brand of humor. A purpose-act ratio emphasizes Conan's motive to put on a hit show, hence his role in co-creating the act by interviewing Louis C.K.

The Organization of This Book

This book is organized around Burke's dramatistic pentad, with each of the five chapters devoted to a central question on one of the elements. While readings have been selected for their emphasis on a chapter's element, it bears repeating that each of the five elements implies the others. Therefore, concentrate on the chapter's element as you read a selection but also contemplate its relationship with others in the pentad. For any assigned reading, ask yourself: What ratios predominate? Act-agent? Purpose-agency? Scene-act? Burke's dynamic model will also allow you to draw connections between readings in different chapters, especially with the aid of the "Making Connections" questions that follow each reading.

Chapter 1 asks, "what takes place when we laugh?" The essays in this chapter introduce the major theories of humor. Their authors adopt a variety of disciplinary perspectives — philosophical, biological, anthro-pological, psychological, and sociological — to understand acts of comedy. Chapter 2 shifts to the comic scene by posing the question, "when and where does humor occur?" This chapter's selections examine the role of context in determining whether something is funny or not. Authors look at potentially offensive and controversial humor, like ethnic and rape jokes, and consider the influence of genre and medium on comic rhetoric. Chapter 3, "who (or what) is a comedian?," zeroes in on the agent of humor. We often laugh due to *who* is saying what as much as what exactly they are saying. Readings in this chapter continue Chapter 2's look at the role that genre plays in generating laughs, and also explore the various ways that professional stand-up comedians exploit identity politics to create humor that critiques prejudice and oppression. Logically enough, Chapter 4 adopts a politically explicit interpretation of comic purpose. Passages in "what is the function of satire in a democratic society?" consider the political efficacy of irony, parody, and satire in the contemporary world. For example: What do late-night comedy shows, fake news programs, and the pranks of activist groups hope to accomplish? Is it possible for a comedy show to do investigative journalism better than traditional news media? Can laughter pave the way to social change? Last but far from least, Chapter 5 turns to the question of agency in humor and asks, "how do you write a comic argument?" While the book's other chapters prompt you to analyze the rhetoric of humor, this chapter invites you to create your own comic rhetoric. Following a couple of how-to essays that provide general advice on writing comedy, you will find a half dozen exemplary pieces of humor meant to inspire you to write your own comic argument. Just keep in mind that although imitation may be the sincerest form of flattery, plagiarism is the fastest way to failure!

A Note on the Questions

Following each of the book's reading selections, you will find three sets of questions designed to help you think critically about the readings and to kick-start your own writing:

- "Understanding the Text" questions aim to facilitate your reading comprehension. These questions ask you to identify and summarize aspects of the text itself, such as its main ideas or persuasive examples, so read the selections closely and annotate liberally. Underlining key passages and writing comments in the margin will help you recall what you have read, and recollection is vital for comprehension.

- "Reflection and Response" questions lead you to examine the text in more depth and breadth. These questions may encourage you to analyze the rhetorical elements and effects of the text; to offer an opinion on the question at issue, problem at hand, or point in dispute; or to think about how a selection relates to your personal experiences. Brainstorming to collect your thoughts before you start composing your answers will help you engage with the ideas of another author in a more profound and structured manner.

- "Making Connections" questions ask you to consider the text in light of other selections in the book. These questions may invite you to put the text into conversation with selections from the same chapter or to relate it to those found in different chapters. Some provide assignments for writing academic essays on issues raised by the author; others prompt you to write research-based analyses of comedic texts pertinent to the selection. You will often be asked to choose your own primary sources (e.g., sitcoms, sketch shows, stand-up routines, jokes, pranks, cartoons, etc.), and to locate applicable secondary sources to support your argument. The "Making Connections" questions in Chapter 5 provide guidelines for writing your own comedic pieces.

In sum, *The Rhetoric of Humor* is a "textbook" symbolic *act* produced in and for the collegiate *scene* by a professorial *agent* with the *agency* provided by The Bedford Spotlight Reader Series for the *purpose* of helping students like you improve their critical reading and writing skills. May the muses of comedy, rhetoric, and academic writing pay your fingertips many visits as you clack away at the keyboard.

Act: What Takes Place When We Laugh?

Laughter is a peculiar phenomenon if you think about it. When you laugh, you momentarily lose control of your body: it emits weird sounds and it shakes awkwardly, sometimes to the point of convulsing. Your hand may even cover your mouth, face, or gut as you try to regain composure. Perhaps even more strangely, laughter can take place in response to very different situations involving many different types of actors and actions. For example, imagine yourself in the following hypothetical scenarios:

- You are running for your life from a stampeding woolly mammoth when the beast suddenly slips and crashes to the earth. You burst into maniacal laughter.
- You can't stop giggling, waving your arms, and kicking your feet as your parents first cover and then uncover their faces and say "peek-a-boo" in high-pitched voices.
- You join a chorus of insults lobbed at an unpopular classmate. Laughing with the crowd on the playground, you feel a terrific sense of belonging as you mock your clueless classmate.
- Your friend replies, "LMFAO." You reread what you previously texted. Mortified, but laughing out loud, you type, "Autocorrect FAIL! XD."
- Your drunk uncle turns to you at the Thanksgiving table and says, "Have you heard the one about the midget fortune-teller who got away with murder? He's a small medium at large. What about the blind man who walks into a bar . . . and a table? And a chair?" You decide it's time for a second glass of wine.
- You work overtime to afford the pricey tickets for you and your spouse to see a famous person stand up on stage for an hour telling jokes about her boring sex life, her lack of parenting skills, her gender troubles, driving while black, the American palate for microwaveable turnovers, and the brazen corruption of politicians and CEOs.
- You lie on your deathbed and recall one of Oscar Wilde's final quips about his wallpaper: "Either it goes, or I do."

photo: FourOaks / Getty Images

In these scenarios, agents like the clumsy mammoth and the autocorrect function in your phone perform funny acts with no cognizance of their comic agency. Although the professional stand-up comedian and the anything-but-professional drunk uncle tell jokes with the purpose of making you laugh, they may or may not succeed. Likewise, there is nothing particularly funny about a deathbed scene or a helpless classmate during recess. What makes these rhetorical situations potentially humorous is the nature of the act itself, whether it be a pratfall, game, put-down, gaffe, joke, or witty thought.

According to Kenneth Burke, who was introduced in the "Introduction for Students," (p. 1), a rhetorical situation exists only if a meaningful act takes place. Unlike motivated human *action*, instinctual animal *movement* lacks the symbolic significance requisite to be rhetoric. (Although evidence suggests that some animals do act humorously, and consciously so, as John Morreall's selection in this chapter acknowledges.) The dramatistic elements of scene, agent, purpose, and agency may be present in a given situation, but rhetoric is unrealizable without an act. Your philosophy professor would say that an act is a *necessary and sufficient* condition for rhetoric, whereas the other elements are merely sufficient. The act serves as the keystone that holds together the elements of Burke's pentad. If the act is funny, the elements coalesce to form the rhetoric of humor.

That's all well and fine, but what exactly makes an act funny? The readings in this chapter introduce several theories of humor that attempt to explain why we find certain acts comic. The late Leon Rappoport, a former professor of social psychology, starts with a survey of general humor theories, including the popular superiority, incongruity, and relief theories. The aforementioned John Morreall, a renowned humor theorist in his own right, approaches the question of why we laugh from the perspectives of evolutionary biology, developmental psychology, and cultural anthro-pology. From the insights of these scientific disciplines, he deduces "the basic pattern in humor." Professor Peter McGraw believes that he, too, has discovered a grand unified theory of why we find certain predicaments funny, as Joel Warner reports in his selection. Sigmund Freud then builds off his early book on the psychoanalytic significance of jokes to theorize about humor as a coping mechanism. This opening chapter concludes with a model essay that analyzes a comedic text using a humor theory, as Jeffrey Klassen applies philosopher Henri Bergson's famous theory to interpret the cult-classic film *Office Space.*

When introducing his dramatistic pentad, Burke liked to cite Thomas Aquinas's definition of God as *actus purus*, or "pure act." Unlike the God of the Western tradition who creates *ex nihilo*, or "out of nothing," human beings always act within a rhetorical situation. Therefore, when reading about what takes place when we laugh, keep in mind the rhetorical context of humor. Think about the ways in which a comic *act* implies the presence of *agents* within a *scene* who have the means (*agency*) to achieve humorous ends (*purpose*).

What Makes Us Laugh

Leon Rappoport

Leon Rappoport (1932–2009) was a professor of social psychology at Kansas State University (KSU) from 1964 to 2003. Known as "Rap" to his friends, he was an avid outdoorsman who published on several topics, including the Holocaust, food, personality, health psychology, psychohistory, and humor. His courses at KSU were popular with students, especially his course on ethnic humor.

In this excerpt taken from his 2005 book *Punchlines: The Case for Racial, Ethnic and Gender Humor*, Rappoport provides a succinct introduction to several foundational theories of humor. Because theories are abstract by their very nature, a common response to learning about them is, "I knew that; I've just never put the idea into words." When reading about the major humor theories, consider if they explain your experiences of humor.

Most people react to theoretical analyses of any type of humor with either boredom or fascination. Boredom is by far the most frequent response, because the concepts involved are often seen as so far removed from everyday life as to appear useless, or the opposite: the concepts seem to be so much a matter of common sense that anybody with half a brain already understands them. Yet some of us become fascinated with the puzzle-solving nature of theory, the idea that it can help us understand why some jokes work and others fail, or why we laugh when we do not think we should, and other things that may at first seem inexplicable. In all fairness, however, it should also be acknowledged that scholars themselves react to theory with boredom or fascination. B. F. Skinner, the famous psychologist of learning, claimed that most theories were not only boring but also a diversion from mapping the concrete determinants of human behavior. The pioneering social psychologist Kurt Lewin, on the other hand, famously suggested that when studying social behavior—and what is more social than humor?—"There is nothing so practical as a good theory." I am with Lewin on this point, even if the theorizing discussed in the following text turns out to hang too heavily over the spontaneous joys of comedy.

One thing that should be made clear immediately, however, is that the theories and research examined [here] primarily concern the *mechanics* of humor—what makes it work—rather than its larger social meaning. . . . By way of introduction, some attention to the remarkably simplistic early efforts to research and theorize about humor during the late nineteenth and early twentieth century can help explain why it became an intriguing topic for psychology in particular.

Toward the end of the nineteenth century, philosopher-psychologists such as William James, whose experiences with depression may have stimulated his interest, clearly saw humor as a significant challenge to the budding science of human behavior. In fact, at one point in his career James spent considerable time searching for the physiological origins of laughter by experimenting with nitrous oxide, the then–newly discovered laughing gas. But he did not get very far with this, and eventually was satisfied to merely describe laughter as an emotional expression of pleasure that has a number of physiological health benefits. The chapter on emotions in his 1890 *Principles of Psychology* text let it go at that, focusing instead on feelings of sadness and depression. At about the same time that James was trying laughing gas, other investigators attempted to study humor by doing systematic experiments on tickling. (One gets a sense here of the charming innocence that characterized the early psychology researchers.) The only substantial finding to emerge from the tickling work was that people only laugh when tickled by others; they are unable to tickle themselves into laughter. We still do not have a good explanation for this, or for the fact that some people are more ticklish than others, but the findings speak to the social nature of laughter.

There were also a handful of studies done on the ability of individuals to remember jokes, and some Darwinian writers speculated that since laughter and smiling require the baring of teeth, these facial expressions may have evolved from a primitive snarling response to aggression. Since so much humor has an aggressive quality, this idea seemed quite plausible. People do, in fact, sometimes mistake an angry grimace for a smile. Later in the 1920s and 1930s, when psychologists were increasingly concerned to establish themselves as respectable scientists, humor studies languished. There were few sources of funding for research on the topic, and it appeared frivolous compared with more significant problems such as learning and motivation.

But psychologists never entirely gave up on humor as a topic for research. 5 Interest in the topic was stimulated in the early 1970s when a comprehensive review of humor research published by Patricia Keith-Spiegel identified several different approaches to the topic. Each approach is distinguished by a particular theme, but all have in common the underlying idea that our humor is an instinct that must have evolved to serve some important purpose for adaptation or survival. The most persuasive evidence for this comes from studies showing that babies generally begin smiling and laughing at about the age of four months. These early infant smiles first occur as a spontaneous response to tickling, and soon become directly linked to pleasurable contact with the mother or primary care giver. Infants also smile spontaneously a little later on when they begin to master any significant new activity, such as crawling or standing up. By the time they are a year old, babies will laugh when adults make funny faces for them. As might be expected, by age two or sooner, they already seem to know that smiling calls up positive responses from adults.

But if laughter is instinctive, how did it evolve, and why do we value it? Among the many quaint ideas that have been suggested, one that holds up pretty well is that it began as a spontaneous expression of triumph after defeating an enemy or killing an animal. According to this view, laughter evolved from hunter-warrior victory cries that were imitated by tribal or family members, perhaps something like the cheering of fans at sporting events, and eventually came to serve as an "all clear, no danger" signal for the whole group. Laughing together then became the basis for sharing a collective sense of well-being. It has been noted that we can see the remains of such behavior today when the leader of a group begins to laugh at something and all the others present take this as a cue to join in, even if they do not know what the laughter is about. Research has also demonstrated that if an individual is placed in a group where everyone else is laughing, he or she will usually join in without knowing why. Once we get past these ingenious speculations about the origins of laughter and humor, however, several more specific explanations for why we laugh come into play.

The earliest and most fundamental of these explanations centers on the time-honored notion of *superiority*. This includes all of the many variations on the theme of laughter as an expression of pleasure at feeling superior to those who appear uglier, stupider, or more unfortunate than ourselves. The superiority theme was already present in the writings of Plato and Aristotle, the work of Hobbes (seventeenth century), Bergson (early twentieth century), and many others. At the most basic level, an immediate sense of superiority is presumably what triggers our laughter when we see someone slip on a banana peel or clowns tripping over their feet and other kinds of slapstick humor. Their mastery of such physical humor is what made silent-film comedians like Charlie Chaplin and Buster Keaton popular all over the world. Pleasurable feelings of superiority are also why we laugh at the victims of practical jokes. Those who sit on a tack or panic when finding a snake in their bed are immediately rendered inferior to ourselves.

Hobbes described this pleasurable sense of superiority as a feeling of "sudden glory." This is why practical jokes seem especially enjoyable to observers if the victim has a high social status. The higher the status of the victim, the greater is the tendency to glory over making fools of them.

Jokes at the expense of people who are clearly of lower status than the observers may also be enjoyed, but in this instance there is usually some need on the part of observers to reinforce their feeling of superiority. People who are uncertain about their superior position or feel a bit guilty about it are the ones most likely to enjoy witnessing the embarrassment or humiliation of others who are supposed to be inferior to them. Carried to its extreme, such humor becomes sadistic, as when prisoners are abused by their guards. Finally, superiority theory can also be applied to account for the more subtle from of pleasure the Germans call *schadenfreude,* that is, the quietly amused feeling of gratification one may experience at witnessing a disliked colleague or supervisor being "taken down a peg" because of a poor performance or embarrassing error.

If there is any single triggering mechanism that most modern scholars and comedians agree offers the most important explanation of humor, it is encounters with *incongruity.* Even those who acknowledge superiority as a fundamental principle argue in favor of incongruity as the basis for feelings of superiority. The reasoning here is that the sense of superiority gained from observing the victim of a practical joke, for example, ultimately follows from the incongruity of the victim's situation. A tack on the chair or snake in the bed is essentially a contradiction to the normal function of chairs and beds, and suddenly plunges the victim into a humiliating experience of incongruity. Another way to distinguish between the superiority and incongruity interpretations of humor is by noting that the former is an ego-enhancing emotion within the individual, whereas incongruity refers to something outside the individual, a quality of the situation "out there," in the environment. Philosophers such as Kant, Hegel, Schopenhauer, and Bergson all discussed incongruities as a source of humor. Kierkegaard suggested that if a dramatic incongruity is seriously threatening, it becomes the basis for sadness rather than laughter. It is funny to see someone get a pie in the face, but not if there is a brick in the pie. One of the hallmarks of a brilliant clown is the way he or she can quickly cycle an audience through moments of humor and sadness.

Examples of nonthreatening incongruities that stimulate humor are 10 commonplace. Young children laugh when they see a parent make funny faces, whereas adults enjoy the absurd routines that were a staple of the Marx Brothers comedies. Groucho could amuse an audience simply by twitching his eyebrows while making nonsensical conversation with matronly ladies. He was also celebrated for the wonderfully incongruous remark, "I would never join a club that would have me as a member." Incongruity has been a perennial source of humor in plays and films where adults act like children, animals speak good English, or males masquerade as females and vice versa. Henri Bergson's discussion of incongruity also emphasized that contradictions between physical appearances and the social character of situations were a prime condition for laughter. In some obvious cases, these involve self-contradictions, as when a high and mighty professor comes to class with his fly open or lets go a loud fart in the midst of a lecture. What the incongruity theory of humor boils down to is our apparently innate tendency to be amused by scenes that are clearly absurd or contradictory. Many cartoonists specialize in sketching such scenes. One of the most famous examples was a cartoon drawn by Bill Mauldin during World War II. Appealing to the cavalry tradition of shooting a horse with a broken leg, the cartoon showed a tearful soldier pointing his forty-five automatic at the hood of a jeep with a broken wheel. The absurdity of the scene was enhanced by the military practice of referring to its mechanized units as "armored cavalry."

> "What the incongruity theory of humor boils down to is our apparently innate tendency to be amused by scenes that are clearly absurd or contradictory."

The *surprise* theory of humor overlaps with incongruity but simply focuses on sudden, unexpected positive events (finding money in the street, getting an A when you expected a C) that are experienced as a happy shock. The seventeenth-century French philosopher René Descartes noted that it was the mixture of joy and shock at the occurrence of a happy surprise that provoked laughter, and both Hobbes and Darwin also mentioned surprise as an important basis for humor. More specifically in *The Philosophy of Rhetoric* published in 1776, George Campbell discussed surprise as a function of incongruity, saying it was the essence of wit to "excite in the mind an agreeable surprise," and this could be accomplished by "debasing things pompous," "aggrandizing things little and frivolous," or arranging ordinary things in unusual ways. Comedians, of course, know very well that a good punch line to a joke should not only resolve an incongruity but also come as a surprising shock to the audience. [M]any stand-up comedians make strategic use of obscenities and ethnic slurs in order to produce a surprising shock effect. A relevant example was the advice old vaudeville comedians would give to beginners, to the effect that if your act is not working, you can always drop your pants to get a laugh. But perhaps the purest case of surprise humor can be seen in the delight of children when a jack-in-the-box pops up.

Ambivalence theory suggests that laughter occurs when we experience conflicting feelings or emotions. Such ambivalence can follow from an incongruity between emotional states. In one of Plato's dialogues, for example, he notes that laughter may result from the simultaneous experience of incompatible emotions. Specific examples suggested by modern theorists emphasize incongruities between joy and sorrow, love and hate, superiority and inferiority, and so on. A familiar common illustration of ambivalence occurs, for example, when people attending a funeral or memorial service find themselves having to stifle laughter when speakers express pious sentiments about the deceased even though many mourners in attendance remember the individual as a hell-raising atheist. Jewish mother jokes can often generate ambivalent feelings because they call up a mixture of affection for the mother and resentment or anger at some of her domineering behavior. Another variation is the mix of emotions that attracts people to roller coasters: on the one hand fear, and at the same time excitement and mastery of the fear, resulting in uncontrollable laughter.

Cognitive theory, rather than focusing on the emotions, emphasizes the intellectual aspects of humor. In this perspective, laughter is viewed as the outcome of creative problem solving, an activity that requires some degree of information processing or the mental manipulation of symbolically represented persons or concepts. A simple example is the joke about Moses coming down from Mount Sinai and announcing to the waiting crowd, "I have good news and bad news. The good news is that I got Him down to ten. The bad news is adultery is still in." In order to get the point, you would have to know who Moses was, what the Ten Commandments were about, the meaning of adultery, and the fact that one of the Commandments forbids it. Even after processing these concepts, if you did not think people enjoyed adultery, the joke would make no sense. In his 1999 book about jokes, the philosopher Ted Cohen sums up this point by emphasizing that many jokes are "conditional"; they will only work on condition that the audience has both the knowledge and information processing ability required to understand them. Another good example of the necessity for information processing goes something like this: A fellow meets an acquaintance and announces that he is going to tell him a great new stupid joke. Knowing the usual stereotype involved in such jokes, the other guy stops him, saying, "I better warn you I'm Polish," at which the fellow replies, "That's okay, I'll tell it to you slowly." This joke may not register immediately because it takes a moment or two to process the concepts involved. Cartoons also frequently require some level of cognitive processing whereby visual and verbal information are linked together in a way that yields an amusing conclusion. A cartoon in my files by Callahan shows a priest with his arms raised toward heaven standing over a man in a wheelchair, and crying out, "Heal!" In the next box the man who was in the wheelchair is shown crouched on all fours, panting like a dog at the

FRENCH ARMY KNIFE

According to the cognitive theory of humor, Michael Crawford's cartoon above will make you laugh only if you have the relevant knowledge (knowing what a Swiss army knife is, what a corkscrew is for, that the French enjoy wine, etc.), to process the information correctly and you agree with the joke's slightly negative stance toward French people. How would the other theories explain how this joke works?

© Michael Crawford/The New Yorker Collection/The Cartoon Bank

feet of the priest. The humor here requires a stereotyped knowledge of faith healing and recognition of the dog training command "Heel!"

In general, cognitive theory emphasizes a critically important aspect of humor that we often ignore because the mental activity necessary to get a joke happens so quickly. An interesting ramification of cognitive theory has been the effort by a few humor scholars to develop a computer program that can generate jokes. They more or less have the computer randomly matching standard straight lines with a variety of punch lines. But the results so far have not been very funny.

Release and relief theory focuses on the tension arousal and release that 15 must accompany virtually all humor. The general principle here is that there can be no laughter without some prior arousal of tension. This is why so many jokes and comedy routines center on emotionally loaded topics such as sex, toilet behaviors, and politically incorrect ridicule of ethnic groups. ("How do you break a Pole's finger? Punch him in the nose." "What do you get when you cross a French whore with a Jewish

American Princess? A girl who sucks credit cards.") Apart from jokes and pie-in-the-face slapstick routines, the tension built up in many stressful real-life situations can also be released in what we call nervous laughter. In the film and TV series *M*A*S*H*, for example, surgeons operating under difficult conditions were shown making wisecracks in order to cope. This frequently occurs in real life among soldiers, police, and others who are in stressful situations. A classic example was in the film *Butch Cassidy and the Sundance Kid*. When the two outlaws can only escape from a posse by jumping from a high cliff into a river, one of them hesitates, saying, "I can't swim," and the other replies, "Don't worry, the fall will probably kill you." Sigmund Freud's psychoanalytic theory provides the most elaborate tension release explanation for humor.

[Freud's] theory first appeared in a 1905 monograph titled *Jokes and Their Relation to the Unconscious*. Major elements of Freud's humor theory are still widely accepted because of their close fit with common experience. Almost everyone is familiar with the concept of the "Freudian slip," whereby we mistakenly say something embarrassing by mixing up similar words. Typically, the mix-up yields some inadvertent expression of aggression or sexuality. I still recall an incident in junior high school, when a very attractive social studies teacher asked our class if anyone knew why the United States led the world in wheat production, and one of my friends raised his hand, shouting, "The invention of the McCormick raper" instead of reaper. Of course, according to Freud the mixing up of similar words is no accident; it represents the expression of a socially unacceptable motive or wish that has slipped past our internal censor.

Briefly, Freud's approach to humor was based on his three-dimensional view of personality in which primitive, socially unacceptable *id* impulses are inhibited or censored by the moralistic *superego*, while the *ego* or conscious self mediates between them. Accordingly, immoral or other unacceptable material that would ordinarily be inhibited can be released when the superego is evaded, or tricked by the ego's ability to package the forbidden impulse merely as humor. The laughter that follows is understood as catharsis: the sudden release of tension. In terms of everyday life, one of the implications of the theory is that we can get away with making all sorts of insulting, aggressive, or sexual remarks so long as they are delivered in a humorous fashion.

Freud's theory, therefore, has it that all jokes and witty remarks, with the possible exception of childish nonsense, like making funny faces, relates directly or indirectly to some sort of forbidden, socially unacceptable behavior. Even funny faces, such as when children thumb their noses or stick out their tongues, can often be expressions of anger or rejection. In fact, research studies have shown that the most frequent themes of jokes center on sex and/or aggression. This is obviously true of all racial, ethnic, and gender jokes, but practical jokes, like putting a tack on the teacher's chair or a bucket of water over the schoolroom doorway, are also clear examples, along with all forms of slapstick comedy. Aggression carried out in the name of fun is easy to see in various initiation rituals, when people are forced to wear buckets over their heads or recite humiliating lines ("I am a plebe; a plebe is lower than whale shit at the bottom of the ocean on a cloudy day"). Any such situation that creates enough tension to stimulate laughter by onlookers can be taken as evidence of how Freud's ideas relate to the Hobbesian theory of superiority. If the implicit presence of aggression in humor sometimes may seem obscure or debatable, no such problem exists when it comes to sexuality. We have an apparently inexhaustible supply of sexual jokes and comedy routines, where males target females, females target males, and both will often ridicule their own gender group.

In addition to jokes based on aggression and sex, there is the wide range of body processes that are considered unmentionable. Freud himself never discussed bathroom behaviors, farts, belches, and nose picking as topics for humor, but insofar as public discussion of such things can arouse tension or anxiety, they provide further evidence for his theory. A striking "pure case" demonstrating this point was comedian George Carlin's seven dirty words routine on a successful comedy record produced about thirty years ago. Carlin simply recorded seven of the obscene words that were at that time not allowed to be used on radio or TV, even though, as he pointed out, everyone had heard them. And if anyone had not heard them, or did not know what they meant, then it could do them no harm. This sort of thing would not have interested Freud, who was contemptuous of what he considered to be vulgar attempts to get laughs. In some of his later writings compiled in 1959, Freud was at pains to distinguish between higher level, healthy forms of humor and low comedy or wisecracks. He called the former a "rare and precious gift" because it helped people to not take themselves too seriously and could serve as a valuable defense against anger and guilt feelings. Low comedy he just called "trash."

Another aspect of Freud's theory that deserves emphasis is that our laughter at the punch line of a joke is an unconscious reflex. For the most part, we seem to either understand or not understand a joke immediately, and laughter is a reflexive, spontaneous response. Cognitive theorists would object that this appearance of things may be deceptive, but if we have to spend much time thinking about a joke in order to decide whether or not it is funny, then it usually is not.

A potent example of how unconscious processes can become a collective group experience occurs when a comedian occasionally "gets on a roll" or begins to "riff" (rapidly free associate) on a topic that resonates with the audience. Psychologically, what happens here is that the comedian's spontaneous stream of thought on a topic somehow harmonizes with that of the audience, and it is as if the performer and people in the audience become intimately linked together. The audience can be seen hanging on the words of the comedian, chuckling or giggling in anticipation of the next punch line, for as long as this sense of harmony lasts. Freud's theory receives yet another boost from stand-up comedians who say that when they are on a roll with an audience, it feels as if they are sharing a sexual orgasm with them. Comedians push the analogy even further by suggesting that the buildup to a punch line is like sexual foreplay that culminates in a rush of orgiastic laughter. When they can bring this off they experience it as a fantastic "high," superior to anything that can be obtained from drugs. Ironically, it is often because they get so high during their performances that comedians have difficulty "getting down" afterward, and they might begin to use drugs just to cool out.

The idea of a shared group unconscious relevant to humor can be further supported by observations of children (every kindergarten teacher knows this) who may begin to giggle together for no apparent reason except that one of them has started giggling. This is fairly common among teenagers as well, who may occasionally look at each other across a room and begin giggling spontaneously, even while trying not to. We have no simple explanations for such behavior. Followers of Carl Jung's analytical theory would likely appeal to his concept of collective or shared unconscious processes: something in the situation triggers off a funny thought or reaction in the collective unconscious of the people involved. More traditional Freudian theorists, however, might describe it as a form of emotional empathy, whereby people may unconsciously sense the feelings of others. For their part, behaviorist learning psychologists would attribute the phenomenon to some sort of simultaneous conditioned response to a stimulus in the situation. All of these explanations still remain as little more than theoretical speculations.

Parenthetically, it may be worth noting that while Freud's ideas about jokes have had a broad impact on the popular culture, that culture has occasionally struck back. A remarkable example of this appeared in a scholarly article by Sachi Sri Kantha published in 1999 under the title "Sexual Humor on Freud as Expressed in Limericks." From a list of six thousand limericks available in collections such as Bennett Cerf's *Out on a Limerick*, the author identified twenty-one that specifically targeted Freud. Here are two of them.

An early psychologist, Freud
had the blue noses° very anneud,
saying, you cannot be rid
of the troublesome Id,
So it might just as well be enjoyed.

Withdrawal, according to Freud,
is a very good thing to avoid
If practiced each day
your balls will decay
to the size of a small adenoid.°

The author went on to offer a sober discussion of the possible reasons why limerick writers, many of them anonymous, might have chosen to create sexual rhymes about Freud, none of which need concern us here. But his suggestion that Freud himself would have been pleased by the attention seems appropriate.

Freud's ideas have never lacked critics, however, and in his 1983 book *Taking Laughter Seriously*, the philosopher John Morreal argues for a less complex theory of humor. In his view, our laughter depends on only three conditions. First, we must experience a shift in our thoughts or feelings, which is usually stimulated by encountering an incongruity. Second, this change must be sudden or unexpected, and third, it must be pleasurable, something that strikes us as amusing. These conditions can be seen in the following joke circulated prior to the Iraq War. A reporter spots George Bush and Colin Powell in a bar having an argument. He immediately approaches and asks what they are arguing about. Bush exclaims, "He doesn't agree with my plan to kill a million Iraqis and a blond with big tits!" "Oh," says the reporter, "why would you want to kill a blond with big tits?" Bush laughs and turns to Powell: "See, I told you nobody would care about a million Iraqis." Of course, this may be amusing only to critics of President Bush, but given the shift imposed by the incongruity between the Iraqis and the blond, and the sudden change triggered by the punch line, this joke and countless others fit the commonsense model proposed by Morreal. Yet there is still something here in line with Freud because the tension aroused by this joke is based on aggression and sex.

Brief as it is, the foregoing review should also make it obvious that if 25 anything, we have an overabundance of general humor theories. Each of them emphasizes one or more answers to the question of what makes

blue noses: informal term for puritanical people.
adenoid: a mass of lymphatic tissue located at the rear of the nasal cavity.

people laugh, but none of them, not even Freud's theory, really covers all of the possibilities. Morreal, for example, deserves praise for offering a broadly inclusive commonsense analysis, but he has little to say about the deeper cognitive or emotional processes involved. In sum, therefore, when it comes to humor theory at large, you pay your money and take your choice because one size does not fit all.

Understanding the Text

1. How is the incongruity theory related to the superiority theory of humor? In your answer, make sure to define both theories in your own words.

2. How does the ambivalence theory contrast with the cognitive theory? What types of evidence does Rappoport cite to support these two theories?

3. Explain Freud's version of the relief theory of humor.

Reflection and Response

4. As a survey of general humor theories, "What Makes Us Laugh" exemplifies an informational instead of argumentative piece of writing. What distinguishes these two modes of writing? Despite Rappoport's intention to inform, does he appear to favor a specific theory over the others? If you think he does, how do you know?

5. Rappoport concludes that "one size does not fit all" when it comes to the ability of humor theories to account for why we laugh (par. 25). What theory struck you as either the most interesting or most persuasive? Why?

Making Connections

6. The first chapter of this book includes the work of a few theorists mentioned by Rappoport: John Morreall, Sigmund Freud, and Henri Bergson (as expounded upon by Jeffrey Klassen). Use Rappoport and one of these readings to analyze a brief comedic text, e.g., a television sketch, stand-up clip, joke, internet meme, cartoon strip, comic character, and so on. Alternatively, conduct outside research on one of these humor theorists, and write an essay that uses his or her work to analyze a more substantial comedic text, for example, a comedy film or television show, stand-up comedian, podcast, humor web site, joke genre, and so on.

7. Rappoport claims that some general humor theories match particular genres of comedy rather closely. For example, he links superiority theory with slapstick and practical jokes, incongruity with clowns and cartoons, ambivalence with Jewish mother jokes, and relief with stand-up. Choose one of these pairings and write an essay that applies the theory to a specific example of the genre. You could, for instance, employ the incongruity theory to analyze one of Gary Larsen's *The Far Side* cartoons.

From Lucy to *I Love Lucy*: The Evolution of Humor

John Morreall

Why did humans as a species develop a sense of humor? How did humor evolve in tribal and then more advanced human societies? How does a sense of humor develop in the psychology of children? Do animals have a sense of humor? One of today's leading scholars in humor studies, John Morreall, addresses these questions and others in this chapter from his book, *Comic Relief: A Comprehensive Philosophy of Humor* (2009).

A professor of religious studies at the College of William and Mary, Morreall founded the International Society for Humor Studies (ISHS), serves as a board member for *Humor: International Journal of Humor Research*, and runs Humorworks, a service that offers employers keynotes and seminars on humor in the workplace. He is also the author of several books on humor, including *Taking Laughter Seriously* (1983), *The Philosophy of Laughter and Humor* (1987), *Humor Works* (1997), and *Comedy, Tragedy, and Religion* (1999).

Television programs about human evolution often dramatize how hominids began to walk upright, use tools, and harness fire, but we never see them laughing. Archaeologists can inspect the leg bone of a pre-human ancestor like Lucy,° from 3 million years ago, to determine how she walked, but there is no funny bone to reveal if or how she laughed. And even with early *Homo sapiens*, there are no funny stone tools or cave paintings. In thinking about how early humans laughed and how humor evolved, then, we have to work with indirect evidence.

Jan van Hooff provided one useful clue. It is that chimpanzees, bonobos, gorillas, and orangutans have a laugh-like vocalization that accompanies a relaxed open-mouth play face, during tickling and rough-and-tumble play. Humans came from the same evolutionary line as these primates, having split off from chimpanzees 6 million years ago, and from the others before that. So it is reasonable to think of our laughter as evolving from a play signal we inherited from a distant ancestor we share with the great apes.[1]

This hypothesis looks more plausible when we consider that young children today laugh during the same activities in which chimps, gorillas, and orangutans show their laugh-like vocalization and play face. Babies first laugh during mock-aggressive activities like tickling,

Lucy: named after the famous Beatle's song "Lucy in the Sky with Diamonds," Lucy is the name of the 3.2-million-year-old skeletal remains of an *Australopithecus afarensis* specimen exhumed in Ethiopia in 1974.

play-biting, and being tossed into the air and caught. Later they laugh in chasing games like "I'm going to catch you and eat you up!" All of these activities would seem dangerous to the child if they were not done in play. Biting, chasing, and grabbing are obviously aggressive. Tickling consists of grabbing and poking vulnerable areas like the stomach and ribs. Throwing a baby, non-playfully, is child abuse. With most babies, even seeing and hearing an adult laugh isn't enough for them to enjoy these aggressive activities, if they don't know the person. But when the mock aggression comes from someone familiar and trusted, who smiles and laughs, the baby usually joins in the play and laughs, too.

Since young children laugh during the same activities as those in which apes show comparable play signals, and since the laughter of the earliest humans evolved from primate play signals, the development of humor in children today, from non-humorous stimuli like tickling, may well reveal how humor evolved in our species. To go beyond mere play to humor, early humans, like children today, had to engage in what Kant called "the play of thought" — "the sudden transposition of the mind, now to one now to another standpoint in order to contemplate its object."[2]

As many psychological studies have shown, the development of humor 5 in children parallels their cognitive development.[3] While most infants don't laugh until four months, Jean Piaget describes a 2-month-old who would throw his head back to look at things from a different angle, bring his head back upright, and then throw it back again, laughing loudly as he swung between perspectives.[4] By eight months, peekaboo makes most babies laugh in a similar way.

As infants develop eye–hand coordination, they manipulate things to bring on these perceptual shifts, and they enjoy not only the shifts but their ability to produce them. Piaget cites the case of a 7-month-old who had learned to push aside obstacles to reach what he wanted:

When several times in succession I put my hand or a piece of cardboard between him and the toy he desired, he reached the stage of momentarily forgetting the toy and pushed aside the obstacle, bursting into laughter. What had been intelligent adaptation had thus become play, through transfer of interest to the action itself, regardless of its aim.[5]

While these laughter-evoking play activities are enjoyable, there is nothing necessarily humorous in them. The stage of development where most theorists begin talking about humor is when young children enjoy exercising cognitive skills in a way they know to be somehow *inappropriate*, rather than just exhilarating. The fun here seems to be in violating a pattern that the child has learned.

Paul McGhee distinguishes four stages in the development of humor. The first, arising in the child's second year, he calls "Incongruous Actions toward Objects." Here the child knowingly does something inappropriate with an object, for fun. Jean Piaget reported that his daughter Lucien picked up a leaf and held it to her ear, talking as if the leaf were a telephone, and laughing.[6] At 18 months, his other daughter, Jacqueline, said "soap" and rubbed her hands together, but without any soap or water. Soon after that, she pretended to eat non-edible things such as paper, saying "Very nice."[7] Piaget accounts for such cases by saying that in treating one thing as if it were another thing, the young child is manipulating mental images, superimposing the schema of telephone, for example, onto the leaf.

The second stage of humor, according to McGhee, is the "Incongruous Labeling of Objects and Events." Once the child is comfortable with the names of things, actions, and events, she can play by misusing words. At 27 months, Piaget's daughter Jacqueline pointed to a rough stone and said, "It's a dog." Asked, "Where is its head?" she said, "There," pointing to a lump on the stone. "And its eyes?" "They've gone!" Three months earlier, Jacqueline "opened the window and shouted, laughing: 'Hi boy' (a boy she met on her walks and who was never in the garden). Then, still laughing, she added: 'Over there!'"[8]

The incongruous labeling of objects and events shades into McGhee's 10 Stage 3, "Conceptual Incongruity." Once children have developed concepts for Mommy, Daddy, dog, cat, etc., which include their standard features, they can violate those concepts for fun. Dogs bark, for example, while cats meow. So when a child thinks of the reverse, that violates her concept and can amuse her. Kornei Chukovsky describes his daughter's first joke, at 23 months:

My daughter came to me, looking mischievous and embarrassed at the same time—as if she were up to some intrigue. . . . She cried to me even when she was still at some distance from where I sat: "Daddy, oggie-miaow!" . . . And she burst out into somewhat encouraging, somewhat artificial laughter, inviting me, too, to laugh at this invention.[9]

Children in Stage 3 are highly visual, and so incongruous pictures amuse them, such as a drawing of an elephant in a tree.

McGhee's Stage 4 is "Multiple Meanings." At about age seven, children can appreciate riddles based on double meanings and phrases that sound the same, such as:

Why won't you ever be hungry in the desert?
Because of the sand which is there.

From age eight on, children's humor gradually becomes more grown-up, with cleverness, funny stories, and style in telling them becoming more important.

As children develop humor, then, they play in progressively more sophisticated ways with mental images, words, and concepts. They think in a way that is disengaged from conceptual and practical concerns—for fun rather than to orient themselves or to accomplish anything. They hold ideas in their heads, but in a way that makes no demands on them. The medium for most of this activity is language, especially language about what the child knows is not real. While make-believe is not necessary for humor, it is usually the easiest way to be sure that what is happening does not make cognitive or practical demands.

For early humans to develop humor, I suggest, they had to acquire this ability to play with thoughts. Playing requires security, as we have said, and life in the Pleistocene era° was more dangerous than the lives of babies today. So I doubt that the first humor on Earth was in a game of make-believe like those of Piaget's daughters. A more likely candidate for the first humor would be a sudden reinterpretation of some perceptual experience, such as what the neuroscientist V. S. Ramachandran calls "False Alarm" laughter.[10] Like humorous make-believe in young children, it involves having a perception or idea without that perception or idea making cognitive or practical demands. To see what might have been involved in this disengaged mental processing, and how it might have benefited early humans, imagine the following scenario.

A band of early humans is walking across the savanna, when they spot a lion in the clearing ahead. They freeze in their tracks for a moment, but then they see that the lion is feasting on a zebra and doesn't even look up at them. With the sudden realization that the lion is not a threat, they laugh, signaling to each other "We're safe. We can enjoy this."

A more sophisticated kind of early humor might have looked like this. 15 A group is sitting around a fire at night, when they see what looks like a horned monster coming through the tall grass. If it really is an invader, then they should be serious and emotionally engaged. Fear or rage would energize them to escape, or to conquer the monster. But what if "the monster" is actually their chief returning to camp carrying an antelope carcass on his head? Then their fear or rage not only will waste time and energy, but could easily lead to pointless killing. In that case, what they need is a quick way to block or to dispel fight-or-flight emotions. They

---

the Pleistocene era: the period from roughly 2 million to about 10,000 years ago; the precursor for the current geological era, the Holocene.

While we have evolved into desk-dwelling *homo sapiens*, we may be able to trace our development of humor back to our ape ancestors.
Panko/Shutterstock.com

need to disengage themselves and play with their perceptions and thoughts, rather than act on them.

They already have laughter as a play signal for potentially dangerous activities like rough-and-tumble play. Here they extend that play signal to a potentially dangerous experience: the horned-monster apparition. When someone in the group realizes that the monster is actually the chief, their cognitive shift evokes the play signal of laughter. That interferes with their breathing, lowers their muscular coordination, and eliminates the rigidity of the torso that is necessary for large motor activities.[11] So the laughing person is obviously no longer about to attack the chief—or even able to do so. The distinctive look and sound of their laughter signals "false alarm" to the others, telling them that they can relax too.[12] Among a group ready to attack or to flee, laughers would stand out for their lack of purposeful action and muscle control, and for their distinctive spasmodic vocal sounds.

The power of that "false alarm" signal shows today in laughter's contagiousness. It spreads quickly through a group, with each person's laughter tending to increase that of the others. That's why television sitcoms use "laugh tracks" and comedy nightclubs put the chairs and tables close together. Indeed, we don't even have to know what people are laughing about in order to "catch" their laughter. If you approach a group of friends laughing hysterically, you may begin to laugh before anyone explains what's funny.

False Alarm laughter is common today in both children and adults. In one psychology experiment, students are told that they will be handling rats. When they approach the cages and see toy stuffed rats, they usually laugh. V. S. Ramachandran tells of being in an upstairs bedroom when he heard a vase crashing downstairs. Thinking there was a burglar in the house, he steeled himself and walked to the top of the stairs, only to see his cat scurrying out of the living room. Instantly, he laughed.[13]

In False Alarm laughter situations, early humans did something more sophisticated than in tickling or mock-wrestling. They played with a cognitive shift, a rapid change in their perceptions and thoughts. The dangerous lion was suddenly a big cat enjoying its dinner. The monster suddenly became the chief. It was this ability to suddenly see things in new ways and enjoy the mental jolt, I suggest, that marked the transition from simple play to humor.

> "It was this ability to suddenly see things in new ways and enjoy the mental jolt, I suggest, that marked the transition from simple play to humor."

Once our distant ancestors had experienced the pleasure in False Alarm laughter repeatedly, they would have started creating similar situations for more fun. And here they would naturally get into make-believe like that of children today. After the tribe laughed on discovering that the monster was their chief, someone may have re-enacted the funny event by putting animal horns on her own head and skulking through the grass. If that got laughs, she might have gotten a bigger set of horns or found a prop that made her look dangerous in a different way.

There are two possibilities with the re-enactment of the Attack of the Horned Monster. It could be done with everyone's knowledge, so that they all enjoyed the discrepancy between the horned monster and their clowning friend. That may have been the first comedy, indeed, the first drama of any kind. Second, the re-enactment could be done as a trick played on someone unaware of the pretending involved. At first that person would be scared, and then perhaps laugh on discovering there was no danger. The pranksters themselves would laugh not just at the horned monster that wasn't a monster, but at the tricked person's initial fear. Something like this was probably the first practical joke. The fun here may have led the laughing band to create other inappropriate-fear scenarios from scratch, such as by putting a dead snake on someone's food. Young children today laugh uproariously when they think they've tricked adults in ways like this.

Impersonating, mimicking, and pretending generally, of course, were central in the development of comedy. Make-believe *with* the audience's knowledge became stage comedy, clowning, mime, satire, parody, caricature, comic storytelling, joke telling, film comedy, and stand-up comedy. Kendall Walton has even argued that such make-believe is at the heart of all the representational arts.[14] Pretending *without* the audience's knowledge became practical jokes, spoofs, pulling someone's leg, *Candid Camera,*° etc.

The big thing that allowed early humans to play with cognitive shifts, and so to engage in humor, was language. The easiest way to play with thoughts is to play with words. And the same change to an upright posture that made laughter possible made speech possible. As Robert Provine explains, "The evolution of bipedalism set the stage for the emergence of speech by freeing the thorax of the mechanical demands of quadripedal locomotion and loosening the coupling between breathing and vocalizing."[15] With speech, humans could recall past funny events like the Attack of the Horned Monster, just as families and friends today tell and retell funny stories from their shared past. They could add fictional details as they retold the stories, or create funny fantasies from scratch. Instead of manipulating things like animal carcasses to create humor, they could simply use words to describe funny situations.

Language also made possible two techniques that became central to comedy—the wild comparison and the wild exaggeration. If someone did something clumsy, someone else could compare them to a turkey or a dodo, and perhaps confer these as nicknames. Refined, that became wit. Exaggeration, perhaps the single most important comic technique, is easier in language and would have started early. Twenty thousand years ago, comments like "He was so scared that . . ." were probably among the top 10 funny lines.

Another source of pleasure made possible by language was playing with the sounds of words, and with multiple meanings, as in puns and double entendres.[16]

Humor eventually became part of all cultures and was institutionalized in dozens of ways, most notably comic storytelling. Hundreds of the world's myths are about trickster figures who play practical jokes and have tricks played on them. Many tricksters are animals, such as Coyote, Crow, and Rabbit in North America, and Reynard the Fox in Europe. The Winnebago, native to what is now Illinois and Wisconsin, had four dozen trickster tales, which other tribes adapted.[17] Here is "Trickster Loses His Meal" as told by the Anishinaabe:

One day Manabozho (Hare) killed a big moose. But as he was about to take a bite, a nearby tree made a loud creaking noise in the wind. Manabozho rebuked the tree for making noise, but as he turned back to his meal, the tree made the noise again. This time he climbed the tree to deal with the creaking branches,

25

Candid Camera: a practical joke reality TV series that has been on and off the air since 1948.

but the wind blew and he got trapped in the fork of the tree. Just then a pack of wolves came along. Manabozho yelled, "There's nothing over here. What are you looking for?" The wolves realized who it was and headed toward the voice. They found the moose and ate every last bit until nothing was left but the bones. The next day the wind shifted the tree branches again, and Manabozho got free. He thought to himself, "I shouldn't have worried about little things when I had something good in my grasp."

Monarchies from ancient Egypt and China to nineteenth-century Europe institutionalized humor in the form of the court jester, giving him permission to poke fun at the ruler and the court as no one else could.[18] Many religions celebrate a jester or fool figure. Islam has Nasreddin. Russian Orthodox Christianity has canonized three dozen Holy Fools. Dozens of North American native tribes have sacred clowns. The Ojibwa call them *windigokaan*; the Lakotah call them *heyokas*. They burlesque leaders and rituals, break rules, and ask questions no one else would. A basic gag is to reverse something, as by wearing clothes inside out or riding a horse backward.

Many ancient religions ritualized anarchic comic behavior not just for priests but for everyone. Hinduism has Holi, a spring festival in which people play practical jokes, douse each other with water and paint, and in general act silly. Eastern Orthodox Christianity celebrates the week after Easter in a similar way, with people playing tricks on each other, as God tricked Satan with the resurrection of Jesus. In Bavaria in the fifteenth through eighteenth centuries, *Risus Paschalis* (Easter Laughter) involved sermons based on funny stories. Before that, medieval Christians had the Feast of Fools and the Feast of Asses, which, like Roman Saturnalia, held at the same time, let people mock authority and tradition, and in general, lighten up. That spirit survives today in Mardi Gras and Carnival.

In Greece in the fifth century BCE, behavior like this gave rise to "*komoidia*," comedy. The word originally meant "the song of the komos," a *komos* being a band of revelers worshipping Dionysus, god of "wine, women, and song." Often held in the spring, these festivals celebrated fertility, and often a huge phallus was carried on a pole or cart. As these events became more scripted, the performances of individual actors were added to the singing of the chorus, and dramatic comedy was born.

The early comedies of writers like Aristophanes, later called Old 30 Comedy, abounded in sex, food, and drink, and often ended with revelry, as at a wedding banquet. Rites of Dionysus sometimes figured in the plot, and male characters wore large leather phalluses. In line with its origins in fertility rites, Old Comedy celebrated country life, and it mocked politicians, rich people, and other city-types. Political figures and institutions were challenged, as in *Lysistrata*, named after the comic heroine who leads the women of Greece in a sex strike to protest their men's constant warfare. The influence of Old Comedy on European literature shows up in writers like Rabelais, Cervantes, and Swift, and in contemporary buffoonery and political satire.

Greek New Comedy, discussed by Aristotle, began in the last part of the fourth century BCE. Its most famous writer was Menander. Though almost all the plays have been lost, they were imitated in the comedies of the Romans Plautus and Terence. Here the chorus has been eliminated, the style is more realistic, and the themes are more domestic and romantic than political and satirical. In place of mockery and fantastic situations are scenes from daily life with bragging soldiers, clever slaves, and young lovers trying to deal with stern fathers. That approach to comedy has been standard ever since, and can be seen in Shakespeare and Ben Jonson, and today in TV sitcoms and romantic comedies.

Given the centrality of language in the development of humor, both in our species and in children today, it's reasonable to think that if other primates developed language, they might develop humor, too. In the last few decades, this hypothesis has been borne out by the gorillas, chimpanzees, bonobos, and orangutans who have learned various languages.[19] The most famous, Koko the gorilla, has over a thousand signs in American Sign Language. While gorillas in the wild have a laugh-like breathing pattern during tickling and rough-and-tumble play, they don't show evidence of the cognitive play of humor. But once Koko had a basic competence in using signs, she began to do what young children do when they have mastered words—she played with them. According to Francine "Penny" Patterson, Koko's trainer and friend, on December 10, 1985, Koko took a folder that she had been working with and put it on her head, signing "hat."[20] Similarly, Moja, a chimpanzee trained to sign by Roger Fouts, called a purse "shoe," and put the purse on her foot to wear.[21] Like Piaget's daughter pretending that the leaf was a telephone, this fits into McGhee's Stage 1 of humor development, "Incongruous Actions toward Objects."

McGhee's Stage 2, "Incongruous Labeling of Objects and Events," can be seen in this exchange between Koko and one of her keepers, Cathy:[22]

The dispute had begun when Cathy showed Koko a poster picture of Koko that had been used during a fund-raising benefit. Cathy had signed to Koko, What's this? by drawing her index finger across her palm and then pointing to the picture of Koko.

Gorilla, *signed Koko.*

Who gorilla? *asked Cathy, pursuing the conversational line in typical fashion.*

Bird, *responded Koko.*

You bird? *asked Cathy, not about to let Koko reduce the session to chaos.*

You, *countered Koko, who by this age was frequently using the word bird as an insult.*

Not me, you bird, *retorted Cathy.*

Me gorilla, *Koko answered.*

Who bird? *asked Cathy.*

You nut, *replied Koko, resorting to another of her insults. (Koko switches bird and nut from descriptive to pejorative terms by changing the position in which the sign is made from the front to the side of her face.)*

After a little more name-calling Koko gave up the battle, signed, Darn me good, *and walked away signing* Bad.

Now sometimes Koko's incongruous labeling of things and people seems to arise simply from annoyance with her trainers, as when she calls them "dirty toilet,"[23] but other times it is accompanied by a play face, and she seems to enjoy misnaming things for its own sake. While she is no Lucille Ball, she seems to show a sense of humor that at least approaches that of kindergartners.

The Basic Pattern in Humor: The Playful Enjoyment of a Cognitive Shift Is Expressed in Laughter

If this account of the evolution of humor is on the right track, we are now in a position to offer a general account of humorous amusement. Today our humor is more sophisticated than that of early humans. We enjoy lots of complex fantasies, as in jokes, movies, and cartoons. Many of our comedies have three or four stories going on simultaneously. With books, television, and DVDs, we can experience amusement while we are alone. We also engage in clever repartee. Despite our sophistication, however, our humor has much in common with prehistoric humor. The basic pattern is that:

1. We experience a *cognitive shift*—a rapid change in our perceptions or thoughts.

2. We are in a *play mode* rather than a serious mode, disengaged from conceptual and practical concerns.

3. Instead of responding to the cognitive shift with shock, confusion, puzzlement, fear, anger, or other negative emotions, we *enjoy* it.

4. Our pleasure at the cognitive shift is expressed in *laughter*, which signals to others that they can relax and play, too.

We can comment on these four aspects of amusement one at a time.

1. The Cognitive Shift

In the jargon of stand-up comedy, a cognitive shift involves a setup and a punch. The setup is our background pattern of thoughts and attitudes. The punch is what causes our thoughts and attitudes to change quickly. In some humor, especially jokes, the first part of the stimulus establishes the background, and the second part serves as the punch. In other humor, our mental background is already in place before the stimulus, and the whole stimulus serves as the punch. If, while taking a walk, we see identical twin adults dressed alike, we may chuckle because that perception conflicts, not with anything else on our walk, but with our assumption that each adult is an individual.

One simple technique in verbal humor is to shift the audience's attention from one thing to something very different, as in Woody Allen's "Not only is there no God, but try getting a plumber on weekends."[24] A more common technique is to make the audience suddenly change their interpretation of a word, phrase, or story to a very different interpretation. Most jokes work that way.

My boyfriend and I broke up. He wanted to get married. And I didn't want him to. (Rita Rudner)

When I was a boy, I was told anyone could become President—I'm beginning to believe it. (Clarence Darrow, while Warren G. Harding was President)

I love cats—they taste a lot like chicken.

Beauty is only skin deep—but ugly goes clear down to the bone.

It matters not whether you win or lose—what matters is whether I win or lose.

Such shifts of attention or interpretation usually fit the pattern Herbert Spencer called "descending incongruity"—they take us from what is "higher" to what is "lower." When McDonald's restaurants began serving Egg McMuffins in the morning, Jay Leno said, "Great! Before, I could only eat *two* meals a day in my car." Here the shift is from advantage to disadvantage. Similarly, in his television feature *On the Road*, about his travels around the USA, Charles Kuralt said, "Thanks to the Interstate Highway System, it is now possible to drive from Maine to California and not see anything."

In humor generally, cognitive shifts tend to be toward what is less desirable, such as failure, mistakes, ignorance, and vices. On television programs featuring funny home videos, for example, the scenes are typically of someone falling down, crashing a bicycle, or sneakily taking the last piece of cake. Comic characters, as Aristotle noted, are worse than average.[25] For all the enjoyment that humor brings, humor is typically not *about* enjoyment, but about problems. Hence Mark Twain's quip that "There is no laughter in heaven."[26]

In general, the greater the contrast between the two states in the cognitive shift, the greater the possible amusement. Woody Allen's jump from asserting atheism to complaining about plumbers takes us from the cosmic to the trivial. But suppose he had written, "Not only is there no God, but innocent people often suffer greatly" or "Not only are doctors' house calls a thing of the past, but try getting a plumber on weekends." Both of those involve transitions, but they are too small and easy to make to have much promise as humor. 40

Victor Raskin has shown that jokes maximize the difference in the cognitive shift by moving from one *script*, or set of background assumptions, to an *opposed* script—from decent to obscene, for example, or wise to foolish.[27] In Mae West's quip, "Marriage is a great institution—but I'm not ready for an institution," the first phrase makes us think of time-honored traditions, while the second phrase makes us think of being committed to a psychiatric hospital.

In funny real-life experiences, the shift does not have to be between opposites, but it usually involves a significant difference between the mental states. We hear a knock at the door and we approach it thinking someone is going to be on the other side wanting to speak to us. In our heads the script is Answering the Door. If we open it to find two Girl Scouts selling cookies, our second mental state follows the first smoothly; everything is normal. We are still Answering the Door. But if we open the door to discover our dog whapping her tail against it, we undergo a cognitive shift. We reinterpret the sound from a person's knocking to a dog's tail-wagging, and drop our expectation that we will be speaking with someone. No longer Answering the Door, we are Letting the Dog In. Those are not opposite scripts, but they are different enough to jolt us. If we enjoy that jolt, that's amusement. A less drastic cognitive change would be less likely to amuse us. Suppose that we opened the door to find a new telephone book that had just been dropped on the porch. This isn't exactly what we expected—no one wanted to speak to us—but it's close. A human being had knocked on the door to alert us to something. So there is much less possibility for humor here.

Most of what I've said about the cognitive shift in humor is familiar to those who know the Incongruity Theory. What I'm doing can be seen as describing what experiencing incongruity is like, without using that often vague term.

2. The Play Mode

There is nothing automatic about enjoying cognitive shifts. Our perceptions, thoughts, and attitudes are the guidance system for our lives, and any rapid change in them threatens our control over what we are doing and what is happening to us. To a lesser or greater degree, when we experience a cognitive shift, we don't know what might happen next or how to proceed. Here the dictionary definition of *puzzled* is illuminating: "to be at a loss what to do." At the minimum, we may be momentarily disoriented; at the maximum, we may see our lives as in danger. So cognitive shifts are potentially disturbing. What biologists call the "orienting reflex" is essential in keeping animals alive, and fight-or-flight emotions equip them to handle surprises when immediate action is called for. So it's perfectly understandable that seriousness is the default mode for us and all other animals. The non-serious play mode is a luxury.

Sometimes the potential disturbance in humor is nothing more than temporary mild confusion, as in listening to non-tendentious word play, and then it is easy to go into the play mode. But most humor, today as in the Pleistocene era, is a reaction to cognitive shifts that could be more threatening, such as facing danger, failing, misunderstanding other people, quarreling with neighbors, etc. Most humor, as we said, has always been about problems.

We have several ways of taking a playful attitude toward problems rather than reacting with cognitive or practical concern. The most obvious is by fictionalizing them. When we tell a joke, draw a cartoon, or produce a film about a fictional situation, we allow our audience the luxury of dropping the concerns they ordinarily have about comparable real situations. Cartoons like those of Charles Addams and Gary Larsen, for example, are full of situations in which someone is about to get hurt or killed. But knowing that those situations are not real, we can treat them playfully. Sympathy doesn't arise to block our enjoyment of the potentially disturbing scene. The more obviously fictional the character is, the easier the play mode is to achieve. Many people are disturbed rather than amused, for instance, by the way the Three Stooges hurt each other with hammers and saws. But I've never heard anyone make similar complaints about the way Roadrunner drops anvils and dynamite on Wile E. Coyote.

45

Even real problems can be treated playfully under the right circumstances. Distance may be enough to do the trick. Last night my wife and I laughed watching a TV news story about two elephants that had escaped from a circus in Toronto. In the video they were ambling down a residential street, defecating on lawns. Had we been two of those Torontonians cowering behind their curtains, however, it's unlikely that we would have been in the play mode to laugh.

The passage of time also permits us to play with what is potentially disturbing. What puzzled, scared, or angered us last year, or even yesterday, may now be the stuff of funny stories. When old friends reminisce, indeed, many of the events they laugh hardest about were crises at the time. As Steve Allen put it, tragedy plus time equals comedy.

Another factor in comic disengagement is one's role—or better, one's lack of role—in the potentially disturbing situation. If at lunch you spill a blob of ketchup on your shirt that looks like a bullet hole, that might strike me as funny. But I'm less likely to be amused by ketchup on my own shirt. As Will Rogers put it, "Everything is funny if it happens to the other guy." For Mel Brooks, "Tragedy is me cutting my finger; comedy is you falling down a manhole and dying."

These and other psychological phenomena disengage us from situations   50
that would otherwise be disturbing. They "aestheticize" problems so that the mental jolt they give us brings pleasure rather than negative emotions.

While I have been distinguishing cases of amusement from cases of negative emotions, there are times when we seem to experience both. On March 18, 1999, for instance, the evening news in Britain featured a story about the comedian Rod Hull, who had died falling off his roof while adjusting his TV aerial during a soccer match. Many viewers laughed but then felt awful for doing so. There is also the category of "black humor," where the same story can evoke amusement, shock, disgust, and even horror. In the simple examples of such cases, I suggest, we experience pleasure and negative emotions sequentially, or we oscillate between them. Some of those who laughed about Hull's death initially enjoyed the odd story, but then stopped enjoying it as they felt guilt over their insensitivity. But things can get more complicated. It seems possible for us to enjoy something and *simultaneously* be disturbed by our ability to enjoy it — "guilty pleasure," we call it. Notice here, though, that the object of pleasure and the object of displeasure are different. Consider those who were amused by the news of Hull's death, and *at the same time* felt guilty. They were disengaged enough from the suffering of Hull and his family to enjoy *the odd way he died*. And, while still enjoying that, they experienced negative emotions about *their own ability to enjoy such a thing*.

3. The Enjoyment

We all know that it feels good to laugh and most philosophical analyses of amusement include pleasure as an essential element. But few philosophers have said much about that pleasure. I want to say three things about the pleasure in humor—it is social, exhilarating, and liberating.

First, the natural setting for humor, as for play generally, is a group, not an individual. Kierkegaard asked a friend, "Answer me honestly . . . do you really laugh when you are alone?" He concluded that you have to be "a little more than queer" if you do.[28] According to Henri Bergson, "You would hardly appreciate the comic if you felt yourself isolated from others. Laughter appears to stand in need of an echo."[29]

It's hard to get into the play mode by oneself. Often when I experience events alone, especially those involving setbacks, I don't see the humor in them until I am later describing them to other people. And even if I experience an event as funny while I'm by myself, it's unlikely that I'll enjoy it *as much* as when I later share it in conversation.

Watching humor on television is even stronger evidence that humor is essentially a social pleasure. Programs with a studio audience, such as the late-night talk shows, game shows, and the ones showing funny home videos try to make "our viewers at home" feel as if they are part of a large group. We see and hear other people laughing, and we laugh. Many sitcoms are recorded in front of an audience, and though we don't see them, we hear their laughter, again to make the experience social. Even sitcoms that are not recorded in front of an audience usually add a "laugh track" to create the same social feeling.

Part of the pleasure of laughing with other people is enjoying their company, of course, and this pleasure can be distinguished from amusement per se. So there is no necessary correlation between the amount of laughter and the degree of amusement. Nonetheless, it seems that things are more likely to amuse us, *and* more likely to make us laugh, when we are with other people.

A second aspect of the pleasure in humor is that it is lively, or as the psychologist Willibald Ruch says, exhilarating.[30] Kant described joking as the "play of thought" and compared it to the "play of tone" in music and to the "play of fortune" in games of chance. In all three, he said, our changing ideas are accompanied by a "changing free play of sensations . . . which furthers the feeling of health" by stimulating the intestines and the diaphragm.[31] In joking,

the play begins with the thoughts which together occupy the body, so far as they admit of sensible expression; and as the understanding stops suddenly short at this presentiment, in which it does not find what it expected, we feel the effect of this slackening in the body by the oscillation of the organs, which promotes the restoration of equilibrium and has a favorable influence upon health.[32]

Whatever we may think about Kant's grasp of physiology here, he understands that amusement is not a sedate pleasure, like looking at a lovely sunset, but a lively delight involving mental gymnastics. Aristotle said that witty people have "a quick versatility in their wits."[33] He spoke of "sallies" of witty remarks, comparing lines in conversations to sudden military attacks. As in an exciting battle, in the best humor we're not sure what might happen next.

My third observation about the pleasure in humor is that it is liberating.[34] In the comic mode, people think, say, and sometimes do all kinds of things that are normally forbidden. Extreme examples are the Roman Saturnalia, the medieval Christian Feast of Fools, and Mardi Gras and Carnival. But even the tamer humor of polite joking challenges authority figures and traditional ways of thinking and acting. It gets us out of mental ruts. As Milton Berle said, "Laughter is an instant vacation." In Greek comedy, even the gods were lampooned, and there is an old saying among Hasidic Jews: If God lived on earth, people would break his windows.

In humor we can poke fun at not just civic and religious authorities, but the whole serious approach to life, including what Robert Mankoff, cartoon editor of the *New Yorker* magazine, calls "the hegemony of reason." Ever since Aristophanes' *The Clouds* ridiculed Socrates, the pedant and the absent-minded professor have been the butts of jokes. Schopenhauer recognized the liberating pleasure here when he said that, "It must therefore be diverting to us to see that strict, untiring, troublesome governess, the reason, for once convicted of insufficiency."[35]

In the humorous frame of mind, we can challenge any standard belief, value, or convention. Dave Barry is typical of gentle humorists who poke fun at society in a way that doesn't stray far from normal thought patterns. Here are his comments on the jogging craze:

Running is the ideal form of exercise for people who sincerely wish to become middle-class urban professionals. Whereas the lower classes don't run except when their kerosene heaters explode, today's upwardly mobile urban professionals feel that running keeps them in the peak form they must be in if they are to handle the responsibilities of their chosen urban professions, which include reading things, signing things, talking on the telephone, and in cases of extreme upward mobility, going to lunch.[36]

But humorists can jolt our mental patterns in deeper ways. Consider the value system implied in this stand-up bit by Rita Rudner:

I love to sleep. It really is the best of both worlds. You get to be alive **and unconscious.**

In humor, we also get to challenge the hegemony of reason by giving free reign to imagination. The pleasure of humor, then, goes far beyond Woody Allen's comment that it's the most fun you can have with your clothes on. Humor gives our minds a workout at the same time it liberates them. Enid Welsford's comment about the traditional comic fool applies to humor generally: it has "the power of melting the solidity of the world."[37] It aestheticizes our experience so that what would otherwise be puzzling, shocking, scary, disgusting, enraging, or saddening becomes the stuff of fun.

4. The Laughter

The last element in this analysis of humorous amusement is the most familiar—laughter. People who have never heard of a "cognitive shift" or the "play mode," or even "humor" and "amusement," know about laughter. Before the late seventeenth century, when "humor" and "amuse" acquired their current meanings, there was only the word "laughter" for what are now called "humor," "amusement," and "laughter." Some languages still do not distinguish amusement as mental from laughter as physical. Of those that do, many have simply imported the English word "humor." Lin Yutang, for example, introduced it into Chinese in 1923, and it is now transliterated as "youmo."[38]

The new concept of amusement was based on laughter. *Amuse* meant "to make someone laugh or smile with pleasure"; *amusement* meant "the state of being caused to laugh or smile with pleasure." And there was no active verb for "to be amused" except "to laugh." As Jerrold Levinson says, "The propensity of the state of amusement to issue in laughter is arguably what is essential to its identity, and underpins the widespread intuition that humor and laughter, though not coextensive, are nevertheless intimately related."[39] That is why Levinson puts the tendency of amusement to issue in laughter at the center of his theory of humor.[40]

When we enjoy a cognitive shift, there is a natural tendency to laugh. 65 We don't learn it any more than we learn the disposition to cry; both emerge in normal brain development. In all cultures, babies begin to smile between 2 and 4 months of age, and to laugh shortly after that. Even babies born blind and deaf smile and laugh. In a normal mother–child relationship, the baby's laughter evokes her own, and a virtuous cycle ensues, each one's pleasure and laughter increasing the pleasure and laughter of the other. That shared pleasure increases the mother's affection for the baby and the baby's attachment to her. Later, as the child interacts with other people, sharing laughter establishes a social bond with them. All this fits well with the idea that laughter is a play signal. Between parent and child; between child and sibling; between friends, lovers, colleagues, etc., laughter sends the message, "We are safe. I enjoy this—you enjoy it, too."

Notes

1. Robert Provine, *Laughter: A Scientific Investigation* (Harmondsworth: Penguin, 2000), 86; Jennifer Gamble, "Humor in Apes," *Humor: International Journal of Humor Research* 14/2 (2001), 169; William Fry, "The Biology of Humor," *Humor: International Journal of Humor Research* 7/2 (1994), 111–26.

2. Immanuel Kant, in *The Philosophy of Laughter and Humor,* ed. John Morreall (Albany: State University of New York Press, 1987), 46, 48.

3. See Paul McGhee, *Humor: Its Origin and Development* (San Francisco: W. H. Freeman, 1979).

4. Jean Piaget, *Play, Dreams, and Imitation in Childhood,* trans. C. Gattegno and F. M. Hodgson (London: Routledge and Kegan Paul, 1991), 91.

5. Piaget, *Play, Dreams, and Imitation in Childhood,* 92.

6. In McGhee, *Humor: Its Origin and Development,* 66.

7. Piaget, *Play, Dreams, and Imitation in Childhood,* 96.

8. In McGhee, *Humor: Its Origin and Development,* 68. See Piaget *Play, Dreams, and Imitation in Childhood,* 120.

9. Kornei Chukovsky, *From Two to Five,* trans. Miriam Morton (Berkeley: University of California Press, 1963), 601.

10. V. S. Ramachandran and Sandra Blakeslee, *Phantoms in the Brain* (New York: William Morrow, 1998), 206.

11. Wallace Chafe, *The Importance of Not Being Earnest: The Feeling Behind Laughter and Humor* (Amsterdam: John Benjamins, 2007), 23.

12. An early version of this account of laughter is in Donald Hayworth, "The Social Origin and Function of Laughter," *Psychological Review* 35 (1928), 367–85. A contemporary version is in Provine, *Laughter: A Scientific Investigation.*

13. Ramachandran and Blakeslee, *Phantoms in the Brain,* p. 205.

14. Kendall Walton, *Mimesis as Make-Believe: On the Foundations of the Representational Arts* (Cambridge: Harvard University Press, 1990).

15. Provine, *Laughter: A Scientific Investigation,* 87.

16. See John Morreall, *Taking Laughter Seriously* (Albany: State University of New York, 1983), 70–2.

17. Paul Radin, *The Trickster: A Study in American Indian Mythology* (New York: Random House, 1972), 6.

18. Beatrice Otto, *Fools Are Everywhere: The Court Jester Around the World* (Chicago: University of Chicago Press, 2001).

19. Gamble, "Humor in Apes," 163–79; Francine Patterson and Eugene Linden, *The Education of Koko* (New York: Holt, Rinehart and Winston, 1985), ch. 16; McGhee, *Humor: Its Origin and Development*, 110–20; Provine, *Laughter: A Scientific Investigation*, ch. 5.

20. Francine Patterson, "Koko: Conversations with Herself," *Gorilla*, 10 (December 1989).

21. Provine, *Laughter: A Scientific Investigation*, 94.

22. Patterson, "Koko: Conversations with Herself," ch. 1.

23. Provine, *Laughter: A Scientific Investigation*, 95.

24. Woody Allen, *Getting Even* (New York: Random House, 1971), 33.

25. Aristotle, *Poetics*, 5, 1449a, in *The Philosophy of Laughter and Humor*, ed. John Morreall (Albany: State University of New York Press, 1987), 14.

26. Mark Twain, *Following the Equator: A Journey around the World* (New York: Harper and Brothers, 1906), ch. 10.

27. Victor Raskin, *Semantic Mechanisms of Humor* (Dordrecht: Reidel, 1984), 107–14.

28. Søren Kierkegaard, *Either/Or*, trans. W. Lowrie, Vol. II (Garden City, NY: Anchor Books, 1959), 331–2.

29. Henri Bergson, *Laughter*, in *The Philosophy of Laughter and Humor*, ed. John Morreall (Albany: State University of New York Press, 1987), 119.

30. Willibald Ruch, *Die Emotion Erheiterung: Alusdrucksformen und Bedingungen* [The Emotion of Exhilaration: Forms of Expression and Eliciting Conditions], unpublished habilitations thesis, Department of Psychology, University of Düsseldorf, 1990.

31. Immanuel Kant, *Critique of Judgment*, in *The Philosophy of Laughter and Humor*, ed. John Morreall (Albany: State University of New York Press, 1987), 45–7.

32. Ibid., 47.

33. Aristotle, *Nicomachean Ethics*, 4, ch. 8, in *The Philosophy of Laughter and Humor*, ed. John Morreall (Albany: State University of New York Press, 1987), 15.

34. Cf. Harvey Mindess, *Laughter and Liberation* (Los Angeles: Nash, 1971).

35. Arthur Schopenhauer, *The World as Will and Idea*, trans. R. B. Haldane and J. Kemp (London: Routledge and Kegan Paul, 1964), 2: 280.

36. Dave Barry, *Dave Barry's Guide to Life* (New York: Wings Books, 1991), 215.

37. Enid Welsford, *The Fool: His Social and Literary History* (Garden City, NY: Doubleday Anchor, 1961), 223.

38. Qian Suoqiao, "Translating 'Humor' into Chinese Culture," *Humor: International Journal of Humor Research* 20 (2007), 277–95.

39. Jerrold Levinson, "Humour," *Routledge Encyclopedia of Philosophy*, ed. E. Craig (London: Routledge, 1998), 565.

40. Ibid.

Understanding the Text

1. What did the evolution of language make possible with regard to humor? How does the development of an individual child's sense of humor (ontogenesis) relate to that of humans in general (phylogenesis)?
2. How does Morreall distinguish between Old and New Greek Comedy?
3. Summarize the four aspects that comprise the basic pattern of humor as laid out by Morreall.

Reflection and Response

4. In terms of evolution, "false alarm" laughter arose from situations where a potential threat proved to be harmless. Laughter signaled that the danger had been defused. Humor proper developed when humans started to simulate "false alarm" situations in order to ease tensions and enhance social bonds. Think about the humor in your own life. When have you experienced "false alarm" laughter? How do you joke around to cement relationships with your family and friends?
5. On two occasions Morreall mentions the laugh tracks that accompany traditional sitcoms. More contemporary sitcoms, especially of the mockumentary variety (e.g., *The Office, Parks and Recreation, Modern Family*, etc.), have tended to do away with the laugh track. Does your experience of canned laughter adhere to Morreall's thoughts on the phenomenon? Do you find laugh tracks obtrusive? Why or why not?

Making Connections

6. While Morreall supplies a cursory look at the science of humor from the perspectives of evolutionary biology, developmental psychology, and cultural anthropology, other scientific fields also have much to say on the subject. Write an academic research essay that either digs deeper into the science of humor in one of the aforementioned disciplines or explores what another field of science (neuro, medical, cognitive, zoological, etc.) has discovered about why we laugh.
7. Review the literature on incongruity theory and write an extended analysis of a comedic text based on your research. Morreall mentions Victor Raskin's script-based semantic theory of humor, for example, but much work exists on the subject, such as sociologist Murray Davis's book *What's So Funny?: The Comic Conception of Culture and Society* (1993).
8. Morreall quotes from several comedians who reflect on the nature of humor. Choose one of these figures or another historically renowned comedian of interest to you, and write a thesis-based research essay that examines how their body of work reflects or contradicts their own views of comedy as well as those of humor theorists.

One Professor's Attempt to Explain Every Joke Ever

Joel Warner

In this feature column written for the May 2011 Humor Issue of *Wired* magazine, freelance writer Joel Warner travels to the Mind Science Foundation's comedy symposium to report on consumer psychologist Peter McGraw's presentation of his benign violation theory (BVT) of humor. Based in Denver, Warner has written for several publications, including *Westword*, *Slate*, and *Grantland*. McGraw is an associate professor of marketing and psychology at the University of Colorado at Boulder, where he runs the Humor Research Lab (HuRL). Together, they authored the book *The Humor Code: A Global Search for What Makes Things Funny* (2014).

The writer E. B. White famously remarked that "analyzing humor is like dissecting a frog. Few people are interested and the frog dies." If that's true, an amphibian genocide took place in San Antonio this past January. Academics from around the world gathered there for the first-ever comedy symposium cosponsored by the Mind Science Foundation.

The goal wasn't to tell jokes but to assess exactly what a joke is, how it works, and what this thing called "funny" really is, in a neurological, sociological, and psychological sense. As Sean Guillory, a Dartmouth College neuroscience grad student who organized the event, says, "It's the first time a roomful of empirical humor researchers have ever gotten together!"

The first speaker at the podium, University of Western Ontario professor Rod Martin, began with a lament over the lack of comedy scholarship. He pointed out that you could fill a library with analyses of subjects like mental illness or aggression. Meanwhile, the 1,700-plus-page *Handbook of Social Psychology*—the preeminent reference work in its field—mentions humor once.

The crux of Martin's argument involves semantics. It takes issue with the imperfect terminology we use to describe the emotional state that humor triggers. Standardizing language would help humor studies earn the respect of related fields, like aggression research. Martin exhorted his audience to adopt his preferred word for the "pleasurable feeling, joy, gaiety of mind" that humor elicits. Happiness, elation, and even hilarity don't quite fit, to his mind. The best word, he said, is *mirth*.

For those curious about the physiology of humor, Helmut Karl 5 Lackner of the Medical University of Graz, Austria, presented his research on the relationship between humor, stress, and respiration.

By tracking breathing cycles and heart rates, he has determined that social anxiety makes things less funny. (Fittingly, he seemed nervous as he read his paper in halting English.) Nina Strohminger, a researcher at the University of Michigan, explained how she's been exposing test subjects to unpleasant odors. She extolled the virtues of a spray called Liquid Ass, which can be purchased at fine novelty stores everywhere. (Her conclusion: Farts make everything funnier.) The audience members take the subject of amusement very seriously, yet they couldn't help but chuckle at this.

Other speakers peppered their talks with multivariate ANOVAs° and mesolimbic° reward systems. Some presented research on whether people with Asperger's syndrome get jokes and how to determine the social consequences of put-downs. But as the sessions wound on, no one had addressed the underlying mechanism of comedy: What, exactly, makes things funny?

That question was the core of Peter McGraw's lecture. A lanky 41-year-old professor of marketing and psychology at the CU-Boulder, McGraw thinks he has found the answer, and it starts with a tickle. "Who here doesn't like to be tickled?"

A good number of hands shot up. "Yet you laugh," he said, flashing a goofy grin. "You experience some pleasurable reaction even as you resist and say you don't like it."

If you really stop to think about it, McGraw continued, it's a complex and fascinating phenomenon. If someone touches you in certain places in a certain way, it prompts an involuntary but pleasurable physiological response. Except, of course, when it doesn't. "When does tickling cease to be funny?" McGraw asked. "When you try to tickle yourself . . . Or if some stranger in a trench coat tickles you." The audience cracked up. He was working the room like a stand-up comic.

Many would assert that this tickling conundrum is the perfect evidence 10 that humor is utterly relative. There may be many types of humor, maybe as many kinds as there are variations in laughter, guffaws, hoots, and chortles. But McGraw doesn't think so. He has devised a simple, grand unified theory of humor—in his words, "a parsimonious account of what makes things funny." McGraw calls it the benign violation theory [BVT], and he insists that it can explain the function of every imaginable type of humor. And not just what makes things funny, but why certain things aren't funny. "My theory also explains nervous laughter,

ANOVAs: analysis of variance; in statistics, ANOVA tests for significant differences between the means of more than two groups.
mesolimbic: in the brain, the mesolimbic pathway is the major transmitter of dopamine, which is connected with reward-motivated behavior.

racist or sexist jokes, and toilet humor," he told his fellow humor researchers.

Coming up with an essential description of comedy isn't just an intellectual exercise. If the BVT actually is an unerring predictor of what's funny, it could be invaluable. It could have warned Groupon that its Super Bowl ad making light of Tibetan injustices would bomb. *The Love Guru* could've been axed before production began. Podium banter at the Oscars could be less excruciating. If someone could crack the humor code, they could get very rich. Or at least tenure.

It's a wintry afternoon in Boulder and a 53-year-old tech worker named Kyle fires up a joint he obtained from a medical marijuana dispensary. After smoking his medicine and waiting 15 minutes for it to take effect, Kyle opens a 10-page printed questionnaire. He sees a photoshopped image of a man picking his nose so vigorously that his finger pokes out of his eye socket. "To what extent is this picture funny?" the survey asks, inviting Kyle to rate the picture on a scale of 0 to 5. He gives it a 3.

Kyle is one of 50 or so marijuana aficionados who have volunteered to take part in a study run by McGraw's laboratory at CU-Boulder—the Humor Research Lab, or HuRL for short. Founded in 2009, HuRL is unorthodox, to put it mildly, even for academia. But McGraw is doing serious enough work at HuRL to have earned two grants from the Marketing Science Institute, a nonprofit funded by respectable organizations like Bank of America, Pfizer, and IBM. The professor and a team of seven student researchers have been asking test subjects to gauge whether *Hot Tub Time Machine* is funnier if you sit close to the screen or far away. They show subjects a YouTube video of a guy driving a motorcycle into a fence over and over again to see when it ceases to be amusing.

> "If someone could crack the humor code, they could get very rich. Or at least tenure."

The medical marijuana patients will help HuRL researchers answer a momentous question: Can smoking pot make things more funny? The answer may seem forehead-smackingly obvious, but according to McGraw it's impossible to know for sure without applying scientific rigor. "Your intuition often leads you astray," he says. "It's only within the lab that you can set different theories against one another." McGraw believes that the tests will ultimately prove that marijuana does in fact make broad sight gags more funny. But he needs more data before he can be certain. He's begun soliciting input from more potheads through Amazon.com's crowdsourcing marketplace, Mechanical Turk.

McGraw didn't set out to become a humorologist. His background is in marketing and consumer decision making, especially the way moral transgressions and breaches of decorum affect the perceived value of things. For instance, he studied a Florida megachurch that tarnished its reputation when it tried to reward attendees with glitzy prizes. The church's promise to raffle off a Hummer H2 to some lucky congregant was met with controversy in the community—what the hell did that have to do with eternal salvation? But when McGraw related the anecdote at presentations, it prompted laughter—a holy Hummer!—rather than repulsion. This confused him.

"It had never crossed my mind that moral violations could be amusing," McGraw says. He became increasingly preoccupied with the conundrum he saw at the heart of humor: Why do people laugh at horrible things like stereotypes, embarrassment, and pain? Basically, why is Sarah Silverman funny?

Philosophers had pondered this sort of question for millennia, long before anyone thought to examine it in a lab. Plato, Aristotle, and Thomas Hobbes posited the superiority theory of humor, which states that we find the misfortune of others amusing. Sigmund Freud espoused the relief theory, which states that comedy is a way for people to release suppressed thoughts and emotions safely. Incongruity theory, associated with Immanuel Kant, suggests that jokes happen when people notice the disconnect between their expectations and the actual payoff.

But McGraw didn't find any of these explanations satisfactory. "You need to add conditions to explain particular incidents of humor, and even then they still struggle," he says. Freud is great for jokes about bodily functions. Incongruity explains Monty Python. Hobbes nails Henny Youngman.° But no single theory explains all types of comedy. They also short-circuit when it comes to describing why some things aren't funny. McGraw points out that killing a loved one in a fit of rage would be incongruous, it would assert superiority, and it would release pent-up tension, but it would hardly be hilarious.

These glaringly incomplete descriptions of humor offended McGraw's need for order. His duty was clear. "A single theory provides a set of guiding principles that make the world a more organized place," he says.

McGraw and Caleb Warren, a doctoral student, presented their ele- 20 gantly simple formulation in the August 2010 issue of the journal *Psychological Science*. Their paper, "Benign Violations: Making Immoral Behavior Funny," cited scores of philosophers, psychologists, and neuroscientists (as well as Mel Brooks and Carol Burnett). The theory they

---

Henny Youngman: (1906-1988), a comedian famous for playing the violin between delivering one-line gags such as "Take my wife . . . please."

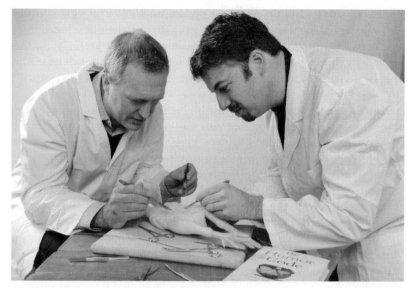

Professor McGraw (left) and Warner (right) dissecting a rubber chicken.
Photo by John Leyba/The Denver Post via Getty Images

lay out: "Laughter and amusement result from violations that are simultaneously seen as benign." That is, they perceive a violation—"of personal dignity (e.g., slapstick, physical deformities), linguistic norms (e.g., unusual accents, malapropisms), social norms (e.g., eating from a sterile bedpan, strange behaviors), and even moral norms (e.g., bestiality, disrespectful behaviors)"—while simultaneously recognizing that the violation doesn't pose a threat to them or their worldview. The theory is ludicrously, vaporously simple. But extensive field tests revealed nuances, variables that determined exactly how funny a joke was perceived to be.

McGraw had his HuRL team present scenarios to hundreds of CU-Boulder students. (Some were bribed with candy bars to participate.) Multiple versions of scenarios were formulated, a few too anodyne to be amusing and some too disgusting for words. Ultimately, McGraw determined that funniness could be predicted based on how committed a person is to the norm being violated, conflicts between two salient norms, and psychological distance from the perceived violation.

The ultimate takeaway of McGraw's paper was that the evolutionary purpose of laughter and amusement is to "signal to the world that a violation is indeed okay." Building on the work of behavioral neurologist V. S. Ramachandran, McGraw believes that laughter developed as an instinctual way to signal that a threat is actually a false alarm — say, that a rustle in the bushes is the wind, not a saber-toothed tiger. "Organisms that could separate benign violations from real threats benefited greatly," McGraw says.

The professor was able to plug the BVT into every form of humor. Dirty jokes violate social norms in a benign way because the traveling salesmen and farmers' daughters that populate them are not real. Punch lines make people laugh because they gently violate the expectations that the jokes set up. The BVT also explains Sarah Silverman, McGraw says; the appalling things that come out of her mouth register as benign because she seems so oblivious to their offensiveness, and "because she's so darn cute." Even tickling, long a stumbling block for humor theorists, appears to fit. Tickling yourself can't be a violation, because you can't take yourself by surprise. Being tickled by a stranger in a trench coat isn't benign; it's creepy. Only tickling by someone you know and trust can be a benign violation.

McGraw and the HuRL team continue to test the theory even as they begin to deploy it in the real world. They've partnered with mShopper, a mobile commerce service, to see whether BVT-tested humor can make text-message product offers more compelling. They've also launched FunnyPoliceReports.com, which aggregates law enforcement dispatches that are likely to amuse readers, such as a woman who called the cops when she was sold fake cocaine.

If the web site sounds sort of like FAIL Blog, that's no accident. McGraw 25 knows Ben Huh, CEO of the Cheezburger Network, who has been using HuRL's findings to help determine what content and features have the potential to be the next big meme. The lolcats baron points to a recent post about a priest cracking down on cell phones in church after a parishioner's "Stayin' Alive" ringtone went off during a funeral. "The benign violation theory applies to that," Huh says. "I'm a guy who makes his living off of internet humor, and McGraw's model fits really well. He's just a lot more right than anyone else."

The conference in San Antonio was the first time McGraw presented his theory to other humor researchers. His well-honed delivery gets a lot of laughs, but his theory ultimately receives the same polite applause as everything else. There are no stunned looks of amazement in the audience, no rumblings of a field torn asunder.

Maybe it's because a discipline that can't even agree on what to call the response elicited by humor isn't ready for a universal theory of humor. At this point, there's still no single way to measure it. (The

International Society for Humor Studies [ISHS] lists 14 tests and scales for measuring humor, from the Multidimensional Sense of Humor Scale to the Humorous Behavior Q-Sort Deck.)

The BVT also has its fair share of detractors. ISHS president Elliott Oring says, "I didn't see many big differences between this theory and the various formulations of incongruity theory." Victor Raskin, founder of the academic journal *Humor: International Journal of Humor Research*, is more blunt: "What McGraw has come up with is flawed and bullshit— what kind of a theory is that?" To his mind, the BVT is a "very loose and vague metaphor," not a functional formula like $E = mc^2$. He's also quick to challenge McGraw's standing in the tight-knit community of scholarship: "He is not a humor researcher; he has no status."

McGraw's lecture did impress Robert Mankoff, cartoon editor at the *New Yorker*, who also gave a presentation in San Antonio. (Fun fact: *New Yorker* cartoons must endure the infamous rigors of the magazine's fact-checkers; just because a cartoon bluebird can talk doesn't mean it shouldn't resemble a genuine Sialia.) After the symposium ended, he offered to provide HuRL with thousands of caption-contest entries to examine. Mankoff says he admires McGraw's work, "and I admire him even more for having the balls to take his theory on the road as stand-up." But he also has a caveat for McGraw and other humor scientists: "All these theories are so general that they're of no use when you're trying to craft a good cartoon." He cites one that he's particularly fond of, an illustration of a Swiss Army knife featuring nothing but corkscrews. The caption reads "French Army knife." No Venn diagram, he says, has ever produced a joke like that.

A Venn diagram illustrating McGraw's benign violation theory (BVT).
Courtesy of Dr. Peter McGraw

It's a half-hour to showtime at Denver's Paramount Theatre and 30
McGraw is milling around in the lobby, hoping to get green-room access
to the comedian Louis C.K. The prof is convinced that his theory works
in the lab, and he's increasingly interested in testing it in the wild. Kind
words from Huh and Mankoff are fine, but the endorsement of a comedian with his own eponymous show on cable would be invaluable. C.K. is
one of McGraw's favorites. "I am fascinated by his ability to make things
funny that I wouldn't have thought could be funny," McGraw says, "how
he portrays his role as a father in an unflattering way."

McGraw gets the go-ahead, and with curtain time closing in, he's
soon sitting in the presence of his idol. The comedian slumps into a
chair, the toll of weeks on the road apparent on his face. Knowing that
he has only a few minutes, McGraw gives a nutshell version of his well-
honed spiel. He lays out the BVT and describes the tickling conundrum
that killed at the humor symposium. But C.K. cuts him off. "I don't
think it's that simple," he says, directing as much attention to a preshow
ham sandwich as to McGraw. "There are thousands of kinds of jokes. I
just don't believe that there's one explanation."

Oof, tough room. His research dismissed, McGraw casts about for another subject of inquiry. Luckily, he'd polled fellow attendees for questions while waiting for an audience with C.K. "A woman in the lobby
wants to know how big your penis is," he says.

C.K. cracks the faintest of smiles, shakes his head. "I am not going to
answer that."

"I wouldn't either," McGraw says. With a chuckle he adds, "But I've
heard that if you don't answer that, it means it's small."

The silence that follows is so thick you could pound in a nail and 35
hang a painting from it. That last remark is a violation, and it isn't
benign. McGraw changes the subject again. "So, you're friends with
Chris Rock?" he says. He wonders whether C.K. could ask Rock for seed
funding, even offering to rename his facility the Chris Rock Humor
Research Lab (CRoHuRL?).

"No," C.K. says. This time, there's no smile.

Sensing that his time is up, McGraw heads for the door. He did get one
valuable takeaway: "My approach to this sort of research needs to be
more professional."

When the show begins a bit later, Louis C.K. has shed all vestiges of
his preshow reticence. It takes only a couple of jokes about slavery to get
McGraw chuckling in his front-row seat. By the time the comedian describes having a bizarre dream about Gene Hackman, the professor is
completely overcome. His body jerks uncontrollably as he emits a series

of deep, braying laughs that end with a little nasal honk. This is full-on mirth.

The other people in the theater are also in hysterics. They don't know exactly why, and maybe it doesn't matter.

Understanding the Text

1. Describe the benign violation theory (BVT) of humor. According to this theory, what factors predict how funny something will be? Provide an example of this theory from the text.

2. Analyze the rhetorical situation of Warner's article. How would you describe the mode and purpose of his writing? What kind of publication is *Wired* magazine? Who comprises its intended audience?

Reflection and Response

3. At one point, Warner calls McGraw's theory "elegantly simple," but in the same paragraph he refers to it as "ludicrously, vaporously simple" (par. 20). He also includes the counterarguments of naysayers like Elliott Oring and Victor Raskin, who question the novelty of McGraw's research as well as his authority. Can you discern Warner's overall take on BVT? How do you think we are supposed to feel about McGraw after having read this piece?

4. What is your view on the validity and veracity of BVT? Can this theory of humor explain your experiences with humor? What is your first impression of professor McGraw? Does he strike you as a credible source? Why or why not?

5. Warner ends the article with an awkward encounter between McGraw and comedian Louis C.K. Why do you think Warner ends the article with this story? What was your reaction to McGraw and C.K.'s interaction?

Making Connections

6. Compare and contrast McGraw's BVT to Morreall's basic pattern of humor from this chapter. How are they similar and/or different? Which one do you find more persuasive?

7. Conduct more research on McGraw's theory. Begin by searching your library's databases for the paper he wrote with Caleb Warren, "Benign Violations: Making Immoral Behavior Funny," and by tracking down a copy of the book that McGraw and Warner wrote together, *The Humor Code: A Global Search for What Makes Things Funny* (2014). After learning more about BVT itself, research academic articles and book reviews that respond to this theory. Defend your own position on BVT in a thesis-driven essay.

Humor

Sigmund Freud

As the founder of psychoanalysis, Sigmund Freud has long been a household name. Most people have at least a passing familiarity with his notion that dreams and parapraxes, like slips of the tongue and errors in memory, reveal unconscious desires. However, Freud also believed that jokes can function as a relief valve for aggressive and sexual inhibitions. In *Jokes and Their Relation to the Unconscious* (1905), Freud argued that we save psychic energy that would normally be spent repressing hostile and carnal feelings by telling "tendentious jokes." Such jokes evade internalized forms of societal censorship and provide us with a licit way to express otherwise forbidden thoughts. In this later essay from 1927, Freud expands upon his version of relief theory by speculating on humor's role in our emotional life. (Note that Freud wrote during a time when gendered language and patriarchal values were conventional. It is up to the savvy reader to decide whether or not masculine pronouns and paternal references detract from Freud's overall argument.)

In my work on *Jokes and Their Relation to the Unconscious*, I considered humor really from the economic point of view alone. My object was to discover the source of the pleasure derived from humor, and I think I was able to show that that pleasure proceeds from a saving in expenditure of affect.°

There are two ways in which the process at work in humor may take place. Either one person may himself adopt a humorous attitude, while a second person acts as spectator, and derives enjoyment from the attitude of the first; or there may be two people concerned, one of whom does not himself take any active share in producing the humorous effect, but is regarded by the other in a humorous light. To take a very crude example: when a criminal who is being led to the gallows on a Monday observes, "Well, this is a good beginning to the week," he himself is creating the humor; the process works itself out in relation to himself and evidently it affords him a certain satisfaction. I am merely a listener who has not assisted in this functioning of his sense of humor, but I feel its effect, as it were from a distance. I detect in myself a certain humorous satisfaction, possibly much as he does.

We have an instance of the second type of humor when a writer or a narrator depicts the behavior of real or imaginary people in a humorous fashion. There is no need for the people described to display any humor;

---

affect: the psychological term for a feeling, emotion, or desire.

the humorous attitude only concerns the person who makes them the object of it, and the reader or hearer shares his enjoyment of the humor, as in the former instance. To sum up, then, we may say that the humorous attitude—in whatever it consists—may have reference to the subject's self or to other people; further, we may assume that it is a source of enjoyment to the person who adopts it, and, finally, a similar pleasure is experienced by observers who take no actual part in it.

We shall best understand the origin of the pleasure derived from humor if we consider the process which takes place in the mind of anyone listening to another man's jest. He sees this other person in a situation which leads him to anticipate that the victim will show signs of some affect; he will get angry, complain, manifest pain, fear, horror, possibly even despair. The person who is watching or listening is prepared to follow his lead, and to call up the same emotions. But his anticipations are deceived; the other man does not display any affect—he makes a joke. It is from the saving of expenditure in feeling that the hearer derives the humorous satisfaction.

It is easy to get so far, but we soon say to ourselves that it is the process 5 in the other man, the "humorist," which calls for the greater attention. There is no doubt that the essence of humor is that one spares oneself the affects to which the situation would naturally give rise and overrides with a jest the possibility of such an emotional display. Thus far, the process must be the same in the humorist and his hearer. Or, to put it more accurately, the hearer must have copied the process in the mind of the humorist. But how does the latter arrive at that mental attitude, which makes the discharge of affect superfluous? What is the dynamic process underlying the "humorous attitude"? Clearly, the solution of this problem is to be found in the humorist himself; in the listener we may suppose there is only an echo, a copy of this unknown process.

It is now time to acquaint ourselves with some of the characteristics of humor. Like wit and the comic, humor has in it a *liberating* element. But it has also something fine and elevating, which is lacking in the other two ways of deriving pleasure from intellectual activity. Obviously, what is fine about it is the triumph of narcissism, the ego's victorious assertion of its own invulnerability. It refuses to be hurt by the arrows of reality or to be compelled to suffer. It insists that it is impervious to wounds dealt by the outside world, in fact, that these are merely occasions for affording it pleasure. This last trait is a fundamental characteristic of humor. Suppose the criminal being led to execution on a Monday had said: "It doesn't worry me. What does it matter, after all, if a fellow like me is hanged? The world won't come to an end." We should have to admit that this speech of his displays the same magnificent rising superior to the real situation; what he says is wise and true, but it does not betray a trace of humor. Indeed, it is based on an appraisal of reality which runs directly counter to that of humor. Humor is not resigned; it is rebellious. It signifies the triumph not only of the ego, but also of the pleasure principle,° which is strong enough to assert itself here in the face of the adverse real circumstances.

> "Humor is not resigned; it is rebellious. It signifies the triumph not only of the ego, but also of the pleasure principle, which is strong enough to assert itself here in the face of the adverse real circumstances."

These last two characteristics, the denial of the claim of reality and the triumph of the pleasure principle, cause humor to approximate to the regressive or reactionary processes which engage our attention so largely in psychopathology. By its repudiaton of the possibility of suffering, it takes its place in the great series of methods devised by the mind of man for evading the compulsion to suffer—a series which begins with neurosis and culminates in delusions, and includes intoxication, self-induced states of abstraction and ecstasy. Owing to this connection, humor possesses a dignity which is wholly lacking, for instance, in wit, for the aim of wit is either simply to afford gratification, or, in so doing, to provide an outlet for aggressive tendencies. Now in what does this humorous attitude consist, by means of which one refuses to undergo suffering, asseverates the invincibility of one's ego against the real world and victoriously upholds the pleasure principle, yet all without quitting the ground of mental sanity, as happens when other means to the same end are adopted? Surely it seems impossible to reconcile the two achievements.

If we turn to consider the situation in which one person adopts a humorous attitude toward others, one view which I have already tentatively suggested in my book on wit will seem very evident. It is this: that the one is adopting toward the other the attitude of an adult toward a child, recognizing and smiling at the triviality of the interests and sufferings which seem to the child so big. Thus the humorist acquires his superiority by assuming the role of the grownup, identifying himself to some extent with the father, while he reduces the other people to the position of children. This supposition is probably true to fact, but it does not seem to take us very far. We ask ourselves what makes the humorist arrogate to himself this role?

pleasure principle: in psychoanalysis, the desire to obtain pleasure and avoid the opposite, that is, pain, discomfort, tension, and so on.

Here we must recall the other, perhaps the original and more important, situation in humor, in which a man adopts a humorous attitude toward himself in order to ward off possible suffering. Is there any sense in saying that someone is treating himself like a child and is at the same time playing the part of the superior adult in relation to this child?

This idea does not seem very plausible, but I think that if we consider 10 what we have learned from pathological observations of the structure of our ego, we shall find a strong confirmation of it. This ego is not a simple entity; it harbors within it, as its innermost core, a special agency: the superego. Sometimes it is amalgamated with this, so that we cannot distinguish the one from the other, while in other circumstances the two can be sharply differentiated. Genetically the superego inherits the parental function; it often holds the ego in strict subordination, and still actually treats it as the parents (or the father) treated the child in his early years. We obtain a dynamic explanation of the humorous attitude, therefore, if we conclude that it consists in the subject's removing the accent from his own ego and transferring it on to his superego. To the superego, thus inflated, the ego can appear tiny and all its interests trivial, and with this fresh distribution of energy it may be an easy matter for it to suppress the potential reactions of the ego.

To preserve our customary phraseology, let us not speak of transferring the accent, but rather of displacing large quantities of cathexis.° We shall then ask whether we are justified in imagining such extensive displacements from one agency in the mental apparatus to another. It looks like a new hypothesis, conceived ad hoc; yet we may recollect that repeatedly, even if not often enough, we have taken such a factor into account when endeavoring to form some metapsychological conception of the mental processes. For instance, we assumed that the difference between ordinary erotic object-cathexis and the state of being in love was that in the latter case incomparably more cathexis passes over to the object, the ego as it were emptying itself into the object. The study of some cases of paranoia proved to me that ideas of persecution are formed early, and exist for a long time without any perceptible effect, until as the result of some definite occasion they receive a sufficient amount of cathexis to cause them to become dominant. The cure of paranoiac attacks of this sort, too, would lie not so much in resolving and correcting the delusional ideas as in withdrawing from them the cathexis they have attracted. The alternation between melancholia and mania, between a cruel suppressing of the ego by the superego and the liberation of the ego

cathexis: in psychoanalysis, libidinal investment in or attachment to an object of desire.

after this oppression, suggests some such shifting of cathexis; and this conception would, moreover, explain a number of phenomena in normal mental life. If, hitherto, we have but seldom had recourse to this explanation, it has been on account of our customary caution, which is surely rather praiseworthy than otherwise. The ground on which we feel ourselves secure is that of mental pathology; it is here that we make our observations and win our convictions. For the present we commit ourselves to an opinion concerning the normal only insofar as we detect it among the isolated and distorted features of the morbid. When once this hesitation is overcome, we shall recognize how greatly the static conditions as well as the dynamic alteration in the quantity of the energic cathexis contribute to our understanding of mental processes.

I think, therefore, that the possibility I have suggested, namely, that in a given situation the subject suddenly effects a hypercathexis of the superego, which in its turn alters the reactions of the ego, is one which deserves to be retained. Moreover, we find a striking analogy to this hypothesis of mine about humor in the kindred field of wit. I was led to assume that wit originates in the momentary abandoning of a conscious thought to unconscious elaboration, wit being therefore the contribution of the unconscious to the comic. In just the same way humor would be a contribution to the comic made through the agency of the superego.

In other respects we know that the superego is a stern master.° It may be said that it accords ill with its character that it should wink at affording the ego a little gratification. It is true that the pleasure derived from humor is never so intense as that produced by the comic or by wit and never finds a vent in hearty laughter. It is also true that, in bringing about the humorous attitude, the superego is in fact repudiating reality and serving an illusion. But (without quite knowing why) we attribute to this less intensive pleasure a high value: we feel it to have a peculiarly liberating and elevating effect. Besides, the jest made in humor is not the essential; it has only the value of a demonstration. The principal thing is the intention which humor fulfils, whether it concerns the subject's self or other people. Its meaning is: "Look here! This is all that this seemingly dangerous world amounts to. Child's play—the very thing to jest about!"

If it is really the superego which, in humor, speaks such kindly words of comfort to the intimidated ego, this teaches us that we have still very much to learn about the nature of that agency. Further, we note that it is not everyone who is capable of the humorous attitude: it is a rare and

In other respects we know that the superego is a stern master: in other works like *Civilization and Its Discontents* (1930), Freud warned against the pathological dangers of the superego inflicting guilt on the ego by repressing its desires. Here, Freud poses a more heroic and less villainous role for the superego.

precious gift, and there are many people who have not even the capacity for deriving pleasure from humor when it is presented to them by others. Finally, if the superego does try to comfort the ego by humor and to protect it from suffering, this does not conflict with its derivation from the parental function.

Understanding the Text

1. What are the two types of humor Freud outlines at the beginning of his essay?

2. What "characteristics of humor" does Freud identify (par. 6)? Why does he attribute these qualities to humor?

3. According to traditional Freudian psychoanalysis, the source of humorous satisfaction derives from "a saving in expenditure of affect" (par. 1)? What kinds of emotions does humor spare a person from experiencing?

4. Explain the role of the superego in the attitude that adults with a healthy sense of humor assume about themselves. Is it accurate to label the humor Freud discusses "self-deprecating"? Why or why not?

Reflection and Response

5. Freud begins with some prefatory remarks on the intersubjective nature of humor: the fact that a person can vicariously experience the enjoyment he or she sees or hears in a humorist's performance. Take a moment to reflect on how your own experiences with humor involve other people. Based on your experiences, how intersubjective is the phenomenon of humor? Can one adopt a humorous attitude without an audience? Are you ever truly alone when you laugh to or by yourself? Explain.

6. In what kinds of situations do you think that humor can have a "liberating and elevating effect" (par. 13)? In what situations might it have the opposite effect of devaluing or repressing?

Making Connections

7. Peter McGraw "insists that [the benign violation theory] can explain the function of every imaginable type of humor" (p. 46). Does McGraw's theory explain the kind of humor Freud discusses in this essay? In other words, is dark comedy benign?

8. Freud illustrates his theory of rebellious humor with an example of gallows humor: "a criminal who is being led to the gallows on a Monday observes, 'Well, this is a good beginning to the week'" (par. 2). Gallows humor is a form of black comedy. Is black comedy as a genre of humor essentially rebellious? Write an essay that uses Freud's essay to analyze the politics of the black comedy found in a comedic text or real-life humorous situation.

He Looked into the Grim Reaper's Eyes and Nervously Laughed

Jeffery Klassen

Jeffery Klassen, a media studies student and frequent contributor to the Montreal-based online film journal *Offscreen*, revisits the famous theory of comedy put forth by French philosopher Henri Bergson. In his collection of essays titled *Laughter* (1900), Bergson located what is comic in the antisocial behavior of individuals who are mechanical, absentminded, and rigid.

In this essay, Klassen finds our collective "symbolic reality constructions" as the source of comedy for being "simple, weak, or flawed" (par. 8). While Bergson claimed that we laugh at others as a way of correcting their aberrant physical, mental, and moral behavior, Klassen uses Mike Judge's cult classic *Office Space* (1999) to suggest that laughter can ridicule the fallibility of society itself.

Henri Bergson's 1900 monograph, *Laughter*, attempts to outline the base elements of comedy. Bergson outlines various maxims of comedy in order to prove his main thesis that comedic texts are those which portray life in a mechanical way. This essay will review Bergson's theory of comedy and show how it can be used in an analysis of the contemporary comedic film *Office Space* ([writ. and dir.] Mike Judge, 1999). In light of seeing the strengths of Bergson's theories this essay will also attempt to offer a sort of experimental modification which, instead of emphasizing the mechanical properties of the comic, explores comedy as something which threatens peoples' psychic/symbolic realities.

Bergson's theory of comedy makes three large claims: 1) laughter is purely intellectual (and not emotional), 2) laughter is used to correct behavior in society and, 3) comedy (that which makes us laugh) can most often be understood as "the mechanical encrusted upon the living" (84). In saying that laughter is purely of the intellect Bergson is trying to understand the "absence of feeling" (63) that accompanies laughter. While we may empathize with comedic characters in stories, Bergson says, we put this aside during moments of the story where we laugh at them—we have a "momentary anesthesia of the heart" (64). There seems to be a strong element of truth to this, especially when we consider that film comedies can be set in the most grim of situations—prison, war, and even the Holocaust. While in real life we would not be able to laugh at people in these dire situations—our moral makeup, cultural or instinctual, requires us to empathize and care for them—film provides us with a temporal, cultural, and spatial distance which allows us to perceive them as objects outside of our reality (even more so with cartoons). However, if realism, grit, or emotionally powerful scenes are added, then the ability to negotiate comedy becomes more difficult, as detail and depth makes it easier for viewers to empathize with a film's subjects. One might argue that some of the greatest comic moments are those which are able to make comedy out of this difficult reality (e.g., *Borat, This is Spinal Tap*, certain types of stand-up, etc.); however, as a general comic principle, we can agree that emotional involvement creates an obstacle to our ability to laugh.

Bergson believes that comedy, at its core, is society's way of correcting unproductive behavior patterns in individuals. His theory holds that people have minds with an infinite capacity when they are not preoccupied with the body and "self-preservation" (73). While our bodies are limited by biology and the laws of physics, our minds have complete freedom to expand and imagine. But it is here, Bergson says, that because of laziness, absentmindedness, or weakness that we often behave in fixed patterns. Laughter, says Bergson, is society's way of maintaining the strength of this shared psychic realm by pointing out the unnecessarily fixed patterning in people's behavior—society sees something "rigid" (73), performs the "social gesture" (73) of laughing at it, and hence the laughed-at individual is inspired by "fear" (73) to change his or her behavior, improving themselves and the shared social world in the process (72–74). This aspect of comedy is obvious to anyone who has been laughed at for doing something stupid. Comedy is full of characters that are pathetic, foolish, weak, or socially deficient in some way. We laugh at these characters as they remind us of general patterns we see in real-life people (comedy is always pointed at the general, says Bergson) (157), and hence we are participating in the correction of general or shared social behavior patterns. This could be why the happy ending is so common in comedy—the director wants to give us the experience of some sort of social weakness being corrected (perhaps if it is uncorrectable, it shows that it is not weak and so, uncomic).

The third major claim, closely related to this "rigidity" of character, is that comedy is fundamentally about the "mechanical encrusted upon the living" (84). Bergson looks at multiple comic forms (the comic character, jokes, what children find funny, etc.) and continually finds this idea at the root. His first example is the humor in watching a running person trip over a rock. What makes us laugh, says Bergson, is that instead of the person acting with a full mind and watching where they are going, they act like absentminded machines, "involuntarily" falling because of "rigidity" and "momentum" (66). Another example is when we laugh at someone because they look funny physically (his example is the hunchback, but an important point is we laugh only to the extent that we can imitate these people). Because we can imitate them, Bergson says, it appears to us that they are acting based on a behavior pattern (the mind instead of the body) and hence we laugh as a form of corrective gesture. In dealing with film comedy, we can see Bergson's thesis most clearly in the body language of physical comedians. Buster Keaton's films have him shooting and springing around sets, running faster than life, and interacting with intricately constructed mechanical sets where much of the laughter comes from seeing him become machine-like as a result. Another example is the Three Stooges as they treat each other not like people but as unfeeling objects. They tumble, whack against each other, crank each others' body parts, walk in circles, and collide (all with mechanical sound effects), making it quite obvious that Bergson's "mechanical encrusted upon the living" thesis can go a long way in pinpointing what it is that makes films funny.

Mike Judge's 1999 comedic film *Office Space* is a good example of 5 Bergsonian comedy. The film is about the humiliating and depressing experiences of working a 9–5 cubicle job where all the main characters despise their lifestyles but continue to live them because they imagine they have no choice. Things change when a hypnotism-session-gone-wrong puts Peter (the main protagonist, played by Ron Livingston) permanently in a relaxed, Zen-like state and he decides from that point on he will live a worry-free life and only do what keeps him stress-free and happy. While others at the office are working extra hard to keep the jobs they hate, Peter shows up when he feels like it, ignores work protocol, and talks to his superiors as equals. The irony [is] that Peter is the only one who succeeds and does well while all his friends are laid off. The most obvious connection to Bergson here is in the fact that the office workers are living a mechanical-like existence based on their behavioral choices. Human beings, at our most free, are not continually bothered about reports or forced to use aggravating fax machines that absurdly never do the job they are supposed to facilitate. The film demonstrates how many people in the real world choose to live in this automaton-like way, and we laugh at this weakness in a way that seems to be laughing and correcting the real world. Another example is in the opening scene of the film where Peter, Samir (Ajay Naidu), and Michael Bolton (David Herman) are sitting in their cars frustrated by the traffic jam, which is so slow that an old man in a walker moves more quickly. The people in their cars are forced into an "involuntary" stillness. As they sit inching forward in their cars, they appear as part of a lifeless, rigid chain of events. Ironically, the weakness we are laughing at in this scene is an inefficiency—rows of slow moving cars—which mimics the hallmark of efficiency: the assembly line.

Another example, perhaps more subtle, is when one employee, Michael Bolton, expresses his extreme annoyance at continually being asked if he is related to the famous singer of the same name, whom he considers to be "a no talent ass clown." The fact that the two names are [the same] is already fitting into Bergson's theory (where repetition and coincidence are signs of mechanical-like activity); however, we also read a certain rigidity and un-free human behavior in the way that Michael repeatedly responds in the same way (with automatic annoyance) every time the subject is brought up. "Why should I change (my name)? He's the one who sucks," he says. This stubborn refusal to change is a hallmark of absentminded behavior. All of this "mechanical" behavior is signified through his facial expressions, voice, and body language, culminating in laughable gags and scenes.

Despite the supporting evidence, Bergson's theory does not seem like it can explain all comic activity, something he himself realized when he referred to his "rigidity is the comic and laughter its corrective" (74) theory as a "leitmotiv" and not a "definition" (74). The most evident sign that "the mechanical encrusted upon the living" theory might not hold up universally is that, as a metaphor, it seems very much a child of its time. At the end of the nineteenth century, the Western world was undergoing dramatic technological developments which [had a drastic impact] on social custom and behavior (developments in transportation, manufacturing, communications, etc.). The term "mechanical," which grows out of this historical condition, may limit its ability to talk exclusively and continually to laughter, a phenomenon that no doubt existed in pre-technological *homo sapiens*. A rewording and rethinking of this metaphor might give us a better concept to further explore the comic. Bergson himself mentions something interesting early on in his essay and then moves forward without returning to it. When commenting on the social gestural aspect of comedy, he describes the "material and "immaterial" aspects of the individual. As social beings, he writes, we take ourselves out of "the struggle for life" (the material aspect of ourselves/the body) and instead "adapt" (73) ourselves to the shared social realm of ideas (the immaterial aspect of ourselves/the mind) in a sort of social contract necessary for the complex functioning of organized society. As society attempts to work together, Bergson says, we use comedy as the appropriate "immaterial" means for getting this "immaterial" realm to act as a harmonious whole (72–74). Perhaps these material and immaterial realms could be further elucidated through Ernest Becker's idea of the human being as "half animal and half symbolic" (Becker 26).

In his 1977 book, *The Denial of Death*, Ernest Becker describes the human dilemma of being "gods with anuses" (51)—infinitely minded yet physically limited in our bodies. In summary, Becker believes that people build their symbolic worlds (language, ideas, concepts) around a fear of death (the body, decay, meaninglessness) and that idea systems are designed to give us a story, or "grand illusion" (56), of immortality. Becker sees religion, government, nationalism, race ideas, career choices, beliefs in love, and just about any form of immaterial concern as being necessary ("vital") lies to keep us sane. For example, the reason we believe in an afterlife is because it gives us a way to live a life, something to keep us going every day (if we had no lie, what would be the point?). His theory explains the zealousness around things like debates around evolution and religious warfare where the reason people get worked up to the point of stress and violence is that their entire immortal existence is at stake. As an experiment in deconstructing Bergson's theory, we can put comedy into this framework and get fruitful results. Maybe comedy, instead of fundamentally seeing rigidity in the realm of the symbolic, is instead more about finding flaws and weaknesses in symbolic reality

> "Maybe comedy, instead of fundamentally seeing rigidity in the realm of the symbolic, is instead more about finding flaws and weaknesses in symbolic reality constructions and, as a result, inching closer to revealing the meaninglessness in life."

constructions and, as a result, inching closer to revealing the meaninglessness in life. The reason why comedy is continually evolving and has proven difficult to pin down in one theory is because it works as a sort of antithesis to all theory—it demonstrates all symbolic systems as inherently human-made and hence fallible. Rather than placing comedy as a creator of puppet-like illusion (making the living seem mechanical), this approach reconsiders comedy as a revealer of truth (as it deconstructs lies). It is certainly not uncommon to hear "it's funny because it's true" when witnessing a stand-up comedian's act. Because our symbolic reality (which is inherently a lie) is vital to our sanity, the act of revealing it as simple, weak, or flawed, threatens us and puts us into a state of fear. This would go a long way in explaining why laughter has often been associated with aggression and fear in other analyses (like Freud, for example). While this theory supports Bergson's "social gesture" argument, it rejects the comedy-as-only-intellectual argument, and modifies the mechanical metaphor to make it more universal. Instead of correcting weakness in "the mechanical encrusted upon the living," laughter now corrects weakness in the symbolic/immaterial man-made world which operates over our material (perhaps "symbolic encrusted upon the living"). Laughter, in this theory, exists as a sign of the violence involved in attacking symbolic reality systems of individuals. If we try to show someone that their fundamental thoughts are foolish, then we are attacking the core of their necessary lie. This stress explains why people don't want to be laughed it—they want to save themselves the trouble of having to readjust their existence in some fundamental, energy-consuming manner.

This experimental revision can be reapplied to *Office Space*. The entire plot of the film is about the way we think about life on the grand scale and, subsequently, act on those beliefs. What is funny about *Office Space*, in general, is that it shows us how our youthful dreams of great careers and wonderful lifestyles often amount to monotony, disrespect, and an overall bad life. While all the characters are clinging to their jobs and hopes of riches and a decent retirement, Peter, who has disregarded this plan, strangely rises to success and is happy as a result. This is further echoed in the happiness of Lawrence, his beer-drinking couch potato friend, who rejects the corporate lifestyle yet is the most content one in the film, acting as another element which debases the corporate lifestyle plan. While it is truth that a Bergsonian mechanical-like function seems to be at play in the opening traffic jam scene, what is perhaps more fundamental is the absurdity that modern society, in its supposed immortal-like plan of ever improving, has instead evolved the world into a place where every morning people are put in torturous situations they can't get out of (the laughable being the threat to our way of technological life). In the scenes where Michael Bolton shows frustration about his name, we might say that this notion of two identical beings is funny because it shows us how absurd the naming system of society is and, hence, how absurd society is—threatening the grand scheme of thought which we all share (the social/symbolic realm of the mind). Continually, the scenes of *Office Space* show that the corporate lifestyle (which many in the real world are living) is foolish, and so the film acts as a threat to this way of life and presumably influences society to change its ways and construct stronger reality systems.

Bergson's theory elucidates many patterns of comedy, and it is still a 10 useful tool for analyzing a contemporary film such *Office Space*. While his theory has many strengths, it still leaves room for adjustment and this essay has provided a modification. While too brief and underdeveloped to be a full-fledged theory, the idea of comedy as reality debaser seems potentially fruitful, and it might be a good stepping stone to explore learning and laughter. The idea of relating learning (which can so often be work) to laughter (which is so often fun) seems like something worthwhile.

Works Cited

Becker, Ernest. *The Denial of Death.* New York: Free Press, 1973.

Bergson, Henri. "Laughter." *Comedy.* Ed. Wylie Sypher. New York: Doubleday Anchor Books, 1956.

Freud, Sigmund. *Jokes and Their Relation to the Unconscious.* New York: Norton, 1989.

Understanding the Text

1. Explain Bergson's theory of comedy and its three main claims.
2. Explain how *Office Space* supports Bergson's original social corrective theory of comedy.
3. Why does Klassen believe that Bergson's theory needs to be updated? How exactly does Klassen revise Bergson's famous theory?

Reflection and Response

4. What concepts play a key role in Klassen's argument? Does Klassen clearly define his central terms?
5. Klassen's essay provides a model for analyzing a comedic text using a theory of humor. If you were to write your own analysis of a comedic text, what attributes of Klassen's essay would you attempt to imitate, and why? What aspects would you try to avoid, and why? In other words, conduct a rhetorical analysis of his argument.

Making Connections

6. Bergson's theory and Bergson-based approaches like Klassen's work well to analyze comedic texts that feature either eccentric characters or dysfunctional social institutions (campuses, hospitals, police departments, etc.). What other comedies can you think of that support either Bergson's or Klassen's version of the social corrective theory of humor? What do these comedies say about the nature of the institutions on which they are focused?

7. Write an essay in which you propose your own theory of humor. Contemplate how theories found in this chapter relate to each other and synthesize those pertinent to your own ideas about what takes place when we laugh. To support your humor theory, provide examples of jokes, comedic texts, and real-life humorous situations.

Scene: When and Where Does Humor Occur?

Rhetoricians use the terms *kairos* and *forum* to refer to the time and place, respectively, of a rhetorical situation. Time and place play a crucial role in whether comedy, as a form of discourse, succeeds or fails. If you tell a joke in one setting, you could be met with raucous laughter. If you tell the same joke in a different scene, you might be dodging flying tomatoes (or worse). When *Jyllands-Posten*, a Danish newspaper, published controversial cartoons of the prophet Muhammad in 2005, many Muslims found the images blasphemous and racist, and over 200 people died in the ensuing protests. Misjudging a comedic context can mean the difference between a riot and a *riot.*

Humor need not target religious idols to incite controversy; humor often covers topics that polite society prefers to ignore. Audiences often respond to sexual and scatological humor with disgust, dark humor with unease, and cringe comedy with contempt. Humorists who choose an inappropriate *kairos* and forum to tackle taboo subjects will get brushed off by audiences for being too vulgar, infantile, or absurd. While humor can provide a relief valve for repressed desires and may ameliorate social tensions, when and where comedy occurs is of utmost importance in determining its ultimate rhetorical effect.

Context includes the cultural and historical circumstances that provide the setting for and influence the meaning of comic acts. In the opening reading of this chapter, magazine writer Caitlin Flanagan criticizes how the specific context of today's college campus is determining whether a comedian's performance will be found hilarious or deemed offensive. Philosopher Simon Critchley then picks up on the idea that "a sense of humor is usually highly context-specific" (p. 80), but he focuses on how the laughter that bonds a particular "we" often comes at the expense of a "them" that is othered, marginalized, and even excluded. The remaining readings in this chapter explore the role played by other aspects of the rhetorical scene of comedy, namely, *genre* (types defined by expected and

photo: FourOaks / Getty Images

repeated conventions) and *medium* (means of communication). Daniel Harris and Katherine Leyton examine the sociology of lightbulb and rape jokes, respectively, while Michael V. Teuth looks at the genre of transgressive humor as it is broadcast on the medium of cable television. Last, Aleks Krotoski and Ian Crouch evaluate the impact that the internet as a medium has had on traditional forms of comedy such as stand-up as well as in creating new genres like the grumpy cat memes.

When reading through the selections of this chapter, consider how scene in its various guises — *kairos,* forum, genre, medium — can either beget or wreck humor. Depending on the context, a humorous message sent may not be a humorous message received.

That's Not Funny!

Caitlin Flanagan

In 2015, famous comedians like Chris Rock and Jerry Seinfeld declared that they would no longer perform at universities because students had become too sensitive and politically correct. Comedic tastes certainly change over time. What people in their fifties and sixties find funny may not necessarily appeal to members of younger generations. Whether an off-color joke will make an audience laugh or cringe also depends on where it is told. What works in the comedy club might not be appropriate for a college campus.

A native of Berkeley, California, with a B.A. and an M.A. degree from the University of Virginia, author Caitlin Flanagan weighs in on the changing context of humor on today's campuses. Flanagan is a contributing editor for *the Atlantic*, where this article appeared in September 2015, and is the author of the books *Girl Land* (2012) and *To Hell with All That: Loving & Loathing Our Inner Housewife* (2004). As you read, ask yourself: Why would a joke that one person finds funny offend someone else?

Three comics sat around a café table in the chilly atrium of the Minneapolis Convention Center, talking about how to create the cleanest possible set. "Don't do what's in your gut," Zoltan Kaszas said. "Better safe than sorry." Chinedu Unaka offered. Feraz Ozel mused about the first time he'd ever done stand-up: three minutes on giving his girlfriend herpes and banging his grandma. That was out.

This was not a case of professionals approaching a technical problem as an intellectual exercise. Money was riding on the answer. They had come to Minneapolis in the middle of a brutal winter for the annual convention of the National Association for Campus Activities (NACA), to sell themselves and their comedy on the college circuit. Representatives of more than 350 colleges had come as well, to book comics, musicians, sword swallowers, unicyclists, magicians, hypnotists, slam poets, and every kind of boat act, inspirational speaker, and one-trick pony you could imagine for the next academic year.

For the comics, the college circuit offers a lucrative alternative to Chuckle Hut gigs out on the pitiless road, spots that pay a couple hundred bucks and a free night in whatever squat the club owner uses to warehouse out-of-town talent. College gigs pay easily a grand a night—often much more—and they can come in a firecracker string, with relatively short drives between schools, each hour-long performance paid for (without a moment's ugliness or hesitation) by a friendly student activities kid holding out a check and hoping for a selfie. For all these reasons, thousands of comics dream of being invited to the convention.

The colleges represented were—to use a word that their emissaries regard as numinous—diverse: huge research universities, tiny liberal arts colleges, Catholic schools, land-grant institutions. But the students' taste in entertainment was uniform. They liked their slam poets to deliver the goods in tones of the highest seriousness and on subjects of lunar bleakness; they favored musicians who could turn out covers with cheerful precision; and they wanted comedy that was 100 percent risk-free, comedy that could not trigger or upset or mildly trouble a single student. They wanted comedy so thoroughly scrubbed of barb and aggression that if the most hypersensitive weirdo on campus mistakenly wandered into a performance, the words he would hear would fall on him like a soft rain, producing a gentle chuckle and encouraging him to toddle back to his dorm, tuck himself in, and commence a dreamless sleep—not text Mom and Dad that some monster had upset him with a joke.

Two of the most respected American comedians, Chris Rock and Jerry   5 Seinfeld, have discussed the unique problems that comics face on college campuses. In November, Rock told Frank Rich in an interview for *New York* magazine that he no longer plays colleges because they're "too conservative." He didn't necessarily mean that the students were Republican; he meant that they were far too eager "not to offend anybody." In college gigs, he said, "you can't even be offensive on your way to being inoffensive." Then, in June, Seinfeld reopened the debate—and set off a frenzied round of op-eds—when he said in a radio interview that comics warn him not to "go near colleges—they're so PC."

When I attended the convention in Minneapolis in February, I saw ample evidence of the repressive atmosphere that Rock and Seinfeld described, as well as another, not unrelated factor: the infantilization of the American undergraduate, and this character's evolving status in the world of higher learning—less a student than a consumer, someone whose whims and affectations (political, sexual, pseudo-intellectual) must be constantly supported and championed. To understand this change, it helps to think of college not as an institution of scholarly pursuit but as the all-inclusive resort that it has in recent years become—and then to think of the undergraduate who drops out or transfers as an early checkout. Keeping hold of that kid for all four years has become a central obsession of the higher-ed-industrial complex. How do you do it? In part, by importing enough jesters and bards to keep him from wandering away to someplace more entertaining, taking his Pell grant and his 529 plan and his student loans with him.

But which jesters, which bards? Ones who can handle the challenge. Because when you put all of these forces together—political correctness, coddling, and the need to keep kids at once amused and unoffended (not to mention the absence of a two-drink minimum and its crowd-lubricating effect)—the black-box theater of an obscure liberal arts college deep in flyover territory may just be the toughest comedy room in the country.

"You can't use logic on these people," Geoff Keith told me over dinner at the Hilton, "or then they think you're a dick." He was about to walk through one of the frigid skyways connecting a cluster of downtown hotels to the Minneapolis Convention Center, where he would perform for 1,000 potential buyers, but he evinced not a trace of anxiety other than to glance at his iPhone now and then to make sure he wasn't late.

> "The black-box theater of an obscure liberal arts college deep in flyover territory may just be the toughest comedy room in the country."

Keith is one of the kings of the college circuit. A few years ago, he was the most-booked college comic, playing 120 campuses. He charges $2,300 for a single performance.

Keith is 31, fast-witted and handsome, possessed of an acute and often witheringly precise ability to assess people and situations. He 10 rocketed into comedy at a young age; at 22 he spent a year and a half on the road, performing with a popular headliner: Pablo Francisco, who let him do half an hour, and allowed him to tell filthy stories onstage. (Keith was a good-looking kid working big gigs in Vegas and Dallas and Chicago; he wasn't short on filthy stories.) For a while he was in danger of becoming too dirty for mainstream audiences, but he's smart and ambitious, so he toned down his material, put together a television reel, and sharpened his crowd work. He now has TV credits and a following. He lives in Los Angeles, where he kills at clubs, goes on auditions, and waits—impatiently, as do all the young and talented people in Hollywood who have passed 30—for the big break.

Until then, there's the college market, and the logic problem. Trying to explain to these kids any of the fundamental truths of stand-up— from why it's not a good idea to hold a comedy show in the cafeteria during lunch hour, to why jokes involving gay people aren't necessarily homophobic—is a nonstarter and only serves to antagonize the customers. The logic problem is also responsible for the fact that many of the comics at the convention weren't very funny, and several of those who *were* funny didn't get much work, despite garnering huge laughs and even standing ovations.

A young gay man with a Broadway background named Kevin Yee sang novelty songs about his life, producing a delirium of affection from the audience. "We love you, Kevin!" a group of kids yelled between numbers. He invited students to the front of the auditorium for a "gay dance party," and they charged down to take part. His last song, about the close relationship that can develop between a gay man and his "sassy black friend," was a killer closer; the kids roared in delight, and several African American young women in the crowd seemed to be self-identifying as sassy black friends. I assumed Yee would soon be barnstorming the country. But afterward, two white students from an Iowa college shook their heads: no. He was "perpetuating stereotypes," one of them said, firmly. "We're a very forward-thinking school," she told me. "That thing about the 'sassy black friend'? That wouldn't work for us." Many others, apparently, felt the same way: Yee ended up with 18 bookings—a respectable showing, but hardly a reflection of the excitement in the room when he performed.

If your goal were simply to bring great comics to a college campus, it would be easily accomplished. You would gather the school's comedy nerds, give them a budget, and tell them to book the best acts they could afford. But then you'd have Doug Stanhope explaining to religious kids that there's no God, or Dennis Miller telling an audience of social justice warriors that France's efforts to limit junk food in schools are part of the country's "master plan to raise healthier cowards." You would have, in other words, performers whose desire is not to soothe an audience but to unsettle it, performers who hew to Roseanne Barr's understanding of comedy: "I love stand-up. I'm totally addicted to it," she once said. "It's free speech. It's all that's left."

College campuses have never been incubators for great stand-up; during the 1960s and 1970s, schools didn't dedicate much money to bringing in entertainers, and by the time they did, PC culture had taken off. This culture—its noble aspirations and inevitable end game—was everywhere apparent at the convention. In the lavishly produced, 144-page brochure, I found a densely written block of text that began with a trumpet blast of idealism—"NACA is committed to advancing diversity development and the principles of equal opportunity and affirmative action through its respective programs"—but wound down to a muffled fart of unintended consequences: "There is no intent to support censorship."

Bringing great artists to colleges is not NACA's mission. Its mission 15 involves presenting for potential employment on American campuses a group of entertainers whose work upholds a set of ideas that has been codified by bureaucrats. And in the comedians' desperate attempts to grasp the realpolitik of the college market—and to somehow reverse engineer an act catered to it—you could see why stand-up is such a singular form: it is mercilessly ineffective as agitprop.°

Because the inclination to hold a convention in Minneapolis in February is not widely shared, the convention center was largely deserted and dystopian. Homeless men, some wearing hospital gowns and ID bracelets under their parkas, slunk quietly inside to keep warm, although if they panhandled or menaced anyone, they were bounced back onto the urban tundra by security guards. Vast expanses of the structure loomed in all directions, and empty escalators wheeled ever upward. During the day, "educational sessions" on topics of inexpressible tedium—"Wave Goodbye to Low Volunteer Retention"—droned on, testament (as are the educational sessions of a hundred other conferences) to the fact that the growth field in higher education is not Elizabethan literature or organic chemistry but mid-level administration.

All of this was enlivened—mightily—by the fact that the doors of the main auditorium regularly swung open for two-hour variety shows. These shows were like episodes of *America's Got Talent*—jolly and sparkly, sometimes diverting and sometimes wearisome—but in contrast to the lectures on volunteer retention, the gloomy convention center, and the gelid metropolis beyond, they came to seem like examples of the highest reaches of human achievement, and it was not mere journalistic zeal that had me thundering down the main aisle to grab a good seat for each new showcase.

The kids in the audience belonged to their schools' student activities committees and had thus been appointed the task of picking the paid entertainment for the next year. I found them, as a type, to be cheerful, helpful, rule-following, and nerdy. They were also—in the best sense of a loaded word—inclusive. "We don't want to sponsor an event that would offend anyone," Courtney Bennett, the incoming president of the student activities board at Western Michigan University, told me. The NACA kids were impossible not to like, although nothing about them suggested a natural talent for identifying original forms of artistic expression. They would cluster around their grown-up advisers like flocks of ducklings to powwow about the performers they had seen. Then, with the casual ease of people spending someone else's money, they would use an app to blast potential dates to the artists they liked. These were the buyers, then: one half of the equation.

The entertainers were the other half. They had come to the event on their own dime, and were trying to do whatever it took to please these

---

agitprop: derived from *agitation* and *propaganda*; refers to political propaganda typically found in art, literature, drama, or music.

young people so that they could get some road work. Their first step might have been to read the convention brochure. NACA, it explained, is dedicated to "promoting the importance" of "eliminating" any language that is "discriminatory or culturally insensitive."

O, Utopia. Why must your sweet governance always turn so quickly 20 from the Edenic to the Stalinist? The college revolutions of the 1960s — the ones that gave rise to the social justice warriors of today's campuses— were fueled by free speech. But once you've won a culture war, free speech is a nuisance, and "eliminating" language becomes a necessity.

The process begins, as such processes always do, in a committee of "undisclosed members." In the fall, an anonymous group of staff and volunteers reviews hundreds of submission tapes to determine which performers will get to showcase their acts at the convention. What this seemed to boil down to, when I looked at the slate of performers who had gotten a golden ticket, was that comics who even gestured toward the insensitive had been screened out, and those whose racial or ethnic background contributed to the diversity of the slate had been given special consideration.

There were comics of Nigerian, Afghan, Pakistani, Indian, Hispanic, and Korean–African American heritage. Some were very good. But others barely had the 15 minutes necessary for a showcase; it was hard to believe they would have the hour needed for college work. Many of these younger artists thought that if they could just get the gigs off this audition, they could then do their regular club act once they showed up on campus. They were mistaken. Tell a joke that upsets the kids, and the next morning the student activities director is going to be on the phone: to your agent, to NACA, and—more crucially—to his or her co-equals at the other four colleges in the region that you booked.

Geoff Keith had counseled Chinedu Unaka and Feraz Ozel not only to work clean, but also to confine any jokes about ethnicity to their own heritage. Unaka delivered an original and interesting set about growing up black in Los Angeles, the son of Nigerian—not African American— parents; Ozel, whose family is Middle Eastern, also did a bit about his cultural background. They were both well received, but they earned few bookings. Who could predict how such jokes would go over back on campus? Zoltan Kaszas, on the other hand, did a cheerful, anodyne set about Costco, camping, and pets. He was the breakout star of the convention. "Look at him," one student group's adviser said to me as more than 40 campus reps clamored for a visit from Kaszas. "His career just got made." Another victory for better-safe-than-sorry.

As I listened to the kids hash out whom to invite, it became clear that to get work, a comic had to be at once funny—genuinely funny—and also deeply respectful of a particular set of beliefs. These beliefs included, but were in no way limited to, the following: women, as a group, should never be made to feel uncomfortable; people whose sexual orientation falls beyond the spectrum of heterosexuality must be reassured of their special value; racial injustice is best addressed in tones of bitter anguish or inspirational calls to action; Muslims are friendly helpers whom we should cherish; and belonging to any potentially "marginalized" community involves a crippling hypersensitivity that must always be respected.

The students' determination to avoid booking any acts that might con-   25
ceivably hurt the feelings of a classmate was in its way quite admirable. They seemed wholly animated by kindness and by an open-mindedness to the many varieties of the human experience. But the flip side of this sensitivity is the savagery with which reputations and even academic careers can be destroyed by a single comment—perhaps thoughtless, perhaps misinterpreted, perhaps (God help you) intended as a joke—that violates the values of the herd.

When you talk with college students outside of formal settings, many reveal nuanced opinions on the issues that NACA was so anxious to police. But almost all of them have internalized the code that you don't laugh at politically incorrect statements; you complain about them. In part, this is because they are the inheritors of three decades of identity politics, which have come to be a central driver of attitudes on college campuses. But there's more to it than that. These kids aren't dummies; they look around their colleges and see that there are huge incentives to join the ideological bandwagon and harsh penalties for questioning the platform's core ideas.

Meanwhile—as obvious reaction to all of this—frat boys and other campus punksters regularly flout the thought police by staging events along elaborately racist themes, events that, while patently vile, are beginning to constitute the free-speech movement of our time. The closest you're going to get to Mario Savio°—sick at heart about the operation of the machine and willing to throw himself upon its gears and levers — is less the campus president of Human Rights Watch than the moron over at Phi Sigma Kappa who plans the Colonial Bros and Nava-Hos mixer.

After Geoff, Keith, and I finished dinner, we made our way to the auditorium and fell in with a group of other comics who were heading over to catch his set. Keith is deeply respected in this crowd: he may

---

Mario Savio: (1942–1996) a political activist best known for his participation in the Free Speech Movement at the University of California, Berkeley, in the mid-1960s.

still be developing his career in the real comedy world, the one where you perform for grown-ups, but he can book as many colleges as he wants.

Keith was dressed not in the understated clothing he wears in comedy clubs, but in an almost clownish getup: bright-pink pants, a green shirt, a polka-dot tie. The outfit was strategic—he didn't want a kid forgetting his name and booking the wrong comic; he would remind the audience to think of him as the guy in the pink pants. Instead of performing for 15 minutes, he would cut his set short at the first big laugh after the 12-minute mark, so that the act would seem to fly by. He would tell jokes about his fiancée's strict father, and getting out of jury duty, and tricking someone by using an English accent. The students would love him, and book him in great numbers, as they always do.

But he would not tell the jokes that kill at the clubs. He would not do 30 the bit that ends with him offering oral sex to the magician David Copperfield, or the one about a seductive woman warning him that she might be an ax murderer, or the one about why men don't like to use condoms. Those jokes include observations about power and sex and even rape—and each, in its complicated way, addresses certain ugly and possibly immutable truths. But they are jokes, not lessons from the gender studies classroom. Their first objective is to be funny, not to service any philosophical ideal. They go where comedy always wants to go, to the darkness, and they sucker-punch you with a laugh when you don't think you should laugh.

And maybe you shouldn't. These young people have decided that some subjects—among them rape and race—are so serious that they shouldn't be fodder for comics. They want a world that's less cruel; they want to play a game that isn't rigged in favor of the powerful. And it's their student activities money, after all—they have every right to hire the exact type of entertainment that matches their beliefs. Still, there's always a price to pay for walling off discussion of certain thoughts and ideas. Drive those ideas underground, especially the dark ones, and they fester.

Sarah Silverman has described the laugh that comes with a "mouth full of blood"—the hearty laugh from the person who understands your joke not as a critique of some vile notion but as an endorsement of it. It's the essential peril of comedy, as performers from Dave Chappelle to, most recently, Amy Schumer understand all too well. But to enroll in college and discover that for almost every aspect of your experience—right down to the stand-up comics who tell jokes in the student union—great care has been taken to expose you to only the narrowest range of approved social and political opinions: that's the mouth full of blood right there.

Understanding the Text

1. According to Flanagan, what kind of comedy can and cannot be performed at contemporary college campuses? How does she characterize the type of comic performers that colleges are looking to book?

2. How does Flanagan address counterarguments to her position about which comedians do and do not get hired to perform on college campuses? Discuss at least two examples of her treatment of positions that oppose her own.

3. What assumptions about the nature of comedy underpin Flanagan's position? For example, what does she mean by claiming that stand-up "is mercilessly ineffective as agitprop" (par. 15)?

Reflection and Response

4. What assumptions about the state of the contemporary university and its students underpin Flanagan's position? Do you agree with them? Does your experience at college fit her descriptions? Why or why not?

5. What do you think those tasked with hiring comedians to perform on campus should consider when making their decisions? What should comedians think about before trying out to perform on campus?

6. Where do you as a college student draw the line between appropriate comedy and jokes that you believe are offensive? Why do you draw the line where you do?

Making Connections

7. Conduct research on the reasons why well-established comedians like Jerry Seinfeld and Chris Rock have become disaffected with performing on college campuses. In an essay that cites at least three sources besides Flanagan's article, defend a thesis on the issue of potentially offensive humor, political correctness, and censorship in the context of the contemporary university.

8. In her concluding paragraph, Flanagan mentions comedian Dave Chappelle (par. 32). Among other reasons, Chappelle stopped doing his Comedy Central sketch series *Chappelle's Show* (2003–2006) because he felt that members of his audience were enjoying his race-based humor for bigoted reasons. In short, they were missing or ignoring the ironic context of his skits. Write an essay on whether or not comedians can be held responsible for an audience who "understands [a] joke not as a critique of some vile notion but as an endorsement of it" (par. 32).

Foreigners Are Funny: The Ethicity and Ethnicity of Humor

Simon Critchley

Simon Critchley is a British philosopher and professor at The New School in New York City who has written several books on ethics, politics, religion, and aesthetics. In *On Humour* (2002), he argues that true humor reveals our shared practices and beliefs while challenging us to question what we regard as common sense. In this way, comedians function much like philosophers, whose job it is to make us think critically about that which we take for granted.

While Critchley's claim about the critical function of comedy is largely normative, he concedes that most humor upholds the status quo by delineating between that which is normal and that which is aberrant. Such humor often pits a superior "us" against an inferior "them." In the following excerpt from *On Humour*, Critchley points out the predictable drawbacks of ethnic and parochial humor but also its potential benefits.

Jokes are like small anthropological essays. If one of the tasks of the anthropologist is to revise and relativize the categories of Western culture by bumping them up against cultures hitherto adjudged exotic, then we might say with Henk Driessen that:

Anthropology shares with humor the basic strategy of defamiliarization: common sense is disrupted, the unexpected is evoked, familiar subjects are situated in unfamiliar, even shocking contexts in order to make the audience or readership conscious of their own cultural assumptions.[1]

The lesson that Driessen draws from this is that anthropologists are akin to comedians, tricksters, clowns, or jesters. The lesson that we can draw from Driessen is that humor is a form of critical social anthropology, defamiliarizing the familiar, demythologizing the exotic, and inverting the world of common sense. Humor views the world awry, bringing us back to the everyday by estranging us from it. This is what I mean . . . when I claim that humor provides an oblique phenomenology of ordinary life. It is a practice that gives us an alien perspective on our practices. It lets us view the world as if we had just landed from another planet. The comedian is the anthropologist of our humdrum everyday lives.

Any study of humor, again like anthropology, requires fieldwork and detailed contextualization. Finally, it is only as good as its examples.

And what makes humor both so fascinating and tricky to write about is the way in which the examples continually exceed the theoretical analysis one is able to give of them—they say more in saying less. For Driessen, the lesson to be drawn from anthropology is the humility of a certain cultural relativism, as a strategy aimed at combating the intolerance and racism of Western ethnocentrism. Now, is the same true of humor? Your sense of humor may not be the same as mine—let us hope it is not for both of our sakes—but does the study of humor lead us to embrace cultural relativism?

The Universal and the Particular

With this question, arguably the most intractable dilemma of humor can be broached: the universal *versus* the particular. Most studies of humor, jokes, and the comic begin by claiming that humor is universal. Apparently there have never been cultures without laughter, although the varieties and intensities of humor vary dramatically. Mary Douglas writes:

We know that some tribes are said to be dour and unlaughing. Others laugh easily. Pygmies lie on the ground and kick their legs in the air, panting and shaking in paroxysms of laughter.[2]

However, to say that humor is universal is, of course, to say almost nothing, or very little. All cultures laugh, just as all cultures have a language and most of them seem to have some sort of religious practice usually involving a belief in a hidden metaphysical reality and an afterlife. So what? The fact that all cultures laugh might be a formal universal truth, of the same order as admitting that all human beings eat, sleep, breathe and defecate, but it tells us nothing at the level of a concrete context, and that is where matters begin to get difficult and interesting.

Humor is local and a sense of humor is usually highly context-specific. Anyone who has tried to render what they believe to be a hugely funny joke into a foreign language only to be met by polite incomprehension will have realized that humor is terribly difficult to translate, perhaps impossible. Although various forms of nonverbal humor can travel across linguistic frontiers, witness the great success enjoyed by the *Commedia dell'arte°* throughout Europe in the sixteenth and seventeenth centuries

---

Commedia dell'arte: a form of improvisational theater popular in Italy in the 16th-18th centuries in which a traveling group of performers donned masks and played stock characters.

and the enduring popularity of various forms of mime and silent comedy, such as Chaplin, Monsieur Hulot, and Mr. Bean, verbal humor is notoriously recalcitrant to translation. The speed and brevity of wit can become tiresome and prolix in another tongue, and a joke explained is a joke killed. In 1921, Paul Valéry noted, "Humor is untranslatable. If this was not the case, then the French would not use the word."[3] But if Valéry is right and the French use humor because it is untranslatable, then might it not be the very untranslatability of humor that somehow compels us? Might not its attraction reside in the fact that it cannot be explained to others, and that humorous *savoir faire*° always contains a certain *je ne sais quoi*?°

Humor is a form of cultural insider-knowledge, and might, indeed, be said to function like a linguistic defense mechanism. Its ostensive untranslatability endows native speakers with a palpable sense of their cultural distinctiveness or even superiority. In this sense, having a common sense of humor is like sharing a secret code. Indeed, is this not the experience of meeting a compatriot in an otherwise foreign environment, on holiday or at a conference, where the rapidity of one's intimacy is in proportion to both a common sense of humor and a common sense of humor's exclusivity? We wear our cultural distinctiveness like an insulation layer against the surrounding alien environment. It warms us when all else is cold and unfamiliar.

Ethos and Ethnos

If, as I have claimed, humor can be said to return us to physicality and animality, then it also returns us to *locality*, to a specific and circumscribed *ethos*. It takes us back to the place we are from, whether that is the concreteness of a neighborhood or the abstraction of a nation-state. The word *ethos* must here be understood in its ancient Greek sense, as both custom and place, but also as disposition and character. A sense of humor is often what connects us most strongly to a specific place and leads us to predicate characteristics of that place, assigning certain dispositions and customs to its inhabitants. The sweet melancholy of exile is often rooted in a nostalgia for a lost sense of humor.

There is a further link to be made here between *ethos* and *ethnos*, in the sense of a people, tribe, social group, or, in the modern world, nation. In relation to humor, this is often vaguely expressed in two ways: first

---

savoir faire: expertise or the ability to speak or act appropriately in social situations.
je ne sais quoi: something that cannot be adequately described; literally "I do not know what."

that "foreigners" do not have a sense of humor; and, second, that they are funny. Such are the powerful basic ingredients of ethnic humor. Recall that George Orwell famously said that the British Empire was based on two fundamental beliefs: "nothing ever changes," and "foreigners are funny."[4] In ethnic humor, the *ethos* of a place is expressed by laughing at people who are not like us, and usually believed to be either excessively stupid or peculiarly canny. In England, the Irish are traditionally described as stupid and the Scots as canny; in Canada, the Newfies and the Nova Scotians assume these roles; in Finland, the Karelians are deemed stupid and the Laihians clever; in India, the Sikhs and the Gujaratis occupy these places. Either way, the belief is that "they" are inferior to "us" or at least somehow disadvantaged *because* "they" are not like "us." Such is the menacing flipside of a belief in the untranslatability and exclusivity of humor.[5]

The facts of ethnic humor are all too well known: the French laugh at the Belgiums, the Belgiums laugh at the Dutch, and the Dutch laugh right back. The Danes laugh at the Swedes, the Swedes laugh at the Finns, and the Finns laugh right back. The Scots laugh at the English, and the English laugh at the Irish, and the Irish laugh right back. The Germans laugh at the Ostfrieslanders and everyone else laughs rather nervously at the Germans. In relation to humor, the Germans are obviously a special case and much could be said about anti-German jokes, whose history stretches back at least 200 years, a case that was obviously not helped overmuch by the events of the last century. German humor is no laughing matter. Ted Cohen relates a splendidly objectionable joke:

The thing about German food is that no matter how much you eat, an hour later you are hungry for power.[6]

This qualifies as what Cohen calls a "meta-joke," where the condition for the joke is the fact you already know the joke about Chinese food invariably leaving one hungry soon after eating. Therefore, this is not just a joke, but a joke about a joke, a sheer play upon form.

It is indeed interesting to note no lesser a personage than George Eliot writing in 1856 in a fascinating essay on the great German wit, Heinrich Heine:

. . . German humor generally shows no sense of measure, no instinctive tact; it is either floundering and clumsy as the antics of a leviathan, or laborious and interminable as a Lapland day, in which one loses all hope that the stars and quiet will ever come.

NEW YORK JEWS   **SAN FRANCISCO CHINAMEN**   **CLEVELAND INDIANS**

*No race, creed, or religion should endure the ridicule faced by Native Americans today. Please help us
put an end to this mockery and racism by visiting www.ncai.org or calling (202) 466-7767.*

NATIONAL CONGRESS OF AMERICAN INDIANS

This poster from the National Congress of American Indians (NCAI) includes
two fictional baseball hats with stereotypical racist images shown beside the
real Cleveland Indians logo (right). By comparing them, the NCAI demonstrates
how the logos appear equally offensive and highlights Critchley's notion that
certain ethnic groups are often prime targets for prejudice and negative
characterizations.

© DeVito Verdi

Warming to her theme, she continues,   10

*A German comedy is like a German sentence: you see no reason in its structure
why it should ever come to an end, and you accept the conclusion as an ar-
rangement of Providence rather than that of the author.*[7]

We should note that Heine got his own back in typical style by describing the English language as the "hiss of egoism" ("Zischlaute des
Egoismus"). Now, such humor is undoubtedly funny. But it is neither innocent, nor to be strongly recommended. The curious feature of the
German case is that the alleged absence of a sense of humor has been
thoroughly internalized by German culture and one often hears one's
German friends bemoaning their lack of a sense of humor.

In my view, the intimate connection between the ethnicity and
"ethicity" of humor must be recognized and not simply sidestepped.
Ethnic humor is very much the Hobbesian laughter of superiority or sudden glory at our eminence and the other's stupidity. It is a curious fact that
much humor, particularly when one thinks of Europe, is powerfully connected to perceived, but curiously outdated, national styles and national
differences. There is something deeply anachronistic about much humor,
and it refers nostalgically to a past whose place in the present is almost
mythical, certainly fantastical. For good or ill, old Europe still has a robust
fantasy life.

There Was a Frenchman, an Englishman and an Irishman . . .

Although I have spent many happy hours thumbing its pages, it is always an open question how much etymological authority one should invest in the *Oxford English Dictionary*. If one consults the entry on "humor," the *OED* states that the first recorded usage of the word to indicate something amusing or jocular occurs in 1682. This is obviously not to say that there was no humor prior to that date, but rather that the association of the word "humor" with the comic and the jocular is an innovation that belongs to a specific time and place: the English language in the late seventeenth century. Prior to that date, humor signified a mental disposition or temperament, as in Ben Jonson's "Every man in his humor," from 1598. The earlier meaning derived from the ancient Greek medical doctrine of the four humors or fluids that made up and regulated the body: blood, phlegm, bile, and black bile (*melancolia*). It is this link between humor and melancholy that Breton suggests in his notion of *humour noir*.°

Thus, the association of humor with the comic and jocular is specifically modern and arises in the period of the rise of the modern nation-state, in particular the astonishing rise of Britain as a trading, colonizing, and warring nation after the establishment of constitutional monarchy in the Glorious Revolution of 1688. . . . The modernity of humor is something also apparent in French accounts of the origin of the concept. Although the English word is originally a French borrowing, from the Anglo-Norman *humour* and the Old French *humor*, it is curious to note that French dictionaries claim that the modern sense of humor is an English borrowing. The *Dictionnaire de l' Académie Française* is quite adamant on this point. "Humor" is a:

[w]ord borrowed from English. A form of irony, at once pleasant and serious, sentimental and satirical, that appears to belong particularly to the English spirit [l'esprit anglais].[8]

With the dissenting voice of Voltaire, who thought that the English had stolen the notion of humor from the comedies of Corneille, French authors in the eighteenth century and as late as Victor Hugo in 1862 refer to "that English thing they call humor."[9]

One finds the same view in Diderot's and D'Alembert's *Encyclopédie*, in a fascinating short article that may have been written by Diderot himself, although the attribution is not certain. "Diderot" writes:

humour noir: black or dark comedy; humor that makes light of morbid subjects like death.

HUMOUR: The English use this word to designate an original, uncommon and singular pleasantry. Amongst the authors of that nation, no one possesses humour, *or this original pleasantry, to a higher degree than Swift. By the force which he is able to give to his pleasantries, Swift brings about effects amongst his compatriots that one would never expect from the most serious and well-argued works,* ridiculum acri, *etc. Thus it is, in advising the English to eat little Irish children with their cauliflowers, Swift was able to hold back the English government which was otherwise ready to remove the last means of sustenance and commerce from the Irish people. This pamphlet has the title, "A Modest Proposal."*[10]

We should note the exemplary place of Swift in this French history as the "plus haut point"° of English humor. This is something continued in Breton, who begins his anthology of *humour noir* with Swift's "Modest Proposal." Breton claims Swift as "the true initiator" of *humour noir,* and as the inventor of "ferocious and funereal pleasantry" (*"la plaisanterie féroce et funèbre"*).[11] Of course, the question of ethnicity returns once again here, for it is curious, indeed paradoxical, to define humor as something essential to *"l'esprit anglais,"* and then to give Swift as the highest example of English humor: the Dean was not exactly English. As Beckett replied when he was asked by an American journalist whether he was English: *"au contraire."* The same reply might also apply to Swift, Sterne, Wilde, Joyce and many other Irish contraries to Englishness. But if Irishness is the contrary of Englishness, then it is important to point [out] that it is an internal contradiction. Humor is a battlefield in the relation between what Richard Kearney rightly calls those national Siamese twins, England and Ireland, locked together in a suffocatingly close, often deathly embrace.[12]

Having the Courage of Our Parochialism

So, humor is what returns us to our locale, to a specific *ethos* which is often identified with a particular people possessing a shared set of customs and characteristics. A sense of humor is often what is felt to be best shared with people who are from the same place as us, and it is that aspect of social life which is perhaps the most difficult to explain to people from somewhere else. That is to say, humor puts one back in place in a way that is powerfully particular and recalcitrantly relative.

15

> "Humor is what returns us to our locale, to a specific *ethos* which is often identified with a particular people possessing a shared set of customs and characteristics."

plus haut point: the highest point.

This point is important because we should not, in my view, shy away from the relativistic nature of humor. When it comes to what makes us laugh, "we must," as Frank Cioffi writes, "have the courage of our parochialism."[13] As I have claimed, humor puts us back in place, whether the latter is our neighborhood, region, or nation. Now it *can* do this triumphantly, and this is the basic feature of ethnic humor. However, it *need* not put us back in place in this manner. It might equally put one back in one's place with the anxiety, difficulty, and, indeed, shame of where one is from, a little like trying to explain the impotent rage of English football hooligans to foreign friends. Perhaps one laughs at jokes one would rather *not* laugh at. Humor can provide information about oneself that one would rather *not* have.

This phenomenon is probably most sharply revealed in the gap between what one found funny in the past and what one now finds funny. Episodes of *Monty Python* that had me innocently rolling on the floor in prepubescent mirth in the early 1970s, and which we—like so many others—laboriously tried to rehearse word-for-word during lunch breaks at school, now seem both curiously outdated, not that funny, and crammed full of rather worrying colonial and sexist assumptions. Equally, as an eager cosmopolitan, I would rather not be reminded of national differences and national styles, yet our sense of humor can often unconsciously pull us up short in front of ourselves, showing how prejudices that one would rather not hold can continue to have a grip on one's sense of who one is.

In this sense, one might say that the very relativity of humor can function as an (un)timely reminder of who one is, and the nature of what Heidegger would call one's *Geworfenheit,* or thrownness. If humor returns us to our locale, then my point is that it can do this in an extremely uncomfortable way, precisely as thrown into something I did not and would not choose. If humor tells you something about who you are, then it might be a reminder that you are perhaps not the person you would like to be. As such, the very relativity of humor might be said to contain an indirect appeal that this place stands in need of change, that history is, indeed, in Joyce's words, a nightmare from which we are all trying to awake.

Comic Repression

A similar point can also be made in Freudian terms. In *The Interpretation of Dreams*, Freud makes a very perceptive remark about the relation between the comic and repression:

Evidence, finally, of the increase in activity which becomes necessary when these primary modes of functioning are inhibited is to be found in the fact that we produce a comic *effect, that is, a surplus of energy which has to be discharged in* laughter, if we allow these modes of thinking to force their way through into consciousness.[14]

The claim here is that I produce a surplus of energy in laughter to cope with my inhibition when repressed unconscious material threatens to force its way through into consciousness. For example, my tight-lipped refusal to laugh at an anti-Semitic joke might well be a symptom of my repressed anti-Semitism. As Freud claims, jokes have a relation to the unconscious; they articulate and reveal a certain economy of psychical expenditure. In this sense, ethnic jokes can be interpreted as symptoms of societal repression, and they can function as a return of the repressed. As such, jokes can be read in terms of what or simply who a particular society is subordinating, scapegoating or denigrating. Grasping the nature of societal repression can itself be liberating, but only negatively. As Trevor Griffiths writes, "A joke that feeds on ignorance starves its audience."[15]

Notes

1. "Humour, laughter and the field: reflections from anthropology," *A Cultural History of Humour*, 227.

2. Mary Douglas, "Do dogs laugh?" and "Jokes" from *Implicit Meanings: Essays in Anthropology* (Routledge, London, 1975), 84.

3. Cited in *Le Grand Robert de la Langue Française,* 10th Edition, Paris, 1985. Vol. 5, p. 288. This text by Valéry is also briefly discussed in the Preface to Andre Breton's *Anthologie de l'humour noir* (Jean-Jacques Pauvert, Paris, 1966), 11.

4. "Boys' Weeklies" from *Inside the Whale and Other Essays* (Penguin, London, 1957), 187.

5. On ethnic humor, the definitive study is Christie Davies's *Ethnic Humor Around the World* (Indiana University Press, Bloomington, 1990), which is a rich, compendious, and extremely helpful work. Davies provides a thorough taxonomy of ethnic humour, persuasively identifying surprisingly common patterns among ethnic jokes from all across the world that can be divided into jokes about the stupid and canny. Therefore, despite the undoubted relativity of the butt of jokes in different contexts, their form remains remarkably similar. Davies outlines the same argument in "Stupidity and Rationality: Jokes from the Iron Cage," *Humour in Society* (Macmillan, Basingstoke, 1988), 1–32, where he views jokes about stupidity not as ethnic jokes viciously directed toward hated others but as a reaction to the excessive rationalization of society. As such, ethnic jokes can be forms of protest. Personally, I have my doubts.

6. Ted Cohen, *Jokes: Philosophical Thoughts on Joking Matters* (University of Chicago Press, Chicago, 1999), 21.

7. George Eliot, "German Wit: Heinrich Heine," in *Selected Essays, Poems and Other Writings,* eds. A.S. Byatt and N. Warren (Penguin, Harmondsworth, 1990), 73.

8. Huitième Edition, Hachette, Paris, 1935, 29.

9. Jan Bremmer and Herman Roodenburg, *A Cultural History of Humour* (Polity, Cambridge, 1997), 1–2.

10. *Encyclopédie, Nouvelle impression en facsimile de la première edition de 1751–80* (Fromann Verlag, Stuttgart-Bad Cannstatt, 1967), Vol. VIII. 353.

11. Breton, *Anthologie de l'humour noir,* 19–21.

12. See Richard Kearney, *On Stories* (Routledge, London, 2002).

13. Frank Cioffi, *Wittgenstein on Freud and Frazer* (Cambridge University Press, Cambridge, 1998), 18.

14. Sigmund Freud, *The Interpretation of Dreams,* trans. J. Strachey (Penguin, London, 1976), 766.

15. Trevor Griffiths, *Comedians* (Faber, London, 1976), 23.

Understanding the Text

1. What does Critchley mean by *ethos* and *ethnos*?

2. What is Critchley's opinion of ethnic humor? Can ethnic humor ever serve a positive purpose? Why or why not?

3. What are the early definitions of the term *humor* that Critchley discusses? Why does Critchley discuss these definitions? How do they relate to his overall argument?

Reflection and Response

4. How does what you currently find funny differ from what you used to find funny? Does your changing sense of humor make you feel uncomfortable about who you have been? How would you characterize your current sense of humor?

5. Critchley provides several examples of ethnic groups — many of them defined by national citizenship — who laugh at other ethnicities. Does such humor, in your experience, pertain to other groups besides ethnicities? Write about a joke that one group of people tells about a "foreign" group that they perceive as inferior.

Making Connections

6. Critchley begins by discussing how "jokes are like small anthropological essays" because they "defamiliariz[e] the familiar" (par. 1). Compare Critchely's idea here to Michael Kimmel's essay (p. 297). How does Kimmel defamiliarize the familiar by providing a "critical social anthropology" (par. 1)?

7. Critchley cites Freud while arguing that "ethnic jokes can be interpreted as symptoms of societal repression, and they can function as a return of the repressed" (par. 19). What societal repressions underpin ethnic jokes currently popular in the United States? What do these jokes reveal about contemporary Americans?

How Many Lightbulb Jokes Does It Take to Chart an Era?

Daniel Harris

Daniel Harris is a cultural critic and the author of a handful of books, such as *The Rise and Fall of Gay Culture* (1999); *Cute, Quaint, Hungry, and Romantic: The Aesthetics of Consumerism* (2000); and *Celebrity: A Star-Studded Look at Consuming Fame* (2009).

In this essay, originally published in the *New York Times Magazine* in 1997, Harris argues that lightbulb jokes — and by extension similar jokes — function as historical artifacts that can reveal much about a particular time and place.

Unlike knock-knock jokes, dead-baby jokes, dumb-blonde jokes, and why-did-the-chicken-cross-the-road jokes, the lightbulb joke is uniquely political. Not only does it make references to current events (how many Canadian separatists, how many Branch Davidians), it also summarizes, in epigrammatic form, the history of the second half of the twentieth century, excoriating in virtually the same breath the illegal immigrant and the gainfully employed bureaucrat, big government and big business, homosexuals and homophobes, shrinks and paranoids. And because the lightbulb joke involves a piece of electrical equipment, it mirrors our ambivalent attitudes toward technology, which, ever since Thomas Edison invented the incandescent bulb in 1879, has become so complex that we can no longer install and repair our appliances without enlisting the services of price-gouging experts. In the lightbulb joke, the ancient literary genre of the riddle demonstrates its versatility and wickedly dissects the problems of the machine age.

The crux of the joke's humor lies in the words "how many" since in most instances changing a lightbulb requires only one person—not the teeming hordes of support technicians and service providers who crowd around the ladder protesting unsafe working conditions and developing special bulb-insertion software. The lightbulb joke is, in spirit, both anti-corporate and anti-Federal, providing a perfect vehicle for satirizing byzantine bureaucracies. It is the ideal joke of an era of upsizing, in which both large corporations and government agencies have bloated staffs that will allow the bulb to be changed only after the completion of environmental impact statements, ergonomic reports, and Civil Service examinations conducted for the Lightbulb Administrator position. It is a deeply American joke, full of the rage of the Republican rebel who despises the social welfare state and advocates instead a pioneering philosophy of self-rule. At the risk of overstatement, you might suggest that the historical roots of the joke's libertarian agenda lie in the colonists' rejection of royalist tyranny and the nineteenth-century frontiersmen's love of personal initiative.

The lightbulb joke is also well suited to an age of consumer protection campaigns and media exposés of the potentially life-threatening dangers of defective products, from exploding gas tanks to leaking silicone breast implants. It resonates with our suspicion of the rapaciousness of specialists eager to make a quick buck at the expense of both our pocketbooks and our physical safety, like the six garage mechanics, five of whom hold the ladder while the other gives the estimate at the end of the month. Within the context of its virtually infinite permutations, the joke transforms the lightbulb into a kind of symbolic Every Commodity, whose purchase and installation is complicated by malfunctioning components and hidden costs. (How many IBM PC owners? Only one, but the purchase of the lightbulb adapter card is extra.)

The joke is peculiarly modern because it makes sense only in an era in which the middle-class homeowner maintains his own property and is unable to afford the servants who, in a long-lost age of cheap immigrant labor, would have changed his bulbs for him. It is at once the epitaph for an obsolete class of household slaves and the patriotic battle hymn of the bedraggled housewife and the diligent handyman who cut their own lawns and unclog their own sinks. In the late twentieth century, we are all bulb changers, participants in a pedestrian task that unites the rich with the poor.

The lightbulb is a highly charged ideological object in our aging 5 democracy—an emblem of normality, of a society that stigmatizes its exceptional citizens, reviling their lack of conformity and mechanical ineptitude as unpardonable evidence of their elitism. The ability to perform this simple household chore becomes a test of one's humanity, and those outcasts who fail are immediately interned in the menagerie of buffoons that the lightbulb joke so mercilessly pillories.

The joke singles out two contrasting groups in its role as an equal-opportunity leveler. On the one hand, it ridicules bungling minorities whose spatulate fingers are ill equipped to handle this fragile glass object, smashing the bulb with a hammer, cutting it in two with a chain saw, or getting drunk until the room spins. On the other hand, it is increasingly used to satirize overeducated scientists who intellectualize a task that involves a mere twist of the wrist, compiling libraries of software documentation or defining Darkness™ as a new industry standard. Simultaneously snobbish and anti-elitist, the joke reflects an identity crisis occurring among angry white males. Hemmed in from below by destitute ethnic groups and from above by incomprehensible aristocracies of white-collar intellectuals, the average citizen holds himself up as the exemplar of common sense, which inevitably prevails over those who refuse to turn the bulb without first completing the software upgrade and drawing up forbiddingly complex contracts governing brown-outs or pratfalls.

The fact that a single joke is used to belittle the supposed deficiencies of minorities and the esoteric skills of the intelligentsia suggests that, in some sense, we equate the tensions caused by ethnic conflicts with the tensions caused by the new hierarchies of knowledge. Both ethnic diversity and profound inequalities of information and know-how are contributing to social unrest, to the demoralizing feelings of inadequacy and competitiveness that are tearing apart a nation already fractured by intolerance. It is not an accident that the same joke is used to ridicule the homeboy and the software designer; both are viewed with distrust as members of subversive minorities.

One of the most surprising features of the lightbulb joke is how the lowly bulb has been used to make fun of the exalted computer, spawning scores of lightbulb jokes about Silicon Valley. (How many hardware engineers? Thirty—but, of course, just like years ago all it took was a couple of kids in a garage in Palo Alto.) Far from streamlining the modern environment, mechanization has made our lives more complex and has needlessly confused straightforward tasks like setting the clocks on our VCRs, paralyzing us with the cerebral intricacies of a chore it has turned into an indecipherable electronic puzzle. The joke catches the machine age in the nostalgic act of clarifying its original purpose—that of making things simpler, faster, easier to use.

The lightbulb joke reflects another form of social unrest. In the not too distant past, it was an uncensored forum for socially acceptable expressions of racism, homophobia, anti-Semitism and misogyny. (How many feminists? Two—one to declare that the bulb has violated the socket and one to secretly wish that she were the socket.) In the 1990s, however, the joke is being turned against its traditional tellers by a gang of comic vigilantes bent on evening the score. It is a joke in turmoil, the battleground of a small civil war in which minorities, who for decades remained in tight-lipped silence as loudmouthed Archie Bunkers taunted them in public, are now talking back, lambasting such groups as homophobes, who

> "The fact that a single joke is used to belittle the supposed deficiencies of minorities and the esoteric skills of the intelligentsia suggests that, in some sense, we equate the tensions caused by ethnic conflicts with the tensions caused by the new hierarchies of knowledge."

Charting an Era with Lightbulb Jokes

Circa 1950
How many Polacks does it take to screw in a lightbulb?
Five—one to stand on a table and hold the bulb in the socket and four to rotate the table.

1960s
How many psychiatrists does it take to screw in a lightbulb?
Only one, but the lightbulb has to really *want* to change.

Circa 1970
How many feminists does it take to screw in a lightbulb?
One—and that's *not funny*!

1980s
How many Reagan aides does it take to screw in a lightbulb?
None—they like to keep him in the dark.
How many Holocaust revisionists does it take to screw in a lightbulb?
None—they just deny that the bulb ever went out in the first place.
How many Communists does it take to screw in a lightbulb?
One, but it takes him about 30 years to realize that the old one has burned out.

1986
How many Ukrainians does it take to screw in a lightbulb?
They don't need lightbulbs; they glow in the dark.

Date Unknown
How many Surrealists does it take to screw in a lightbulb?
A fish.

Early 1990s
How many baby boomers does it take to screw in a lightbulb?
Ten—six to talk about how great it is that they've all come together to do this, one to screw it in, one to film it for the news, one to plan a marketing strategy based on it, and one to reminisce about mass naked bulb-screwing in the 1960s.
How many Gen Xers does it take to screw in a lightbulb?
Two—one to shoplift the bulb so the boomers have something to screw in and the other to screw it in for minimum wage.

1990s
How many Microsoft executives does it take to screw in a lightbulb?
None—Bill Gates will just redefine Darkness™ as the industry standard.

Circa 1991
How many LA cops does it take to screw in a lightbulb?
Six—one to do it and five to smash the old bulb to splinters.

1995
How many O. J. jurors does it take to screw in a lightbulb?
None of them believe it is broken.

1997
How many Dolly clones does it take to screw in a lightbulb?
As many as you'd like. As many as you'd like.

change the bulb with sterile rubber gloves because it is possible that a gay person with AIDS just touched it. The scapegoats have been elevated from the butt of the joke to the joke tellers, a promotion that mirrors their increasing integration into society. While very little has been done from 1879 to the age of the politically incorrect to improve Edison's invention, the lightbulb joke has been constantly reinvented.

Understanding the Text

1. According to Harris, what is the "crux of the [lightbulb] joke's humor" (par. 2)? Which characteristics of lightbulbs does Harris think are important to the joke's effectiveness?

2. In what ways does the lightbulb joke chart the second half of the twentieth century? How is the joke "peculiarly modern" (par. 4)?

3. What forms of social unrest does the lightbulb joke reflect? How did the joke evolve in the 1990s, according to Harris?

Reflection and Response

4. How does the list of lightbulb jokes that accompanies Harris's essay help support his arguments? Did you know enough about the historical context of these jokes to get them? Were any offensive to you? How about funny? Why or why not?

5. Harris claims that "the lightbulb joke has been constantly reinvented" (par. 9), but his essay was published in the late 1990s. Are you familiar with any contemporary lightbulb jokes? How is this joke form being reinvented for the twenty-first century?

Making Connections

6. Simon Critchley notes that "ethnic humor is very much the Hobbesian laughter of superiority or sudden glory at our eminence and the other's stupidity" (p. 83). Write an analysis of how lightbulb jokes, ethnic or otherwise, exemplify the superiority theory of comedy. Are there any versions of the joke that complicate the dynamic between "our eminence and the other's stupidity"?

7. Harris begins his essay with the assumption that the "lightbulb joke is uniquely political" (par. 1). Conduct research on another controversial kind of joke (e.g., dead-baby, dentist, dumb-blonde, lawyer, yo' mama, etc.), and write an essay that historicizes its cultural and political significance.

Laughing It Off

Katherine Leyton

In 2012, a woman heckled comedian and TV host Daniel Tosh during his stand-up routine at the Laugh Factory by saying, "Actually, rape jokes are never funny." He doubled down in response by telling more rape jokes. The disputed incident resulted in a media firestorm, with several famous comedians weighing in on the issue.

One of the more thoughtful responses to the controversy came from Toronto poet and writer Katherine Leyton, whose "Laughing It Off" was published by *Bitch* magazine in 2013. Leyton was the first Al and Eurithe Purdy A-Frame writer-in-residence, and her work has appeared in the *Malahat Review*, *The Edinburg Review*, and *The Globe and Mail*.

"I was dating a guy, and we were going to sleep together, and he said he wasn't a condom guy—who isn't a condom guy?!"

Last autumn I sat in a Toronto comedy club and watched my good friend, comedian Alexandra Howell, perform a joke about being sexually assaulted.

"Anyway, I didn't really know him that well and I definitely wasn't willing to sleep with him without a condom. But he was really fucked up that night. He was an alcoholic and a drug addict, and at some point during the night he entered me without a condom on, even though I had clearly said I didn't want that. I pushed him off and he didn't fight me. He just rolled over." Howell's audience was uncomfortable at this point but starting to laugh, mostly because of Howell's delivery. "I didn't feel attacked—I was more pissed off than anything. But I didn't kick him out of the house. In fact, I went on a date with him again. And thinking back on this I ask myself: How much am I willing to put up with for the sake of a warm body next to me? I guess I'm willing to put up with just a dash of rape."

I laughed along with the audience, then immediately felt ashamed—my friend's assault was upsetting, not funny.

I confessed my guilt to Howell afterward. "But I gave you permission 5 to laugh!" she responded. She explained that by telling the joke, she felt she was controlling how people reacted to her experience while simultaneously negotiating her own feelings about the incident. She found it therapeutic. "But [making that] experience part of my routine speaks to the level of trauma I experienced," she admitted. "If I suffered a sexual assault [that] I personally found more traumatizing, I don't know if I'd be able to make it part of my comedy routine."

When Howell told me this, I couldn't help but wonder how desensitized to sexual assault we have become—to the point where a woman can find experiencing it only moderately traumatizing and an audience can laugh at it.

After all, we live in a culture where two high-school football stars in Steubenville, Ohio, were found guilty of raping a teenage girl and major news outlets responded by lamenting the loss of the young men's bright futures. America is a country where one in six women will be a victim of rape or attempted rape in her lifetime and only 3 percent of convicted rapists will ever spend a day in jail. Within this cultural context, laughing at a rape joke is not a simple thing. If we have not collectively proven that we fully understand the atrocity of rape, it's worth asking if comedians should be making jokes about it. In the summer of 2012, the popular Comedy Central host Daniel Tosh sparked a tempest of online controversy when he responded to a female heckler during a set at the Laugh Factory by saying it would be funny if she got raped "by like, five guys." After the incident, the feminist backlash via social media effectively caused Tosh to apologize, albeit begrudgingly.

More recently, comedian Sam Morril found himself at the center of an online media storm after feminist journalist Sady Doyle wrote about jokes she'd seen him perform that used raping women and rape victims as the punch line. She quoted statistics about the high incidence of rape in America and asked: "Given these numbers, what's the benefit of presenting yourself to an audience—which is likely to contain some women, and some assault victims—as someone with an interest in raping and hitting women? Even as a joke? Where's your payoff there?"

While male comics are quick to defend their right to tell rape jokes, they rarely have an eloquent explanation as to why, beyond "there are no boundaries in comedy" or "comedians should be able to joke about anything." Dane Cook responded to the Tosh controversy by saying to whomever had been offended by the joke, "It's best for everyone if you just kill yourself."

Every time a guy like Tosh or Morril turns rape into an easy punch line, it gets harder to believe that male comics who perform (or defend) these kinds of jokes don't understand the pervasiveness of rape in America or the devastation it causes. Women comprise 90 percent of rape victims in America—we are, as a group, oppressed by rape.

But when the oppressed joke about their oppression, different rules apply. Amy Schumer, Sarah Silverman, Wanda Sykes, Phoebe Robinson, Nikki Glaser, Lisa Lampanelli, Lena Dunham, Whitney Cummings, and Tina Fey are just a few examples of the female comedians who have performed or written jokes about rape—what compels them?

Some female comics tell jokes that clearly target rape culture, such as one classic skit by veteran comedian Sykes. "Even as little girls we're taught we have something everybody wants—you gotta protect it, you gotta be careful, you gotta cherish it. That's a lot of fucking pressure! I would like a break! You know what would make my life so much easier? Wouldn't it be wonderful if our pussies were detachable?" The joke goes on to detail situations where you could leave your "detachable pussy" at home, mainly to avoid the chance of rape.

Likewise, Chicago-based comic Ever Mainard has a long joke that expertly exposes rape culture. The bit details how Mainard, while walking alone one night, came across a man in an alley and suddenly found her mind flooded with the lifetime of warnings she's received. "Never walk alone at night," she yells urgently into the microphone. "If you walk alone at night, you'll get raped! You need a man to survive, unless he's following you at night!" She jokes there should be a game show for women called *Here's Your Rape!*

In a game show-host voice, she goes through the scenarios women have been taught to dread: "Wait a minute—a suspicious van in a dark parking lot next to your car? Wait a second, what's that? Your keys fell? You're fumbling around? *Here's Your Rape!*" The joke allows the audience to feel how frightening and exhausting it is for women to live under the constant threat of rape, while also demonstrating the absurdity of carrying the burden to protect ourselves from it.

> "I feel that comedians really have a tool that most people don't. People let their guard down in comedy; they start laughing at something that may or may not offend them if they were just having a conversation, and because they're laughing about it, they slowly start to think about it."

Having run an open-mic night for 15 years, Mainard has seen countless male comics tell bad rape jokes purely for shock value, and she wanted to contribute a different kind of rape joke to the dismal landscape. "The response I've had, especially from a lot of my guy friends, is that it changed their perspective," says Mainard. "They've never thought about rape jokes from a woman's perspective."

"I think comedy is the best way to bring up sensitive subjects, when you're doing it intelligently. I feel that comedians really have a tool that most people don't. People let their guard down in comedy; they start laughing at something that may or may not offend them if they were just having a conversation, and because they're laughing about it, they slowly start to think about it."

And then there's the other type of rape joke women tell—the up-for-interpretation, not-sure-why-I'm-laughing, "that's offensive" kind, like the Sarah Silverman quip "I was raped by a doctor . . . which is so bitter-sweet for a Jewish girl."

"Whenever I'm watching a movie where they have a hot actor portraying a rapist," begins a joke by Cleveland-born comic Phoebe Robinson, "I think: This girl complains too much, you know? It's not rape if he's hotter than you, okay? Fucking be grateful, all right?"

Robinson, who writes a popular blog called *Blaria* and is an occasional contributor to *The Huffington Post*, received negative attention for the joke online after it was mentioned in a 2011 *New York Times* article on how female comics were breaking taste taboos with controversial jokes.

When I spoke to Robinson over the phone from her home in New York, 20 she told me her intention was to make fun of Hollywood, not rape. "It was more of a commentary on, like, 'Oh, you're just going to have someone like Brad Pitt portray a rapist, a date rapist?!' You know what I mean? I was making fun of that concept. It wasn't supposed to be like 'Haha, rape!' It was more like, 'Hollywood is ridiculous.'"

Robinson no longer performs the joke. "I'm kind of in the zone where [rape] is not really something I care to talk about right now in a way that I think will be interesting for me and for the listener." While she doesn't outright say it's because it might do harm, she implies it. "I think there's waves of being intrigued by a touchy subject and wanting to tackle it, and then kind of backing off of it because you don't think you can bring anything to it or it just doesn't interest [you] in a way that maybe it did before."

Although Robinson admits some rape jokes may not contribute anything positive to the discussion of rape, she doesn't think they're a problem in themselves. "I do think there is a rape culture that's very problematic in America, but I don't think saying 'No one make a rape joke' is going to rectify that. A serious discussion needs to happen—whether it's about how [rape is] represented in movies and on TV or in real life—and [about] the fact that there's not really an open dialogue about sexual abuse in this country. I think that's far more problematic than someone making a joke like I did about hot actors being cast as rapists."

Robinson is right: America does need to open a dialogue about sexual abuse, but jokes like her Hollywood-rapist bit, which asks the audience to laugh at a rape victim (albeit a fictional one) and suggests rape might actually be pleasant for the victim, provides the perfect opportunity to have that dialogue and possibly even demonstrates why such a discussion is still necessary.

Not everyone would agree. Like Robinson, shock comic Lisa Lampanelli believes rape jokes aren't going to do any damage. "If you're going to see a comedy show, you're not looking to that comedy for direction on how to conduct your life," she says. "If you're doing that, you've gotten your signals crossed way before you walk into a show."

For Lampanelli, who has been dubbed "The Queen of Mean" and is   25
wildly popular for her offensive stand-up routines that employ jokes based on stereotypes about race, gender, and sexual orientation, a comedian's only responsibility is to make the audience laugh, no matter how offensive the content.

"It's not like you're putting out views that people should aspire to. We're not making speeches. We're doing jokes. If suddenly I go and decide to do a speaking-engagement series where I expound on the greatness of rape and getting AIDS through unprotected sex, that is a different context—it's not supposed to be funny, it's just some crazy bitch doing a speaking tour. It's someone trying to influence people in a serious way."

Lampanelli used to tell a joke where, in mock seriousness, she says she just heard about yet another woman getting raped while jogging in Central Park—saying this was proof that exercise is bad. "You never hear about a fat bitch getting raped while sitting at home eating Doritos and watching *One Life to Live*." Another joke of hers posits that rape is a good excuse for cheating. Lampanelli says these are actually jokes about her own self-esteem—concerns about being lazy and out of shape, for example, or being too much of a coward to admit infidelity.

Rape may just be a means to an end here, but, like Robinson's bit, these jokes rely on harmful concepts ingrained in our culture: that women are responsible for protecting themselves from rape, for example, or that rape only happens to certain types of women. If these notions still comprise part of our collective psyche, can jokes like Lampanelli's and Robinson's work to subtly reinforce these ideas?

Lampanelli gives an emphatic no. "I think audiences are smart enough to see if somebody means something real in their material. They don't go back and see 'em two or three times if they think, 'Oh, gosh, that guy really doesn't like Asians, that guy really does think people should be raped.' It's kind of like dogs—they have a sense of who is good and who is bad. They're not stupid."

This may be comforting logic, but it fails to consider how many of us,   30
men and women, may have internalized messages from the rape culture in which we exist. Rape awareness campaigns still call upon women to protect themselves from attack by limiting their freedom of movement, and some rape victims will chastise themselves for being out at night in a particular spot alone. Lampanelli's logic, and her comedy, ignores that. Just as Lampanelli's jokes about race are problematic because we still live

in a racist society, her jokes about rape fall flat politically because of how entrenched we are in rape culture.

Whether or not Lampanelli believes the stereotypes she jokes about or not is almost irrelevant. Reveling in—rather than deconstructing—stereotypes discourages the process of rethinking how they are constructed and propagated. In Lampanelli's case, it's up to the audience to critically engage with her Central Park jogger joke—her goal is just to get them to laugh.

And for survivors in the audience who have experienced victim-blaming or been accused of secretly liking their rapes, such a joke might not be so funny. "I forget that people blame rape victims. Because in my mind it's so obviously not their fault that I don't even initially or instinctually remember that that might not be seen," says Georgea Brooks, a comedian who works between Los Angeles and Toronto and has a few jokes that hinge on rape and sexual assault.

How the audience interprets these jokes—or is possibly triggered by them—has become a concern for Brooks. "I think some women comedians think because they're a woman, and because maybe they have been victims of sexual assault, they feel like they can make rape jokes. I think it's kind of like how black comics sometimes make fun of black people and it's okay because they're black, but the difference is that the audience knows that person's black whereas the audience doesn't necessarily know that I have—or that someone has—suffered sexual assault, and so I do really worry about making people hurt. I don't mean to hurt anyone." Brooks's comparison is problematic, but her point—a comedian's identity matters—is valid. An individual who has experienced a trauma has the right to speak about it however they choose, and just speaking about that trauma is important: We must hear the experiences of the oppressed in order to understand that oppression better.

It is interesting that Brooks, Lampanelli, and Howell have all incorporated jokes about their own sexual assault into their routines. Brooks tells a joke about how in Montreal she was once followed by a man in a car who masturbated as she rode her bike home. She was extremely traumatized by the event and told me that she went to tell two male friends about it, thinking they'd be incensed and would respond by being protective. "And they weren't. And I thought, well, you know what, that's funny, that's funny that nobody will help me. Nobody is protective of me. And I thought, I guess I can frame this in a funny way that's ironic and that's a joke. And for me that's the only comfort I could get out of the situation."

Brooks admits she often uses comedy to deal with issues she doesn't 35 know how to cope with. Turning this particular experience into a joke helped her feel like she'd conquered the situation. "That guy following me for half an hour while I watched him stroke his dick—it was awful. And it could have really affected me negatively; it could have taken me back a few steps in my life path, potentially. And when I turn it into a joke, I'm like, you will not hold me back, I will use this. . . . It makes me feel stronger."

Brooks admits this act of turning her sexual assault into a joke may have been selfish since she had not fully considered the consequences of performing it in front of audience members who may feel triggered by the scenario. Nevertheless, in a rape culture that still teaches women to feel shame and fear about openly discussing sexual assault, the candor and confidence Brooks demonstrates while discussing this experience is refreshing, and provides one model for how women can talk about being victims.

For Lampanelli, comedy has the same cathartic value. During a writing session for a new Broadway show she's doing about her life with food and men, Lampanelli was reminded of a near–date rape experience she had in college. "I'm a freshman, I'm from a small town in Connecticut, and I'd never had any guy try to force himself on me. I got really lucky that he took no for an answer. [So] yes, this was a painful, horrible thing to happen, but it's generated into a joke about myself—like, 'Wow, how unattractive must I be if my date rapist takes no for an answer?' It makes you feel even worse about yourself. So again it's targeted at myself and people who can relate to the stuff you go through with self-esteem."

Lampanelli may be joking, but the assertion that her date rapist taking no for an answer is some sort of insult is a dangerously harmful message.

"People think we put a lot more thought into jokes than we actually do. If it's fucking funny, then it's fucking funny," she says. "I'm not a social commentator, I'm not somebody who sets out to hurt anybody, but I simply don't pander. You know what? If it's funny to make fun of cancer, rape, AIDS, and you get a really good laugh off of it and people are made happy and it takes the piss out of the subject matter, then I just do it."

Laughter does provide momentary relief, and rape and rape culture are certainly things many women deserve relief from, but at what cost does that relief come? Laughing at rape is different than laughing at cancer because we still have not collectively acknowledged the destruction caused by rape—not only on victims but on society as a whole. When Brooks tells the joke about her sexual assault, there is a danger of allowing both herself and the audience to take the incident—and therefore sexual assault in general—less seriously. At the same time, she is highlighting the absurdity of a culture where people feel comfortable laughing at sexual assault, while using it to move on from the experience herself.

Brooks isn't sure herself if the joke ends up doing more harm or more good, but she isn't surprised so many female comics tell jokes about rape. "I think a lot of female comics talk about [sexual assault] because it happens so much. I think that for a stand-up, [whether you're] male or female, it's so important to be able to talk about everything that's going on and to be able to be comfortable in talking about those things. And I think female stand-ups are just starting to feel really comfortable about being themselves and talking about these issues."

Diana Love is a comedian based in Toronto who performs two jokes about rape, one using it as a punch line. When I ask her if she ever worries someone in the audience will misunderstand her intentions and think she is condoning or trivializing rape, she compares that to blaming Marilyn Manson for Columbine.

Last summer, a man was sexually assaulting women in the Toronto neighborhood where Love lived, and the threat of rape was all too real for her. "I felt really unsafe walking down my own street. I had a car pull up to me one time and I just started running. It could have been nothing, but I was scared. But what am I going to do? Not leave my house? Yeah. I feel very strongly about my right to tell rape jokes."

Love's feeling is understandable. When female comics tell rape jokes they are taking control of the narrative about rape—they are, however briefly, no longer victims of rape culture. Of course, not all rape jokes are created equal, and it's problematic when female comedians employ harmful stereotypes about rape as if they were truths, or when they dismiss victims of rape, or rape itself—in these cases they risk empowering themselves by oppressing other women. Nevertheless, their position as individuals in a group that clearly understands how real the threat of rape is adds a layer of complexity to any joke they tell. Every female comic I spoke with understood (as much as one can without having been through it) how devastating rape is. Unlike male comics, the majority of whom do not have to worry about rape on a regular basis (although men do, of course, suffer rape), women tell jokes from a position in which they are very much aware of their own vulnerability, a fact that automatically changes the nature of the joke. This isn't to say that women cannot tell rape jokes that contribute to rape culture by reinforcing the myths the culture is built on—they can, and do. Such jokes, however, don't just work in a single way. When a woman tells a rape joke—even a "bad" one— it can also be an expression of power, control, and therapy (however fraught with contradiction), and a nebulous offer to women in the audience to momentarily relieve themselves from the burden of rape culture.

At the end of all my interviews for this article I asked each comic if 45
they had a favorite rape joke. Georgea Brooks recounted something her
roommate — a fellow comedian — had said one day after they got coffee
together. As they were leaving Starbucks, some men leaning on nearby
cars began shouting inappropriate, sexual things at them. Back in the
car and out of earshot of the guys, Brooks's friend said, as if speaking
directly to them: "It's not that I don't want to date you — it's that I don't
want to get raped by you." "That's my favorite rape joke," says Brooks.
"Because it was in real life, it wasn't even on stage."

Understanding the Text

1. To create an academic argument, authors write the voices of others into
   their essays. Summarize a few of the positions on telling rape jokes that
   Leyton puts into conversation.

2. In your own words, paraphrase Leyton's central argument or thesis. Then
   cite a passage that you believe reflects her primary claim.

3. According to Leyton, why have many male comedians' defense of rape
   jokes fallen flat? How do their justifications differ from those of some
   notable female comedians?

Reflection and Response

4. When making a joke, as when composing an argument, context matters.
   According to Leyton and the comedians she quotes, what contextual
   factors — cultural, historical, rhetorical, etc. — determine whether a rape
   joke is humorous or derogatory?

5. Do you agree with Leyton's assessment of Lisa Lampanelli's views on rape
   jokes? Look up Lampanelli's jokes, as well as some of the other comedians'
   rape jokes that Leyton mentions, to inform your opinion.

Making Connections

6. In the previous chapter, Leon Rappoport (p. 13) and John Morreall (p. 25)
   argued that, according to the relief theory of comedy, humor can serve a
   therapeutic function. Leyton agrees but with reservations: "Laughter does
   provide momentary relief, and rape and rape culture are certainly things
   many women deserve relief from, but at what cost does that relief come?"
   (par. 40). Using these as well as outside sources, write an essay that
   discusses the potential benefits, limits, and drawbacks of comedy as a
   form of therapy for traumatic experiences.

7. In response to the Laugh Factory incident, comedian Daniel Tosh tweeted,
   "all the out of context misquotes aside, i'd like to sincerely apologize." Read
   several of the commentaries on the Tosh controversy and write an essay in
   response to Tosh's comments and apology.

Breaking and Entering: Transgressive Comedy on Television

Michael V. Tueth

Michael V. Tueth is a professor of Communication and Media Studies at Fordham University. A Jesuit priest with a background in theater, Tueth has also written two scholarly books on comedy: *Laughter in the Living Room: Television Comedy and the American Home Audience* (2005) and *Reeling with Laughter: American Film Comedies from Anarchy to Mockumentary* (2012).

In "Breaking and Entering," which was originally published in Mary M. Dalton and Laura R. Linder's 2005 edited collection *The Sitcom Reader: America Viewed and Screwed*, Tueth contextualizes the animated television show *South Park* (1997–within the long history of transgressive comedy.

Over the years, most television comedy has behaved itself. In the early days, however, a few memorable exceptions tried to break the rules. In the 1950s, when *Father Knows Best* and *The Adventures of Ozzie and Harriet* provided the models for husbandly behavior, Jackie Gleason approached forbidden territory in his portrayal of a loudmouthed braggart on *The Honeymooners*. Gleason's character would threaten to retaliate against his wife's remarks, "one of these days," by sending her "to the moon, Alice, to the moon!" Milton Berle's drag routines, Red Skelton's drunken characters, and Ernie Kovacs's effeminate Percy Dovetonsils were similar mild violations of the social taboos of middle America that kept well within the traditions of slapstick and vaudeville comedy. Such outlandish comedy, however, was apparently too risky for the networks. *The Ernie Kovacs Show* survived only a few months on nationwide television in 1952–1953. *The Honeymooners* lasted only one full season (1955–1956) in its situation comedy format. Gerard Jones claims that its portrayal of a working-class couple barely making ends meet and constantly on the verge of argument "played on deep anxieties" and were a "harsh reminder of a conflict being ardently denied by popular culture" (G. Jones, "Honey" 113).

Fifteen years later, Norman Lear's creations dared to speak the unspeakable, provoking frequent complaints from defenders of good taste. In Lear's breakout success, *All in the Family*, Archie Bunker's bigotry, his daughter Gloria's feminism, and his son-in-law Mike's liberal atheism all served to shock sensibilities across the ideological spectrum of the

1970s (Adler). Lear continued this pattern with the treatment of abortion on *Maude*; homosexuality on *Mary Hartman, Mary Hartman*; and the anger of African Americans verging on reverse racism on *Sanford and Son* and *The Jeffersons*. The programs were followed by two of the most popular situation comedies of the 1980s and 1990s, *Roseanne* and *Married . . . with Children*, both of which thrived on offensive attitudes, outrageous behavior, taboo topics, and the language of insult.

Almost all of these instances of groundbreaking comedy appeared on major networks during prime time, and most of them were cast in the conventional context of family situation comedies. They were all subject to the pressure of network standards and practices, the threats of viewer boycotts, the sensibilities of their sponsors, and the usual consensus in favor of "least offensive programming" to appeal to the huge viewership commanded by the three major networks (MacDonald, "One Nation" 118–24). A new pattern has emerged with the advent of cable television, however. Less burdened with FCC [Federal Communications Commission] regulations, less dependent on sponsor support, and less hampered by the need to achieve blockbuster ratings, cable television has enjoyed the opportunity to appeal to a narrower demographic. In some cases, this has resulted in bold new comedy that dares to offend, transgressive comedy that revels in shock and tastelessness. The most successful of these new comedies has been Comedy Central's biggest hit, *South Park*, an animated cartoon that made its debut during the summer of 1997. Despite its TV-MA rating (unsuitable for children under 17) and its later time slot of 10 p.m., it became instantly popular, achieving a record-high rating for a cable series of 6.9 by February 1998. Its popularity has continued.

South Park, with its presentation of "alien abductions, anal probes, flaming farts, and poo," has been described as "gleefully offensive and profoundly silly, juxtaposing cute and crude, jaded and juvenile" (Marin 56–57). Using childlike cut-out figures, the show follows the adventures of four nine-year-old boys in a small mountain town (named after an actual county in Colorado notorious for alien sightings). The show's creators, Trey Parker and Matt Stone, portray it as a "poisoned place in the heart, a taste-free zone where kids say the darndest, most fucked-up things" (Wilde 34). The foul-mouthed boys, Stan, Kyle, Cartman, and Kenny, constantly heap abuse on each other, utter racist and other politically insensitive epithets (like "Stan's dog's a homo"), question all authority, and obsess about flatulence, excrement, and other bodily functions. Stan, the leader of the group, vomits every time he encounters his semi-girlfriend, Wendy. Kenny, criticized by the others because he is poor, faces a horrible death in almost every episode only to reappear the following week. Other prominent characters include: Stan's Uncle Jim, a gun-rights fanatic; Jim's Vietnam-vet buddy, who speaks through a voice box; the school cook, Chef, the only African American in the town, who shares his fantasies and advice about sexual matters with the awe-struck boys; and Cartman's mom, described by the other boys as a "crack whore." The other adults—teachers, parents, and town officials—are generally portrayed as repressed, frantic, or otherwise unworthy of any child's respect. The one exception may be Jesus Christ, who, dressed in his familiar white robe and sandals, serves as the nice-guy host of a local cable-access show. It all adds up to a ribald, irreverent comedy with a "joyous lack of self-restraint . . . stridently, relentlessly, gloriously, and hilariously outrageous" (Mink).

Like the alien visitors who menace their town, these four nasty little   5 boys have invaded the world of American pop culture and taken it by storm. The inevitable feature film, *South Park, the Movie: Bigger, Longer, and Uncut*, was released to high critical praise and big ticket sales in the summer of 1999. Meanwhile, its phenomenal success emboldened both cable and broadcast networks to attempt their own treatments of taboo subjects with varying degrees of success. In September 1999, for example, the FOX Network introduced with heavy marketing fanfare its new comedy, *Action*, replete with four-letter words (bleeped-out but easy to lip-read), outrageous sexual misbehavior, and viciously self-absorbed characters. The network executives were counting on what they saw as "the rapid disappearance of most taste and language restrictions in mass media," with *South Park* as the prime example (Cartier and Mifflin C10).

Not everyone has shared the general enthusiasm for *South Park*. Peggy Charren, founder of Action for Children's Television, suspects that despite the TV-MA rating, many children watch the program. She was particularly concerned about the characters' use of racial slurs, indicting such language as "dangerous to the democracy" (Huff). Dale Kunkel, a professor of communication at the University of California, Santa Barbara, questioned the motives of the producers and the network. He noted that "the humor and the whole orientation of the show is adolescent-oriented humor, rejecting authority, flouting convention. . . . They say they don't want the teen audience, yet the nature of the content is significantly targeted to appeal to that audience" (Huff). Two grammar schools in New Jersey went so far as to send letters home urging parents to stop their children from watching the show (Starr).

Concern about the influence of mass communication on the general citizenry has followed every advance in mass circulation, from the penny-presses and lurid dime novels of the nineteenth century, to the nickelodeons at the turn of the century, to the hysteria-inducing *War of the Worlds* radio broadcast in 1938, and on into the present. But the debate increased in volume when television invaded the living rooms of the nation, often serving as the new baby-sitter. What McLuhan° envisioned as the new family hearth has become unusually powerful, not only in shaping but also reinforcing mainstream values. Television has become the culture's primary storyteller and definer of cultural patterns by providing information and entertainment for an enormous and heterogeneous mass public.

The success of *South Park* and similar television comedy represents the mainstreaming of a new comic attitude previously displayed only in more marginal settings. This attitude is new enough to television to shock yet creative enough to fascinate viewers. Transgressive comedy, climbing through the window of television, has broken into the American home.

This type of comedy is best identified in terms of its purpose. In his study of "the purpose of jokes," Freud first considers "innocent" jokes, such as puns and other plays on words, that are enjoyed for their cleverness and playfulness with no further purpose and which usually evoke a chuckle of moderate amusement. He then deals with "tendentious jokes" that seem to provoke much more laughter and therefore are probably serving some deeper psychological purpose. Freud sees only two such types of purposive humor: "it is either a hostile joke (serving the purpose of aggressiveness, satire, or defense) or an obscene joke (serving the purpose of exposure)" (Freud 97). His explanation of the higher amount of pleasure derived from these two types of humor, especially the obscene, derives directly from his view of "civilization and its discontents":

> It is our belief that civilization and higher education have a large influence in the development of repression, and we suppose that, under such conditions, the psychical organization undergoes an alteration (that can also emerge as an inherited disposition) as a result of which what was formerly felt as agreeable now seems unacceptable and is rejected with all possible psychical force. The repressive activity of civilization brings it about that primary possibilities of enjoyment, which have now; however, been repudiated by the censorship in us, are lost to us. But to the human psyche all renunciation is exceedingly difficult, and so we find that tendentious jokes provide a means of undoing the renunciation and retrieving what was lost. (Freud 101)

Since civilization and education remove "the primary possibilities of enjoyment" found in uninhibited aggression and sexual activity, in Freud's view, certain types of humor allow us to "retrieve what was lost,"

McLuhan: Marshall McLuhan (1911–1980), a media theorist famous for the quip "the medium is the message."

to regress to the more primal state of childhood with its accompanying lack of inhibitions. It is particularly pertinent to this study that, as Freud proceeds to analyze the operation of the smutty joke, he observes that its sexual material can include anything that is "common to both sexes and to which the feeling of shame extends, what is excremental in the most comprehensive sense" (Freud 101). He specifically refers to "the sense covered by sexuality in childhood, an age at which there is, as it were, a cloaca° within which what is sexual and what is excremental are barely or not at all distinguished" (Freud 97–98). The farting, vomiting, and verbal spewing of the *South Park* boys vividly display such interconnection.

Freud distinguishes the obscene joke, with its purpose of exposure, from the hostile joke, which serves the purpose of aggressiveness or defense. Satirical comedy is one form of such aggression, attacking its target from a sense of outrage and with the hope of some reform. Juvenal catalogued the moral corruption of Rome; Molière ridiculed the religious hypocrites, the lying doctors, and the miserly parental tyrants of Louis XIV's Paris; Pope and Dryden derided the vanity and foppery of London society; Heller, Vonnegut, Kubrick, and other twentieth-century artists have employed absurdist techniques to oppose the stupidities of modern warfare and military culture. Such is the grand aggressive tradition of satire: human reason's warfare on human folly.

> "Transgressive humor has no such moral purpose. Instead of trying to change or eliminate human foolishness, certain comic writers and performers deliberately revel in the lower forms of social behavior."

10

Transgressive humor has no such moral purpose. Instead of trying to change or eliminate human foolishness, certain comic writers and performers deliberately revel in the lower forms of social behavior. Unlike the intellectual wit and verbal sophistication of the satirical tradition, transgressive humor regresses to the infantile. Rather than portraying the objects of its humor in hopes that witty ridicule and public shame might provoke change, transgressive humor does not expect or even desire a change, for then the fun would end.

Transgressive humor does share one element with satire: both comic methods depend upon a basic consensus of standards and boundaries; otherwise, the joke would not be pleasurable. The societal taboos must remain so that one can experience the delight of the entry into

---

cloaca: the common opening for the intestinal, urinary, and genital tracts of some animal species.

forbidden realms, a childish joy in simply breaking all the adult taboos, a pleasure indulged in for the sake of exposure of the impulses we have all been forced to repress.

In another overlap with satire, transgressive humor, purposely or not, can sometimes serve general satirical purposes by its faux-innocent or playful criticism of ignorance, prejudice, or stereotypes. For example, in a transgressive context, the articulation of an offensive word or the performance of an offensive action operates to transform stigmatization into empowerment. The appropriation of the insult by the intended target disempowers the insult. The use of the word "nigger" by Black comedians, rappers, and urban street-talk in general and the use of the epithet "queer" by gay groups from academia to performance art serve precisely this purpose while adding an element of threat to those who would attempt to use these words against them. Gay comedy reverts to "camp" and Black comedy employs "homey" style for much the same purposes (Core 5–15). Appropriation of the insulting attack disempowers the attacker.

Transgressive humor sometimes adds a subtle twist to this formula. While the comic speaker may not be a member of the target group, the speaker may attempt to signify his or her solidarity with the group by joining in their appropriation of the hostile or outrageous language or actions. Such seems to have been the intent of an attempt at transgressive humor which resulted in considerable confusion and offense, a blackface act performed by the television star Ted Danson at a Friars Club roast° of the African American comedian Whoopi Goldberg in 1993. The routine had been written primarily by Goldberg, who was in a relationship with Danson at the time. In the long tradition of the Friars Club roasts, Danson's routine was sexually explicit with many references to Black sexual stereotypes, outrageous sexual positions, and Goldberg's anatomy. Danson also joked about racist social stereotypes, reporting that when he brought Whoopi to meet his family, they asked her to do the laundry and wash the dishes and offered to drive her to the nearest bus stop when she had finished. Many prominent African Americans in the audience were deeply offended, including former Mayor David Dinkins and television talk-show host, Montel Williams, who cancelled his membership in the Friars (Williams).

In the ensuring controversy, Goldberg defended the routine as their 15 response to the volume of hate mail and openly racist threats she and Danson had received. "We thought it would be a good idea if we sort of

Friars Club roast: the private New York Friars Club holds an annual roast of one its members, who consist mostly of comedians and celebrities.

dispelled that word" (qtd. in Williams). The comedy writer Bruce Vilanch, who may have contributed material to the sketch, added, "Ted's plan was to defuse the whole (racial) thing with jokes up front" (Williams). The actor Burt Reynolds offered two arguments in favor of the humor: first, the traditionally raucous context of Friars roasts that combine tasteless-ness with affection; and second, Goldberg's sensitivity to racial offensive-ness, saying, "She's tuned in to what would be degrading to Blacks. Times have changed, and we've gone past that" (Thomas). In an interview on the Black Entertainment Television Network, Danson added another ar-gument in defense of the sketch, saying, "We are a racist nation. It's time maybe we started talking" ("Danson 'Proud'"). In other words, such humor brings unpleasant realities into public consciousness. Even aca-demic experts offered some defense of Danson's comedy. Elise A. Williams, associate professor of English at the University of the District of Columbia and an expert on African American humor, commented that even though jokes based on racial stereotypes are particularly troublesome in a mixed-race setting, "I would rather have a comedian push the truth as far as he or she possibly can . . . tease, or move the stereotype to a kind of carica-ture as a way of *deflating* it" (Mills) [emphasis mine].

Another oblique technique is to place the transgressive remarks or actions in the mouth or body of a character for ironic effect. For instance, in *All in the Family*, when Archie Bunker refers to "jungle bunnies," "chinks," or "fags," his obvious ignorance was intended by Lear to serve as a satire of racism. Audience surveys at the time of the show's initial run, however, indicated that many viewers identified with Archie's big-otry and failed to see the irony that Lear intended; they saw the show not as satire but as an outrageous expression of many viewers' socially forbid-den racial resentments (Vidmar and Rokeach, qtd. in Adler, 123–38). Similarly, the *South Park* children's emotional and mental immaturity and undeveloped impulse-control allow them to speak the unspeakable and act out the forbidden behavior. The adults to whom the program is ostensibly targeted are presumed to understand and enjoy the irony and satire, but such a viewer reaction cannot be guaranteed. One viewer's sat-ire may be another viewer's secret truths.

In fact, if the humor is truly outrageous, it is not properly considered satire but merely a case of truly bad taste. Freedom to engage in such transgressive humor has even found a legal basis, most famously in the case of Larry Flynt, who was sued by Jerry Falwell for intention to inflict emotional distress. In 1983, Flynt's *Hustler* magazine ran a parody Campari liquor ad depicting the famous televangelist as intoxicated and confessing that his first sexual experience had been with his mother in an outhouse. This crude joke qualifies as transgressive rather than satirical. It was not intended as a criticism of any specific behavior of the Reverend Falwell; there was no evidence or public awareness in 1983 of any alcoholic or sexual misbehavior by Falwell. It is better understood as misbehavior on the part of the magazine, a besmirching of a respected moral authority, like the eternal portrayal by adolescents of their high school teachers or administrators in outrageous behavior. In the same spirit, Flynt could just as easily have decided to target Mother Teresa or the Dalai Lama. Such was the understanding behind the decision in the first court's decision on the case before it finally made its way to the Supreme Court as a First Amendment case. It was precisely the general understanding that the portrayal of Falwell was not intended to be taken as truth that robbed the joke of any satirical or libelous power and made the prosecution change its case to one of "emotional distress." The unanimous Supreme Court decision reaffirmed the protection of parody as included in "the recognition of the free flow of ideas." Chief Justice Rehnquist's decision stated, "freedom to speak one's mind is not only an aspect of individual liberty . . . but essential to the quest for truth and the vitality of society as a whole" (*Hustler Magazine v. Jerry Falwell* 51). It is worth noting in this context that the Supreme Court decision came at a time when many of the Reverend Falwell's televangelist colleagues were being exposed for financial fraud and sexual misconduct, and such a portrayal of Falwell could have been interpreted as an accusation of guilt by association, yet the Supreme Court ignored such an interpretation.

While precedents for the outrageous comedy of *South Park* could readily be found in the practices of various folk cultures, the more mainstream influence can be traced to the long tradition in European societies of organized periods of anarchy and official societies comprised of common people as well as the highly educated that regularly violated, and often criticized, the standards and practices of their culture. In Enid Welsford's classic study of the social and literary history of the fool in Western culture, she describes the phenomenon of "misrule" which appeared in European culture from Roman days until the Renaissance. She refers us to Lucian's *Saturnalia* and its description of the "Liberties of December" at the time of the winter solstice, when "for a short while masters and slaves changed places, laws lost their force, and a mock-king ruled over a topsy-turvy world" (Welsford 201). In the first centuries of the Christian era, there were even instances of the clergy engaging in public folly, in which "mighty persons were humbled, sacred things profaned, laws relaxed and ethical ideals reversed, under the leadership of a Patriarch, Pope, or Bishop of Fools" (Welsford 201). In the cathedral towns of twelfth-century France, the Feast of Fools was an annual occurrence, during which even the Mass was burlesqued. Instead of waving censers of incense, the clergy would swing chains of sausages. Instead of sprinkling the congregation with holy water, some of the sacred ministers would be doused with buckets of water. Sometimes an ass was brought into the church, and "on these occasions solemn Mass was punctuated with brays and howls" (Welsford 202). The celebrant would conclude the liturgy by braying three times (*ter hinhannabit*), and the people would respond in similar fashion. According to Welsford, such sacrilegious frivolity was often accompanied by satirical verse, topical plays, and burlesque sermons as expressions of the lower clergy's criticism of the Church for whom they were the official exponents.

The official Church, of course, persistently condemned such behavior so that eventually people in secular associations took up the roles of seasonal fools. Groups such as the Societes Joyeuses flourished from the end of the fifteenth to the middle of the seventeenth century. Welsford describes them as:

associations of young men who adapted the traditional fool's dress of motley, eared hoods, bells and baubles and organized themselves into kingdoms under the rule of an annually elected monarch known as Prince des Sots, Mere-Folle, *etc. . . . which enabled them to keep up a running commentary on the affairs of their neighbours and to indulge a taste for satire and social criticism. (205)*

With the disappearance of the religious festivals of folly, we seem to lose any account of this behavior among the lower classes, but there is considerable documentation of the continuation of such frivolity among the upper classes. This pattern of annual interruptions of the ordinary routine, with temporary suspension of law and order, remained popular in England, with the traditional feast of the "boy-bishop" among the choirboys of the English cathedrals and in the Christmas Revels of the Lord of Misrule among university students, at the Inns of Court, and in the English and Scottish royal courts of the fifteenth and sixteenth century. In France, the holiday tradition became a permanent feature among the upper classes. What had been seen as a social safety-valve, an "annual interruption of the ordinary routine, marked by a temporary suspension of law and order," developed into a "permanent and legal recognized institution, whose members . . . were pledged to more or less continuous representation of the whole of society as a 'great stage of fools'" and the social satire that had been "the occasional by-product of the Feast of Fools became the whole business of the Societes Joyeuses" (Welsford 205). Welsford describes the development as a change in the understanding of the purpose of a fool:

The Enfants-sans-Souci emphasized the idea of folly as a mask for the wise and armour of the critic. Their "Misrule" was no temporary relaxation of law and order, but a more subtle and permanent reversal of ordinary judgments. It was the wisdom of Mere-Folle to display the folly of the wise. (218)

One is left with the question of whether the transgressive humor of *South Park* and similar television shows is meant to be a mere relaxation of all prevailing norms, like the early Saturnalia and Feasts of Fools, or as a constant satirical commentary on the powerful and famous. Should the foul-mouthed children of *South Park* be considered our boy-bishops (fools for a day) or our *Enfants-sans-souci* (year-round fools)? Since such comedies appear on a weekly basis throughout the year, should they be understood as a break in the week's routine or the regular weekly meetings of the global village idiots? Can the viewing of such programming offer an opportunity for a "more subtle and permanent reversal of ordinary judgments"? Can such programming be truly oppositional and not just a holiday from the prevailing hegemony?

Fiske's approach° to the "pleasure and play" of television viewing 20 seems to opt for the oppositional interpretation, describing some readings of the television texts as expressions of resistance to the prevailing norms. He points to Lovell's study of female oppositional readings of soap operas and Schwichtenburg's account of the stylistic excessism and fetishism in *Miami Vice*, where "it is important to render pleasure out of bounds" (Lovell, Schwichtenburg 47). Fiske comments:

*This sort of pleasure lies in the refusal of the social control inscribed in the "bounds." While there is clearly a pleasure in exerting social power, the popular pleasures of the subordinate are necessarily found in resisting, evading, or offending this power. Popular pleasures are those that empower the subordinate, and they thus offer political resistance, even if only momentarily and even if only in a limited terrain. (*Television Culture 230*)*

The crude language and the offensive actions of the characters on *South Park* seem to develop what Fiske goes on to describe as "an alternative semiotic strategy of resistance or evasion" (240). As a model of such cultural resistance, Fiske uses the example of the carnival:

. . . not in its more overtly political or even revolutionary [sense] of attempting to overthrow the social system. Rather it refers to the refusal to accept the social

---

Fiske's approach: John Fiske (born 1939), a media scholar, is famous for rejecting the notion that television viewers watch shows uncritically.

*identity proposed by the dominant ideology and the social control that goes with it. The refusal of ideology, of its meanings and control, may not of itself challenge the dominant social system but it does resist incorporation and it does maintain and strengthen a sense of social difference that is a prerequisite to any more direct social challenge. (*Television Culture *242)*

One final observation of Fiske's is particularly relevant to the comedy of *South Park* and other animated comedies of recent years. The self-referential nature of much of the humor creates what Fiske has called an "empowering inversion of viewer relations" (242). Beavis and Butthead spend considerable time watching and commenting on the music videos typical of MTV, the very channel that carries the show. *The Simpsons* and *King of the Hill* provide frequent visual jokes about the art of animation and the existence of their characters as products of animators and not actual persons. One of the most sophisticated examples was *The Simpsons* episode that took the viewers behind the show, as MTV does with *Behind the Music*, and interviewed each of the main characters as if they were actual actors looking for other work. This conspiracy between the creators and viewers to acknowledge the artifice of television primes the viewer to question the legitimacy of any televised versions of "reality."

If the comedy of *South Park* can be understood as genuinely oppositional, how long can it continue? Will its ability to shock and offend be somehow disempowered and "domesticated," as Gitlin maintains happened to the Norman Lear comedies of the 1970s ("Prime-Time Ideology" 522)? Will it spawn enough successful imitators, as television megahits tend to do, that eventually the irreverence, irony, and shock will become the familiar comic landscape of television? Since Gitlin ascribes the softening of *All in the Family*'s edges to commercial decisions, perhaps the greatest hope for transgressive comedy lies in the viewer-driven nature of cable television as opposed to the broadcast networks' subservience to their advertisers. Alan Ball, Academy Award–winning writer of *American Dream*, has remarked that he chose to write his dark comedy, *Six Feet Under*, for HBO because "network TV works as a vehicle for marketing. . . . They want as large an audience as possible . . . primed by the fantasy in the shows for the fantasy of the products" (qtd. in Friend 83). Ball and others believe that commercial-free cable television offers an alternative situation, connecting more esoteric programming with a more select but highly appreciative target audience. This seems to be borne out by the popularity of several taboo-breaking cable programs like *Oz, Sex and the City, The Osbournes*, and *The Sopranos*, as well as the less sophisticated revelry of *WWE Smackdown*. If this is the case, cable television offers viewers who delight in the violation of cultural taboos their best hope of indulging their antisocial appetites. Every week, they can join the foolish company of Stan, Kenny, Cartman, and Kyle and enjoy the carnival while it lasts.

Works Cited

Adler, Richard, ed. All in the Family: A Critical Appraisal. New York: Praeger, 1979.

Cartier, Bill, and Lawrie Mifflin. "Mainstream TV Bets on 'Gross-Out' Humor." New York Times 19 July 1999: C1+.

Core, Philip. Camp: The Lie That Tells the Truth. New York: Delilah, 1984.

"Danson 'Proud' of Racial Act at Roast." Arizona Republic Oct. 25, 1993: B8.

Fiske, John. Television Culture. New York: Routledge, 1987.

Freud, Sigmund. Jokes and Their Relation to the Unconscious. New York: Norton, 1960.

Friend, Tad. "The Next Big Bet." New Yorker 14 May 2001: 83.

Gitlin, Todd. "Prime-Time Ideology: The Hegemonic Process in Television Entertainment." Television: The Critical View. Ed. Horace Newcomb. New York: Oxford UP 1994 ed. 516-37.

Huff, Richard. "'South Park' Fuels Truth-in-Labeling Debate." New York Daily News 5 Mar. 1998: 103.

Hustler Magazine v. Jerry Falwell, 485 US 46. US Supreme Court 1988.

Jones, Gerard. Honey, I'm Home! Sitcoms: Selling the American Dream. New York: St. Martin's, 1992.

Lovell, T. "Writing Like a Woman: A Question of Politics." The Politics of Theory. Eds. Francis Barker, Peter Hulme, Margaret Iversen, and Diana Loxley. Colchester: U of Essex P, 1983.

MacDonald, J. Fred. One Nation Under Television: The Rise and Decline of Network Television. Chicago: Nelson, 1994.

Marin, Rick. "The Rude Tube." Newsweek 23 Mar. 1998: 55-62.

Mills, David. "What's So Funny?" Washington Post 26 Oct. 1993: 5.

Mink, Eric. "'South Park' Comes up a Hallo-winner." New York Daily News 29 Oct. 1997: 89.

Schwichtenburg, C. "Sensual Surfaces and Stylistic Excess: The Pleasure and Politics of Miami Vice." Journal of Communication Inquiry 10.3 (1987): 45-65.

Starr, Michael. "'South Park' Net Cries 'Foul.'" New York Post 20 Mar. 1998: 120.

Thomas, Karen. "Friars Take the Heat for Their Tradition of Tasteless Humor." USA Today 12 Oct. 1993: 3D.

Welsford, Enid. The Fool: His Social and Literary History. Gloucester, MA: Smith, 1966.

Wilde, David. "South Park's Evil Geniuses and the Triumph of No-Brow Culture." Rolling Stone 19 Feb. 1998: 34.

Williams, Jeannie. "Whoopi's Shock Roast/Danson in Blackface Leaves Many Fuming." USA Today 11 Oct. 1993: 2D.

Understanding the Text

1. According to Tueth, what is the difference between satire and transgressive humor? Does *South Park* blur the boundaries between these two genres of comedy?

2. For Tueth, which one of Burke's dramatistic elements is most important for identifying trangressive comedy? Why is it so crucial to this form of comedy?

3. How are contemporary television shows like *South Park* related to the "long tradition in European societies of organized periods of anarchy" (par. 18) that characterized the medieval carnival?

Reflection and Response

4. One might say that Tueth has penned an exploratory essay because it raises several questions that it does not answer. Respond to one of these unanswered questions. For example, Tueth writes, "One is left with the question of whether the transgressive humor of *South Park* and similar television shows is meant to be a mere relaxation of all prevailing norms, like the early Saturnalia and Feast of Fools, or as a constant satirical commentary on the powerful and famous" (par. 19). What do you think?

5. At the end of the essay, Tueth lists other self-referential animated comedies that resist dominant ideologies. Do you believe that animation allows cartoons to be more transgressive than live-action fare? Write about a more recent animated comedy such as *The Boondocks*, *Adventure Time*, *Bob's Burgers*, *Rick and Morty* or *Archer* that you believe is "genuinely oppositional."

Making Connections

6. Tueth notes that cable has provided more opportunity for transgressive comedy than network television. With the advent of web television, has truly groundbreaking comedy become the province of shows produced by subscription streaming services such as Netflix, Amazon, and Hulu? Analyze a web comedy series in light of Tueth's observations about transgressive television.

7. Considering that television is not just a medium but also an extremely lucrative industry, does it even make sense to talk about transgressive programs? Do any other forums for or genres of comedy strike you as potentially more subversive? Why?

What Effect Has the Internet Had on Comedy?

Aleks Krotoski

A journalist and broadcaster, Aleks Krotoski also has a Ph.D. in social psychology, hosts the *Guardian* podcast *Tech Weekly* and the BBC Radio 4 program *Digital Human*, and is the author of the book *Untangling the Web* (2013).

In 2011, the *Guardian* published Krotoski's essay, "What Effect Has the Internet Had on Comedy?," which provides a glimpse into Krotoski's work on how humans behave and interact with the web. Her essay provides a cursory look at why certain types of humor are popular online.

"The Internet is made of cats," *Huffington Post* cofounder Jonah Peretti once told me. He was, of course, referring to the frankly obscene number of pictures and videos of cats in ridiculous situations, wearing silly outfits, doing hilarious things that are littering every corner of the web.

If the hype is to be believed, cats are the epitome of modern web humor. They are the eternal subject of silly, one-click laugh fodder, from Maru, the Japanese YouTube kitty superstar most famous for jumping in and out of cardboard boxes (91 million views) to the cast of thousands photographed in compromising positions and labeled with poorly spelled captions on the internationally lauded icanhascheezburger.com. But these moggies are more than memes. They explain why we are able to relate to one another online.

It's not surprising that so much of online content is comedy; the library of psychological and anthropological research describes humor as the glue that helps to define communities and keep them together. Psychologist Dr. Rod Martin, who has published extensively on the role of humor in mental and physical health, describes it as a coping mechanism: we seek to clarify a unified reality through our interpersonal communications, but when that unified reality isn't forthcoming—because we inevitably look at the world through different frames of reference and have different interpretations of what's happening around us—we poke fun at our inconsistencies, which allows us to smooth them over because we are able to embrace the contradictions.

It's also an essential part of our social development. From a young age, we are influenced by what our social group defines as funny. We conform to that for the sake of keeping the peace, to feel like we belong, and to function to our greatest capacity in our small section of the world. Now, we share much of our online interaction on social networks such as

Facebook with people we know, in an environment that sociologist Ray Oldenberg would call a "third place": a space such as a café or pub, where we can extend the bonds we have with one another through light-hearted, often humorous interaction.

But beyond Facebook, the web is still an overwhelmingly anonymous place. It has historically had so few default social cues that we've spent much of our online time asking one another, "Age/Sex/Location?" to identity the most appropriate way to chat. Humor gives us, the anonymized strangers, instantaneous common ground. And that explains why social scientists and communication scholars have found so much banter in our everyday online conversations.

It also explains the ephemeral and quick-fix nature of most online comedy. Let's face it; LOLcats and a Japanese moggie jumping into boxes aren't exactly high-brow. But across the ocean of possible new friends online, they are the only cornerstones we have to establish connections between one another and to find people like us. We rely on universals. One of these, in the early twenty-first century, appears to be cats.

Professor Jim Hendler, a veteran of the internet of the 1970s, says that "second perhaps to pornography, humor was a major force" in the first two decades of the net. "The kind of humor that worked best online in the 1970s and 1980s was countercultural stuff that chimed with the nature of what we were doing," he says. "Those of us using email lists on the ARPAnet° were hiding the fact from our advisers. Cats really came into the story with the addition of images and web technologies."

The limitations of the medium—when a computer screen only had 20 lines of 80 characters—also set the scene for the format of what works in modern online comedy. "Reading anything long took a long time and was boring," says Hendler. Now that we have images, audio and video, successful jokes and puns are even briefer, a feature that Martin Trickey looked for as one of the BBC's comedy commissioners for multiplatform.

Trickey has identified four characteristics that work: brevity, topicality, authenticity, and self-containment. "You don't need to know anything about where it came from or where it is going," he says. What this translates into is quick hits, rather than ongoing vignettes. "The attention span of the online audience is incredibly short. If we haven't got you in the first 10 seconds, we have probably lost you. It makes character development difficult and long-running narrative impossible."

Hence the reliance of most successful online humor on current events and what can appear to outsiders as a series of in-jokes. Importantly,

ARPAnet: Advanced Research Projects Agency Network, one the foundational technologies of the internet funded by the U.S. Department of Defense.

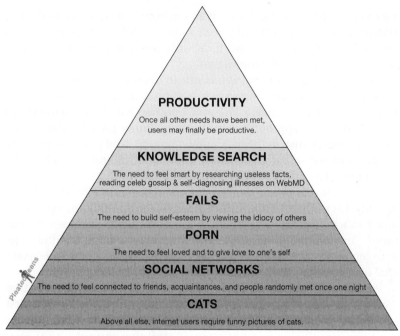

Maslow's Hierarchy of Internet Needs

This parody by Jeff Wysaski tweaks psychologist Abraham Maslow's famous "Hierarchy of Needs" pyramid, listing our most fundamental internet needs at the bottom. Not surprisingly, our need for cats is the most fundamental.
© www.pleated-jeans.com

although they may not look like the pinnacle of cultural sophistication, these jokes are transformed into postmodern satire and parodies, as people develop derivatives. They become the bedrock for culture.

"As humans, we grasp commonality and share what we find funny with our group to demonstrate our belonging."

Although rare, some comedians are able to foster ongoing relationships with their audiences. Peter Serafinowicz has used YouTube and Twitter for self-promotion and to play with different ways of being funny. "Immediately you've got a huge audience, and not just locally, but globally," he says. The videos he published with his brother James raised his profile in the United States significantly, and won him a TV contract with Channel 4.

Serafinowicz has also relished the interactivity of a medium such as Twitter, which he says replicated, in some ways, an offline, live experience.

"Twitter is very satisfying for a comedian: to think of a funny quip, to put it up, and to have people re-tweet it or react to it." He also loves how the 140 characters forces him to think shorter. "Brevity is the soul of wit," he says. "It's really helped me hone my one-liner skills."

As humans, we grasp commonality and share what we find funny with our group to demonstrate our belonging. Now, thanks to the rise of social networks, little memes can spread like wildfire, and can be adapted and transformed. The pervasiveness of silly pictures of cats is simply our way of creating a unified reality out of nothing. Humor is the heart and soul of the web. It makes it the place we want to be.

Understanding the Text

1. Why does Krotoski claim that it's "not surprising" (par. 3) that so much internet content is comedy?
2. According to Krotoski, why does so much online humor feature cats?
3. What makes internet comedy successful?

Reflection and Response

4. What kinds of online humor do you enjoy? What is your favorite comic web site to visit?
5. The Oulipo literary movement believed that constraints were the key to invention. When confronted with certain parameters or obstructions, an artist must think innovatively to be creative. For comedians, the internet as a medium poses what we might call creative limitations. How does the internet pose creative limitations? In what ways do the constraints of the internet inspire invention of comedic content? What unique benefits of the medium allow it to flourish in new ways?

Making Connections

6. Krotoski's column begins with references to several theories of humor, including those of Dr. Rod Martin. How do these ideas connect to and/or complicate the scientific theories discussed by John Morreall (p. 25)?
7. Matt Buchanan (p. 131) writes about one type of humor found on Twitter — parody accounts. Research another form of comedy made possible by social media networks such as Twitter. Is this kind of humor pioneering, or does it hark back to older types of comedy?
8. If the proliferation of sites like *College Humor*, *ClickHole*, and *Funny or Die* and YouTube comedians like Jenna Marbles, HolaSoyGermán, and PewDiePie are any indication, comedy is thriving on the internet. Research and write an argumentative essay or profile about a comedic text or performer from the web.

Is Social Media Ruining Comedy?

Ian Crouch

Ian Crouch is a writer whose work on culture, sports, and books has appeared in several online journals such as the *Paris Review* and the *New Republic*. He has worked as a web producer since 2009 for newyorker.com, which is where he originally published "Is Social Media Ruining Comedy?"

In this piece, Crouch investigates how the internet has complicated the comedy scene for "well-established straight men" (par. 7) comics like Bill Burr. Burr is an American comedian and actor in his late forties who hosts *Bill Burr's Monday Morning Podcast.* When reading Crouch's.piece, think about how social media has changed the comedy industry for better and for worse.

The trailer for the comedian Bill Burr's new special on Netflix, *I'm Sorry You Feel That Way*, begins with a disclaimer: "If you have strong religious beliefs, politically correct opinions, or are easily offended by crude language and sexual innuendo CONSIDER YOURSELF WARNED." The potential viewers being warned away are those who might take exception to Burr calling Jesus Christ "some bearded baby" or referring to adoption as a form of human recycling. About midway through the eighty-minute set, Burr tells a story about how his father didn't want his kids getting hugged because he was afraid they'd become gay. He says that his dad might have been on to something, before pausing to admonish the audience: "Let me finish before you start blogging, okay?" The subject here, as with a lot of Burr's comedy, is the nature of offense—the people likely to take it, and why he thinks that they shouldn't bother.

Despite the disclaimer about political correctness, this special is Burr's most progressive—the least likely to offend the kinds of people who have been accused of policing comedy in recent years for any sign of transgression. He makes fun of gun owners and talks about the hypocrisy of religion. He doesn't, as he has in the past, make white-people-are-like-this, black-people-are-like-that jokes. He doesn't say "fag" anymore (it was always as a joke on homophobic, insecure straight men, but it still sounded like a slur). And he has backed away from the full-blown misogyny that marred his previous special, *You People Are All the Same,* in 2012. ("This time, I made a note that I wasn't going to trash women, because I thought I overdid it on my last one," he recently told *The Hollywood Reporter.* "I looked back and watched it and thought, Jesus! Does this guy need a hug or what?"

Still, Burr has decidedly not become a feminist. Much of his humor involves him impersonating women while saying vain, childish, and stupid things—he pitches his voice high and screws up his face. In 2008, he described women as "psycho robots that don't run out of batteries." This time, it's "You just want to keep them calm. Just keep them calm, like a rescue dog, right?" Watching the special, I laughed at these jokes, at the same time knowing that it would be perfectly reasonable for someone to find them mean-spirited and retrograde. They are both of these things, and saying so means that I am the kind of hypocrite who laughs and then, later, attempts to explain away or renounce that laughter. This might make me a bad comedy fan, or at least a bad Bill Burr fan—the kind of anxious, worried, score-keeping blogger whom he so often ridicules.

On a recent episode of Jerry Seinfeld's web series, *Comedians in Cars Getting Coffee*, Burr complained about the sensitivity of modern comedy audiences. "There's this new level of, like, selfishness when you go to a comedy club—where they'll watch you for forty minutes and take everything as a joke, and then all of a sudden you'll hit a topic that's sensitive to them, and then all of a sudden you're making statements," he said. Seinfeld asked Burr if he thought that the culture was becoming more "respectful," and if that meant people couldn't be funny anymore. Burr responded, "If I'm saying something and I'm joking, then I'm joking. This is the deal, those people who get offended like that, if they want to see stand-up comedy, they should hire a comic for a private show and go, 'These are the topics you can talk about and these are the topics you don't.' So you come into the hostile environment of a comedy club, and we get to say whatever we want."

> "The hostility between comedians and audiences has long been central to comedy, but the nature of that relationship is changing now that technology has knocked down the walls of the comedy club."

Burr is making an argument that downplays the cultural power of 5 the comedian—I'm just telling jokes here—while defending the comedian's absolute and essential requirement of free speech to pursue his art. It is similar to a statement that Louis C.K. made in an interview with *Slate*, in 2011, after Tracy Morgan was accused of homophobia (during a performance in Nashville, Morgan said that he would kill his son if he came out as gay.) "It's a dumb thing to take at face value," Louis said of the angry online response to Morgan's bit. "You'd have to be a moron. And if you do, you are not allowed to laugh at any more jokes. You are not allowed to laugh at any jokes that have any violence or negative feelings attached to them, ironically or otherwise." The hostility between comedians and audiences has long been central to comedy, but the nature of that relationship is changing now that technology has knocked down the walls of the comedy club.

Even though comedians are public performers, they can be an antisocial bunch, and these days a certain set of very famous older male comics sound as if they mostly want to be left alone. In a recent interview, Chris Rock said that American culture had reëmbraced the political correctness of the nineties, and that the infiltration of cell phones and social media into the comedy club has spoiled that space for performers. Something said in front of a small crowd a few drinks deep in the middle of the night can easily be shared with a sober mass of people sitting upright in their chairs browsing the internet the next day. Every performance has become a de-facto national set, even the ones in which a comedian is riffing or failing through new material. "There are a few guys good enough to write a perfect act and get onstage, but everybody else workshops it and workshops it, and it can get real messy," Rock said. "It can get downright offensive. . . . But if you think you don't have room to make mistakes, it's going to lead to safer, gooier stand-up. You can't think the thoughts you want to think if you think you're being watched."

Stand-up has always been about thinking while being watched, and it can be a bit grating to hear celebrity comics like Rock, Louis, and Burr gripe about feeling powerless in a fight against an army of hecklers on the web. (For every critical voice, there are hundreds of fans hanging onto their every word, and who have no problem laughing at a little casual racism or misogyny.) It isn't that these comedians are Luddites (Burr, for example, hosts his own podcast and has talked about the various ways in which the web has been good for his career). Rather, they are responding to the ways that technological innovation has changed the very definition, and composition, of an audience. Other things are changing as well. These complaints about the web's restrictive atmosphere are being made by well-established straight men in a field that has, until recently, mostly been the province of straight men. Contemporary audiences are more attuned to social power dynamics in comedy: the high-profile controversies involving comedians in recent years have all started with a straight man making a joke about a less-empowered segment of the population: Tracy Morgan talking about gays, in Nashville, in 2011; Daniel Tosh joking about rape at a club in Los Angeles, in 2012; Bill Maher drawing connections between Islam and violence during a segment on his HBO show earlier this fall.

And, as the world of comedy itself has become more diverse—thanks in large part to the web—subjects like homosexuality, sexual assault, and Islam are no longer the exclusive province of straight men, but of gay, female, and Muslim comics as well. Today, more people would prob- ably rather hear a joke about the nebulous uncertainties of sexual con- sent told by Amy Schumer ("We've all been a little bit raped. Like, not totes consensch") than by Bill Burr ("Choke me, but let me breathe, but kind of scare the shit out of me a little bit.") It is not that Schumer is allowed to do it because she is a woman and Burr isn't because he is a man. Instead, it is Schumer's perspective, as well as her gifts as a per- former, that make her better suited to tell a better joke. For someone like Burr, meanwhile, the comedy bar is now much higher and harder to clear. A rape joke by a man has to be really funny and socially acute to be worth hearing.

If the world has become a less safe place for daring, iconoclastic com- edy, as people like Chris Rock have suggested, that may also be because of the very influence that Rock and other comics have in American culture. As comedy has emerged as an essential art form, with its stron- gest voices looked to as formidable social critics, the whole enterprise has taken on an earnest gravity that is often at odds with its original purpose—laughter. One response from comedians has been to play down their authority and to mock the people who parse their every word. It is what Burr is doing when he says, "Just because you took what I said seriously doesn't mean I now meant it." Or when, during his spe- cials, he backs off from his own most outlandish bits, by telling the audi- ence, as he does this time, "I know I'm a fucking moron," or as he did, in 2008, while telling a joke about pedophiles, "It's just a theory, people. Don't take this shit too seriously."

Yet such a position is a slight to comedy. For one thing, Burr is selling   10 himself short: as well as being a gifted joke-writer and a sharp performer, he has all kinds of smart things to say about hypocrisy, consumerism, and the rage that lives in the hearts of modern American men—as his bits on Black Friday, Steve Jobs, and Lance Armstrong demonstrate. And while the internet can be unnervingly adept at fostering groupthink and ginning up nearly anything to the level of scandal, it's false to suggest, as Burr does, that all the criticism that comedians face is merely "manufac- tured outrage."

Controversy has always been the lifeblood of comedy. As people such as Chris Rock and Louis C.K. have argued, in order to be funny, to be meaningful, to transcend the hacky and the inane, comedians have to say things that other people are afraid to say, and, by making us laugh, force us to admit some things about ourselves that we would be unwill- ing to cop to in the cold light of day. The best comedy has to be offen- sive, or at least offensive to someone, in order to prove that it is good— that it is doing something useful beyond just filling time and selling cocktails. Any comedian who purports to be shocked when the manifestly shocking thing that he says gets a lot of attention can't be telling the truth. It is dangerous when criticism leads to censorship, or self-censorship, because controversy and scandal are also signs that a comedian is doing something right.

As for Bill Burr, his often-upsetting and even menacing comedy about women should not be dismissed merely as uninspired, possibly offensive jokes. There is something deep and dark in this material for Burr, and it's not surprising that it provokes strong and divergent responses from his audience. It was heartening to see Burr own up to the missteps in his previous special, but this is not the same thing as wanting to see him be punished by the culture or forced to abjectly apologize. Comedians become boring with their edges sanded away. Such a thing seems unlikely, anyway, in Burr's case. For now, he is continuing on a kind of take-it-or-leave-it personal evolution. As he says in his latest special, "If you're being a dick, then yeah, apologize. But other than that, go fuck yourself."

Understanding the Text

1. How does Crouch believe that the internet has altered the world of comedy? Does Crouch think that innovative web technologies are ruining or renewing the comedy scene?

2. What assumptions about the nature of comedy underpin Crouch's argument? Are these assumptions descriptive (i.e., beliefs about what the world *is* like) or prescriptive (i.e., beliefs about what the world *should be* like)? Do they strike you as justifiable?

Reflection and Response

3. Burr implies that the selfishness and sensitivity of contemporary audiences have made them forget that the comedy club is a "hostile environment" (par. 4) where comedians can joke freely about offensive topics. Do you agree that the comedy club is a rhetorical situation in which anything goes? What if a stand-up performance is recorded and distributed online? Do different roles apply for virtual as opposed to in-person forums of comedy?

4. In your experience, what times and places provide safe havens for irreverent comedy? Do you think that any of these situations support Crouch's claim that "the comedy bar is now much higher and harder to clear" (par. 8)?

Making Connections

5. In "That's Not Funny!," (p. 70) Caitlin Flanagan discusses the line comedians must walk between being funny and offending their audiences, particularly on college campuses. What responsibility do you think

comedians have to be aware of their audiences' sensibilities? Are audiences obliged to allow comedians to perform without reservations? Why or why not?

6. Watch a few episodes of Jerry Seinfeld's web series *Comedians in Cars Getting Coffee*. How do the settings featured in this show — car interiors, coffee shops, restaurants, etc. — free the comedians to hold candid conversations with Seinfeld? What concerns do the comedians share about today's comedy scene? Conduct follow-up research on how one of the interviewed comedians uses the internet to promote their comedy.

3 | Agent: Who (or What) Is a Comedian?

Who in your family or group of friends is the funniest? What is it about this person that makes them so hilarious? Are they witty, goofy, klutzy? Do they tell funny stories and jokes? Do they act inappropriately? Do you and your friends laugh *with* or *at* this person?

While the humorous scene comprises part of a comic act's appeal, as Chapter 2 argued, another part is due to the individuals involved — both the funny actors and the audiences they crack up. Although the title of "comedian" is typically reserved for those paid to make us laugh, anyone can be a comic agent. Comic agents need not even be people, let alone professional performers. For example, internet cats, robots that "FAIL," and young kids who say the darndest things act without any intention to make us laugh, and yet they do. Might the locus of humor lie with the agent who perceives an act to be funny rather than the agent who performs a comic act, as incongruity theorists argue? Is humor, like beauty or art, a subjective matter?

The audience for a humorous act certainly plays a crucial role in determining what is funny. On the web site *Funny or Die*, for example, internet surfers vote on whether videos, images, articles, and songs are funny or whether they should "die" and be removed from the site. In a very direct way, users choose the site's content; the comics who create material without considering who exactly will view, read, or listen to their material do so at the peril of their success. Nevertheless, we should not exaggerate the role of the audience at the expense of the author. Some folks are objectively funny or, at least, funnier than most. What is it about such people that makes them great comedians?

One answer is that we like them or like to hate them. As master rhetoricians, comedians construct a compelling *ethos*, or ethical character. While *logos* and *pathos* refer to how a speaker persuades an audience with logical and emotional appeals, respectively, *ethos* includes those rhetorical strategies intended to persuade an audience that the writer or speaker is

photo: FourOaks / Getty Images

an intelligent and virtuous character who is a credible and reliable source. The modern word *ethics* derives from this ancient Greek word, which makes sense because *ethos* appeals establish authority by emphasizing the principled conduct of an author. If a speaker demonstrates a sense of reasonable morality, we find them trustworthy and are more likely to agree with what they say. Kenneth Burke took *ethos* one step further, arguing that such appeals make an audience identify and feel "consubstantial," or of one essence, with the author. Parents, friends, teachers, politicians, and businesses have all used this same strategy at some point to try to convince you to identify with their motives.

Ethos matters to comedians as much as it does to traditional authorities. More comedy than you might suspect contains an ethical motive. A long-standing technique of humorists is to adopt a persona who lacks *ethos* for the precise reason of reaffirming ethical standards. Comedian Amy Schumer employs this rhetorical strategy when she plays the role of a libertine, misogynist, or subservient woman. We laugh at the immoral behavior of her ironic performances to affirm correct behaviors and ethical beliefs. Other comedians like Chris Rock take a more sincere approach, bluntly and even antagonistically defending higher moral ground. Laughing at a joke by Rock indicates our agreement with his views. Laughing through the entirety of one of his albums signifies our identification with him as a humorous moralist. Beyond characters played and personas adopted, comedians' actual identities also influence how their comedy is received. When we learn about a comedian's sordid past, substance abuse, or struggles with depression, our view of their comedy changes. Who can now watch *The Cosby Show* without thinking about its titular character being an alleged serial rapist, for example?

All the writers in this chapter analyze the diverse characteristics and personas that comic agents adopt to establish their credibility as comedians. In the first reading, Matt Buchanan, an editor for *The Awl,* argues that it is better not to know the author when it comes to parody Twitter accounts because anonymity is key to a form of internet humor where the author pretends to be someone else. Next, novelist Chris Bacheleder harkens back to the humor theories in Chapter 1 as he explains how to turn an incident with his young daughter and a dead chipmunk — an unlikely comic duo — into a conventional joke. Professor of film studies Tama Jeffers McDonald then considers a different sort of objective comic agent than an unfortunate animal: genre itself, specifically the romantic comedy (romcom) genre. The remaining selections in this chapter turn to the question of how stand-up comedians get laughs by playing with identity politics: Amanda Lynch Morris examines the rhetoric of American Indian stand-up comedy; Alan Shain reflects on his own stand-up routine as a form of disability activism; and Karley Sciortino and Jennifer Reed comment on the feminist and queer comic performances of women, respectively.

The writers in this chapter ask you to reflect on the comic agent in the rhetoric of humor. As you read these selections, consider the *ethos* of not only the comic agent being analyzed but also the author of the reading conducting the analysis.

Why Twitter Parody Accounts Should Stay Anonymous

Matt Buchanan

If you are on Twitter, you may have come across tweets from anonymous users impersonating just about anyone famous, from Steve Jobs and Mark Zuckerberg to Jesus Christ and God. Matt Buchanan, a former science and technology writer for the *New Yorker* online, addresses the anonymity, art, and humor of parody Twitter accounts in this 2013 piece. Buchanan is currently based in New York City as an editor for *The Awl*, an online cultural blog founded in 2009 that publishes long-form essays.

Earlier this month, after maintaining anonymity for three years, Josh Friedland, a freelance writer, announced that he was behind @RuthBourdain, a Twitter account that combined the food writer Ruth Reichl's often rapturous accounts of food with the sarcasm and vulgarity of Anthony Bourdain.° The account was an occasionally funny and often profane deflation of America's current overblown food culture ("Jesus. This fucking cold, gray city. Snorting salmon roe off tiny pancakes. Golden showers of lemon. Money shot of sour cream. New York."), and the author accumulated 71,000 followers. Since revealing himself, Friedland has posted only four tweets to @RuthBourdain, all in reference to the revelation of his identity. The account is, for all intents and purposes, salted earth: rare is the parody Twitter account that remains funny after the author unmasks himself.

Parody accounts are, oddly, one of Twitter's most distinguishing features. Anyone can have virtually any username on the service, as opposed to Facebook and Google Plus, which require users to display their real names. While fake Twitter accounts are sometimes created in an attempt to deceive, they're just as often meant to be humorous and have become a routine reaction to practically every news event, a fact lamented by Alex Pareene in the *New Republic*. Most fake Twitter accounts are, in fact, unfunny; some are in poor taste, like the fake Tsarnaev brother accounts that emerged almost immediately after the two were identified as suspects in the Boston Marathon bombing. But at their best, they ascend to "the highest cultural rung" of "the making-fun-of-others department," as Louis Menand wrote of parody in the magazine in 2010. "Part of the enjoyment

---

Ruth Reichl's often rapturous accounts of food with the sarcasm and vulgarity of Anthony Bourdain: Reichel and Bourdain are celebrity American chefs, food writers, and television hosts.

people take in parody is the enjoyment of feeling intelligent," Menand noted. "Not everyone gets the joke." The highly self-selected audience necessary for parody presents itself automatically on Twitter, which allows its users to choose exactly whom to follow.

@BPGlobalPR, created in May 2010, by the comedian Josh Simpson, was perhaps the first Twitter parody to receive truly mainstream attention; the account was a brutal skewering of BP's milquetoast response to the Gulf oil spill as well as of Twitter's deployment in modern corporate communications. The resulting effect is surreal on its own; this, in turn, makes Twitter an exceptional vehicle for parody. "A parody is an imitation of an imitation: its target is the manner of representation itself," Menand wrote. "If the original is solemn, then solemnity must be what is solemnly lampooned." @BPGlobalPR began with a tweet declaring "We regretfully admit that something has happened off of the Gulf Coast. More to come"—a straightforward post—before it transitioned to producing more outwardly absurd tweets like "BP has pledged 75 million dollars towards the 40 billion dollar cleanup cost. #makingitright." This is only a short distance from a typical BP tweet downplaying the Gulf crisis, like "Scientists report largely no oil impact on wildlife in #Alabama coastal marshes: http://bit.ly/ZPTPeN via @aldotcom."

> "Rare is the parody Twitter account that remains funny after the author unmasks himself."

Not knowing the man behind the Twitter curtain—that it could be anybody openly mocking one of the wealthiest and most powerful corporations in the world—was key to @BPGlobalPR's initial sense of frisson. By the time Simpson eventually revealed himself as the creator, there was little left to say.

When Dan Sinker, the head of the Knight-Mozilla OpenNews project, created the @MayorEmanuel account, which spun the former White House chief of staff Rahm Emanuel's infamous volcanic temperament into a full-fledged Twitter personality, he thought he needed to maintain his anonymity throughout Emanuel's 2010–2011 Chicago mayoral campaign. "The minute the identity is revealed, something really does fundamentally change," said Sinker, who unmasked himself and stopped updating the account after the election was over. He cited the example of Dan Lyons's *The Secret Diary of Steve Jobs*, a parody blog supposedly written by Jobs that lost most of its comedic potency after Lyons revealed himself as the author, as instructive. "You're not mistaking this as the actual person," Sinker said. "But you're able to suspend your disbelief and enter into the logic of the world of that parody account easier when you don't automatically assign an additional author or face to it."

"I have multiple personalities and they are all following me on Twitter."
CartoonStock

What's most powerful about Twitter parodies, according to Sinker, is that "if you're following the account in real time, it's popping up within the context of the rest of the reality you have built in Twitter." The unreal and the real are combined in a single stream. An @MayorEmanuel tweet admonishing voters to "VOTE, BITCHES" appears at the same time that the actual Rahm Emanuel tweets "Hey hey hey . . ." or CNN reveals the results of the election. In this sense, Twitter seems to be a powerful answer to a fundamental problem parody has faced over the past several decades: as Menand noted, "the barrier between the authentic and the parodic has collapsed." If parody is everywhere, if it is diffuse, it requires a medium that can properly contain and convey it—a real-time outlet. (This is also why Stephen Colbert's character works so beautifully via tweets, outside of the constraints of his television show.)

Yet Twitter also constantly undermines the parody it creates. The primary currency of social media is fame, and it is fame that drives the authors of popular parody accounts to uncloak themselves, destroying the account in the process. If fame is all the authors of parody accounts care about, as @MayorEmanuel wrote in one of his last tweets, "it's pretty clear that the party's over."

Understanding the Text

1. Buchanan opens with a story about Josh Friedland's parody Twitter account, @RuthBourdain. What purpose does this anecdote serve for his argument?

2. According to Buchanan, what characteristics must a parody Twitter account exhibit to be successful?

3. Why is it important for a parody Twitter account to be anonymous? What effect does knowing the identity of the real tweeter have on an account's followers?

Reflection and Response

4. What parody Twitter accounts have you followed yourself or heard of? Analyze the humor in two or three accounts. (If you are unfamiliar with the genre, look up a few lists of the top parody Twitter accounts online.)

5. Do you agree with Louis Menand's claim that "the barrier between the authentic and the parodic has collapsed" (par. 6)? If you do, what might account for this collapse? Who today is blurring the line between irony and sincerity, and how? What is their motivation?

Making Connections

6. Buchanan cites articles from Alex Pareene in the *New Republic* and Louis Menand in the *New Yorker* to develop his argument. Locate and read these pieces. Then write an essay that responds to the debate over the efficacy of parody Twitter accounts.

7. In 2014, a kerfuffle erupted over a tweet posted by @ColbertReport. Research this event, including activist Suey Park's #CancelColbert hashtag, and write an essay that responds to Buchanan's suggestion that "Stephen Colbert's character works so beautifully via tweets" (par. 6). The readings in Chapter 2 should also help you develop and support your position.

8. Parody Twitter accounts about BP's response to the 2010 Deepwater Horizon oil spill and Rahm Emanuel's 2010–2011 campaign to be reelected Chicago's mayor demonstrate that the genre is a bona fide vehicle for satire. After reading through the selections in Chapter 4 on the purpose of satire in a democratic society, write an argumentative research essay on parody Twitter accounts that skewer politicians or comment on political issues.

The Dead Chipmunk: An Interrogation into the Mechanisms of Jokes

Chris Bachelder

Chris Bachelder is an associate professor of creative writing at the University of Cincinnati and the author of the novels, *Bear v. Shark* (2001), *U.S.!* (2006), *Abbott Awaits* (2011), and *The Throwback Special* (2016). In this examination of the craft of joke telling, which originally appeared in the February 2011 edition of *The Believer,* Bachelder follows an opening anecdote about his daughter and a dead chipmunk with a systematic analysis of jokes and what they do. Bachelder poses the question, "Where, precisely, is the joke located? Where is it emerging: from the content or from the speaker?" (par. 20). His wide-ranging ruminations on humor theories, authors like Don DeLillo and Kurt Vonnegut, and the American sitcom *The Office* lead him to conclude that the comic often resides in the incongruity between the jokester and the joke itself.

I. Anecdote

One day in August I went to campus to make some copies and retrieve a book from my office. My three-year-old daughter came with me as my "helper." I had packed her a muffin and some milk, and I had promised her we would have a picnic when I finished what I had to do. After she helped me by pushing all the buttons in the elevator and spinning around fast in my swivel chair, we left the building, and I began to look for a good place for our picnic. I spotted a shady bench in a small courtyard, and I pointed the way. As we approached, however, I noticed, directly in front of the bench, a dead chipmunk splayed beneath a cloud of flies.

"Honey," I said, putting my hand on her shoulder, "let's look for another place." I know by now I can't shield or distract my children from all unpleasant things, but if I had the choice, I would rather not picnic by a dead animal and answer the inevitable barrage of questions about the chipmunk's condition.

"Why?" she asked.

"Let's just keep looking," I said.

"Why?" she asked. 5

With my hand on her shoulder I managed to turn her away from the bench. "This is just not a very good spot," I said. "How about over there?"

"Why, Dad?" she asked, trying to turn back around.

"There's something over there," I said, in effect rendering the bench irresistible.

"What is it?"

"It's a chipmunk," I said.   10

"Chipmunk?" She shook free from my hand and looked back toward the bench.

"Let's go, honey," I said. "That chipmunk is not alive."

My daughter took a couple of steps toward the bench and stopped. Evidently she spotted the chipmunk. "Why?" she asked.

"It's dead," I said.

She turned back to me, her face clouded with worry. I knelt down beside   15 her, put my hand on her head. "Let's just go somewhere else," I said.

"Yeah, Dad," she said quietly. "We don't want the dead chipmunk to eat our food."

II. Notes

(1) I see now what happened. My daughter and I went to campus, and we became unwitting elements in the spontaneous generation of a joke. All of the requisite materials—protective father, inquisitive child, snacks, dead animal—were combined on a pleasant morning, and a joke was created. When joke genesis occurs in the real world (or even on a university campus), we have the opportunity to learn a great deal about jokes. How are they formed? What are their conditions and variables? Why— or how—are they funny? And what exactly is to be gotten when we *get it*?

(2) A character in Don DeLillo's novel *Americana* says, "Underwear is humorous and only the undemocratic mind interrogates humor." The idea here, I think, is that funniness belongs to individual citizens. Don't tread on me, don't try to tell me what is funny and why. The analysis of humor is, in its suppositions, presumptuous and dictatorial. The comic— and its mechanisms—should not be decreed from above. And, of course, this seems righteous and correct, but nevertheless I'd like to figure out why DeLillo's funny statement on funniness is funny. I am, that is, compelled to analyze the humor in a sentence that warns against the analysis of humor. ("We murder to dissect," sayeth Wordsworth.) The statement is comic, in part, because of the abrasion between the low-minded (underwear) and the high-minded (democracy, interrogation). The sentence yokes the sad banality of underwear and the noble abstraction of democracy—the reader must hold both in her mind, and the tension produces comic energy. Also, *humorous* is funnier than *funny*. Underwear is actually

funny—those words belong to the same register—and yet *Underwear is funny* is not very funny. *Humorous* elevates the diction to a more formal level, and the slight mismatch between the noun and its adjective is comically ironic in its effect. That the interrogation of humor is undemocratic is a moderately difficult point. It is not immediately evident, and thus not immediately funny; it takes some thought to figure this out. But the sentence does not rely on its meaning for its humor. In fact, the connection between democracy and the interrogation of humor is not really intended to be funny—it's a point of some substance—and it might be the case that the statement is funnier before we comprehend it. The sentence is funny immediately (before we understand it) because of the surprising elements that it contains. There is, in addition, a kind of umbrella irony at work. The keen, formal, interrogative, analytical voice of the sentence is here issuing a warning against interrogation and analysis. Someone capable of articulating this point is clearly not someone content to let the comic properties of underwear go unexamined—not to mention the fact that in this strongly worded verdict, the speaker is undemocratically castigating the undemocratic—so ultimately the sentence floats off into a kind of ludicrous paradox.

(3) The chipmunk story is, if not *funny*, at least *comic*, which is to say it has a comic form. The story, in fact, is shaped almost precisely like a joke. I can tell it as a joke rather than an anecdote if I make three simple changes:

(a) First, I have to shift from the first person ("One day in August I went 20 to campus. . . .") to a very general third ("So a man and his daughter. . . ."). Jokes are rarely if ever in the first person. The personality and idiosyncrasies of a narrator are irrelevant to the mechanism of the joke, and in fact they distract from the joke's operation. (The exception here is the stand-up comedian, who in the course of an act or a career develops a kind of literary persona that is capable of generating a second-order or dramatic irony. The joke, that is, achieves more power from the friction between its content and its teller. Potentially offensive jokes, in particular—jokes about race or women—can become more complicated when there is an overarching question of narrative intent. This is the Sarah Silverman Effect: *Did she mean that? Is this act an act?* Where, precisely, is the joke located? Where is it emerging: from the content or from the speaker? Am I laughing at the offensive joke, or am I laughing at the ironic persona who holds such offensive and ridiculous positions? This gag can be thoughtfully or haphazardly executed. At its worst it is a craven mode, its practitioners lobbing bombs behind the Fortress of Irony.) In literature, a first-person narration tends to reveal something about the narrator—we find a meaningful gap, large or small, between what the narrator understands and what we as readers understand. Jokes as a rule are not dependent upon this kind of revelatory technique; while jokes depend upon irony (more below), they do not tend to utilize the irony that obtains in first-person narration. It is difficult, that is, to imagine a standard joke (not a comedian's joke) that uses an unreliable narrator. (Though not, of course, in the context of a novel, where a man telling a dirty joke might very well reveal more about himself than he intends.) One reason is that jokes, which use a clear, simple setup and a final, surprising punch line, can't afford to be that subtle or slippery. Another reason is that jokes point outward, not inward. They tend to be about language or groups of people or about the human condition in general. Thus our chipmunk joke requires the universal "man and his daughter."

(*b*) The second step in joke conversion is to shift the joke from past tense to present to create more immediacy and energy, and to signify the story's superficiality, its tonal purview, its *jokiness*. Present tense is part of the joke's code (a man walks into a bar). Past tense moves us tonally toward fable, allegory, or tale (the genres of wisdom and instruction), which use the sense of the deep past as displacement, as a means of arriving at truths. Past tense creates gravity; present tense, levity.

(*c*) Finally, I must delete the few vivid and particularizing details. Vivid description, used in literature to render a character or a scene unique and credible—lifelike—is a disruption in jokes. In the idiom of information theory, description acts as noise in a joke, weakening the signal, threatening the joke's "information." If I say, "A priest walks into a bar. He sits down on the stool and the bartender notices he has a chipped tooth . . . ," the receiver of the joke will expect that tooth to be relevant to the setup and the punch line. If it is not relevant, it endangers the joke's effect by leading our attention astray. A joke teller is a devious shepherd, and must herd all listeners to the Punch Line Deployment Zone, where they will be ambushed (by a kind of misinformation). In a literary context, the priest's chipped tooth is revelatory or at least suggestive, though it needn't be, in terms of the narration, strictly relevant or propulsive. That the detail is unnecessary is in fact a virtue in the context of the post-Chekhovian story. Particularizing detail is necessary, that is, precisely to the extent that it is unnecessary. One of the qualities Nabokov admired in "The Lady with the Little Dog" is that the story is in effect all noise, no information. "There is no special moral to be drawn," Nabokov writes, "and no special message to

> "A joke teller is a devious shepherd, and must herd all listeners to the Punch Line Deployment Zone, where they will be ambushed (by a kind of misinformation)."

be received." Chekhov's narrator, Nabokov notes, "seems to keep going out of his way to allude to trifles, every one of which in another type of story would mean a signpost denoting a turn in the action ... but *just because these trifles are meaningless*, they are all-important in giving the real atmosphere of this particular story" (italics added). A joke, though, carries information in its setup. Atmosphere, if it is valuable, is valuable only to the extent that it carries the joke forward and establishes a clear code or pattern that can be disturbed by the punch line.

(4) If we retain the basic form but change the point of view and verb tense, and if we streamline the anecdote to render its particulars more bland and general, we have this dead-chipmunk joke: A man and his young daughter are out for a walk and a picnic on a beautiful summer day. After an hour of walking, the girl becomes tired and hot and hungry, and so the father says, "Okay, honey, let's look for a good spot for our picnic." "Why?" the girl asks. "Because we're hungry," the father says. "And as soon as we find a nice shady place, we'll have our picnic." Soon he sees a perfect spot—it has soft grass to sit on, it's in the shade of a tall and beautiful tree, it even has an old tree stump to use as a table. The father takes the girl's hand and says, "Let's go right over there beneath that big tree." "Why?" the girl asks. "Because," the father says, "it's a perfect spot for our picnic." They walk to the tree, and just as the father is about to spread the blanket on the ground, he sees a dead chipmunk nearby in the grass. Not wanting his young daughter to see the dead animal, the man quickly picks up the blanket, takes his daughter's hand, and says, "Sweetheart, I've got an idea. Why don't we move to that tree over there." "Why?" the girls asks. "It's a much better place for a picnic," he says. The girl starts to ask why, but then she sees the chipmunk. "Dad, look, it's a chipmunk!" she screams. The father turns the girl away from the chipmunk, and he kneels down in the grass to talk to her. "Honey, the chipmunk is dead," he says. "Let's go over there for our picnic." The girl stares at the chipmunk, then looks at her father. Her eyes are beginning to water and her lips are quivering. "Yeah, Dad," she says. "We don't want that dead chipmunk to eat our food."

(5) Kurt Vonnegut called jokes *mousetraps*. This metaphor fits into a traditional conception of humor as a form of violence. (Freud theorized that humor is an act of aggression.) Much of the language of comedy is hostile. We say of funny people that they *kill* us or *slay* us. A comic will say that a joke *killed*, which is the opposite of *bombed*. We say of wit that it is either *dull* or *sharp*, and a sharp wit might be called *rapier*. Dull humor *clubs us over the head* or even *bludgeons us*. We describe wit as *mordant* and *sardonic*. The root of *mordant* is the Latin *mordere* ("to bite"), and the root of *sardonic* is the Greek *sardonios*, referring to a plant on the

island of Sardinia that (according to legend), when ingested, makes you laugh so hard you *die*. By comparison, Vonnegut's mousetrap is fairly innocuous, though illuminating. To be certain, there is an element in joke telling of entrapment by lure, and there is a sense that the receiver (the *victim*) *walks into* the joke, following desires or expectations toward the punch line. As many jokes work by swift and precise reversal (of expectation or logic), you could call the very form of the joke cunning and aggressive. Punch lines—they're called *punch* lines—are often short and sharp. They are brutal in form if not content. If the receiver of the joke does not feel punched, he might feel as if he has been blindsided or as if he has suffered a kind of logical whiplash. Vonnegut, though, wasn't talking explicitly about the violence of joke telling. He was talking about the craft of joke telling, the mechanism of the joke. The joker sets the trap—just as there is potential energy stored in a compressed spring, there is tension in the joke's setup—then springs it. The punch line snaps, harnessing and releasing the joke's energy.

(6) The mousetrap is a good way to speak of a certain kind of joke that snaps shut. The punch line is final and utter, a closing, a flipping of a switch. Once you "get it," you've gotten it. Here's a joke: The Invisible Man walks into the doctor's office. He goes to the front desk and tells the receptionist he's here for his appointment. The receptionist says, "Please wait here, I'll go tell the doctor." A moment later she returns and tells the Invisible Man, "I'm sorry, I'm afraid he can't see you right now."

(7) When Mr. Irony renounces irony in Padgett Powell's exceedingly funny story "Mr. Irony Renounces Irony," he must choose a suitable conceptual replacement for the ironic. He chooses the childlike term *surprisy*, trying in effect to salvage a comic vision of life by purging cynicism and emphasizing wonder. (That the substitution of *surprisy* for *ironic* is inescapably ironic adds another comic dimension to the story.) *Surprisy*, though, is actually just about the best anyone has ever been able to do to account for humor. *Surprisy* is our prevailing theory for why our species laughs, which is after all a weird thing to do. Most theories of humor—most notably the Incongruity Theory—posit that humor grows out of surprise. As Pascal wrote a long time ago, "Nothing produces laughter more than a surprising disproportion between that which one expects and that which one sees." *Surprise* here is kind of an umbrella term, and there are many ways of articulating surprise—incongruity, wordplay, reversal, non sequitur and all logical fallacy, the mixture of high and low, vulgarity, inappropriateness, and, of course, irony, which can be formulated as a (surprising) *difference* or *gap*: between what is said and what is meant, between what happens and what we expect to happen, between what a character knows and what a reader/viewer knows.

(Sarcasm being the crudest form of irony: "Analyzing humor. Yeah, that sounds like a blast." The mental processing of irony involves recognizing the gap and interpreting it.) Laughter, according to the Incongruity Theory, can be seen as the physiological response to the cognitive act of resolving the surprise. Some theories of humor (the Ontic-Epistemic Theory° is a real knee-slapper) contend that funny things short-circuit the brain, causing a fleeting cognitive lockup or a kind of tiny metaphysical stroke. In this model, a joke creates a small tear in our notion of the real, the brain rushes in to mend the rip, resolve the incongruity, and our subsequent smile or chuckle or guffaw is an act of profound relief. Humor, then, emerges in a sense from terror, as the mind gets a tiny peek at the void, then quickly nails a board over the crack to preserve its illusion of mastery, control, meaning, order, reality.

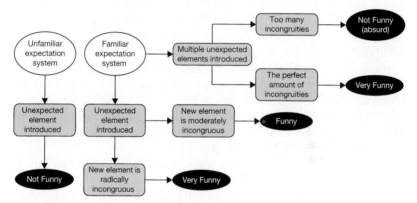

A simplified model of humor according to the Incongruity Theory.

(8) All of this happens almost instantaneously, of course, and none of it enters our consciousness. (And so, like a lot of psychological theory, including almost all of Freud, these claims are unverifiable and thus not even scientific. But it's still fun to think about.) If we could somehow adapt the kind of slow-motion technology CBS uses for its golf coverage, we might be able to watch what happens when the brain receives a joke, let's say, the Invisible Man joke above. We would see, first of all, that the joke creates anxiety, a heightened state of awareness and tension. The joke is a threat. There is, superficially, the real worry that we might not get it, that we might be made to look foolish. But the more dire threat exists at

Ontic-Epistemic Theory: a theory of humor proposed by Peter Marteinson that argues that the comic arises when we perceive a disjunction between social being, which is constructed and ultimately fictional, and material reality, which is objective and real.

the level of language and meaning. *He can't see you right now.* The word *see* means different things, and the mind must confront this multivalence, a fundamental instability of language. It's a crisis of reference, correspondence. To think, to communicate, we need words to stand for things. This is just a dumb pun, but it opens up to chaos, to Babel. This Invisible Man joke is *dangerous*—it's a virus that threatens to crash the entire meaning-making system. At this point—remember, this is slo-mo—the joke-receiving mind regains its composure, then enters the breach to isolate and quarantine the pun. *See*, in the context of the joke, means only two things, just two. *Can't see you right now* is figurative—in medical argot, it means the doctor is busy. And *can't see you right now* is literal—the patient is invisible. The mind can hold these two meanings down, contain them, recognize them simultaneously. What a relief! The world as we know it is preserved. The mind can then order the mouth to laugh, or, better yet, to groan. The mind can order the mouth and hands to do that drum thing that people do after bad jokes, but to do it—this is important—in a way that seems to make fun of doing the drum thing after bad jokes. . . . All of this, more or less, occurring in a split second.

(*9*) A *pun*—like any mousetrap joke—is what we might call a one-alarm joke. The brain jumps out of bed, slides down the pole, races to the scene, and "gets it"—i.e., sees both meanings at once, resolves the ambiguity, thus restoring order and security. It's a kind of infection control. This activity of our Cognitive First Responders is experienced as pleasure, whether or not it is based in abject fear.

(*10*) (A pun is, on rare occasions, witty, though it is rarely if ever funny. Most often, puns are dreadful, though if puns are employed relentlessly and conceptually, as in Shakespeare and Joyce, they can achieve power, though not necessarily comic power. As Doctorow writes of Joyce's *preconceived aesthetic*: "I will pun my way into the brain's dreamwork." Punning can be an assault on consciousness and order, a way to evince a frightening instability beneath the seen and the known. Puns suggest (demonstrate) that meaning is slippery, that other meanings lurk behind words like spirits. In Shakespeare, punning is related to the preoccupation with doubling, with ambiguity, with sleeping and dreaming, with the question of the real. A pun is the linguistic analog of the forest in *A Midsummer Night's Dream*, and it might be comic, but it's also kind of spooky.)

(*11*) Some jokes, though—call them three- or four-alarm jokes— manage to punch multiple holes in our ontic-epistemic fabric. (Well, that's all right, because we like the way it hurts.) Faced with a breakout of the surprisy, the brain must recognize and resolve these numerous incongruities, and the mending process is sequential. Each surprise comprises two or more elements (what we expected and what we received).

For each surprise, the mind must do more than one thing at once, simultaneously holding the incongruous elements. The brain can do more than one thing at once, but it can't do *more than* more than one thing at once *at once*. One surprise at a time, that is. A joke like this does not snap like a mousetrap but pops like a string of firecrackers. The process of *getting it* is not instantaneous.

(12) On an episode of *The Office*, Pam sets up Michael with her friend Julie. As Michael and Julie get to know each other, Michael asks her about her work. Julie says, "I'm an ESL teacher." Michael says, "Really? See, I didn't think you could teach that. I thought that was something you were born with. What am I thinking right now?" To which Julie answers, "Are you thinking I said ESP?" We can analyze this sequence, but one way to know a multi-alarm joke is by sensation. You can feel certain jokes rattling through your mind like Plinko chips. This particular joke is not outrageously complex, but it doesn't resolve instantaneously. When Michael says, "What am I thinking right now?" we must scramble, in the middle of their conversation, to break the joke down into meaning: *Julie teaches English as a Second Language and Michael thinks she teaches extrasensory perception. Wow, is he dumb.* This is very basic dramatic irony—there is a gap between what Michael understands and what we understand—but it is expressed rapidly and indirectly. With a degree of wit, that is, and a respect for the audience. We have to execute at least three steps here. First, since Michael does not actually say *ESP*, we have to convert "What am I thinking right now?" into the proposition "Michael thinks she means ESP." Second, we have to recognize the difference between what Michael thinks to be true (ESL is ESP) and what we know to be true (ESL is not ESP), and, third, we have to interpret that difference (Michael is an idiot). If we can process this incongruity, it feels nice. (Aristotle thought humor arose from a feeling of superiority.) We are inclined to laugh, but there is not time. Michael's line is not delivered as a zinger, and there is no laugh track to slow the scene. Julie's answer is coming quickly on the heels of his question, so we have to stay alert. The dumb irony in Michael's line is a joke, but it's a setup, not the punch line. Without hesitation Julie says, "Are you thinking I said ESP?" A good way to ruin a joke is to explain it, and Julie's line seems at first merely to be explaining the ESL/ESP confusion in case we didn't catch it on the fly. And indeed, she is subtly recapitulating for our benefit, but she is also extending and layering the joke. Julie could have said, "I have no idea what you're thinking. I teach ESL." That line does one thing only, hammering home the single joke so that absolutely nobody will miss it. But Julie's question introduces further incongruity. The substance of her question is that Michael is mistaken about her ability to read

minds — *Are you thinking I said ESP? Because that's not what I said. You obviously think I can read minds, but I can't.* But in answering Michael's question about what he's thinking, Julie is in a sense *actually reading Michael's mind*—he had in fact thought that she meant ESP. She disavows mind-reading ability precisely in the act of mind-reading. This is a classic paradox, a logical impossibility originating, in this case, from the incongruity between what she is saying and what she is doing. And, alas, the mind's work is not quite done because this paradox has comic meaning. It isn't paradox for paradox's sake; it must be interpreted: Michael is so transparent that his mind can be read by an ESL teacher. In a sense, Michael was so outrageously wrong about ESP that he was right—Julie can read minds.

(*13*) (Most viewers of *The Office* do all of this without any analysis, of course. The mind does its work, the mouth laughs. We are largely unconscious of the mechanisms of the joke and the activity of our minds. Viewers know it's comic—they don't need to know why. Understanding or articulating the joke is not the same thing as getting the joke, and it is not, thank god, requisite. An explanation of the joke is in fact an explanation of how we almost immediately got it, even if the joke made us scramble.)

(*14*) A man walks into a diner for lunch. He looks on the menu board and reads the day's specials: cheese sandwiches for two dollars and hand jobs for five dollars. He walks up to the counter, where a pretty woman at the register says to him, "So, what can I get you today?" And the man says, "Yeah, why don't you go wash your hands and then make me a cheese sandwich." This is—I decree it—a sophisticated and nuanced joke, and all the more so because it initially appears to be such a stupid and flimsy joke. There are, in and around this diner gag, multiple incongruities existing at different orders or levels. The most basic and readily graspable incongruity is about appetite or hunger—the man surprisingly chooses food over sexual gratification. The specific elements of the joke accentuate this initial incongruity. It's lunch, not dinner (at dinner we might expect him to be hungrier), and it's a cheese sandwich and not, say, a roast-beef sandwich. (Meat would be latently sexual and masculine in the joke, and choosing meat over sex would not be as surprising.) *Cheese sandwich* is funny here because it's so innocuous, so nonsexual, such a powerful underdog when pitted against sexual contact (though admittedly *hand job* is also comic and not raunchy, not the stuff of erotic fantasy or wish-fulfillment). Certainly this is a joke that depends on gender stereotype to create incongruity—the man here is (surprisingly) not acting like a man. In this way the joke is sexist, but its sexism ultimately targets women. The man is ridiculous because he is acting like a not-man, i.e., a woman. But there is more going on, including a tonal incongruity in the punch line. The man's lunch order, which can be delivered in the manner of a cowboy, is vaguely sexual. He's literally *ordering*, and it registers like dirty talk. There is obvious irony here, a gap between *what* he orders and *how* he orders. He's not really acting childlike or innocent or "feminine." He's acting worldly and stereotypically masculine: he knows what he wants and he's asserting it. This argues against the point about sexism above but probably introduces another form of sexism. The man is toying with the woman, he doesn't need her (though she is pretty), he is not vulnerable to her explicit sexual availability, and in fact he prefers a vegetarian sandwich to her touch. In comic tradition, men are brought low, made foolish, by sexual desire, and here you might say there is a reversal of that potential reversal in which the woman becomes the fool: the man spurns sex, orders a comic food item, and *still* retains his masculinity and dominance. (At any rate, we can be certain that the joke trades on gender because the man and the woman are not interchangeable—the joke would lose force and meaning if we switched their roles. It might, in fact, cease to be a joke altogether.)

(*15*) Okay, but I think the joke also operates on a higher plane, at the level of joke telling itself. To fully *get it*, the mind must confront meta-joke incongruity. When the man reads the sign in the diner—cheese sandwiches and hand jobs—the joke suddenly opens up into incongruous space. It becomes a dirty joke, first of all, but more fundamentally it becomes a joke. Major incongruity is introduced before the punch line. Why would a diner offer hand jobs and cheese sandwiches? That's absurd and illogical—it's not what diners *do*. (This is the joke's ontological threat, its challenge to the idea of diner-ness, which in effect is a challenge to the very concept of the real. It is startling, says the Ontic-Epistemic Theorist of Humor, for the brain to be reminded that diners are part of social reality, that their characteristics are made, not discovered, and that a diner is fundamentally different from, say, a tree.) Consequently, our minds sound the alarm, issue a red alert. Cognitively, we rush into the joke space opened up by the absurd or unreal diner, and there we prepare for further surprise as a pretty woman behind the counter asks what this man wants. We are now in a heightened state of incongruity-readiness. All hands on deck. But then: the man orders a cheese sandwich. . . . So it's not, after all, a dirty joke. The imagination had opened out into prurience—even though I know this is not a *real* diner, I can contain it and allow for the lascivious action to come—but the man's order is not dirty. It is literally clean ("go wash your hands," he says). The man does not step through into the alternative reality of a dirty joke, or of any joke at all. He does not enter the incongruous world created by the setup. The setup, that is, is a trick, a kind of bait and switch. The receiver of the joke steps into the joke space—we are ushered into the dirty diner by the joke's premise—but the joke doesn't take place there. The man in the diner remains in the real world, a real diner. Unlike us, he has not been forced to realize that *diner* is a social construct and not a natural kind. He is not suffering from ontological shock. He is hungry and he wants a sandwich for lunch. He does, more or less, what anyone would do. He is a consummate straight man, and the straight man rarely delivers a punch line. And in fact, the man in the diner does not really deliver a punch line, either. (Note that his order is not elegantly rhythmic or punchy. It's artfully prolix.) He is not making a joke. Generally speaking, a man ordering a sandwich in a diner is not funny or surprising or incongruous in the least, and yet his order is surprising because the joke has lured us out of the real, and, in the context of the unreal, the real has the power to startle us once more. The paradox is that we expect to be surprised and we aren't, which is a tremendous surprise. A non–punch line in the slot of the punch line is a kind of grand meta-joke punch line. This is a *Gotcha!* joke, and a simple, beautifully designed experiment conducted on the mind. In deceptively refusing to play by the rules of jokes, this joke reveals the activity of the joke-receiving mind. In a way it *plays a joke* on the mind. By not working, it shows us how jokes work. Ultimately, the joke is that you thought it was going to be a joke and it wasn't a joke.

(16) Now you try one. Read the following joke and then explain why 35 it is funny. (Answers below, in note 24.) A man walks into a bar holding an octopus. He sits on a stool, puts the octopus on a stool beside him, and announces, "This octopus is a musical genius. He can play any instrument in the world. If you bring an instrument up here, I'll bet you a hundred dollars this octopus can play it." There is a great commotion in the bar, and someone eventually comes forth with a guitar. The man takes the guitar and hands it to the octopus. The octopus slowly extends its tentacles all over the guitar, feeling the tuning keys, the fret board, and the strings. Then he uses the tips of three tentacles to press down strings, and with another tentacle he gently strums a G chord. The man with the octopus gets his hundred dollars and says, "Who else wants to bet? I'll bet you one hundred dollars this octopus can play whatever instrument you bring." A few minutes later, a guy comes up to the bar and gives the octopus a flute. The octopus takes the flute with two tentacles, and with its others it begins to probe the instrument, gingerly touching the lip plate, the keys, the tuning slides. Then it raises the flute, puts the mouth hole beneath its beak, arranges its tentacles on the keys, and blows a decent C-major scale. The man collects his money and

says, "All right, anyone else? Anyone else want to bet me that this octopus can play any instrument you give him?" Just then a man bursts through the door with a bagpipe. "Here," he says, handing the bagpipe to the octopus. Once again, the octopus extends its tentacles all over the instrument, touching and probing the bagpipe. The tentacles gingerly move over the blowstick, the drones, and the bag. This happens for quite some time, the octopus continuing to touch the bagpipe without playing it. Eventually the bartender comes over and says to the man next to the octopus, "Well, buddy, is he going to play it or not?" And the octopus says, "*Play* it? If I can get these pajamas off, I'm going to fuck it."

(*17*) Let's return, at last, to the chipmunk anecdote that is so easily rendered as a joke. The germ of this undemocratic interrogation is my daughter's comment "We don't want the dead chipmunk to eat our food." When she said it, I immediately felt the kind of cognitive whirring that signifies multi-incongruity resolution. I was struck with that glazed, faraway look that is so inappropriate for a picnic. Before I "got it," before I understood why it was comic, I understood *that* it was comic, that it was in essence the punch line of a joke. This joke has a simple, archetypal premise (on a beautiful day a man and his daughter are looking for a place to picnic); a complication (the man sees a dead chipmunk); a brilliant straight man (the father); a reversal (the girl gets the last word); tonal complexity (gravity and levity intertwined); well-calibrated variables (picnic [not bar], dad [not mom], girl [not wife], chipmunk [not dog]); a rhythmic and patterned sequence of dialogue (the girl's repetition of "Why," as well as the short beat before the punch line that misleadingly implies that the girl is upset about death); and numerous ironies that cannot be processed simultaneously or immediately. I'm not claiming that the joke is hilarious, only that its form and composition provide an opportunity for the exploration of the phenomenon of humor. The anecdote's inherent jokeness makes it an ideal case study in what jokes are and what they do.

(*18*) The initial incongruity is obvious, and it resides within the girl's statement. Dead chipmunks don't eat. Dead chipmunks don't do anything, and they particularly don't take nourishment. Also, the girl says, "We don't *want* the dead chipmunk to eat our food," rather than "The dead chipmunk *might* eat our food." The introduction of her desire— what she wants and doesn't want—deepens the incongruity: What the girl and dad don't want the chipmunk to do is irrelevant; death has removed the chipmunk from the sphere of their desires. Further, the girl's phrasing implies that the dead chipmunk, given half the chance, *will eat* their food. For her, moving to another spot is not a precautionary measure; it's an emergency procedure. But the illogical punch line opens up into further incongruity when it is regarded in the larger context of the situation and the interlocutors. The girl's statement is decidedly not an instance of *wit*. If an adult delivers this line—say, an adult in an Oscar Wilde play—then we have the operation of wit, an intentionally ironic and absurd statement intended to create laughter or pleasure. Again, this young girl is not displaying wit. (The acme of my three-year-old daughter's wit is a mock threat, delivered through gasping laughter, to poop on her older sister's bed.) Her fear that the dead chipmunk will eat her food is real, and thus the punch line is an example of dramatic irony, an incongruity between what she understands and what the receiver of the joke understands. Dead chipmunks don't eat (irony 1), and the girl doesn't know that dead chipmunks don't eat (irony 2). The force of the second irony is the funny/sad realization that the girl has no conception of death and is just concerned about her lunch. The identity of the speaker is crucial to the force and meaning of the joke. (Imagine, for instance, if the punch line was delivered by the man's witty, grumpy teenage daughter. The irony is still doubled, but the second irony is pointed in a different direction. It becomes a mordant, sarcastic jab at the father. "Yeah, we don't want the dead chipmunk to eat our food." In other words, "You are an idiot, Dad, for being so worried about that stupid chipmunk. I hate you. Can I have a car?" Or a spouse could deliver the line in a way that was either vicious derision or affectionate kidding, etc.). The first irony (dead creatures don't eat) is not that compelling, but if the irony is doubled by context (who is speaking and to whom), the line becomes more complex. Years ago, the young daughter of a coworker told me a joke. She said, "Why did the man throw a stick of butter out the window?" Before I could even respond with my obligatory *I don't know, why?*, the girl said, "Butterfly! Joke! Joke! Joke!" And then she laughed and laughed. Here the joke is not funny at all, and in fact is barely coherent. What is funny is that the girl thinks you activate a joke by yelling the word *joke*. (And I laughed when she told her "joke," no doubt reinforcing her misconception.) She has no idea what a joke is or what it does, and it is this second-order irony that is comic.

(*19*) The father in the chipmunk joke is worried. His earnest fear drives the joke and sets up the punch line. (The perfect straight man appears not to know he is in a joke, and, as I actually did not know I was in a joke, I gave an amazing performance.) The father does not want his daughter to see a dead animal, doesn't want her to direct her stereotypical childlike curiosity (established with a pattern of *whys*) to the abstract notion of death. He doesn't want to have to explain the idea of death, and he also wants to protect her. His desire and his expectations propel the joke and lay the groundwork for a comic reversal. In the punch line, the girl—surprise—*also* wants to go elsewhere. She is so oblivious to death that she is not even curious about it. Like her father, she is also afraid, though her concern is primal. She is hungry, she wants her food, she doesn't want something else to eat her food. And so a further surprisy element arcing over the joke is that the father is indeed protecting his daughter, but not at all in the way he intended. This is the final work to be done in processing the joke: the daughter's dramatically ironic punch line—an unwitting expression of what she does not understand—actually serves to illuminate what the *father* doesn't understand. He doesn't understand how his child thinks or what she thinks or what she wants. He hasn't accounted for her *hunger*, her *aliveness*. The child's irony points not simply to her innocence but to her father's abstraction. Her ignorance ultimately reveals his ignorance, and this is the comic reversal, the wise adult brought low.

(*20*) For all of its superficial, mouths-of-babes cuteness, the joke is dark and elemental: death, food, fear.

(*21*) The elements and variables of the joke are essential to the quality, strength, and vector of surprise. Just as a teenage daughter creates a different effect than a three-year-old daughter, and a cheese sandwich creates a different effect than a roast-beef sandwich, a dead chipmunk is significantly different from, say, a sleeping chipmunk. The joke needs an unconscious creature, but there are varieties of unconsciousness, and death happens to be funnier than sleep. Death, pain, and suffering are often the very conditions of humor. (There were no jokes in Eden, as Donald Barthelme said.) Underlying this joke is the fact that all living things die—including, of course, the father and the daughter—but the daughter does not understand this yet. The brute fact of mortality is awful to contemplate, and the girl's ignorance is poignant—she will in the years to come fall from this state of blissful not-knowing into an awareness of death, and that, believe me, is sad. But gravity often enhances a joke, or, more precisely, gravity is often inseparable from the joke. A joke brings us close to the most uncomfortable truth, but then allows through its punch line a *release* of anxiety and fear. It has been said many times before that humor arises from pain, that laughing and crying are similar responses, though no one has said it as well as Kurt Vonnegut:

Laughter is a response to frustration, just as tears are, and it solves nothing, just as tears solve nothing. Laughing or crying is what a human being does when there's nothing else he can do. Freud has written very soundly on humor—which is interesting, because he was essentially such a humorless man. The example he gives is of the dog who can't get through a gate to bite a person or

40

fight another dog. So he digs dirt. It doesn't solve anything, but he has to do something. Crying or laughing is what a human being does instead. I used to make speeches a lot, because I needed the money. Sometimes I was funny. And my peak funniness came when I was at Notre Dame, at a literary festival there. It was in a huge auditorium and the audience was so tightly tuned that everything I said was funny. All I had to do was cough or clear my throat and the whole place would break up. This is a really horrible story I'm telling. People were laughing because they were in agony, full of pain they couldn't do anything about. They were sick and helpless because Martin Luther King had been shot two days before. The festival had been called on the Thursday he was shot, and then it was resumed the next day. But it was a day of grieving, of people trying to pull themselves together. And then, on Saturday, it was my turn to speak. I've got mildly comical stuff I do, but it was in the presence of grief that the laughter was the greatest. There was an enormous need to either laugh or cry as the only possible adjustment. There was nothing you could do to bring King back. So the biggest laughs are based on the biggest disappointments and the biggest fears.

"We wouldn't want the sleeping chipmunk to eat our food"—that punch line is still ironic, it still activates the joke, but it's not as funny because it's not unsettling. A sleeping chipmunk makes the joke light and silly, ephemeral. The dead chipmunk gives the joke weight, a tangled tone, and a reason to be told. Humor is, as Gregory Bateson° said, "the great alternative to psychosis."

(*22*) A sleeping animal shades the joke lighter. For a darker shade—for more comic impact—the joke requires something dead. The identity of the dead thing is another of the joke's variables. Real life supplied us with a chipmunk, and that works fairly well. A chipmunk is more poignant than a lizard, less manipulative and unsettling than a puppy. It's a small mammal—it's cute—but it's skittish and undomesticated. A squirrel can water-ski, but a chipmunk can't. (Besides, let's face it, *chipmunk*, like *bagpipe* and *hand job,* is just a funny word.) A dead walrus introduces absurdity. A dead baby introduces shock and tastelessness. A dead soldier or senator might turn the joke political. A dead member of a racial or ethnic group introduces taboo and extreme offensiveness. In his famous story "The School," Donald Barthelme exploits this spectrum of gravity, this hierarchy of dismay. Edgar, the narrator and a teacher, is disconcerted by the number of things that have died at the school during the year. First, the pet snakes died. Then the trees that the children

Gregory Bateson: (1904–1980) an English anthropologist whose work traversed a series of multidisciplinary topics, such as epistemology, cybernetics, ecology, and systems theory.

planted. ("All these kids looking at these little brown sticks, it was depressing.") Then herb gardens. Then gerbils, white mice, a salamander. ("Well, now they knew not to carry them around in plastic bags.") Then tropical fish. ("Of course we *expected* the tropical fish to die, that was no surprise. Those numbers, you look at them crooked and they're belly-up on the surface. But the lesson plan called for a tropical-fish input at that point, there was nothing we could do, it happens every year, you just have to hurry past it.") And then the story turns: "We weren't even supposed to have a puppy. . . ." Then a Korean orphan. Then "an extraordinary number of parents" and "the usual heavy mortality rate among grandparents, or maybe it was heavier this year." And finally two children from the school. "I forgot to mention Billy Brandt's father," Edgar then inserts, "who was knifed fatally when he grappled with a masked intruder in his home," a sentence that is as much about polluted language as it is about Billy's deceased father. Because of Barthelme's tone and comic phrasing and the inexorable escalation stipulated by form, this sequence remains comic throughout, but the quality of our laughter shifts as we encounter puppy, orphan, parents, grandparents, students. You could say that the story gets funnier in precise correlation to the severity and gravity of its content. The ironic gap between *what* is being told and *how* it is being told grows wider and wider, causing greater discomfort and greater humor. If you could watch a film of an audience hearing a reading of "The School," you would see a lot of interesting faces. You would see bodies reacting to incongruity, even dramatizing it, hands cupped over laughing mouths.

(23) Does the dead-chipmunk joke work if it's a mother and a daughter out on a picnic, or a mother and a son, or a father and a son? If you choose a different parent/child permutation, I think the joke remains a joke, but just barely. Father/daughter is the most compelling and comic permutation, for gendered reasons that may not be good but are nonetheless real. The father as straight man is necessary for irony because the father is, stereotypically, the protector, but also, I would argue, because the father is a stereotypical bumbler. (When this caricatured bumbling is embraced by men, as it often is, it becomes a way to avoid domestic work, and their partners suffer. In my home this phenomenon is called, with various degrees of gentleness, *feigned incompetence*.) A mother, who is aware of her child's needs and desires, and who possesses a natural wisdom and a special connection to the child, would not be as effective in creating the preconditions for a comic reversal. And though the joke could function with a boy, a girl probably creates—again, stereotypically—more of a sense of innocence and vulnerability and pathos.

(*24*) Here are the answers to the octopus joke above:

- There is a disjunction not only between a real octopus and a talking octopus, but between the octopus that appears to be mute in the joke's setup and the octopus who passionately delivers the punch line. Suddenly, we are reoriented—we learn that this creature is not just some primitive musical prodigy but a disgruntled, articulate, foulmouthed, sexually frustrated, and poignantly mistaken bar trick. The premise—the octopus's fine musicianship—is not in fact the joke's central incongruity.

- There is a powerful comic disjunction between the silly wholesomeness of *pajamas* and the vulgarity of *fuck*.

- There is a surprising connection (a visual joke) made between a bagpipe's plaid bag and pajamas. Given the octopus's sensuous treatment of the first two instruments, we are prepared for a dirty joke involving the octopus and the bagpipe. So the surprise is not the sexual joke, which we see coming, but the manner of its deployment. A joke must surprise surprisingly. The proposition on which the joke is constructed—*a bagpipe looks like an octopus in pajamas*—is startlingly true, but it's nonsensical. Just as *pajamas* and *fuck* are linguistically disjunctive, pajamas and octopi are visually (even ontologically) disjunctive.

- And yet the benighted octopus does not realize the joke. He is not being witty. This is standard dramatic irony—we know the octopus is wrong, and further we understand why he has made this error. This knowledge gives us a sense of superiority, control, and relief.

(*25*) "Less perfect times," Barthelme said, "are likely to produce a great many jokes, variously inflected; thus, the Twentieth Century staggers toward its close in a blizzard of one-liners." It seems safe to say that the late-century blizzard has been upgraded to a shit-storm: YouTube pratfalls, laugh-track zingers, wacky ringtones, digitally altered JPEGs, Twitter fights. (When singer Aimee Mann implied that Ice-T was a bad actor, Ice-T recommended via Tweet that Mann "Eat a hot bowl of Dicks," etc.) These one-liners, though, are not the jokes of yesteryear, not the tell-me-if-you've-heard-this-one joke. That kind of a joke—a priest, a pilot, and a farmer, etc.—has vanished, though it lives on in irony. If I come up to you and say, "So a man walks into a bar with an octopus," you would immediately register not one but two incongruities—there's the octopus in the bar, certainly, but the prime incongruity is that I am, dad-like, telling you a joke. I know jokes are dumb and I'm telling one anyway—this is the perfunctory and completely unsurprising irony.

Isn't it incongruous that I would try to be funny doing something that's expressly not funny? Get it? (But, hey, wasn't it kind of funny anyway? Do you like me? What's that gnawing feeling? Where's my smartphone? I'm lonesome.) Incongruity used to reside within the joke, and now it resides within the telling. The irony has retreated from the punch line, back through the joke canal, and into my mouth, where it coats all that I say. What a joke accomplishes now is, primarily, the derision of joke telling and the kind of person who would do it. And without concentration or thought, I can make my tone do this—I can signal to you, through intonation and expression, a nuanced system of cues, that my joke is only joking. Think about how complicated this procedure is, telling a joke while indicating my awareness of the stupidity of telling a joke. And the ease with which we can all send and receive these signals suggests how fluent we are in not-meaning.

(*26*) We speak of wit as *sharp* or *dull*, *quick* or *slow*. We also call wit *dry*, 45 though we don't speak of *wet* wit. We should, because it's a useful term (though probably oxymoronic). We don't speak of wet wit because it's the dominant mode. Wet wit is wet in the sense of being *all wet* (i.e., full of it), and it's wet in the sense that it has a slick, protective coating—it's dripping, it's slippery with fear, nothing can stick to it. If dry wit is a kind of deadpan insinuation, wet wit is exuberant noncommitment, a celebration of procedure, style, technical merit. But really, here I'm just back to the tired old jeremiad about irony and conviction. Instead of denouncing or renouncing irony—that genie won't go back into the bottle—I'd like to tell you what happened when I googled *wet wit*. What happened when I googled *wet wit* is that I received—*wit* being a dialectal form of *with*—a lot of very dirty hip-hop lyrics. And that was—add a short wet beat here—pretty surprisy.

Understanding the Text

1. Bachelder's essay begins with an anecdote that he proceeds to turn into a joke by analyzing its humor. What are the steps in what Bachelder calls "joke conversion" (note 3b), i.e., the transformation of raw anecdotal material into the comic form of a full-fledged joke? How does the joke in note 4 differ from the opening anecdote?

2. Why is the dead-chipmunk joke funny? What conditions, elements, and variables are "essential to the quality, strength, and vector of surprise" (note 21) in this particular joke?

3. *Irony* is one of the key words in Bachelder's examination of the mechanisms of jokes. How does he define this term? What types of irony create humor?

4. What does Bachelder say about the nature of puns and wit?

Reflection and Response

5. Bachelder comments on novelist Don DeLillo's claim that "only the undemocratic mind interrogates humor." "The analysis of humor is," Bachelder argues, "in its suppositions, presumptuous and dictatorial" (note 2). In your opinion, does Bachelder manage to interrogate humor in a democratic manner, or does he write in an elitist style? What *ethos* does he attempt to establish? Might a certain amount of elitism be necessary to analyze humor, and therefore it is not a vice to be avoided but a virtue to be cultivated?

6. In note 16, Bachelder tells a joke about a musical octopus and invites you to explain why it is funny. He provides answers in note 24. What does his interpretation of the octopus joke leave out? Are there elements of this joke that detract from its humor?

7. What do you think of the unusual structure of Bachelder's essay? Why does he number (and letter) his paragraphs? What does this organizational scheme let him accomplish as a writer?

Making Connections

8. Although this essay appears in the chapter on the comic *agent*, what other elements of Kenneth Burke's dramatistic pentad does Bachelder examine with regard to the rhetoric of humor? Which "ratios" might appear most vital to joke telling for Bachelder?

9. Bachelder has consciously crafted an essay to explain the mechanisms of jokes, but his central example involves a comic story in which the agents did not intend to be funny. Reflecting on the experience, he writes, "My daughter and I went to campus, and we became *unwitting elements* in the spontaneous generation of a joke" (note 21, emphasis added). Later he states outright, "We are largely unconscious of the mechanisms of the joke and the activity of our minds" (note 13). Write an essay on the role of agency and intent in humor. Refer to Bachelder's essay as well as Sigmund Freud's theories of humor as discussed by Rappoport (p. 13), Critchley (p. 79), and Peterson (p. 216).

10. Bachelder cites the episode "Happy Hour" from the sixth season of the American sitcom *The Office* (2005–2013). Use Bachelder's essay to analyze a different episode from this award-winning show or from another mocku-mentary television series (e.g., *The Comeback, Reno 911!, Summer Heights High, Trailer Park Boys*, etc.).

Romantic Comedy and Genre

Tamar Jeffers McDonald

Tamar Jeffers McDonald is a professor of film studies at the University of Kent's School of Arts. Her research focuses on a variety of Hollywood issues, from stardom and performance to genre and costume. This reading originally appeared as a chapter in her book-length study, *Romantic Comedy: Boy Meets Girl Meets Genre*, which was published by Wallflower Press in 2007 as part of their Short Cuts series of "introductory texts covering the full spectrum of film studies." In this excerpt, McDonald introduces the conventions of the romantic comedy, but she also argues with some long-standing assumptions about the genre.

*G*enre is a French word meaning "type" or "kind." Thinking about film genres, therefore, employs ideas about different types or kinds of films. Deciding a film fits within a well-defined genre can be a way for film critics to dismiss it since genre films are often assumed to be made in Hollywood, to strict guidelines, as mass-oriented products. To a certain extent, "genre film" has as its implicit opposite the notion of the "art film"; furthermore, genre films carry connotations flavored with "American, low-brow, easy," while assumptions about art films include "European or independent, high-brow, difficult." While genre critics have worked to unsettle these assumptions, contesting the idea that *all* genre films are inevitably "popcorn movies," even genre criticism itself has culturally authorized some types of film, like westerns and gangster films, more than others. Romantic comedy is, arguably, the lowest of the low. Even a book setting out to review 600 "Chick Flicks" ends up admitting its own lack of taste:

It's about time we confessed: we might love the great and the good, but we can also adore the cute and the ridiculously bad, as long as the leading man is handsome or the story—no matter how cheesy—makes us laugh, makes us cry, or makes us hot. (Berry & Errigo 2004: 1)

Romcoms are viewed as "guilty pleasures" which should be below one's notice but, Jo Berry and Angie Errigo suggest, which satisfy because they provide easy, uncomplicated pleasures. I dispute this idea, however, and think that the appeal to audiences of such films is more complex, especially if the viewer is inhabiting a position where conflicting pulls of realism and fantasy are operating, as in my own reactions to *The Prince and Me* (2004).

It is not only romantic comedies that are assumed to provide simple options for enjoyment: all genre movies seem straightforward because of their adherence to a recognizable formula. However, actually considering the elements of a genre and the expectations audiences have of different genres *critically* requires work and detachment. Since the 1970s film theorists have studied genre to problematize it, to question both what makes a film fit a genre and what "genre" itself constitutes. Steve Neale and Rick Altman, for example, both . . . point to the intrinsic hybridity of genre films. While such multiple address, appealing to more than one audience sector through specific generic traits, can be assumed to be a characteristic of recent films, Neale demonstrates that hybridity has a longer history (2000: 2) and Altman notes that film marketing has always attempted to maximize audience appeal by proliferating the number of genres to which a film can belong (1998). These writers also indicate that most movies of whatever genre have a love story as one of their component strands, which can be highlighted or played down in the film's marketing.

> "Actually considering the elements of a genre and the expectations audiences have of different genres *critically* requires work and detachment."

Despite—or perhaps because of—the large numbers of such films which reach us in cinemas and at home every year, what actually constitutes a romantic comedy is seldom debated. Geoff King suggests that the common occurrence of both romance and comedy within many other film genres generates difficulties in appreciating what precisely constitutes the romcom: "Defining romantic comedy as a clear-cut genre is difficult because of the prevalence of both its constituent terms in popular film" (2002: 51). Because these films seem so transparent (they are all about love, boy meets girl, and so on), precise definitions of their characteristics are not often attempted, with the result that a whole slew of films with very different topics of focus are given the same label. For example, some theorists, such as Mark Rubinfeld (2001), treat Cameron Crowe's *Jerry Maguire* (1996) as a romantic comedy, although the romance and comedy elements in the narrative seem overwhelmed by the accent on personal growth, sentiment, and the establishment of a familial unit rather than a couple.

Of course, film reviews and the works of theorists are not the only factors which delimit genre: production and marketing also provide sites where genre gets defined. Films come to audiences prepackaged as generic products through marketing material, advertising and, eventually, as DVDs and videos. Romcom film posters, which are frequently reproduced as DVD covers, employ very consistent tropes to market their products, involving emphasizing the central couple. Movie taglines, one-liners teasing the viewer by summing up or forecasting the narrative, also help direct audience assumptions about films, implying what genre is being employed and thus what outcome we can expect from a particular movie. For example, the tagline for *Kate and Leopold* (2003), "if they lived in the same century they'd be perfect for each other," embodies the whole film's trajectory in just thirteen words: the named pair will meet through time travel and fall in love.

What qualities justify a film's inclusion within the romantic comedy genre? We will examine two Kirsten Dunst vehicles to try to assess them. *Bring It On* (2000) has Dunst as a high school student involved in a cheerleading contest and trying to win the heart of her best friend's brother, Cliff (Jesse Bradford), while *Get Over It* (2001) presents the same actor as a high school student involved in a school musical and trying to win the heart of her brother's best friend, Burke (Ben Foster). In my opinion, however, only the second of these is a romantic comedy. *Bring It On*'s main goal is to expose the problems of incidental daily racism affecting the lives of a troupe of black cheerleaders, a project it makes no easier for itself by following the events from the point of view of this troupe's main *white* rivals. In this film Dunst's character, Torrance, wants to win the contest and she wants to win the boy, but the contest is more important and the love aspect secondary, although this is the one she succeeds in. *Get Over It*, by contrast, clearly reveals that all Dunst's actions as Kelly are motivated by her love for Burke: while she does win a part in the musical, her goal throughout is to help Burke get over his old girlfriend and fall in love with her.

While both of these films are enjoyable enough, the variation in the emphasis on the central couple's romance is, for me, what excludes *Bring It On* from romantic comedy status, but confers it on the other Dunst vehicle. *Get Over It*'s emphasis on the aspirational love story seems a crucial factor, which leads to the following master definition of films within this genre:

[A] romantic comedy is a film which has as its central narrative motor a quest for love, which portrays this quest in a lighthearted way and almost always to a successful conclusion.

Note that, unlike David Shumway's° "boy meets girl . . ." formula, I do not suggest that the romcom is inevitably heterosexual; . . . however, despite

David Shumway: professor of English at Carnegie Mellon University and author of the book *Modern Love: Romance, Intimacy, and the Marriage Crisis* (2003).

several independent films portraying gay or lesbian relationships—such as *Go Fish* (1994), *Saving Face* (2004), *Touch of Pink* (2004), and *Imagine Me and You* (2005)—enjoying some audience and/or box office success, mainstream films have yet to follow this example.

Observe also that the above definition does not insist that romcoms are necessarily funny, although this might seem implicit in the term "comedy." I have used the word "lighthearted" in the definition to signal that, while films of the genre generally end well and may elicit laughs along the way, I am also aware of the importance of tears to the romantic comedy. I want to acknowledge the mixed emotions these films commonly both depict and elicit.

Crying frequently occupies an important space in the narratives of the romantic comedy: as an index of the pain a lover feels when apart from the beloved, when rejected or lonely. As noted, crying—about love, romance and other romantic films—is central to *Sleepless in Seattle*. This film certainly conforms to the definition offered above in that its central driving device is a quest for love: both Annie and Sam are seeking the perfect partner. Comic moments occur on the path to the successful conclusion, when the two are united. But tears also play a fundamental part in the narrative: Annie, engaged to the steady and dull Walter (Bill Pullman), is both moved hearing Sam testifying to his love for his dead wife on the radio and envious of the strength of his devotion, which she realizes is missing from her own relationship. Tears are the result of both of these feelings and guarantee that, since she can be moved to tears by Sam's love, Annie merits its inheritance.

Noting the importance of tears in the romcom is an act of the active analysis of components within the genre's toolkit. For various reasons, considered in detail below, the romantic comedy is often perceived to be so obvious in its construction that its components are *not* analyzed. Furthermore, if critical attention is turned on the genre, often what would be legitimated as a *trope* (a recurrent element) in a genre which has some credibility, is dismissed as a *cliché* in the romantic comedy—even by its theorists (see, for example, King 2002: 58). Thus, although the romantic comedy is one of the most *generic* of genres, heavily reliant on stock elements, personae and even dialogue ("I love you!"), the rudimentary machinery of the genre still needs investigation.

Generic Elements

Three key components warrant consideration in assessing the internal attributes of film genres, descending from the surface deeper into the film: the visual characteristics, narrative patterns, and wider ideology.

Visual Characteristics

We identify film genres by the kind of images found in them and, in turn, these images then become laden with a symbolism dependent on their genre: they become icons and their study within a genre dignified with the title of "iconography."

Colin McArthur, in a very useful article from his 1972 book-length study of the gangster film, provides a guide to looking at iconography within a genre which can assist the study of the romantic comedy. While subsequent work on the romcom has been alert to narrative shifts in tone and confidence (Henderson 1978; Neale 1992; Paul 2002), consideration of the *visual* aspects of the genre has not greatly advanced. McArthur suggests that iconography can include locations, props, costume, and even stock characters (in the western these might be the barman, the saloon gal, the grizzly-bearded prospector). In the romantic comedy we will see such iconographic uses being made of settings (almost uniformly the contemporary romantic comedy now has an urban location), props (consider the repetition within the genre of articles associated with weddings, as well as flowers, chocolates, candlelight, beds), costume (the special outfit for the big date), and stock characters which most often include the unsuitable partner; here the characters who will be a couple by the film's end both start out with an unsuitable partner, illustrating the rightness of the central romance by being plainly wrong, as with Joe's (Tom Hanks) girlfriend Patricia (Parker Posey) and Kathleen's (Meg Ryan) boyfriend Frank (Greg Kinnear) in *You've Got Mail*.

Narrative Patterns

Films in the same genre share more than just key characters and props, however; they also utilize similar narrative patterns, both small and larger ones. For example, at the very smallest level there are the tropes, occurrences which happen repeatedly within genres. As McArthur notes, when we see a car coming down a dark alleyway toward someone in a gangster film, we recognize that the driver is going to try to kill that someone; a moment of peace often precedes a bloodbath, as in the scenes of quiet restaurants before a drive-by shooting. On a larger scale, another common generic pattern of the gangster movie is the rookie gangster's rise through the ranks, as he takes on bigger and bolder crimes, inherits the flashy dress sense, bigger guns and even the girlfriend of the big boss. At the level of the largest pattern, we anticipate a narrative arc displaying the rise and eventual fall of the mobster, a man who uses unlawful means to achieve the American Dream of riches and success.

Looking at the narrative patterns in this way, from the micro to the overarching level, the genre's key themes emerge. In gangster films the immigrant working-class character wants success but tries to achieve it illegally, so is ultimately punished by death. By contrast, the theme of the musical is that hard work and determination committed to the enjoyment of *all* is the best way for the *individual* to be happy and successful. When advancing precepts in this way (do not rob banks, do work hard in your community) narrative patterns go beyond themes to indicate the ideology of the society creating them (Grant 2007).

The romantic comedy can also be seen repeating the same narrative 15 patterns, from the wider story arc to the smaller tropes. As Shumway notes, the basic plot of all mainstream romantic comedies is boy meets, loses, regains girl. Within this master pattern smaller moments also recur with regularity. The "meet cute" was often employed in romantic comedies of the classic period in Hollywood: in this trope the lovers-to-be first encounter each other in a way which forecasts their eventual union. Billy Wilder, first a scriptwriter, then a director, is one of the foremost proponents of the "meet cute"; he is supposed to have kept a notebook of ideas for cute meetings where the eventual couple would meet in a humorous, unlikely, or suggestive manner (see Sikov 1998: 121; Chandler 2002: 80). One of the most twee "meet cutes" comes in screwball comedy *Bluebeard's Eighth Wife* (1938), which Wilder scripted: the couple first cross paths in a department store where he wants to buy only the top half of a pair of pajamas and she the bottoms. The form of the meeting here assures the audience that, although the couple may at times seem to hate each other, they will eventually reunite because they belong together as much as the top and bottom halves of pajamas do.

Other frequently occurring tropes include the wedding derailed by one partner running away; the masquerade, in which one or both of the central characters pretends to be someone else; and the embarrassing gesture—this has one of the lovers submitting to public humiliation in order to prove that love is more important than dignity. . . .

Ideology

The ideology of a genre can both reflect and contest the anxieties, assumptions, and desires of the specific time and specific agencies making the film. Gangster films generally tout the value of accumulating personal wealth, even while the genre tacitly acknowledges, through the lawless actions and ultimate fate of its gangster figure, the difficulties of achieving that goal. Thus these films underscore the American capitalist ideology of *legally* earning wealth, even while allowing audiences the vicarious pleasures of violating such legal strictures.

The basic ideology the romantic comedy genre supports is the primary importance of the couple. While this is usually the heterosexual, white couple, certain films from the 1990s onward have attempted to widen the perspective to include gay and black couples. None, however, has tried to suggest monogamous coupledom itself is an outmoded concept; even *Annie Hall*, possibly the most radical film in choosing to deny the audience an ending with the couple's union, does not suggest the goal of finding one's true love is no longer desirable, merely impossible.

At the heart of every romantic comedy is the implication of sex, and settled, secure, within-a-relationship sex at that. Shumway's "Exhibit A" of plots, with boy meeting girl, thus exists to dress up the naked fact that Western, capitalist society has traditionally relied on monogamy for its stability, as well as on procreation for its continuance. Shumway suggests that romance and marriage have opposing goals, which explains both real-life endemic dissatisfaction with the married state and the need for romantic comedies to end before the couple embarks on married life (2003: 21). The ideology of "one man for one woman" can thus be seen to underlie these films in order to assure stability in Western, capitalist society; but films do not just reflect reality, they help to create it too. In giving the audience a high degree of closure with the happy ending in films of this genre, are romantic comedies benign, supplying an on-screen fantasy of perpetual bliss usually lacking in real life? Or do they negatively promote daydreams, making audiences long for a perfection which can, realistically, never be accomplished, leaving people dissatisfied with themselves and the relationships they do have? Perhaps both; a closer look at what the underlying ideology of the romantic comedy wants to foster in its audiences indicates why film studios go on and on providing fairytales for adults.

Although the current romantic comedy, with its awareness of divorce, 20 biological clocks, myths about the shortages of single men and other simultaneous impulses toward and reasons against coupling, seems to have acknowledged the difficulties of finding true love, it nevertheless continues to endorse the old fantasies. This illustrates the strength of the ideological mandate toward coupling and the industries which depend on romance to make money. It may seem cynical to view romantic love as an ideal which supports capitalist consumerism, but the self-dissatisfaction such films breed can create a vulnerable space which advertisers have been only too quick to target. This fact is self-reflexively considered in *Kate and Leopold*. In a scene where the viewer can almost hear the iconography and generic tropes being ticked off the list (candlelight, romantic music, star-lit cityscape, slow dance) the couple (Meg Ryan and Hugh Jackman) enjoy a romantic dinner for two and she admits having never had much luck with men. When Leopold suggests perhaps she has not yet met the right one, Kate seems to step out of the film for an instant to comment on the whole romantic comedy genre and the industries it nourishes:

Maybe . . . Or maybe that whole love thing is just a grown-up version of Santa Claus, just a myth we've been fed since childhood so we keep buying magazines and joining clubs and doing therapy and watching movies with hip-hop songs played over love montages, all in this pathetic attempt to explain why our Love Santa keeps getting caught in the chimney.

Kate here testifies to her own consumption of items which both reinforce the ideas of romantic love (movies and magazines) and which she hopes will help to make her eligible for romantic love herself (health club membership and therapy, for a better outside and inside). The possibility of gaining romantic love just seems to be the bait that companies dangle before consumers in order to ensure we continue buying their products.

While most romantic comedies do not want to hint that the whole edifice of true romance might be as mythical as Santa, we as audience members, consumers, and film scholars need to remember that big business relies on our urge to make ourselves loveable through the consumption of goods (make-up, shoes, underwear, grooming products, mood music, seductive dinners—and films). Hollywood is just one of these big businesses, and if we can accept that product placement in a film operates to sell more Coca-Cola and Nike products, why not also view the fantasy of romantic love as a product being no more subtly endorsed?

Exposing the tools used by a particular romcom can help examination of the underlying ideology the film reflects. While there are, of course, very sensitive micro-analyses of specific films, there seems to be a prejudice against subjecting such fluffy trifles to intense critical scrutiny. Even people who make (and make money from) such films seem to acknowledge that the genre is less worthy than others, as a comment from Garry Marshall, director of *Pretty Woman* (1990) intimates: "I like to do very romantic, sentimental type of work . . . It's a dirty job but somebody has to do it" (cited in Krämer 1999b: 106). While Marshall's comment can be dismissed as ironic, sarcastic, or perverse, it still taps into an awareness of a prejudice against the romcom, an assumption of cultural lowliness, which needs to be considered and perhaps contested; this contestation is assisted by investigating the elements involved in the genre. Marshall's comment could equally apply to the work of analyzing romantic comedies and their constituent elements, which simply has not been achieved in numbers comparable to works on other genres. Let us consider some of the reasons which may account for their low status.

One aspect mitigating against these films is their seeming transparency, with films like *You've Got Mail, Sleepless in Seattle,* and *Failure to Launch* (2006) appearing so naked in their project to get their men and women together by the last reel that it seems pointless to look for further motive or intent. The genre's simplicity thus deflects proper interrogation. Geoff King proposes this very transparency makes such films "particularly effective vehicles for ideology. Their implicit 'don't take it too seriously' helps, potentially, to inoculate them against close interrogation" (2002: 56).

Another criticism frequently leveled, particularly against contemporary romcoms, is that they repeatedly go over old ground without adding anything original to the mixture of traditional soundtrack songs, picturesque urban views, and initially antagonistic, ultimately blissful male and female protagonists (Hampton 2004). Reviews regularly note the adherence to generic blueprints seeming stale now: American film-trade weekly *Variety*, for instance, found *How to Lose a Guy in 10 Days* (2003) conforming to "trite formula" (Koehler 2003: 68); the reviewer for British critical magazine *Sight and Sound* agreed, feeling that the film's romance was "underdeveloped" and its ending "disappointingly cloying" (Wood 2003: 50). Repeatedly these two publications dismiss the narratives of romcoms as demonstrating a clichéd emptiness: condemning them for "rote vacuity" (Matheou 2003: 48), for being "slick but slight" (Felperin 2005: 26).

One further reason for the habitual critical contempt of romantic comedies may be its association with a female audience: romcoms are popularly supposed to be "chick flicks": the subtitle to Berry and Errigo's book of that title is *Movies Women Love.* To emphasise the point, they include ten films they view as, by contrast, being more male-oriented, male-centered films. Not only do romcoms usually present their stories from the perspective of their female lead character, detailing her feelings and thus privileging her within the film as the site of audience identification, but they are marketed to women, as the special summer 2006 . . . World Cup tie-in advertising for *Imagine Me and You* made clear. They are thus also assumed to appeal largely to women audience members, in the same way as were the "Women's films" of the 1940s (see Krämer 1999a and 1999b). These films—intense stories with strong, well-defined central female roles, about women suffering and sacrificing for love and family—were also critically downgraded until subject to a revisionist rescue mission by feminist film scholars in the 1980s (Modleski 1984; Mulvey 1986; Doane 1987); perhaps the current wave of critical investigation will do the same for the romantic comedy.

By assuming a largely female consumption of romantic comedies, scholars and critics alike disparage them, unconsciously or not; even now in the twenty-first century, women are still supposed to be more interested in gossip, relationships, and clothes than important topics. Like fashion, which has long been held in low critical esteem and whose scholars have to work hard to justify their interest, romantic comedies may suffer from their association with female consumers despite the fact that, as the section on ideology indicates, these films do not actually speak solely to female interests and desires but are aimed more inclusively at both genders. The myth of perfect love appeals to both sexes, and the narratives of romantic comedy films themselves demonstrate that *both* women and men have to change and adapt to deserve love: if, annoyingly, in the masquerade plot which occurs as such a regular trope in this genre it is usually the man who is conning the woman, such films as *Pillow Talk*, *How to Lose a Guy in 10 Days*, and *Lover Come Back* (1961) do demonstrate that, once the woman has discovered his deceit, the man has to change his ways in order to deserve her love again. In illustrating, too, that the romcom male has a nice apartment, designer clothes, an expensive music system, and an enviable physique, the romantic comedy possibly encourages the men in the audience to remake themselves as fitter, more glamorous, and possessing more and better consumer durables. Thus, regardless of the association of women audiences with the genre, the ideology which underpins it seeks to sell love, and products, to everyone.

As a final note, it should be emphasised that these various sub- and dominant genres are neither *all-inclusive*—that is, there were always romantic comedies being made at the same time as, for example, the screwball, which did not fit with the style of that subgenre—nor mutually *exclusive* in that it is possible to read *Pillow Talk* both as a sex comedy and as a romantic comedy. It should be recognized that screwball comedy was therefore not the *only* kind of romantic comedy in the 1930s, although it now seems to have been the most dominant; similarly, the sex comedy and the 1970s radical romance were not the only types of romantic comedies being made, but the cycles they belong to have emerged, over time, as the most influential to the genre's development. By contrast, the recent Neo-Traditionalist romantic comedy seems to be more numerous than influential; perhaps at this point in film history, when the romantic comedy seems forced to side either with the conservative narratives, like *Kate and Leopold*, or the more explicit gross-out films, such as *The 40 Year Old Virgin* (2005), the genre itself is waiting for a new impetus which will renew its energies and lead it in more interesting directions.

Works Cited

Altman, Rick (1998). "Reusable Packaging: Generic Products and the Recycling Process," in Nick Browne (ed.) *Refiguring American Film Genres: History and Theory*. Berkeley: University of California Press.

Berry, Jo and Angie Errigo (2004). *Chick Flicks: Movies Women Love*. London: Orion Books.

Chandler, Charlotte (2002). *Nobody's Perfect: Billy Wilder, A Personal Biography*. New York: Simon and Schuster.

Doane, Mary Anne (1987). *The Desire to Desire: The Women's Film of the 1940s*. Bloomington: Indiana University Press.

Felperin, Leslie (2005). Review of *Imagine Me and You*, *Variety*, 24-30 October, 26.

Grant, Barry Keith (2007). *Film Genre: From Iconography to Ideology*. London: Wallflower Press.

Hampton, Howard (2004). "True romance: on the current state of date movies," *Film Comment*, November/December, 30-4.

Henderson, Brian (1978). "Romantic comedy today: semi-tough or impossible?," *Film Quarterly*, 31, 4, 11-23.

King, Geoff (2002). *Film Comedy*. London: Wallflower Press.

Koehler, Robert (2003). Review of *How to Lose a Guy in 10 Days*, *Variety*, 3-9 February, 68-9.

Krämer, Peter (1999a). "Women first: *Titanic*, action-adventure films, and Hollywood's female audience," in Kevin Sandler and Gaylyn Studlar (eds) *Titanic: Anatomy of a Blockbuster*. New Brunswick, NJ: Rutgers University Press, 108-31.

———— (1999b). "A powerful cinema-going force? Hollywood and female audiences since the 1960s," in Melvyn Stokes and Richard Maltby (eds) *Identifying Hollywood's Audiences: Cultural Identity and the Movies*. London: British Film Institute, 93-108.

Matheou, Demetrios (2003). Review of *Hope Springs*, *Sign and Sound*, May, 48.

Modleski, Tania (1984). "Time and desire in the women's film," *Cinema Journal*, 23, 3, 19-30.

Mulvey, Laura (1986). "Melodrama in and out of the home," in Colin McCabe (ed.) *High Theory/Low Culture: Analyzing Popular Television and Film*. Manchester: Manchester University Press, 80-100.

Neale, Steve (1992). "The big romance or something wild?: Romantic comedy today," *Screen*, 33, 3, 284-99.

———— (2000). *Genre and Hollywood*. London: Routledge.

Paul, William (2002). "The impossibility of romance: Hollywood comedy, 1978-1999," in Steve Neale (ed.) *Genre and Contemporary Hollywood*. London: British Film Institute, 117-29.

Rubinfeld, Mark D. (2001). *Bound to Bond: Gender, Genre and the Hollywood Romantic Comedy*. New York: Praeger.

Shumway, David R. (2003). *Modern Love: Romance, Intimacy and the Marriage Crisis*. New York and London: New York University Press.

Sikov, Ed (1998). *On Sunset Boulevard: The Life and Times and Billy Wilder.* New York: Hyperion Books.

Wood, Anna (2003). Review of *How to Lose a Guy in 10 Days, Sight and Sound,* May, 50.

Understanding the Text

1. What is *genre*? What does this concept entail?
2. McDonald asks, "What qualities justify a film's inclusion within the romantic comedy genre?" (par. 5). What answers does she provide?
3. The *Oxford English Dictionary* defines *ideology* as "a system of ideas and ideals, especially one which forms the basis of economic or political theory and policy." According to McDonald, what is the basic ideology of the romantic comedy (romcom) genre? What ideological functions does the romcom serve in American society?

Reflection and Response

4. Have you seen any of the films mentioned by McDonald? What about other romantic comedies? Reflect on your experience with this genre. What do you think about romcoms? Do you enjoy them? Why or why not?
5. Although classified as comedies, romcoms are not necessarily funny according to McDonald's definition of the genre. Instead she adopts a more classical definition of the word *comedy* when she writes, "films of the genre generally end well and may elicit laughs along the way" (par. 7). Do you agree that a lighthearted tone and happy ending take precedence over actual laughter in romcoms? Do you think this is enough to qualify a film as a comedy? Why or why not?

Making Connections

6. McDonald concludes that the romantic comedy "genre itself is waiting for a new impetus which will renew its energies and lead it in more interesting directions" (par. 27). Her piece is a bit dated though, having been published in 2007. Research and write an essay about a recent film (or television show) that challenges traditional romcom conventions, if not reinvents the genre altogether. For example, have you seen a romcom that exhibits transgressive humor (see Tueth, p. 103)?
7. Romcoms are not the only type of comedy films. Other genres of comedy include slapstick, screwball, dark, bawdy, cringe, musical, action, stoner, caper, and even horror. "The intrinsic hybridity of genre films" makes for a seemingly endless array of possible combinations (par. 2). Write a critical review of a hybrid comedy film. Pay close attention to the film's combination of generic elements, including its visual characteristics, narrative patterns, and ideological values.

Native American Stand-Up Comedy

Amanda Lynch Morris

The ancient Greek philosopher Aristotle divided rhetoric into three different genres: forensic, deliberative, and epideictic. Forensic rhetoric refers to legal discourse within judicial contexts, and it renders past actions just or immoral. Deliberative rhetoric involves political discourse within decision-making contexts, and it advises on the pros and cons of future actions. Epideictic rhetoric includes discourses of praise and blame within current ceremonial contexts, and it shapes public opinion about what society should believe and value.

Amanda Lynch Morris teaches at Kutztown University, where she served as the director of the university writing center for three years. In 2014, she became a staff writer for *Bitch Flicks*, a web site "devoted to reviewing films and television through a feminist lens." Morris, professor of multiethnic rhetorics, claims that American Indian comedians use the epideictic form of rhetoric in their stand-up routines. In this excerpt from a 2011 article published in *Rhetoric Review*, an academic journal, Morris argues that humorous epideictic rhetoric celebrates and praises American Indians while challenging the assumptions of non-Native audiences about indigenous experiences.

"Three Indians walked out of a bar sober . . ." Vaughn Eaglebear looks around at the reservation casino audience, scanning the room amidst the hesitant half-giggles, amused murmurs, and one shout of "that's right!" biding his time to complete the punch line. After a full fifteen seconds, he delivers, "It could happen."

My task is not to define Native American comedy or to theorize about stand-up comedy as John Limon does in *Stand-up Comedy in Theory, or, Abjection in America*,[1] or even to delineate what makes Native American comedy particularly "Native American."[2] Rather, I argue that contemporary Native American stand-up comedy is a form of epideictic rhetoric in the contact zone of the performance space, using generic conventions of stand-up comedy, traditional elements of Native humor, and Aristotelian strategies to challenge what audiences think they know about Native experiences in this land.[3] Instead of the academic arena, this contact zone is the theatrical stage in varying locations (reservation casinos, comedy clubs and festivals, cable television), and the invested parties are the Native American comedians and their Native and non-Native audiences. In order to successfully challenge deeply held beliefs about Native peoples and their experiences in this particularly loaded contact zone, Native comedians employ a wide variety of techniques and rhetorical strategies that comfortably straddle the disciplines of comedy, Native American Studies, and classical rhetoric.

Specifically, Native American stand-up comedians construct epideictic performances with concrete and personal stories, active voice, and repetition of ideas, bodily and facial gestures, and a dynamic revision response to each audience. I suggest that Native American comedy is particularly epideictic in that Native comedians must deal with "praise and blame" because of the tense history they share with and against a potentially white-majority audience. Native comics must balance declamation and play (the cornerstones of such rhetoric) in order to achieve the requirements of comedy as a genre and the intentional "education" of a white audience, or camaraderie with a Native audience. These are more than just superficial comedic performances purely for entertainment or even for education. Native American stand-up comedy is an amalgamation of these objectives but also reaches beyond these boundaries into the realm of historical pain and contemporary lived realities. The potential result may be the necessity for Native comics to privilege praise and blame over other comedic aims.

> "Native American stand-up comedy potentially functions as a resistance strategy for cultural survival and as a criticism of mainstream culture, politics, and beliefs about First Nations peoples."

Despite feeling some resistance to defining Native American comedy (particularly stand-up performances), I offer a potential definition that goes beyond these four characteristics: Native American stand-up comedy teases the audience, relies on self-deprecation for much of its humor, incorporates stories "built on the oral tradition," and as a form of public discourse goes beyond entertainment into the persuasive realm of epideictic rhetoric by arguing for Native peoples' inherent right to survival and sovereignty in the twenty-first century (Don Kelly qtd. in Taylor 62). As a result, Native American stand-up comedy potentially functions as a resistance strategy for cultural survival and as a criticism of mainstream culture, politics, and beliefs about First Nations peoples. Implicit in this resistance and criticism is praise for the living realities experienced by indigenous peoples. In fact, sometimes the praise and blame are explicit in Native American stand-up, as Don Burnstick, Howie Miller, Jim Ruel, and others show in their performances.

While Native American comedians are trained and practiced in Western stand-up forms, they are adept at mediating between the worlds of indigenous experiences and Euramerican ignorance of the mess, mayhem, and trauma of our shared histories. This mediation is similar to the negotiator role[4] that Pindar's lyric poems played in fifth century BCE. According to Jeffrey Walker's discussion of Pindar's "commissioned" lyric poetry for public celebrations of chariot race victors, "[t]he poem is part of a public, civic ritual and as such is an instance of public, civic discourse" (23). Walker argues that the form of the lyric poem, in service of this public event, is often considered to be outside the domain of rhetoric. In reality, however, Pindar's lyric poems were not purely artistic, aesthetic entertainment; rather, they were an integral inclusion to the epideictic rhetorical performance. Both the lyric poem in fifth century BCE and the Native American stand-up comedy performances of today are commissioned and composed for a public purpose, as well as sharing an outsider status as simply entertainment rather than powerful and convincing forms of discourse that can create social and cultural change. These comedians are enacting more than just a superficial performance for entertainment, although that is certainly one of the objectives—to make people laugh.

When I met the Pow Wow Comedy Jam team in Everett, Washington (February 2009), Vaughn Eaglebear did not do the "Three Indians walk out of a bar sober" joke because there were six people in the audience for their 10:30 p.m. show at Marson's Comedy Club and only two were Native Americans. The "Indians walked out of a bar" joke only seems funny with an insider audience—Native Americans who understand the realities of alcoholism in their midst and who can likewise be self-referential about it and laugh at themselves. This joke does not work the same way with a primarily non-Native audience. When I asked the Pow Wow Comedy guys about this, Marc Yaffee (Navajo) first pointed to the fact that there are only three million Native Americans, so the built-in audience is smaller. When I pushed him on this, he said that the content or subject matter they deal with, particularly the topics that are specific to Native experiences in this land, are sometimes difficult for mainstream audiences to hear and understand. In his oral "foreword" to the Pow Wow Comedy Jam's DVD, *Joke Signals*,° Oneida comedian Charlie Hill expresses his appreciation for what these "young fast guns" are doing and also sets up the important potential of Native comedians to

---

Joke Signals: a play on the Native American film *Smoke Signals* (1998). The film is based on Sherman Alexie's short story "This Is What It Means to Say Phoenix, Arizona" from his book *The Lone Ranger and Tonto Fistfight in Heaven* (1993).

change how we see ourselves, our nation, and how we talk and think about Native peoples:

I think what they're doing is wonderful . . . it's new to America simply because they don't know who we are . . . I like that these guys get you to laugh with us and not at us. . . . These guys bring a lot of intelligence and different, distinctive points of view. . . . These guys being from four different cultural backgrounds is like an alliance of Indian nations . . . you know, we've tried before, we've fought the government and they beat us . . . we've signed treaties and they broke every one of them. . . . We've tried everything . . . but now the new Pow Wow Comedy Jam, they're gonna take this land back one joke at a time.

In Drew Hayden Taylor's *Me Funny* (2005), Ian Ferguson writes, "The most surprising thing for most non-Natives is that Indians are funny in the first place" (127). Also contributing a chapter [to Taylor's book], Thomas King (Cherokee/Greek) writes,

In the last five years or so, Native humor has become a minor subject of discussion—not so much on reserves or in urban centers, mind you, but within the academy, where the creation and explication of such subjects is encouraged and where it can lead to publications and promotions. And in this regard, two things have happened. One, we've decided that Native humor exists, and, two, we've come up with a general definition. Or description. Or good guess. (169–70)

Darby Li Po Price predates the sentiments of Ferguson and King in "Laughing Without Reservation: Indian Standup Comedians" from his very first line: "Contrary to the dominant conception of Indians as humorless, stoic, and tragic, humor and comedy have always been central to Native American cultures" (255).

Cherokee intellectual Jace Weaver takes up the existence of Native peoples, writing in his introduction to *That the People Might Live*, "It is important that Native cultures be seen as living, dynamic cultures" as opposed to the colonialist assumptions of cultural stasis and death: "It is a vision of the 'Indian as corpse,' and the stasis box is only a thinly disguised coffin. An extinct people do not change. Their story is complete" (8, 18). In America especially we have become disturbingly comfortable with this idea; perhaps this might be one of the reasons why, when we are confronted with Native American comedians exploring issues that touch on this sacred assumption, we're not quite sure how to react. Surely, not with laughter?! Thomas King actually offers a wise perspective on this, writing, "There are probably cultural differences in humor, but I suspect what makes Native people laugh is pretty much what makes all people laugh. . . . We are at our best when we laugh at ourselves" (qtd. in Taylor 181).

Contact Zones, Epideictic Rhetoric, and Disciplines

Using the recovered text by Guaman Poma° as a prelude to her argument in 1991 ("Arts of the Contact Zone"), Mary Louise Pratt presents the concept of contact zones as "social spaces where cultures meet, clash, and grapple with each other, often in contexts of highly asymmetrical relations of power." Specifically, she claims that Poma "exemplified the sociocultural complexities produced by conquest and empire," written as it is in two languages and two styles that reproduce both Inca knowledge and customs and European writing styles and customs (34). Pratt also introduces the related ideas of an "autoethnographic text" and "transculturation." Pratt claims that transculturation is a phenomenon of the contact zone, quite a useful concept outside the academic setting, and when applied to Native American stand-up comedy, can provide a sensible theoretical space in which to examine how this particular type of speech operates and what the benefits are for the participants.

Related to contact zones is the interdisciplinary academic field of Native American Studies, arguably a contact zone in and of itself. This field provides useful definitions for studying Native American comedy. Consider Jace Weaver's 2007 *American Indian Quarterly* assessment of "The Current State of Native American Studies" in which he suggests that Native American Studies has an "interdisciplinary character," is "comparative in nature," and "must seek to understand the material from the perspective of Natives," while maintaining a commitment to Native American community (235, 236). Thus far, only Drew Hayden Taylor and Darby Li Po Price have undertaken studies of Native American stand-up comedy. Furthermore, while Native scholars such as Vine Deloria, Jr., and Gerald Vizenor do address Native humor, neither includes Native American stand-up in their studies, *Custer Died for Your Sins* and *Manifest Manners: Narratives on Postindian Survivance*, respectively. In *Custer* Deloria, Jr. writes,

Laughter encompasses the limits of the soul. In humor life is redefined and accepted. Irony and satire provide much keener insights into a group's collective psyche and values than do years of research. It has always been a great disappointment to Indian people that the humorous side of Indian life has not been

---

Guaman Poma: (1535–1616) Quechuan nobleman who chronicled the injustices of the Spanish conquest of indigenous Andes peoples.

mentioned by professed experts on Indian Affairs. Rather the image of the granite-faced grunting redskin has been perpetuated by American mythology. (146)

Additionally, in *Manifest Manners* Vizenor focuses primarily on Native American literature and refers to Alan Velie as "the first scholar to observe the comic and ironic themes in Native American literature. His interpretations were literary, a wise departure from the surveillance of the social sciences. The tribes were tragic, never comic, or ironic, in the literature of dominance" (79).

One question that arises is why Native stand-up comedy was excluded from these rich investigations into Native American humor.[5] For instance, Oneida comedian Charlie Hill has been performing stand-up comedy since the 1970s and is fairly well known in comedy circles, having crossed over into the mainstream by appearing on the *Richard Pryor Show* in the 1970s, performing on the *Tonight Show* when Johnny Carson was at the helm, and performing at mainstream American venues to this day. Perhaps my examination will begin to provide some insight and potential answers to this question, or perhaps the problem is that Native American Studies scholars have been so busy trying to validate their theoretical stances and argue for the inclusion of a long and rich intellectual tradition of writing that goes far beyond fiction and poetry that none of them has had the opportunity to expand their Native humor studies further afield than literature. Notably, Ellen Cushman's article on Native American scholars and the rhetoric of self-representation still focuses on scholars within the academy. The publication of her article in *College Composition and Communication* affirms an interest in Native American theoretical work and opens the academic door for more research into Native American rhetorical productions such as stand-up comedy.

Turning now to classical rhetoric, I need not go further than Aristotle's ⟨10⟩ *Rhetoric* for the necessary definitions and elements. Particularly applicable to Native comedians is Aristotle's conception of epideictic oratory in which the speaker typically praises or censures someone and is concerned primarily with the present. Aristotle advises us to "take into account the nature of our particular audience when making a speech of praise; for, as Socrates used to say, it is not difficult to praise the Athenians to an Athenian audience" (199). Interestingly, this advice converges with John Limon's stand-up comedy theory that the audience makes the joke, which two of the Pow Wow Comedy Jam members dispute. However, all of these sources seem to agree on the importance of audience and catering the message (or comedy) to that particular audience. Not only that, a deeper examination of Native American stand-up comedy in particular reveals its shared characteristics with traditional epideictic rhetoric.

First of all, stand-up comedy is an art form and therefore has aesthetic and ethical dimensions; comedy is ceremonial and has its rules and rituals; comedy is oriented to public occasions and can be celebratory (as with "in" jokes such as "Drunk Indian" jokes and words such as *snaggin'*, *ayyeez*, *frybread*, and so forth). Interestingly, comedy is usually concerned with the audience's belief in the present, something that Native American comedy diverges from when the comedians reference the past (land loss, broken treaties, and so forth). In this case the audience's potential belief that contemporary Native peoples either don't exist, or should already be well integrated into Euramerican lifeways, becomes a point of tension when a Native American comedian references the past to remind the audience that the past is actually present. Hence, Native comics must necessarily use epideictic rhetorical strategies to reflect and resist their shared position with the audience between "praise" and "blame" about the past and present. Related to this idea is the observation that comedy can also eulogize or lament the loss of someone or something such as a culture, way of life, or land, as well as censure those responsible for that loss and advocate a political course of action for the survivors and their allies. In this respect comedy is concerned with practical knowledge useful in guiding everyday action; therefore, *at its base comedy is a form of moral education* that can connect people across time, space, and cultures. However, one of the dangers inherent to Native American stand-up comedy is the potential to deepen divisions between people, or create indifference, depending on the audience and how a particular audience receives the comedic messages.

More recently, Lois Agnew investigates the challenges of the epideictic genre as a form that can potentially facilitate communication among people with different views. In "'The Day Belongs to the Students': Expanding Epideictic's Civic Function," Agnew suggests that an epideictic encounter can "serve the educational function of constructively interrogating and reimagining public values," even in her example of a violent audience response to a college commencement speech (147). She reminds readers to recall Aristotle's "assumption that any discussion of praise or blame necessarily involves a broader exploration of the public values that would shape the audience's assumptions concerning the definition of those terms" (150). Citing many contemporary genre theorists, Agnew reiterates that epideictic's power may reside in its "dynamic capacity to shape the community's identity." Interestingly, Agnew's keen assessments all connect with Native American stand-up comedy practices, especially when she accentuates the need for speakers and audiences to come together in a cultural moment where they also "creatively work against those boundaries in order to establish a communicative act that has more than formal significance" (151). The idea of the modern epideictic encounter she defines and explores here dovetails nicely with my observations of Native comedians in the contact zone of the performance space with invested participants.

Finally, the specific performance space where comedy lives deserves some attention. In 1987 journalist Betsy Borns interviewed the top stand-up comics of the 1980s to create *Comic Lives: Inside the World of American Stand-Up Comedy*. Borns calls the comedy club "a stormy sea of conflicting purposes," emotionally seducing audiences with the "promise of catharsis through laughter" (14). Focusing on different audience dynamics and how an audience reacts to various types of jokes, and allowing those comics to ruminate about audiences (among other topics), Borns suggests that an "audience's attitude toward a comic's material depends on its members' general range of acceptance" (18). However, she also argues that "stand-up is satire and . . . is also planting some serious seeds. Logic dictates that if you want to get a message across and the frontal lobe is locked, you go in through the back door" (28). Laughter is the key to unlock this door. According to Dana Sutton in *The Catharsis of Comedy*, "Like a sneeze, a laugh can be described as a species of orgasm: a sudden, irreversible, and only partially voluntary discharge of something accumulated and pent up. As such, it is an example of the kind of entropy-achieving event described by Aristotle, of the sort that people find inherently pleasurable" (20). Therefore, if we begin with the premise that catharsis[6] is a process of purgation (in tragedy the feelings purged would be fear and pity; in comedy the question remains as to which feelings are being purged), then this "experience that the spectator undergoes" has the potential to alter that spectator (Sutton 3). Sutton further suggests that "comic catharsis is a process with social implications" (30). This assessment certainly seems to apply to Native stand-up comedy performances—the audience laughs to purge its own fears and anxieties of being implicated as villains in the ongoing shared history.

Continuing the focus on message and audience, in *Performing Marginality: Humor, Gender, and Cultural Critique*, Joanne Gilbert investigates the "elements of contradiction, interaction, and spontaneity inherent" in the medium of stand-up comedy:

Audiences pay to laugh and to be laughed at. And comics wield rhetorical power in a context in which the marginal are not only accepted but valorized. Within the topsy-turvy world of stand-up comic performance, hierarchies are inverted, power relations are subverted, and a good time is had by all. Because it can avoid inflaming audiences by framing incisive—even incendiary— sociocultural critique as mere "entertainment," comedy is undeniably a unique and powerful form of communication. (xxi)

Indeed, it seems that Native American comedians are redefining the place of laughter with regard to performance in a contact zone. How and why people laugh can be explained physiologically, physically, and psychologically, but none of these explanations are satisfying in relation to a Native American comedian and his audience. Sitting in a dark comedy club face to face with a Native comedian who looks you in the eye as he weaves a story that implicates you in uncomfortable ways but still makes you laugh almost involuntarily—how to explain this? Yes, laughter is an expulsion of air; Freud called it a release of psychic energy, and some situations may result in nervous laughter, but these explanations fall short of why we laugh at the stand-up's direct attack on our sense of self. Perhaps only those who have a high sense of self-esteem, a fairly deep awareness and knowledge of the shared histories of Native and non-Native peoples in this land, and who have a willingness to accept criticism would truly find these comedians funny. When I showed my freshman composition students a set by Jim Ruel, only a handful laughed out loud. In their reflective analyses, these students wrote about not understanding land loss, the problem with Thanksgiving, stereotypes, and historical issues that are still present for Native peoples. In addition, these same students enjoyed Ruel's performance and felt they missed out on something, so even though they didn't laugh out loud, they understood the performance was meant to be funny and the seeds of serious ideas were successfully planted.

Native American stand-up comics create a much more complicated   15
performance than many non-Native stand-up comics; theirs is a performance not simply for superficial entertainment. Charlie Hill's idea that the Pow Wow Comedy guys will "take this land back one joke at a time" is a powerful one. Land loss resolved by comedy and laughter? Perhaps this is not as absurd as it seems at first blush. If more people experience the comic stories of American Indian comedians where serious ideas are planted through the back door and not the frontal lobe, as Borns suggests, then over time our overall conceptions of Native peoples may change. For instance, one outcome might be that more people realize that indigenous peoples are still present and visible and are not vanished relics of the past. And quite frankly, getting these ideas through stand-up comedy is a lot more fun than reading a history textbook. Laughter opens up the brain and unlocks the back door, but as my students demonstrated, even when laughter isn't front and center, the ideas still penetrate.

Finally, Richard Zoglin investigates the sociocultural effect that stand-up comedy had on the American mind-set in the 1970s in *Comedy at the Edge: How Stand-Up in the 1970s Changed America*. Zoglin seems to take a more sober and less celebratory approach in suggesting that the sense of adventure that was rampant in 1970s heroic and social commentator comics "has been replaced by the programmed predictability of a General Motors assembly plant. The comics all sound pretty much alike these days, with the same patter to loosen up the crowd, the same recyclable loop of stand-up topics (sex, New York subways, commercials for Viagra)" (2). I'm not sure if Zoglin has seen any Native American comics perform, but in my experience with them and their work, it is entirely possible that this group of comics, with a unique perspective on American experience, might be the "brilliant and radical artists" of our generation, potentially influencing how we see the world, perhaps changing the way we talk and think, and, of course, making us laugh at each other and ourselves, as the best comedy does (6).

Notes

1. Limon's one-sentence summation of his theory is, "What is stood up in stand-up comedy is abjection," and he pulls heavily from Julia Kristeva's concept of abjection, which he defines as "abasement, groveling prostration" (4). Looking at the comedy of Lenny Bruce, Richard Pryor, Ellen DeGeneres, and many others, Limon writes with a cultural-studies point of view, declaring, "Stand-up itself has the structure of abjection insofar as comedians are not allowed to be either natural or artificial (Are they themselves or acting?). . . . All a stand-up's life feels abject to him or her, and stand-ups try to escape it by living it as an act" (6).

2. Plenty of people have done this. In fact, in Taylor's book, *Me Funny*, several Native comedians and humorists define Native or Aboriginal comedy. Don Kelly (Ojibwa) suggests the claim that Native humor is "the comedy of coping—a response to troubled times, dark days, and oppression" is contradictory. Rather, he argues, "Perhaps the last couple of centuries have sharpened and honed our wit, but laughter has echoed across Turtle Island for centuries. . . . Comedy is well-trod ground, but Native stand-up comedy is wide-open terrain. There are no boundaries and no borders. It's undiscovered country. And our people are experts in navigating new territory" ("And Now, Ladies and Gentlemen" 62–65).

3. I thank *Rhetoric Review* reviewers Oscar Giner and Daniel Schowalter for their valuable suggestions and recommendations that improved this article. My sincere appreciation goes out to them for their time and consideration.

4. Walker cites Leslie Kurke's 1991 *The Traffic in Praise*: "Pindar's epinikia negotiated social and political tensions between wealthy aristocrats . . . and non-aristocrats, at a time when the social power of the traditional warrior-aristocrat was being displaced (though not eliminated)" (24). Clearly, the idea that an artistic form can have this sort of persuasive authority is not new.

5. One could also put the study of Native American stand-up comedy in the context of more ancient Native American comic forms such as the sacred clowns who heal through laughter. For instance, the heyoka of the Lakota perform satires to teach and reflect certain behaviors of the audience to shape the moral and ethical boundaries of the community. Heyokas act

contrary to convention and violate the boundaries of rules, social norms, and taboos in order to provide guidance about what those boundaries, rules, and taboos are. Although it is tempting to compare modern indigenous comedians with the traditional sacred clowns (or trickster figures) or to suggest that these comedians are consciously breaking with these traditional forms, I am not comfortable with either direction. Rather, I would like to acknowledge that humor and comedy in some form has been and remains ubiquitous with Native American peoples.

6. In the absence of a traditional critical construct to explain the psychic and emotional processes of comedy, I rely on a term borrowed from tragedy, using *catharsis* as a correlative, but not as a proven, exemplar.

Works Cited

Agnew, Lois. "'The Day Belongs to the Students': Expanding Epideictic's Civic Function." *Rhetoric Review* 27.2 (2008): 147–64.

Aristotle. "Rhetoric." *The Rhetorical Tradition: Readings from Classical Times to the Present.* 2nd ed. Ed. Patricia Bizzell and Bruce Herzberg. New York: Bedford/ St. Martin's, 2001. 169–242.

Borns, Betsy, ed. *Comic Lives: Inside the World of American Stand-Up Comedy.* New York: Simon & Schuster, 1987.

Cushman, Ellen. "Toward a Rhetoric of Self-Representation: Identity Politics in Indian Country and Rhetoric and Composition." *College Composition and Communication* 60.2 (2008): 321–65.

Deloria, Vine, Jr. *Custer Died for Your Sins.* Norman: U of Oklahoma P, 1988.

Gilbert, Joanne R. *Performing Marginality: Humor, Gender, and Cultural Critique.* Detroit, MI: Wayne State UP, 2004.

King, Thomas. *The Truth About Stories.* Minneapolis: U of Minnesota P, 2008.

Limon, John. *Stand-Up Comedy in Theory, or, Abjection in America.* Durham, NC: Duke UP, 2000.

Pow Wow Comedy Jam. Marc Yaffee, Jim Ruel, Vaughn Eaglebear, JR Redwater. Personal interview and e-mail. February 2009–April 2009.

———. *Joke Signals.* Dir. Barbara Holliday. Perf. Marc Yaffee, Vaughn Eaglebear, Jim Ruel, and JR Redwater. H2F Comedy Productions, Inc., 2005. DVD.

Pratt, Mary Louise. "Arts of the Contact Zone." *Profession* 91 (1991): 33–40.

Price, Darby Li Po. "Laughing without Reservation: Indian Standup Comedians." *American Indian Culture and Research Journal* 22.4 (1998): 255–71.

Sutton, Dana Ferrin. *The Catharsis of Comedy.* Lanham, MD: Rowan & Littlefield, 1994.

Taylor, Drew Hayden. *Me Funny.* Vancouver, BC: Douglas & McIntyre, 2005.

Vizenor, Gerald. *Manifest Manners: Narratives on Postindian Survivance.* Lincoln: U of Nebraska P, 1999.

Walker, Jeffrey. "The View from Halicarnassus: Aristotelianism & the Rhetoric of Epideictic Song." *New Definitions of Lyric: Theory, Technology, and Culture.* Ed. Mark Jeffreys. New York: Garland, 1998. 17–48.

Weaver, Jace. "More Light Than Heat: The Current State of Native American Studies." *The American Indian Quarterly* 31.2 (2007): 233–55.

———. *That the People Might Live.* New York: Oxford UP, 1997.

Zoglin, Richard. *Comedy at the Edge: How Stand-Up in the 1970s Changed America.* New York: Bloomsbury, 2008.

Understanding the Text

1. How do the American Indian scholars and stand-up comedians Morris cites characterize Native American humor and the genre of stand-up comedy?

2. To comprehend Morris's argument requires understanding her use of several key concepts. How does she define *contact zone*, *epideictic oratory*, and *catharsis*? What other terms are central to her argument? Directly quote from Morris's essay when necessary.

3. How do American Indian stand-up comedians use epideictic rhetorical strategies?

Reflection and Response

4. Morris published this article in a peer-reviewed academic journal. What aspects distinguish her writing as academic? What are the benefits of this style? What are the drawbacks? Cite specific examples from Morris's essay to support your answers.

5. Morris includes comments by American Indian comedians on the difference between performing for Native versus non-Native audiences. What role do you believe an audience's identity plays in responding to the humor of a minority comedian? Do you feel as if you, like the first-year writing students Morris discusses, fail to grasp the entirety of a comedian's jokes whose identity you do not share?

6. Does your experience confirm Morris's assessment that *"at its base comedy is a form of moral education* that can connect people across time, space, and cultures" (par. 11)? Do you think that comedy can serve the same function as a history textbook? Why or why not?

Making Connections

7. Watch the *American Indian Comedy Slam* (2010) or performances from members of the Pow Wow Comedy Jam posted online. Write an analytical essay on how one of these comedians gets laughs using epideictic rhetorical strategies. What other comedic rhetorical strategies do they employ besides epideictic ones? Chart this comedian's performance using Kenneth Burke's dramatistic pentad (p. 3).

8. The comedians that Morris cites are all men. Research female American Indian comedians like the Ladies of Native Comedy (Teresa Choyguha, Tonia Jo Hall, Adrianne Chalepah, and Deanna M.A.D.). Write an essay on how their comedy is similar to and/or different from their male counterparts.

Perspectives on Comedy and Performance as Radical Disability Activism

Alan Shain

Comedian and multidisciplinary artist Alan Shain begins his autobiographical commentary by stating, "I consider myself a disability activist who is using the arts to effect equality" (par. 1). Indeed, Shain's web site (www.halicamedia.com/shain) relates that his "zany outlook on airport travel, tobogganing, eating chocolate — and everything in between" delivers laughs with "a heavy dose of disability politics, touching issues around physical access, employment and attitudinal barriers." Shain's comedic approach reflects his educational background: He received a B.A. in political science and sociology and an M.A. in social work.

In this excerpt from a 2013 publication in the *Journal of Literary & Cultural Disability Studies*, Shain reflects on his own stand-up routine as a disabled comedian and his aims as a disability activist. As you read, think about what his goals are and how he is able to accomplish them through comedy.

I consider myself a disability activist who is using the arts to effect equality. More specifically, I have chosen the vehicle of comedy and humor as a way of bonding with an audience in order to promote critical thinking and dialogue around the meaning of disability. According to the late comedian Victor Borge,° humor is the shortest distance between two people.[1] I remember discovering at a young age the power of laughter to make others feel comfortable around me. I realized that if I could make people laugh, they were more flexible in including me as a disabled person.

My performance career began over 20 years ago in stand-up comedy. Though I have since branched out into theater and storytelling, comedy and humor remain prominent features of my performance practice. I have performed in a variety of venues such as nightclubs, professional theater halls, high schools, as well as conference and community settings across North America, Australia, England, Bermuda, and Taiwan. My comment here focuses on the artistic and cultural choices that I make within my work to engage audiences within a critical discussion around impairment and disability. Evidence of actually promoting

Victor Borge: (1909–2000) a Danish comedian and pianist.

critical dialogue, however, lies only in the circumstantial evidence of my having sustained a 20-year career, plus a handful of reviews, and feedback from the audience.

Stand-Up Comedy

Modern stand-up comedy is dominated by personal and social commentary. Most comics discuss issues and topics that they feel strongly about, which may include their gut feelings, their fears, their anxieties (Carter 4). The issues I have chosen to discuss highlight the barriers that I face as a disabled person. For example, I typically begin my act by recounting going out to dinner with my brother:

When we sat down, the waiter addressed my brother with the question, "How many menus do you want?" I decided to answer that question with, "Well, there are two of us sitting at the table. Why don't you bring us four menus?"

I start this way because the subject of the joke is an everyday activity to which everyone can relate. People expect to be able to walk into a restaurant, be given a menu, and be served without incident. I tell the story as if I expect to be able to do this as well. My delivery is lighthearted, told with *a funny thing happened to me* type of tone. The humor arises from my exaggerated response. Yet it is precisely *my response* that frames the way the waiter reacts to me as ludicrous and absurd.

Beginning my act in this way works to establish a rapport. Since I typically perform in mainstream venues, I am likely to be seen as an outsider by much of the audience. John Morreall notes the bonding effect of shared humor, "especially" when it is "based on either some perceived strength in the group or some shortcomings in opponents of the group" (67). Here, the shortcoming is in the waiter. I tell the story as if members of the audience would never do what the waiter did. They are treated as my confidant—as if we are in this ludicrous situation together. My tone is not instructional. I am obviously enjoying the waiter's awkwardness and I am inviting the audience to share this enjoyment. The majority of my audience likely shares the viewpoints that I am ridiculing. The nature of this joke forces the audience to identify with me not getting a menu. Yet they probably also strongly identify with the waiter's uncertainty about how to deal with me because of my impairments. This joke always gets a huge laugh precisely because the audience identifies with the waiter. Comedy and humor has allowed me to make fun of the audience's own ideas of disabled people.

Disability oppression is not a hot topic within comedy by any stretch of 5 the imagination. Impairment and disability still remain taboo topics within our culture—particularly when combined with intimacy and sexuality. Comedy has enabled me as a performer to cross these types of boundaries. Morreall highlights the social bonding that can be created through humor and laughter (67). In his discussion of humor and politics, he notes the rapport politicians can cultivate with a particular audience by making funny comments. This social bonding "seems to work especially well when the humor is based on either some strength in the group or some shortcoming in opponents of the group" (67). He further references Konrad Lorenz in noting that laughter forms divisions as well as bonds between people: "If you cannot laugh with the others, you feel an outsider even if the laughter is in no way directed against yourself or against anything at all" (67).

David Mitchell and Sharon Snyder state that dominant treatments of disability within literature and film construct characters with impairments as deviant (2). As such, disabled characters are typically the outsiders. Yet my use of humor constructs characters (such as the waiter) as the outsiders. The audience is therefore laughing *with* me *at them*, the outsiders, the people who are focused on my individual limitations. We might consider a joke as an example:

My friends keep trying to pick out a girlfriend for me, and they are not very good at it. Not at all! Every time they see a woman go by in a wheelchair, they point her out to me, "Hey, look, Alan! There's one for you!" I say, "Come on! She's 85 years old!"

This addresses the popular attitude that disabled people should only date disabled people. On another level, it addresses the notion that disabled people are not competent at dating. My friends feel they have to find dates for me. Treating this with humor allows a mainstream audience to feel as though they are *insiders* to my experience, while at the same time directly attacking notions that they likely hold themselves. On several occasions, I have been approached after a show by people commenting that they were shocked that they had done some of the things I had ridiculed. However, they also said that they loved the show—perhaps precisely *because* they were shocked.

In discussing the potential ethical limitations on humor, Sharon Lockyer and Michael Pickering comment that comedians are often expected to "push at accepted boundaries, attempt to shock us and shatter our illusions" (14). Shawn Chandler Bingham and Alexander Hernandez note black comedian Richard Pryor's ability to address race relations in front of white audiences in the 1960s, and Margaret Cho's ability to discuss her bisexuality within mainstream venues in claiming that "the audience–comedian interaction is one of the few areas where topics of race, class, gender and religion can be openly explored" (339). I would add to this list the topic of disability oppression.

My work incorporates the social model of disability° by making a fundamental distinction between bodily impairment and socially constructed disability. It is the response I receive to my impairment—not my impairment itself—that is the fodder for ridicule.

Victoria Ann Lewis points to a long line of disability comedy troupes, stand-up comics, and performance artists who use humor to shed light on the political reality of disabled Americans. For example, she illustrates the way in which a comedic sketch of "a quadriplegic buy[ing] some food and [trying] to eat it . . . kick[ing] off a media frenzy [. . .] strips bare the social perception of disabled people as being incompetent" (101). Humor allows a direct attack on dominant approaches to disability that frames disabled people as dependent and in need of caretaking.

Morreall discusses the ways in which humor can promote critical 10 thinking: "The humorous mind looks for incongruity, and that is frequently a discrepancy between what people should be and what they are" (72). This follows the incongruity theory of humor, which holds that a situation is humorous when there is some type of discrepancy that we enjoy in some way. My work highlights the discrepancy between the ways people *should* react to me and how people *actually* react to me as a disabled person. In noting the playfulness of humor, Morreall comments that exaggeration is designed to entertain rather than to deceive (68). It is this playful quality of comedy and humor that I believe also opens audiences up to thinking critically about disability and inclusion. By using exaggeration in my own reaction to the ways I am treated, these types of discrepancies are pointed out playfully for the enjoyment of the audience, as in my joke about going for a job interview:

> "My work highlights the discrepancy between the ways people *should* react to me and how people *actually* react to me as a disabled person."

The first question I got asked was not about my education level or my working skills—no. The first question I got asked was "Are you impaired?" Well, I had

---

social model of disability: the idea that society disables people by not accounting for individual differences, as opposed to the medical model that locates disability within bodies that do not conform to what is considered "normal." The social model argues that impairments need not become disabilities if society were structured in a way to accommodate them socially, institutionally, and economically.

had a couple of drinks, but I didn't know it showed! The interviewer clarified what he meant. He said, "By impaired, I mean is there something about you which completely segregates you from everyone else? Something physical perhaps?" I answered with, "Now that you mention it, I'm extremely good looking!" So, I got the job!

My reaction to the interviewer is contentious. This is my comment on the failure of employment equity for disabled people. After 30 years of countless government-funded studies and initiatives, the majority of disabled people remain either unemployed or underemployed. This is a serious issue. Yet I chose to treat this issue humorously, as an effort to promote critical thinking among mainstream audiences surrounding employment and disability. By exaggerating the interviewer's treatment of me as well as my reaction to his treatment, the discrepancy between my own expectations and what I actually receive is highlighted in a playful way. It is the focus on my impairment that is framed as the problem, rather than my expectation of a fair interview—and a job! In actual fact, we rarely even get to the interview stage in the first place.

Morreall comments that humor is often for its own sake and not necessarily trying to accomplish anything (68). Humorous messages are aimed more at the imagination than the intellect. While this is true, I have found that it is precisely because of this that humor can also be a powerful way to drive home a point or a message.[2]

Notes

1. See Granirer.

2. This seemed to resonate in the reviews. For example, one reviewer called the play "An emotional slice of reality," writing, "A simple plan [to go out on a date], yes, but not so for someone with a physical disability" (34). The Ottawa Sun led their review of the 1999 Ottawa Fringe Festival with the headline "Bus best ride at Fringe" and gave my play 5 stars. Another reviewer wrote, "A thoughtful one-man comedy about sex and the single wheelchair guy [...] which drives home one fiery point: Society treats the disabled like little children. [... Mark] has a hot date with Linda. [...] The only problem is that he has to rely on unreliable Handi Transit which plays all sorts of havoc with his carnal urges. What's nice about this very realistic tale is the way Shain conveys a powerful human message without sounding bitter or resentful" (Kives).

Works Cited

Bingham, Shawn Chandler, and Alexander A. Hernandez. "'Laughing Matters': The Comedian as Social Observer, Teacher and Conduit of the Sociological Perspective." *Teaching Sociology* 37 (2009): 335–52. Print.

Carter, Judy. *Stand-up Comedy: The Book.* New York: Dell, 1989. Print.

Granirer, David. "Stand up for Mental Health." Web. 17 May 2013.

Lewis, Victoria Ann. "The Dramaturgy of Disability." *Points of Contact: Disability, Art and Culture.* Ed. Susan Crutchfield and Marcy Epstein. Ann Arbor: U of Michigan P, 2000. 93–108. Print.

Lockyer, Sharon, and Michael Pickering, eds. *Beyond a Joke: The Limits of Humour.* New York: Palgrave Macmillan, 2005. Print.

Mitchell, David T., and Sharon L. Snyder. *Narrative Prosthesis: Disability and the Dependencies of Discourse.* Ann Arbor: U of Michigan P, 2000. Print.

Morreall, John. "Humour and the Conduct of Politics." *Beyond a Joke: The Limits of Humour.* Ed. Sharon Lockyer and Michael Pickering. New York: Palgrave Macmillan, 2005. 63–78. Print.

Understanding the Text

1. How does Shain treat his audience? What effect does his story of the prejudiced waiter have on his audience members?

2. What prejudices about disabled people does Shain's comedy ridicule? How does he make light of being oppressed as a disabled person?

3. Why does Shain choose to treat the serious topic of disability humorously? What does he hope to accomplish?

Reflection and Response

4. Based on Shain's remarks, it seems that other people focusing on an impairment may be more of a hardship than the impairment itself. Do you or does someone you know have an impairment? Has humor been a way to cope with not only the condition but also others' reactions to it?

5. Have you ever heard of anyone who is an activist comedian or thought about the possibility that humor can be a vehicle for social justice? What methods do comedians like Shain use to make their point while making their audiences laugh? What might humor be able to achieve that other forms of activism cannot? Are there any potential drawbacks to mixing humor with activism? Explain.

Making Connections

6. In theorizing about his work, Shain relies heavily on John Morreall, who also appears in Chapter 1 (p. 25) of this text. Conduct research on this humor theorist. Begin by tracking down the work that Shain cites, and write a literature review of Morreall's work.

7. Among other stand-up comic techniques, Shain uses exaggeration to highlight incongruities between how he is treated versus how he should be treated (par. 10). Research other comedians with disabilities (e.g., Zach Anner, Josh Blue, Ally Bruener, Chris Fonseca, Shannon DeVido, Stella Young, Maysoon Zayid). What comic techniques and rhetorical devices do they employ? Do they share Shain's methodology for creating a joke?

Why Amy Schumer Is an Amazing Feminist

Karley Sciortino

Karley Sciortino is a sex-positive writer, blogger, and self-identified feminist. She writes the column "Breathless" for vogue.com, which is where this piece originally appeared on July 23, 2015. Her web site *Slutever* covers issues concerning sexuality and relationships, and her videos have appeared in *Vice* and *Purple*.

In this article, Sciortino praises Amy Schumer for promoting feminist causes in her television sketch comedy show *Inside Amy Schumer* and 2015 film *Trainwreck*, although she has some reservations about the latter. When reading this essay, think about how the subversive comedy of feminists relates to the ways in which stand-up routines by disability activist Alan Shain (p. 179) and the American Indian comedians profiled by Amanda Lynch Morris (p. 167) address audiences who do not share their identity.

"How many feminists does it take to screw in a light bulb?" a guy friend of mine recently asked me.

Me: "I don't know. How many?"

Him: "That's not funny!"

While I *did* laugh at the joke, I probably incriminated myself by following up that laugh with an argument about why, in fact, feminists *can* take a joke. *Okay*?! Of course, my primary defense was the god that is Amy Schumer, whose Emmy-nominated Comedy Central show *Inside Amy Schumer* and new movie *Trainwreck* have made her the radical front-runner of feminist comedy.

Amy is the feminist the world needs right now. With people clamor- 5 ing for equality in seemingly all arenas, Schumer's smart, hilarious satire takes aim at issues like equal pay, gender inequality, sexual double standards, reproductive rights, and sexist stereotypes. Basically, the same issues that smart women have been screaming about for ages—except that Amy's words actually manage to echo beyond the choir.

It was her now-infamous "Last F**kable Day" sketch, in the beginning of Season 3, that really changed the game. Starring Tina Fey, Julia Louis-Dreyfus, and Patricia Arquette, the skit mocks the Hollywood double standard by commemorating Louis-Dreyfus's last date of sexual viability. It went viral—it now has more than 3.5 million hits on YouTube—and suddenly everyone was watching, men and women both.

Basically, Amy's made "women's issues" something that dudes want to tune in for, which is sort of a miracle, considering that most of the guys

I know would rather amputate a limb than read *Jezebel*.° Say "rape culture" at a dinner party and legit every dude's eyes immediately glaze
over. But Amy has a sneaky power for tricking men into paying attention
by presenting her agenda as hilarious comedy. It's sort of like when
moms hide vegetables inside of meatballs so their kids don't know what
they're eating.

Amy is 34, grew up in Manhattan and Long Island, and was a stand-up
comedian for about nine years before launching her show on Comedy
Central. She found success at the height of the female comedy wave, a
movement that began with women like Tina Fey, Amy Poehler, and
Kristen Wiig, and continued with Melissa McCarthy, Mindy Kaling, Lena
Dunham, and *Broad City*'s Abbi and Ilana. (Let's all hope Christopher
Hitchens, who famously argued that women aren't funny, is eating crow
in his grave.) Her show opts for sketch comedy at a time when our four-
minute attention spans prefer entertainment in the short form, and her
brand of comedy feels perfectly of-the-moment.

Amy's not the first political comic, obviously, or the first to point out
that women get the short end of the stick. But she has differentiated herself—and perhaps risked her career—by making it her main gag. She's
pushed everything one step further than her predecessors: She's more
political, more self-deprecating, and more unapologetically sexual in a
way that young women today really respond to, and need.

Maybe it's just me, but I've always thought there was something   10
inherently feminist about being a slut and not being ashamed about it.
The sexual double standard seems to be fading (in liberal, educated circles, anyway), but an unapologetic, sexually hedonistic woman is still
taboo. I've been ranting for years about how we need more slutty female
role models—intelligent, successful, sex-positive women, acting as living proof that having a lot of sex does not mean you're a bad person, or
doomed. And then Amy came along, and I literally praised the slut gods!
In her comedy, Amy (and her characters alike) are proudly promiscuous.
She doesn't subscribe to the idea that wearing a microdress and being
taken seriously are mutually exclusive. In a way, Amy is to millennials
what Madonna was to women in the eighties—proof that you can be
smart, political, funny, and aggressively sexual, all at the same time.

Which means she gets a lot of criticism, of course, often for her looks.
This isn't surprising, given the internet's deep-seeded, misogynous troll
culture, full of sad bros for whom successful, confident women inspire

Jezebel: a feminist blog founded by Anna Holmes in 2007 and owned by Gawker
Media.

Model Amber Rose (left) and Schumer (right) in a scene from *Inside Amy Schumer*.
Everett Collection, Inc.

infinite amounts of rage. But their barrage of shallow insults has become amazing fodder for Schumer's comedy, as in the "12 Angry Men" sketch, an episode-long parody of the classic film in which twelve jurors deliberate over whether Amy is hot enough to be on TV. It stars the likes of John Hawkes, Paul Giamatti, and Jeff Goldblum, and it's a hysterical comment on the absurd hypocrisy by which men evaluate women.

But Amy's comedy is in no way man-hating. (She's clearly DTF.) It's more complex than that. She doesn't praise all women or villainize men. One of her common schticks is the mockery of the Basic Bitch, a self-obsessed yet insecure white girl with a passion for white wine, selfies, and blacking out. Another major target is the women's magazines that feed us bizarre "tips" on how to be a man-pleasing sex-bot: "Take a 5-hour Energy and pour it inside your vagina right before you have sex!" Or: "Be Asian!"

She's also not afraid to take on heavy subjects, as with her sketch slaying Bill Cosby supporters. She's also managed to make a successful rape joke—not an easy task—many times over, most hilariously in the *Friday Night Lights* parody, in which a football coach (Josh Charles) implements a "no raping" rule for his players, igniting outrage in town.

The baffled players retaliate with a slew of objections, that is, "What if my mom is the D.A. and won't prosecute. Can I rape?"

Potentially her most hard-hitting sketch, "A Very Realistic Military Game," addresses sexual abuse in the military. In it, Amy and her boyfriend are about to play a combat video game. Before the "action" begins, Amy's player, who's female, gets raped. Amy's increasingly confused when the game asks her if she wants to report the rape—"Of course!"—after which her character is sent to the Pentagon, where she has to fill out tons of boring paperwork. She ends up under character assassination, and the whole game just becomes red tape and lawyers, which causes her boyfriend to lose interest and leave the room, until the case is ultimately dismissed. The scene ends with Amy shouting a simple but powerful statement: "This game sucks!"

There *has* been one slight bump in the road for me, though. Last week 15 I saw the release of Amy's first feature film, *Trainwreck*. The format is a pretty standard romcom, except the typical gender roles are reversed— Amy plays the emotionally stunted party girl who won't let her lovers sleep over, hates cuddling, and can't be tied down, while her love interest (Bill Hader) is the sweet, together, monogamy-minded costar who wants Amy to commit.

There are a lot of great things about the movie—it's definitely funny, and it starts off following an unapologetic, sexually adventurous girl with an ostensibly good writing job. But in the third act, things get a bit puritanical in a disappointing, confusingly un-Amy way. During a major fight, Amy's boyfriend tells her: "It does bother me that you smoke pot and drink a lot and sleep with a lot of guys. It doesn't make me feel safe." This ultimately leads Amy to admit to her sister that she's "broken" and doesn't feel that she deserves love, hence her destructive lifestyle. The lifestyle entails drinking and smoking a lot of weed, but also includes her sexual behavior—her sex life is lumped in with the negative. Then there was this awful montage in which she throws out all the alcohol in her house. (Do people really do that?) Basically, the film reverted to the standard Hollywood "reformed slut narrative." In the end, Amy simply needs to assimilate and be more like her normal, married sister in order to be happy and lead a fulfilling life.

> "What's truly spectacular about Amy is that her comedy appeals to everyone, which is what modern feminism is truly about — bringing men and women together."

It's probably my stalker-grade fanaticism for Amy that makes me want to blame Hollywood for pushing her hand in this more conventional direction. The slut-shaming element just felt like the antithesis of the message of her show. Why couldn't *Trainwreck* Amy simply have fallen in love and started a monogamous relationship? No one's against love and dating! Why did she have to denounce her sexually adventurous past as destructive (*and* throw out a lot of expensive alcohol)?

But these are small quibbles. What's truly spectacular about Amy is that her comedy appeals to everyone, which is what modern feminism is truly about—bringing men and women together. It's like what Emma Watson urged in her inspirational HeForShe speech at the UN: In order to redefine gender roles for both women and men, we have to invite men into the conversation and make gender equality a social issue, rather than a "female issue." Amy Schumer is doing more to spread the feminist message than anybody has in a long time.

Understanding the Text

1. What kinds of evidence does Sciortino provide to support her argument that Amy Schumer is the "radical frontrunner of feminist comedy" (par. 4)?

2. What potential counterarguments to her position does Sciortino address? Why is she somewhat disappointed by Schumer's film *Trainwreck*?

3. What assumptions does Sciortino hold about comedy and feminism? How does the style and tone of her writing reveal her assumptions?

Reflection and Response

4. Sciortino claims that "Amy has a sneaky power for tricking men into paying attention by presenting her agenda as hilarious comedy" (par. 7). Her observation echoes many others who have commented on the ability of comedians to popularize feminism on the sly. What are the benefits and drawbacks of mainstreaming feminism in this way? Do you think this is an effective strategy? Why or why not?

5. What is your opinion of Schumer's comedy? If you are unfamiliar with her work, watch an episode of *Inside Amy Schumer* or popular clips of her stand-up performances. Do you agree with Sciortino's assessment of Schumer? Why or why not?

Making Connections

6. Sciortino notes that Schumer has made rape jokes and a romcom. Write an analysis of either Schumer's comedic treatment of rape or of her film *Trainwreck*. Cite either Katherine Leyton's piece (p. 94) or Tamar Jeffers McDonald's selection (p. 155) in your analysis.

7. Sciortino makes a passing reference to the late provocative English author Christopher Hitchens, and his article, "Why Women Aren't Funny,"

published by *Vanity Fair* in 2007. A year later, that same magazine published television critic Alessandra Stanley's rebuttal, followed by Hitchens's counterargument. Read these pieces as well as other sources (like Ellie Kemper's 2015 *GQ* piece "Can Men Be Funny?"), and write a research essay on the issue of women in comedy.

8. Although all of the comedians mentioned by Sciortino are women, nearly all happen to be white. Schumer herself has been criticized for having a blind spot around race. Write an essay on women comedians and their various approaches to the intersection of gender and race/ethnicity.

Sexual Outlaws: Queer in a Funny Way

Jennifer Reed

Jennifer Reed is an associate professor in the Department of Women's, Gender, and Sexuality Studies at California State University, Long Beach. She is the author of the book *The Queer Cultural Work of Lily Tomlin and Jane Wagner* (2013). Her work on Roseanne Barr, Ellen DeGeneres, postfeminism, and *The L Word* has appeared in *Feminist Media Studies*, *The Journal of Popular Culture*, *Journal of Popular Film and Television*, and the anthologies *Third Wave Agenda* (1997) and *Queer Popular Culture* (2011).

This piece on the queer comedy of Lily Tomlin, Paula Poundstone, and Margaret Cho first appeared in the academic journal *Women's Studies* in 2011. Tomlin, Poundstone, and Cho are American stand-up comedians, actors, and writers. When reading about their work, think about its relation to that of more recent women comedians, like those discussed by Karley Sciortino (p. 185).

The most important feminist cultural work done by mass-mediated women comedians of the last generation has been a result of their subversions of heteronormativity. Over the last 30 years or so, there have been a relatively large proportion of women comedians in U.S. mainstream comedy who work outside of the terms of heteronormativity in a variety of ways. Sandra Bernhard and Margaret Cho, for example, are two comedians who share a kind of sexual outrageousness and hypersexual personae that break all the rules of heteronormativity not only because they talk about sleeping with both men and women but because they own their sexual desire and are never defined by their relationships to men. Kathy Griffin, like Cho, is well-known for outrageous behavior and language—decidedly unladylike—and for her active address to gay men, whom she calls "my gays." Paula Poundstone has spent her stand-up career insisting that she has no interest in any sexual relationship at all. Lily Tomlin, Ellen DeGeneres, and Rosie O'Donnell spent large parts of their early careers maintaining a kind of silence around their own sexual identities in their work until they came out publicly as lesbians. Wanda Sykes also recently came out as a lesbian, although she had spent a good deal of her act talking about sex with men. Taken together, they all have created some distance around heteronormativity.

I concentrate here particularly on the work and public personae of Lily Tomlin, Margaret Cho, and Paula Poundstone as illustrative examples because of the significant differences between them. Their comedic work, public personae, and use of media are all very different from each other, and together they span the last generation of comedy. More important though, they represent three different challenges to heteronormativity. They occupy very different sexual subjectivities, but all of them create a subjective space in the gaps between categories, occupying a liminal space, which is how I identify them as queer. Tomlin's career spans over four decades, the first three of which she did not publicly and explicitly claim a lesbian identity. In 2000 she "came out" officially. Cho, a queer icon, is married to a man, and identifies publicly as gay, as a "fag hag," and as a "slut," among other labels. Poundstone identifies publicly as non-sexual and creates her persona partly around the fact that she has no interest in a sexual relationship to anyone of any gender. Even more central to her public self is her identity as mother to her three children. She defines herself primarily through her relationship to her family by telling funny stories about her life with them, sans father or any other adult, thus recasting mundane familial life.

They are comedians who have mostly addressed mixed audiences as entertainers first, and have forged long careers in a variety of mass media. This is in distinction to performance artists or others like gay and lesbian comics who address more specialized and politicized audiences. As what can be termed "mainstream entertainers," the queer feminist cultural work they do is at times explicitly feminist but is at its subversive best when it is not topically political. It is uniquely useful because it addresses a common public from a queer place.

What Is So Funny about Queer?

A useful definition of queer for my purposes is Alexander Doty's, developed in his book, *Making Things Perfectly Queer*. For Doty, queer is not a fixed category of identity but what he calls "an open and flexible space" (xv). "Queerness . . . is a quality related to any expression that can be marked as contra-, non-, or anti-straight" (xv). It is a purposely imprecise word, as its primary aim is to challenge strict demarcations of sexual and gendered identities. It can be applied to any "binary outlaw" (xvi). Ian Barnard, further makes the point that queer is not the opposite of straight. He writes, "Queer doesn't seem to have a clearly definable polar opposite, except, perhaps non-queer, a category whose content is as difficult to specify as queer itself is a slippery identity" (11). As different as they are from each other, what all these comedians share is that they refuse a sexual binary of heterosexual/homosexual. There is no singular claim of identity, or object of desire. Most important here is that queer challenges heteronormativity, another term that can be defined for our purposes borrowing from Samuel Chambers:

Heternormativity means, quite simply, that heterosexuality is the norm, in culture, in society, in politics. . . . Heteronormativity emphasizes the extent to which everyone, straight or queer, will be judged, measured, probed and evaluated from the perspective of the heterosexual norm. It means that everyone and everything is judged from the perspective of straight. (178)

By intervening into such deeply naturalized social arrangements, these comedians "make heterosexuality strange" (134) as Richard Dyer notes we must do to denaturalize it. They do it by occupying liminal sexual space: by refusing heteronormativity and not claiming homosexuality. Through a variety of media including stand-up live shows, videos, cable specials, television series, appearances on talk shows, books, and web production, they create public personae that encourage spectators to identify with a queer subject positioning, or in the gap, the space, that is not straight or gay.

The queer gesture in humor, and the humorous gesture in queer, is 5 the mining of this liminality. I rely here on a conception of humor developed by philosopher Simon Critchley. His argument is that what we find deeply funny, what he calls "true humor," are the social forms, structures, and categories which we are able to see as arbitrarily set—including those that are internal to our own subjectivities—and our understanding that we have a blind attachment to and investment in

"Queerness and humor both work through a willingness to delve into an indeterminate space between formal structures or categories that define normative human life."

them. Critchley defines what he calls "true humor" in his book, *On Humor*: "Humor is precisely the exploration of the break between nature and culture, which reveals the human to be not so much a category itself as a negotiation between categories" (29). That is, we laugh at the recognition that our very state of being is unstable, and often lies in between the seemingly stable categories. We laugh when we see the seams exposed, and can identify it as a common human experience.

Humor is by definition social because we laugh out of feeling connected to others in this experience, defined by this liminal state, and our being caught slipping out of our stable façade. Queerness and humor both work through a willingness to delve into an indeterminate space between formal structures or categories that define normative human life. The experience of the indeterminacy of the categories we count on to operate in public is what is exploited to make us laugh, and queer is the exploration of the slippage from straight. Critchley writes that humor produces "a consciousness of contingency" (10). The same, of course, can be said of queer. This common principle makes humor an effective vehicle in which to explore queer politics. The large number of contemporary women comedians who can be read as queer testifies to the nice fit between strategies; and the long history of camp among men, especially in mainstream contexts, is another example of the compelling blend between humor and queer.[1]

The blend works so well because "true humor" is more about us laughing at ourselves—and specifically the contradictions within ourselves—than at others, and according to Critchley, "does not wound a specific victim and always contains self-mockery" (12). It works by pointing to the liminality of human existence, and our shared experience of that. By exploring the lines between our spiritual and animal natures, and between all of the other significant binaries through which we define our human experience, we not only acknowledge the limitations we share as humans, but that also then means that we do not rely on an Other to make us laugh. "True humor" always involves a level of identification, the opposite of Othering. Queer perspectives facilitate Critchley's description of "true humor" through the denaturalizing and destabilizing of sexual structures and identities, landing us in the liminal space of gender and sexuality, and finding the humor in the recognition that the stable veneer of gender and sexuality is not true for anyone, including ourselves.

Tomlin, Cho, and Poundstone have developed funny, queer public personae over many years in many media, and that history is part of the meaning they make. The creation of a queer space is not found so much in one joke, or a series or jokes, or a self-conscious construction of queerness, but in a body of work over an extended period of time that creates a queer public presence.

Lily Tomlin

Tomlin has been a well-loved television, film, and performance comic since 1969, when she debuted on *Laugh-In*. Most well-known for the characters she began to create on that show, she also developed a reputation for her commitment to feminist politics, and although there was no elaborate charade to closet her sexuality, she did not publicly discuss it. For most of her career she operated publicly as a single woman in a not very well-kept secret about her partnership with her writer, Jane Wagner. Tomlin's body of work is quite large; I focus here on one bit from the mid-1970s when she was at the height of her fame for the characters she performed like Edith Ann, Ernestine, Mrs. Beasley, and Sister Boogie Woman, among many others.

At this point, reviews of her work and profiles of her life observe consistently that her characterizations are particularly rich and moving because they are not set up for the audience to laugh at, but make room to identify with.[2] Interestingly, she is also often noted to be mysterious in terms of her personal life. Embedded in the praise and admiration of her ability to bring such humanity to her characters is the assertion that we do not know who Lily Tomlin actually is. There is a gap where her personal story should be in a dominant culture that did not have a place for lesbian subjectivity that was not pathologized. Although not labeled queer, Tomlin occupied a queer subject position at that time. Not quite straight and not explicitly lesbian, Tomlin's very persona, constructed through her work and the commentary about her work and her person, presented a subject outside the bounds of heteronormativity.

Her characters were not necessarily queer, but the perspective she offered in the performance of them often was. As Suzanne Lavin argues in her book, *Women and Comedy in Solo Performance*, many of Tomlin's characters were women who suffered under the constrictions of womanhood. I would add here that it was the confines of straight womanhood in particular that oppressed them. Mrs. Beasley, for example, is a character Tomlin has done in many contexts over decades. The comedy in that character comes from the prudish-seeming, un-self-aware, trapped housewife that we both laugh at and with. That is, Mrs. Beasley is married and lives a very ordinary and stifled life, but we are not led to see her as a victim, nor as a hero or a martyr. We are to read her as "a real person, like yourself," as she says so often. She is positioned as a woman trapped by the terms set up by ordinary heteronormative life, and we identify with her humanity. There is no simple object of ridicule in this character, including her, even as there is plenty to laugh at about her. This characterization is typical for Tomlin in that she "does not wound a specific victim and always contains self-mockery" (Critchley 12). That is, one of the things Tomlin consistently does is make us cognizant that what we are laughing at are the social structures in which we are all haplessly implicated.

A more explicitly queer position is evident in her piece, "Tell Miss Sweeney Goodbye." This bit appeared on her album *Lily Tomlin: Onstage*, which is from her 1970s Broadway show *Appearing Nitely* and has been performed in different venues, including the 1986 benefit performance in Los Angeles at the NOW twentieth-year anniversary celebration, and is part of her "An Evening of Classic Lily Tomlin," currently touring the

United States. In this monologue, Tomlin both narrates as her adult self and experiences, as her second-grade self, her infatuation with her teacher, Miss Sweeney. She captures the essence of an enthusiastic, smart little girl who moves from a feeling of humiliation and alienation to the first day of second grade when she "finds the best reason in the whole world to like school. Miss Sweeney." The child Tomlin is entranced by Miss Sweeney's look, and voice and laugh. She says, "I could always make her laugh when I wanted to, and I almost always wanted to." The bit goes into the rich fantasy life of this girl, intensely attached to her teacher. Part of the fantasy is about where she fits in with Miss Sweeney and her boyfriend. She envisions the boyfriend coming to see Miss Sweeney and says, "I couldn't see them, but I knew exactly what they were doing. And my blood was pounding at the thought of monogram pushing against monogram." She is sure he will ask her to be in their wedding and to come live with them.

The performance takes seriously the queer desires and complex feelings of love of a seven-year-old girl in a very funny and touching exploration that at once particularizes and generalizes her experience. As is true of all of Tomlin's character work, "Tell Miss Sweeney Goodbye" makes the audience laugh with a feeling of identification and not objectification. In this bit in particular, when combined with Tomlin's position outside of the heteronormative paradigm, in a liminal sexual space herself, we are encouraged to read the queer there—the longing that is not contained in the normative subjectivity of a little girl. This characterization bursts those seams, first by staging a little girl with complex desires at all: for recognition, for knowledge, and for Miss Sweeney. It also takes it out of heteronormativity and drops it in no particular place at all. So while it directs us out of heteronormativity, it does not direct us necessarily to a next place—it allows us to linger in the space created there, with no fixed destination.

Paula Poundstone

Poundstone performs in a suit and tie, has long hair and wears red lipstick. She could easily pass as a lesbian, but has consistently denied those rumors by saying that she is not interested in sex with anyone, and calling herself "nonsexual" in interviews, in her book, and on stage. In her Bravo special *Look What the Cat Dragged In* (2006), she interrupts a story about writing her book to say:

I don't like sex at all. There it's been said. . . . I'm sure there is something horribly wrong with me sexually; I have no doubt of that. And that if I went to a

*sex therapist every day and talked for hours and journaled and took medication
and watched educational films and worked with plastic figurines, I'm sure that
it could be overcome . . . but quite honestly from where I am sitting now I can't
imagine any physical sensation that I would enjoy more than sleep. I'm a single
working mom with three kids, ten cats, a big stupid dog, a bearded dragon lizard, a bunny, and an ant farm. I don't go to bed at night. I pass out. The idea
that I go to my bedroom at night and there'd be someone in there with whom I
had to have another activity . . . is just upsetting to me.*

In this bit, she gives a couple of reasons: exhaustion and possible
pathology. Of course, she is making fun of the idea of pathologizing
what feels normal to her. In interviews she gives other reasons, like,

*I honestly thought that you weren't supposed to be sexually active until you were
an adult. It was behavior that was not good. So by the time I was an adult, I was
so far behind. Apparently nobody else followed that rule. By the time I became
an adult, I was back in the beginner class. Everybody else was a scary expert on
the diamond trail. And I didn't want anything to do with anybody. (Kusner 3)*

In her book, *There Is Nothing in This Book I Meant to Say*, she interrupts her
chapter on Helen Keller to write: "I am not a sexual person. I don't have
sex. My manager does, though, and knowing that has, so far, been enough
for me" (71–72). She goes on to tell a story that her manager told her about
her own sexual encounter with a mutual acquaintance that ends with her
telling Poundstone that the guy wanted to be tied up to her headboard:

*I screamed with laughter and a dash of outrage when she told me. I asked if
she could have just written him out a citation this time and wait till their
next date to actually handcuff him. Part of me felt bad for having such an im-
mature reaction to the story. I know I am the one who is different here, but I cannot relate at all. I could never tell anybody what I want. I'm too shy. I couldn't
even tell someone, "Could you move your foot? You're stepping on my neck." (72)*

Her active lack of interest in sex is a continual, if tangential preoccupation. It is an important part of her identity. Her discussion about it
though, does not make it a problem to be solved. In fact, it works on the
kind of self-mockery that invites identification, and thus connection. To
laugh at these jokes is to laugh at the relatable fear of intimacy many
people share, but it is not dependent on a particular object of desire, or
lack thereof. It is also to laugh at the absurdity of the rules of normative
adulthood, which of course are deeply intertwined with heteronormativity. At the same time, her take on her own sexuality explicitly pushes

against the social norms of heterosexual womanhood, without pointing to another particular destination.

Combined with her gender-bending signature look, Poundstone plays 15
with gender as well. She was the correspondent for *The Tonight Show* in 1993 to President Clinton's first inaugural. There is a bit she does that is available on the video-sharing web site, youtube.com, in which she gets lessons from an expert in etiquette, Marjebelle Stewart. Poundstone appears awkward in a taffeta lavender dress with a plunging neckline, pearls, gloves, and hair ornaments and takes her lessons on how to sit and stand and shake hands very seriously. Appearing in what looks like drag, she highlights the disjuncture between sex and gender, even as she is not claiming lesbian space.

Drag has been more readily used by men than by women as a way to play with the sex/gender system.[3] The campy performance of gender made famous by drag queens has a long and noble tradition as a comedic strategy, and as a queer strategy, as Judith Butler made clear in *Gender Trouble*. By denaturalizing femininity (not to mention middle-class manners) from a female-identified body, Poundstone queers the drag queen tradition. Looking as unnatural and awkward as a male-bodied performer might in a taffeta dress, Poundstone emphasizes here the absolute put-on of this version of femininity, while deemphasizing the binary opposition that normally is part of the joke.

Margaret Cho

Cho's very different style starts with her look, which is much more conventionally feminine, and she talks about sex all the time. She talks about gay male sex, and her own sex life with men and women. She is explicitly political in her work and talks about the many ways racism, misogyny, and homophobia manifest themselves in contemporary culture. The way she talks about sex is always within a politicized context, and the aim of the joke is not an Other, but a hypocritical social system. She is well-known for having starred in the first sitcom about an Asian American family in 1994, called *All-American Girl*, and for exposing the racist and sexist machinations in the production of that show in her first one-woman comedy show, *I'm the One That I Want* (1999). She went on to produce film versions of her stand-up shows, *Notorious C.H.O* (2001), *Revolution* (2003), *Assassin* (2005), and *Beautiful* (2009).

Cho grew up in San Francisco in the 1970s and 1980s and credits the gay men and drag queens she knew there for teaching her how to be herself and be courageous about it. "If it were not for gay men, I would not talk to men at all . . . I am heterophobic," she said in *I'm the One That*

I Want. In one bit in *I'm the One That I Want,* she talks about her experience as a comic on a lesbian cruise and ends up saying:

I had sex with a woman on ship. And I went through this whole thing . . . Am I gay? Am I straight? And I realized, I'm just slutty . . .

That has been her basic stance ever since.

On her blog, for example, she wrote in September 2008:

Regarding Palin°
Tuesday, September 23rd, 2008
I am being accused of sexually objectifying Sarah Palin, and I did it because I think it is funny—mostly because she is anti-gay, and would like people like me to be sent to a camp where we can study the bible with other gays and lesbians and have electrodes placed on our privates until we are forced to become heterosexual—like her and um, Track. So I said I would like to do rude things to her, because frankly, I like pussy, and I am not giving it up anytime soon—no matter what the "Christians" have to say about it. Gay sex is monumentally more fun than straight sex. God made it that way, so we would stay gay! He wants us to persevere! Stay strong!! Gay sex is better than straight sex. Sorry, it just is—I should know—I have liberal amounts of both. And Sarah Palin is missing out.

And in an interview in 2009: "I refer to myself as gay, but I am married to a man. Of course, I've had relationships with women, but my politics are more queer than my lifestyle." She married artist/writer/straight man Al Ridenour in 2003, and says they have a different relationship than most: "It's not a traditional situation. It's not a committed marriage. We're just friends who share space. My parents don't understand it. They just send us Yahoo E-cards wishing us well" (Leo). Her parents are fixtures in her public life, and were regulars on her 2008 VH1 reality show, *The Cho Show,* but her husband was not mentioned. Cho's public persona is clearly explicitly queer. She uses a variety of media to craft a self-conscious queer image.

However, all of these comedians play with the form, the structure of heterosexuality, and they maintain occupancy outside of its terms. That is feminist simply because from the position of women, it necessarily means refusing the position of object to men's subject. It is queer because they do it without another narrowly-defined sexual identity or object of desire that would justify their choices, or make them comprehensible in the

Palin: Sarah Palin was the former governor of Alaska and vice presidential nominee of the Republican Party in the 2008 election.

terms of heteronormativity. Over a span of at least 30 years, through many different media, using very different strategies, all of these comedians create queer feminist cultural interventions, addressed to large audiences.

Central to Cho's queer persona is her outrageous image. She is quoted on her blog in the press for *Beautiful*, "This show is really about how we should feel beautiful. When you feel beautiful, you're going to have more of a willingness to use your voice to speak. And there are a lot of dick jokes. A whole lot." This is one of innumerable examples of Cho moving outside of acceptable womanhood to position herself as indifferent to men's approval. Poundstone's performance of her distance from, and discomfort with, conventional femininity combined with her verbal dexterity and quick wit, especially in her long interactions with audience members, removes her from normative feminine subjectivity. Tomlin's characterizations of women caught in the trap of gender and her own very public feminist politics also make her challenges to dominant gender systems very clear. For all of them, the break from heteronormativity is explicit, but not dependent on realigning with another singular sexual identity. In a context of feminist, or even postfeminist consciousness, the queer intervention they make is in the still-naturalized normative power of heterosexuality. The promise of both queer and humor here, in mass mediated contexts, to very mixed audiences, is the emotional opening they both create and exploit.

Notes

1. Alexander Doty writes about this in his *Making Things Perfectly Queer*. The classic work on this topic is perhaps Esther Newton's *Mother Camp: Female Impersonators in America*, U of Chicago P, 1979.

2. A representative list of articles from the mid-1970s, when Tomlin was getting the most attention for her character work includes: Louise Bernikow, "Excuse me, do you know who Lily Tomlin is?" in *Playboy* July 1976; Ellen Cohn "Lily Tomlin: Not Just a Funny Girl," *New York Times Magazine* June 6, 1976; Jack Kroll, "Funny Lady," *Newsweek* March 28, 1977; Cover Story, "Lily . . . Ernestine . . . Tess . . . Lupe . . . Edith Ann . . ." *Time* March 28, 1977; Vito Russo, "A Special Interview Starring Lily Tomlin," *The Advocate* January 14, 1976; Tracy Young "Don't try to laugh along with Lily Tomlin," *New Times* May 27, 1977.

3. See for example, Jill Dolan, *The Feminist Spectator as Critic*, University of Michigan Press, 1988, and Judith Halberstam, *Female Masculinity*, Duke University Press, 1998.

Works Cited

Barnard, Ian. *Queer Race: Cultural Interventions in the Racial Politics of Queer Theory.* New York: Peter Lang, 2003.

Chambers, Samuel A. "Revisiting the Closet: Reading Sexuality in *Six Feet Under.*" *Reading Six Feet Under.* Eds. Kim Akass and Janet McCabe. New York: I.B. Taurus, 2005. 174–190.

Cho, Margaret. www.margaretcho.com/blog. Accessed May 18, 2009.

Cho, Margaret. *I'm the One That I Want.* Video Recording 1999.

Critchley, Simon. *On Humour.* New York: Routledge, 2002.

Doty, Alexander. *Making Things Perfectly Queer.* Minneapolis: U of Minnesota P, 1993.

Dyer, Richard. "Straight Acting." *The Matter of Images: Essays on Representations.* New York: Routledge, 1993, 133–136.

Kusner, Daniel A. "Androgynous, Asexual, and Amply Amusing." *Dallas Voice* June 28, 2007. yahoo.com/transgendernews. May 2009.

Lavin, Suzanne. *Women and Comedy in Solo Performance: Phyllis Diller, Lily Tomlin and Roseanne.* New York: Routledge, 2004.

Leo, Alex. "Margaret Cho: I Refer to Myself as Gay, but I Am Married to a Man," HuffingtonPost.com. March 28, 2009. May 2009.

Poundstone, Paula. *Look What the Cat Dragged In.* Live Performance recorded by Bravo TV, November 2006.

Poundstone, Paula. *There Is Nothing in This Book I Meant to Say.* New York: Three Rivers P, 2006.

Tomlin, Lily. *Lily Tomlin: Onstage.* Sound recording BMG, 2003.

Understanding the Text

1. How does Reed define *heteronormativity*?

2. What makes queer comedians queer, according to Reed? How does she use Simon Critchley's concept of "true humor" to support her assertions about "the compelling blend between humor and queer" (par. 6).

3. How do Lily Tomlin, Paula Poundstone, and Margaret Cho each perform queerness in their comedy? What similarities and differences exist between these comedians' queer identities?

Reflection and Response

4. Reed attributes Tomlin's success to her audience's ability to identify with the characters she performs. What comedians or comic characters do you identify with and why? Would you characterize any of them as queer "sexual outlaws"?

5. Margaret Cho makes an interesting comment when she says that her "politics are more queer than [her] lifestyle" (par. 19). Do you agree with Cho's assumption that one's politics can differ from one's lifestyle? Explain your answer.

Making Connections

6. Reed relies heavily on the work of Simon Critchley, who also appears in Chapter 2 of this text. How does Critchley's argument in "Foreigners are

Funny" (p. 79) relate to Reed's article? How is queer "true humor" unlike ethnic humor? Conversely, how is ethnic humor akin to heteronormative and sexist humor?

7. Research and write about the history of women stand-up comedians in the twentieth and twenty-first centuries. Use at least one book and one academic article on the subject as secondary sources to support your argument.

8. Write an analytical profile piece about a stand-up comedian in the model of Reed's discussions of Lily Tomlin, Paula Poundstone, and Margaret Cho. Address this comedian's comic persona and performance style. Does he or she do characters and imitations, or does he or she play a version of him- or herself by telling jokes that are personal and more or less autobiographical? How would you characterize the identity politics of this comedian?

FourOaks / Getty Images

4

Purpose: What Is the Function of Satire in a Democratic Society?

C omic agents, like those from the previous chapter, have at least one purpose in common: they want to make the audience laugh. Depending on the act and the scene, the message and the context, their comedy may also be motivated by other goals and aspirations. A comedian may aim to educate, outrage, philosophize, ridicule, provide relief, break the ice, cope with dire circumstances, rail against injustice, connect with others, entertain, and, of course, get paid. Regardless of the specific purpose, the comic performer wields influence by making us laugh. Comic agents may affirm, offend, challenge, or up-end our values, opinions, sensibilities, and even behaviors. In short, they exercise the powers of persuasion.

This chapter concentrates on the purpose of a particular genre of humor: satire. The *Oxford English Dictionary* defines *satire* as "the use of humor, irony, exaggeration, or ridicule to expose and criticize people's stupidity or vices, particularly in the context of contemporary politics and other topical issues." In other words, satire is a kind of comedy that exhibits an ethical purpose — to reform those guilty of folly or wickedness — that depends on a concomitant sociological purpose — to understand the social roots and implications of immoral ideas and behaviors. Because the genre requires the public use of reason, it has democratic origins, having derived from ancient Greek society and flourished during the Enlightenment, when the Western world transformed from medieval to modern beginning in the sixteenth century.

Satire can be classified by its intended target and the severity of its criticism. The plays of the ancient Greek Aristophanes lampooned people and institutions. A recent example of this sort of satire would be the late Robin Williams's definition of *politics*: a combination of *poli*, a Latin word meaning "many," and *tics*, meaning "bloodsucking creatures." Menippean satire, on the other hand, skewers general mental attitudes, which come to be embodied by social types like the bigot (e.g., Archie Bunker from

All in the Family) and the seducer (e.g., Barney Stinson from *How I Met Your Mother*). The aforementioned targets of satire can be subjected to the mild and lighthearted mockery of Horatian satire, which gently reprimands folly, or the abrasive and contemptuous derision of Juvenalian satire, which savagely ridicules evil. The type of satire you choose should match your purpose, topic, and audience. You may satirize your friends and folks you like, for example, to make them better, and your enemies and people you don't like to take them down a notch. When the line between the two becomes unclear, as it did with Stephen Colbert's roast of President George W. Bush at the 2006 White House Correspondents' Dinner, controversy ensues.

In the interest of narrowing the scope of this chapter further, the following reading selections all examine political satire within the context of contemporary democratic society — a highly relevant topic considering how tenuous popular government is these days. The chapter begins with two selections that assess the role of satire in the wake of the recent *Charlie Hebdo* shooting in 2015, in which two members of the terrorist group Al Qaeda attacked the offices of the French satirical newspaper *Charlie Hebdo*, killing 11 and injuring 11 others. Millions of people, including over 40 world leaders, met in Paris days later for a national unity rally and marched under the slogan *Je suis Charlie* ("I am Charlie"). The demonstration attempted to draw a clear line of demarcation between those in solidarity with freedom of speech and those sympathetic to terrorism. Needless to say, the issue is more complex than this simple either/or dichotomy. Since being founded in 1970, *Charlie Hebdo* has incited controversy for its incendiary depictions, especially its offensive cartoons of Muslims and the Islamic prophet Muhammad. Cartoonist Joe Sacco uses his medium to criticize *Charlie Hebdo*'s satire for being "vapid" and to depict the reaction from freedom of speech advocates as being motivated more by anger than reason. In the following essay, author Tim Parks agrees with Sacco but adds that globalization has complicated the purpose of satire because publications are now read online by people who do not share the same values or ethical codes.

The chapter's remaining readings trace a genealogy of political satire in the United States from the middle of the twentieth century to today. Academic Russell L. Peterson laments the cynical humor about current events in the stand-up routines of late-night talk-show hosts, which he contrasts with the genuine satire found — ironically enough — on fake news programs. *New Yorker* columnist Elizabeth Kolbert extends Peterson's analysis to the politicians who appear on late-night talk and variety shows and their use of preemptive self-mockery, which she views as an "unsettling development." Writer Steve Almond adopts a position contrary to Peterson's laudatory view of fake news satire, criticizing Jon Stewart and Stephen Colbert for engendering passivity and political disaffection. Amber Day, Assistant Professor of English and Cultural Studies, has a more positive take on parodic news shows, a genre she believes enjoys the success of satiric documentaries and ironic pranksters in turning comedy into a form of activism. *Harvard Political Review* writer Daniel J. Kenny, who caps off the chapter, agrees with Day's assessment, at least when it comes to *Last Week Tonight with John Oliver*, which he argues has supplanted its parodic news predecessors by doing political satire that closely resembles investigative journalism.

The tight-knit selections of this chapter form a coherent narrative on the purpose and efficacy of contemporary political satire. With further research, you will be able to write an argumentative essay that joins this important conversation about democratic humor. Thus, when reading the selections, consider the varied purposes of contemporary political satirists. What kinds of satire do they employ and to what end? What virtues do they defend in lashing the vices they target? How would the world be different if these satirists were taken as serious instead of only joking? What is the most effective form of contemporary political satire?

On Satire: A Response to the *Charlie Hebdo* Attacks

Joe Sacco

Joe Sacco is an award-winning cartoonist who lives in Portland, Oregon. Sacco, who is Maltese-American, works in the genre of comics journalism. He has commented on the Gulf, Bosnian, and Iraq Wars, as well as the Israeli-Palestinian conflict, with what *The Guardian* calls his "compelling combination of eyewitness reportage and graphic art storytelling techniques." His recent titles include *Days of Destruction, Days of Revolt* (2012), an account of poverty in the United States co-written with Chris Hedges; *The Great War* (2013), a 24-foot-long panorama of the first day of the Battle of the Somme; and *Bumf* (2014), a satire of Western foreign policy.

When reading Sacco's response to the *Charlie Hebdo* shooting, which was originally published by *The Guardian* in 2015, think about how he uses text and images to construct an argument about the purpose of satire.

First published in *The Guardian*. © Joe Sacco, 2015.

take the piss: a British colloquialism for taking liberties at the expense of others.

Understanding the Text

1. What is the purpose of the panels of the black man and of the Jew? How do these panels contribute to Sacco's overall argument? What other images does he use to get his point across?

2. Whom does Sacco satirize in this piece? Why does he choose this target?

3. Sacco titles this cartoon "On Satire." What central claim does he make about satire? In other words, what is his thesis?

Reflection and Response

4. Sacco writes that "satire is meant to cut to the bone. But whose bone? What exactly is the target? And why?" How would you answer these questions? What do you think is and is not an appropriate target for satire? Explain why you feel this way.

5. Because Sacco's cartoon strip represents his personal reaction to the *Charlie Hebdo* shooting, he uses the first-person pronoun "I" and draws a cartoon version of himself in the text. Reflect on Sacco's self-depictions and the ethos he creates in this piece. Does the fact that Sacco shares the occupation of the victims give him a certain authority to comment on this event?

Making Connections

6. Sacco mentions that when cartoonists "draw a line, [they] are often crossing one too." Many of the readings in Chapter 2 deal with the line between humorous and offensive material. Use Sacco's piece as well as selections from Chapter 2 to write an essay on when and where satire *should* cross the line.

7. Research *Charlie Hebdo*'s brand of satire, especially its controversial anti-Islamic images; look into the firing of Maurice Sinet that Sacco mentions; and read the reactions to the shooting from a variety of sources, for example, the next selection in this chapter, which is from Tim Parks (p. 210). Then write an argumentative essay on satire and the *Charlie Hebdo* shooting.

8. Compose your own satirical cartoon on a target that you believe deserves to be ridiculed. Make sure to use both images and text to get your point across.

The Limits of Satire

Tim Parks

Tim Parks is Associate Professor of Literature and Translation at the University Institute for Modern Languages in Milan. He is a prolific novelist and, as an émigré to Italy, has written a handful of nonfiction books about his adopted country. He writes essays for the *London Review of Books* and a blog for the *New York Review of Books*, where "The Limits of Satire" was published in 2015.

In this response to the *Charlie Hebdo* shooting, Parks reminds us that, with satire, as with all forms of rhetoric, "Where we're coming from and who we're writing to is important" (par. 11). In a world connected by the internet, it becomes even more incumbent upon satirists to be aware of their own cultural assumptions as well as those of all kinds of different readers.

What does satire do? What should we expect of it? Recent events in Paris inevitably prompt these questions. In particular, is the kind of satire that *Charlie Hebdo* has made its trademark—explicit, sometimes obscene images of religious figures (God the Father, Son, and Holy Spirit sodomizing each other; Muhammad with a yellow star in his ass)— essentially different from mainstream satire? Is it crucial to Western culture that we be free to produce such images? Do they actually *work* as satire?

Neither straight journalism nor disengaged art, satire alludes to recognizable contemporary circumstances in a skewed and comic way so as to draw attention to their absurdity. There is mockery but with a noble motive: the desire to bring shame on some person or party behaving wrongly or ignorantly. Its *raison d'être*° over the long term is to bring about change through ridicule; or if change is too grand an aspiration, we might say that it seeks to give us a fresh perspective on the absurdities and evils we live among, such that we are eager for change.

Since satire has this practical and pragmatic purpose, the criteria for assessing it are fairly simple: if it doesn't point toward positive change, or encourage people to think in a more enlightened way, it has failed. That doesn't mean it's not amusing and well-observed, or even, for some, hilarious, in the way, say, witty mockery of a political enemy can be hilarious and gratifying and can intensify our sense of being morally superior. But as satire it has failed. The worst case is when satire reinforces the state of mind it purports to undercut, polarizes prejudices, and provokes the very behavior it condemns. This appears to be what happened with *Charlie Hebdo*'s images of Muhammad.

raison d'être: something's primary purpose.

Why so? Crucial to satire is the appeal to supposed "common sense" and a shared moral code. The satirist presents a situation in such a way that it appears grotesque and the reader who, whatever his or her private interests, shares the same cultural background and moral education agrees that it is so. The classic example, perhaps, is Jonathan Swift's *A Modest Proposal* of 1729. Swift's target was Protestant England's economic policy in Catholic Ireland and the disastrous poverty this had created. After paragraphs of statistics on population and nutrition, we arrive at the grotesque:

> "Crucial to satire is the appeal to supposed 'common sense' and a shared moral code."

I have been assured . . . that a young healthy child well nursed, is, at a year old, a most delicious nourishing and wholesome food, whether stewed, roasted, baked, or boiled; and I make no doubt that it will equally serve in a fricasie, or a ragoust.

By selling their children for food, the pamphlet claims, the poor can save themselves an expense and guarantee themselves an income. Disoriented, every reader is made aware of a simple principle we all share: you don't eat children, even Irish children, even Catholic children. So if those children are not to be left to starve, something else in Ireland will have to give.

This appeal to what we all know and share becomes more difficult 5 when satire addresses itself to people from different cultures with different traditions. In this regard, the history of *Charlie Hebdo* is worth noting. It grew out of a left-wing magazine, *Hara Kiri*, later *Hebdo Hara Kiri* (where Hebdo is simply short for *hebdomadaire*—"weekly"), which was formed in 1960 to address national political issues and subsequently banned on a number of occasions. When it was banned in 1970 over a mocking headline about Charles de Gaulle's° death, its editors reopened it under a different name to avoid the ban, calling it *Charlie Hebdo* to distinguish it from a monthly magazine, *Charlie*, that some of the same cartoonists were already running. Charlie was Charlie Brown, but also now, comically, Charles de Gaulle. Its focus was on French politics and when it was felt to have overstepped the mark, the democratically elected French government was in a position to impose a temporary closure. It was a French affair.

Wound down for lack of funds in 1981, *Charlie Hebdo* was resurrected in 1991 when cartoonists wanted to create a platform for political satire

---

Charles de Gaulle: (1890–1970) the eighteenth president, from 1958 to 1969, of France.

about the first Gulf War. With this explicitly international agenda, the relationship between satirists, readers, and targets became more complex. The readers were the same left-wing French public, used to seeing fierce attacks on all things sacred, but the targets sometimes lay outside France or at least outside mainstream French culture. In 2002 the magazine hosted an article supporting controversial Italian author Oriana Fallaci and her claims that Islam in general, not just the extremists, was on the march against the West. In 2006, *Charlie Hebdo*'s cartoons of Muhammad and reprint of the Danish cartoonist *Jyllands-Posten*'s controversial Muhammad cartoons led to the paper's selling 400,000 copies, rather than the normal 60,000 to 100,000. Popularity and notoriety had arrived through mockery of a target outside French culture but with which an aggrieved minority in France now identified.

Sued by the Grand Mosque, the Muslim World League, and the Union of French Islamic Organizations, the paper's editors defended themselves, insisting that their humor was aimed at violent extremists, not at Islam itself. Islamic organizations didn't see it that way. While President Chirac criticized satire that inflamed divisions between cultures, various politicians, Hollande and Sarkozy included, wrote to the court to defend the cartoonists, Sarkozy in particular referring to the ancient French tradition of satire. Eventually the court acquitted the paper and freedom of speech was upheld. But the effect of the cartoons had been to inflame moderate areas of Islam. The ancient French tradition of satire was creating more heat than light. It was also uniting French politicians usually opposed to each other against a perceived threat from without.

It is said, by contrast, that Christian leaders have now grown used to their religion being desecrated and pilloried in every way. This is not entirely the case. In 2011, *Charlie Hebdo* noted that while Muslims had sued the paper only once, the Catholic Church had launched thirteen cases against it. In the 1990s, writing satirical pieces for the Italian magazine *Comix*, I had my own experience of the difficulties of attacking the Church through satire. In this case too an issue of cultural blindness was involved. Reacting to yet another Vatican condemnation of abortion, even in cases of rape, I suggested that if the Catholic Church really cared about abortion it might perhaps change its position on contraception and actually manufacture condoms with images of the saints, or perhaps even prickly hair-shirt condoms, or San Sebastian condoms, so that love-making would be simultaneously an indulgence and a penitence, and people would be mindful of their Lord even between the sheets. *Comix* refused to publish.

This was not, I believe, a question of self-censorship or lack of courage on the magazine's part. The editors of *Comix* were perfectly ready to attack the Church on issues of abortion and birth control. They just didn't think that the idea of people having sex with condoms showing their favorite saint was the right way to go about it. Too many of their readers—mostly Catholic by culture if not practice—would be offended; it would not help them to get distance and perspective on the debate. Knowing Italy and Italians better now, I reckon they were right. It was my Protestant background and complete carelessness about images of saints and virgins that made me unaware of the kind of response the piece would have stirred up.

Most likely, however, that same Italian public would have had no problem with the drawings of Muhammad that provoked the massacre at *Charlie Hebdo* last week, because they, like me, but unlike the vast majority of Muslims, set no value on the image Muhammad. When I see *Charlie Hebdo*'s cartoon entitled "Muhammad overcome by fundamentalists," showing a weeping Muhammad saying, "It's tough being loved by assholes," I smile and take the point. For a Muslim reader perhaps the point is lost in the offense of a belittling representation of a figure they hold sacred.

Where we're coming from and who we're writing to is important. Not all readers are the same. In *The Satanic Verses* (1988), Salman Rushdie includes a dream sequence where the prostitutes have the names of Muhammad's wives. There are also various provocative reinterpretations of Islam, but certainly nothing that would disturb a Western reader, and in fact the novel was on the shortlist for Britain's Booker Prize for fiction without even a smell of scandal in the air. Only as publication was approaching in India and the paper *India Today* ran an interview with Rushdie did the controversy begin in earnest, with riots, deaths, and eventually the Ayatollah Khomeini's *fatwa* calling for Muslims to kill Rushdie.

It is, in short, this mixing of cultures and immediate globalization of so many publications through the internet that makes satire more problematic as the Swiftian appeal to the values we share becomes more elusive. In the *Inferno* Dante could imagine Muhammad in hell, his body obscenely split open—"from the chin right down to where men fart"—as fit punishment for his crime of religious schism. *The Divine Comedy* was not intended for publication in India. Needless to say any such representation of Christ would have been unthinkable.

The following questions arise: Now that the whole world is my neighbor, my immediate internet neighbor, do I make any concessions at all, or do I uphold the ancient tradition of satire at all costs? And again, is a culture that takes mortal offense when an image it holds sacred is mocked a second-rate culture that needs to be dragged kicking and screaming into the twenty-first century, *my* twenty-first century, that is? Do I have the moral authority to decide this?

In his response to the attack on *Charlie Hebdo* in Paris, the cartoonist Joe Sacco makes the distinction between the right to free expression and the sensible use of it. One might be free, he says, to draw—as he does to illustrate—a black man falling out of a tree with a banana in his hand, or a Jew counting money over the entrails of the working class, but of what possible use are these images? And actually, of course, we're not free. In Italy and Germany it is illegal to display certain images that recall Fascism and Nazism. Denial of the Holocaust is a crime in France. In the United States and Britain, our freedom—in practice—to indulge in racist, anti-Semitic, misogynist, and homophobic insults has been notably limited, at least since the late 1980s when notions of "political correctness" became increasingly pervasive. Even *Charlie Hebdo* fired a cartoonist for anti-Semitism. None of these restrictions have proved a great loss, at least for me.

Joe Sacco's take on the tragedy in Paris is smart. In raising the question of the usefulness or otherwise of a cartoon, rather than remaining fixated on the question of freedom of speech, he reminds us of the essentially pragmatic nature of satire. However grotesque and provocative its comedy, its aim is to produce an enlightened perspective on events, not to start riots. At this point, and notwithstanding a profound sense of horror for the evil and stupidity of the terrorist attack on the magazine's offices, one has to wonder about *Charlie Hebdo*'s pride in constantly dubbing themselves a "Journal Irresponsable." The current edition of the paper [January 14, 2015] shows Muhammad in such a way that his white turban looks like two balls and his long pink face a penis. The Prophet is being dubbed a prick. He holds a *Je suis Charlie* placard and announces that all is forgiven. The print run was extended to 5 million copies after a first run of 3 million sold out; this up from a standard run of 60,000. Is it likely this approach will help to isolate violent extremists from mainstream Muslim sentiment?

Understanding the Text

1. How does Parks define satire? What does Parks mean when he identifies the purpose of satire as "pragmatic" (pars. 3, 15)?

2. What has made satire more problematic in contemporary times? How does the history of *Charlie Hebdo* exemplify the difficulty of assessing satire's effectiveness?

3. How does the personal anecdote in pars. 8 and 9 support Park's overall argument? What is his overall argument? What other pieces of evidence does he provide to support his thesis?

Reflection and Response

4. Parks asks a series of questions in paragraph 13. How would you answer these questions?

5. Parks lauds cartoonist Joe Sacco's "take on the tragedy in Paris [as] smart" (par. 15). Did reading Parks's essay alter your perspective of Sacco's cartoon (p. 208)? Why or why not?

6. What is your take on the quality of satire produced by *Charlie Hebdo*? Write a response to Sacco's and Parks's reflections on satire in the wake of this event.

Making Connections

7. Parks notes that defenders of *Charlie Hebdo* placed the publication within "the ancient French tradition of satire" (par. 7). Does the United States have a tradition, albeit shorter, of satire? Are there American examples of satire raising problems with freedom of speech? Write an essay on a particular strand of American satire.

8. In a 2015 article for *BBC Magazine* entitled "What's the Point of Satire," novelist Will Self compares the objective of satire with a famous description of journalism: each should "comfort the afflicted and afflict the comfortable." Would Sacco and Parks agree with Self? Write an essay in which you respond to Self's claim on the purpose of satire. Cite specific examples of historical satire or satire on current events to support your assertions.

Losing Our Religion

Russell L. Peterson

Russell L. Peterson teaches American Studies at Iowa University, where he serves as an Adjunct Assistant Professor. This excerpt comes from the first chapter of his book, *Strange Bedfellows: How Late-Night Comedy Turns Democracy into a Joke*, which was published by Rutgers University Press in 2008. In his wide-ranging discussion, Peterson distinguishes between the political comedy of genuine satire and the anti-political comedy of mainstream late-night comics. He argues that, in contrast to satire's upholding of democratic principles, the comedy found on late-night network television breeds cynicism that undermines a government of, by, and for the people.

On the second Saturday after Easter [in 2006], the city of Washington, D.C., witnessed a miracle of sorts. The president of the United States appeared before the assembled members of the White House Correspondents Association accompanied by an uncanny doppelgänger. This apparent clone, who stood stage right of the commander in chief at a matching podium, not only looked and sounded like George W. Bush, he seemed to give voice to the president's subconscious thoughts: "Here I am at another one of these dang press dinners. Could be home asleep, little Barney curled up at my feet. Nooo. I gotta pretend I like being here. Being here really ticks me off. The way they try to embarrass me by not editing what I say. Well, let's get things going so I can get to bed."[1]

The president's double, actor Steve Bridges, did a heckuva job reproducing his voice and gestures, and the crowd loved it. The members of the media elite erupted in laughter when George W. Bush's "inner voice" pronounced the first lady *"muy caliente."* It was the funniest and most elaborate presidential comedy routine since Bill Clinton's "Final Days" video, back in 2000.

But this wasn't the miracle, just a clever bit of stagecraft. The miracle came after the Dueling Bushes routine, when Comedy Central's faux pundit Stephen Colbert stepped up to the lectern. What he said was not in itself so remarkable; the content of his routine was very much of a piece with the tongue-in-cheek right-wing pontificating seen four nights a week on *The Colbert Report*—a few of the jokes were even recycled from the show. What made his monologue startling—even awe-inspiring—was the fact that although the primary target of Colbert's ironic attack, the president of the United States, was sitting not six feet away from him, he pulled nary a punch. "The greatest thing about this man is, he's steady," proclaimed the comedian, with his impenetrable mock-sincerity. "You know where he stands. He believes the same thing Wednesday that he believed on Monday, no matter what happened Tuesday. Events can change; this man's beliefs never will." The president squirmed, his mottled face betraying the effort behind a strained smile. The audience, who had greeted the Bush/Bridges act with full-throated laughter, now sounded subdued, lapsing at times into uncomfortable silence. Colbert appeared undaunted. It was a brave and bracing performance, demonstrating what the comedian would call (in character) *muchos huevos grandes*.

That we live in a country where one can publicly criticize the head of state is, of course, a kind of miracle in itself, one we perhaps too often take for granted. But to see *this* president—whose administration has specialized in intimidating critics and marginalizing dissent—mocked so mercilessly, to his face, in front of a cozy gathering of Washington insiders (who would suffer their own share of Colbert's satirical punishment that night), was like witnessing Moses calling down a plague of frogs on Pharaoh and his courtiers. That is, if Moses had been funny.

Yet the mainstream media, whose shindig this was, appeared to leave   5
all memory of Colbert's astonishing performance in the banquet hall, along with the parsley on their plates. Monday morning's *New York Times* ran a bubbly account of the president's "double" routine without so much as mentioning Colbert's name. Television news, both network and cable, followed suit, fawning over the video of the Bush "twins" as if it were the latest baby panda footage but avoiding any reference to the evening's controversial headliner.[2]

While the diners and the media corporations they represented seemed to be experiencing selective amnesia, though, the internet was going Colbert-crazy. Liberal blogs sang his praises, while conservative commentators condemned him for disrespecting the nation's chief executive (something most of them had little problem countenancing when that office was held by Bill Clinton). Someone launched a "Thank You, Stephen Colbert" web page, which in no time had registered the gratitude of thousands of netizens who felt that President Bush had for too long been treated far too gently by the mainstream press.[3]

When this cyber-rumbling began to grow too loud to ignore, a few members of the diners' club decided they had better say something. But they succeeded only in proving their critics right: the mainstream media's belated response to Colbert was characterized by groupthink and a preoccupation with style over substance. (Sure, his jokes pointed out some unpleasant truths, but did he have to be so blunt about it?) "The only thing worse than the mainstream media's ignoring Stephen Colbert's astonishing sendup of the Bush administration and its media courtiers," wrote *Salon*'s Joan Walsh, "is what happened when they started

Former President Bush (left) looks on as Colbert (right) mocks him at the White House Correspondents' Dinner.
AFP/Getty Images

to pay attention to it." Indeed, from *Hardball*'s human airhorn Chris Matthews—who began his Siskel-and-Ebert bit with fellow irony-challenged critic Mike Allen of *Time* magazine by asking, "Why was he [Colbert] so bad?"—to Lloyd Grove of the *Daily News* to the *New York Observer*'s Christopher Lehman to alternative-media-emeritus Ana Marie Cox (formerly of the Wonkette blog, now safely ensconced in the media mainstream as a Time-Warner columnist, cable news bloviator, and, incidentally, Mrs. Christopher Lehman), the pundit establishment seemed to be on the same page. "The dreary consensus," noted Walsh, was that "Colbert just wasn't funny."[4]

What is and isn't funny is, of course, a subjective judgment, but there may have been more to this near-unanimity among the top tier of television and print journalists—who happen to comprise most of the guest list at events like the White House Correspondents Dinner—than the fact that they all share remarkably similar tastes. "Why so defensive?" asked the *Washington Post*'s media critic, Dan Froomkin.[5] Perhaps it was because a mere comedian had not only embarrassed the press corps's guest of honor but had also shown up his hosts by beating them at what was supposed to be their own game: speaking truth to power. The Fourth Estate is called that because it is meant to act as an extragovernmental check on the judicial, legislative, and executive branches. But the news media's compliant behavior in the wake of 9/11 and the run-up to the invasion of Iraq, their failure to aggressively pursue a raft of administration scandals, and even the cozy ritual of the Correspondents Dinner itself belie that adversarial ideal. Colbert used the occasion to backhandedly chide the press for their lazy complicity: "Here's how it works: the president makes decisions. He's the decider. The press secretary announces those decisions, and you people of the press type those decisions down. Make, announce, type. Just put 'em through a spell check and go home. . . . Write that novel you got kicking around in your head. You know, the one about the intrepid Washington reporter with the courage to stand up to the administration. You know—fiction!"

It's hard to imagine a sharper critique of the press's failure to act as a watchdog, short of hitting Wolf Blitzer in the schnozz with a rolled-up newspaper. Colbert's real achievement, however, lies not in policing the standards of another profession but in asserting those of his own: for if "speaking truth to power" is part of the journalist's job, it is the satirist's primary mission—a higher calling, in fact, than merely being funny.

But if Colbert was just doing his job, why did it make the audience so 10 uncomfortable? If this was just a case of satire fulfilling its function, why call it a miracle? Because, in spite of the fact that comedy *about* politics is now as common as crabgrass, political comedy—that is, genuine satire, which uses comedic means to advance a serious critique—is so rare we might be tempted to conclude it is extinct. Seeing it right there in front of God, the president, and the press corps was an astonishing moment, which stood out from the mundane rituals of politics and the press commonly seen on C-SPAN, *Meet the Press*, and the nightly news. It was like seeing an ivory-billed woodpecker alight on your satellite dish.

So "miracle" is indeed the word. Though some branded Colbert a heretic (the *Washington Post*'s nominally liberal columnist Richard Cohen called him a "bully" for picking on the poor president), others saw him as a satirical evangelist, a Jonathan Edwards° who took his text from the First Book of Jonathan Swift.[6°] If the president and the press didn't laugh very much during the course of this sermon, it was because they recognized themselves as the sinners in the hands of an angry comedian.

Of course, it is possible that Colbert approached the dais with no mission in mind beyond making 'em laugh—though one suspects he and

---

Jonathan Edwards: (1703–1758) American preacher and theologian of the first Great Awakening who is best known for his sermon "Sinners in the Hands of an Angry God" (1741).
Jonathan Swift: (1667–1745) Anglo-Irish writer and cleric famous for his satirical essay "A Modest Proposal" (1729) and book *Gulliver's Travels* (1726).

his writers are smart enough to know what they were getting into. Even if most of its practitioners would be loath to admit it, satire is a moral art. It calls on people and institutions to do their duty, as when Colbert scolded the press for their recent toothlessness: "Over the last five years you people were so good—over tax cuts, WMD [weapons of mass destruction] intelligence, the effect of global warming," he said, wistfully. "We Americans didn't want to know, and you had the courtesy not to try to find out. Those were good times, as far as we knew."

This is the satirist as revivalist preacher, calling his congregation back to the True Faith. And in America—which, despite the efforts of the Christian Right, remains a secular nation—the name of that Faith is Democracy. Its holy book is the Constitution, its clergy the Supreme Court and our elected representatives, its congregants We the People, its rituals voting and vigilance. Like other faiths—but unlike other governmental systems, which are held in place primarily through the threat of force—democracy depends on the devotion of its followers to sustain it. Some of the people, some of the time, must keep on believing that our electoral choices matter, that if we speak out our voices will be heard, that our representatives truly represent our interests. It's a tall order, but if we were to abandon all hope that democracy could endure—if democratic apathy reached the point of democratic atheism—our national faith would go the way of the cults of Baal, Zeus, Quetzalcoatl,° and other unemployed divinities.

Thankfully, our civic religion has not yet reached its moment of Nietzchean doom.° But its tenets—equal justice for all; government of, by, and for the people—have been subjected to a subtle yet constant and corrosive barrage of blasphemous derision. It echoes from the office water cooler to the corner bar, to the corridors of government itself. Most seductively, it rings out amidst the pealing laughter that emanates from millions of Americans' televisions each night.

The Lesser of Two Weasels: Anti-Political Comedy

While genuine satire arises from a sense of outrage, the topical jokes   15
heard in mainstream late-night monologues are rooted in mere cynicism. Unlike satire, which scolds and shames, this kind of comedy merely shrugs. Unlike Colbert, whose appearance at the Correspondents Dinner

---

Baal, Zeus, Quetzalcoatl: *Baal* is a Semitic word for "lord" or "master." Zeus was the god of sky and thunder in ancient Greek mythology. Quetzalcoatl was a Mesoamerican deity and important god in Atzec mythology.
Friedrich Nietzsche: (1844–1900) was a German philosopher who argued that a period of widespread nihilism—the belief that life is intrinsically meaningless—would follow Western society's realization that "God is dead."

evoked a democratic revivalist, Jay Leno, David Letterman, and Conan O'Brien are evangelists of apathy.

The difference is easier to discern if we go back to a presidential election year. So pick up that remote, hit rewind, and keep going, all the way back to 2004:

Political pundits are saying President George W. Bush has made gains in two key states: dazed and confused. (Letterman)

You see the pictures in the paper today of John Kerry windsurfing? . . . Even his hobby depends on which way the wind blows. (Leno)

Earlier today, President Bush said Kerry will be a tough and hard-charging opponent. That explains why Bush's nickname for Kerry is "Math." (O'Brien)

"While genuine satire arises from a sense of outrage, the topical jokes heard in mainstream late-night monologues are rooted in mere cynicism. Unlike satire, which scolds and shames, this kind of comedy merely shrugs."

Kerry was here in Los Angeles. He was courting the Spanish vote by speaking Spanish. And he showed people he could be boring in two languages. (Leno)[7]

A larger sampling would prove, as this selection suggests, that the political jokes told by network late-night hosts aim, cumulatively, for a bipartisan symmetry. Although election season "joke counts" maintained by the Center for Media and Public Affairs do not show a perfect one-to-one balance of jokes aimed at Democratic and Republican nominees, as the election got closer, a rough equity emerged, suggesting that George W. Bush was no more or less dumb than John Kerry was boring.[8] So it is in every presidential election year. Even in between, care is taken to target the abuse at "both sides," even if, during the Bush years, it has often meant resorting to time-worn Monica Lewinsky jokes. Maintaining this equilibrium is understood as one of the ground rules of the genre—a tenet so well established that an industry-specific cliché has arisen to describe those who embrace it: "equal-opportunity offenders [EOO]."

The phrase, or the ideal it expresses, is typically brandished by late-night comics as a shield against charges of bias. But it is a paradigm embraced even more fervently by journalists who write about comedy. Bill Maher, Robin Williams, and Carlos Mencia—even an Israeli/Lebanese comedy team who bill their show as *The Arab-Israeli Comedy Hour*—have been celebrated in press accounts as equal-opportunity offenders. Being branded an EOO by the journalistic establishment is something like getting the Good Housekeeping Seal of Approval, though the honor is bestowed with some subjectivity. Sarah Silverman is praised by the *Milwaukee Journal Sentinel* for being one, and criticized by the *Houston Chronicle* for not being enough of one.[9]

To offend unequally, on the other hand, is offensive indeed. Page 1 of the August 22, 2004, *New York Times* Arts and Leisure section features a telling juxtaposition of two articles concerning topical comedy. At the top of the page, the *Times* frets that a few of those making jokes about President Bush have transgressed the boundaries of "just kidding" and crossed the line into genuine (gasp!) satire. Though Jon Stewart, for example, "has repeatedly insisted that he's nonpartisan," his jokes about the incumbent "have started to seem like a sustained argument with the president." A comedian using humor to express an opinion? *J'accuse!*° Yet below the fold, the *Times* toasts *South Park* creators Matt Stone and Trey Parker's upcoming film, *Team America*, which promises to "take aim at sanctimonious right-wing nutjobs and smug Hollywood liberals alike." Parker takes the opportunity to assert his EOO bona fides: "People who go [to the film] will be really confused about whose side we're on. That's because we're really confused." Ah, that's what we like to see—fair and balanced comedy.[10]

Journalists' peculiar devotion to the equal-opportunity offender ideal results from a tendency to project their own profession's standards of objectivity onto comedians. Expecting Jay Leno to play by the same rules as Anderson Cooper is a bit like squeezing apples to get orange juice, but conventional wisdom seems to take this conflation of journalistic and comedic ethics for granted—the Pew poll, after all, asks its respondents to consider *The Tonight Show* and CNN side by side. Comedians' own reasons for maintaining balance, however, have little to do with abstract notions of fairness; it's more a matter of pragmatism than idealism. As Jay Leno put it, once a comedian takes a political side, "you've lost half the crowd already."[11] These guys are in show *business*, after all, and it doesn't pay to alienate 50 percent of your potential viewers. Such bottom-line considerations, incidentally, help explain why *The Colbert Report* and *The Daily Show* can afford to be more politically "risky" than Leno's show: a little over a million viewers—a narrowly interested but loyal core—amounts to a pretty respectable audience for a cable show like the *Report*, but for *The Tonight Show*, which averages 6 million viewers nightly, it would be a disaster.[12]

The bigger difference between the network and cable shows' humor has to do with what the jokes say, not how many of them are aimed at

20

J'accuse!: French "I accuse." Also, the title of an open letter written by novelist Emile Zola in 1898 that accused the government of anti-Semitism.

Democrats versus Republicans. On closer examination, the only political thing about the mainstream jokes quoted above is that they happen to be about politicians. They are personality jokes, not that different from the ones those same comedians tell about Paris Hilton or Ozzy Osbourne—just replace "dumb" and "boring" with "slutty" and "drug-addled." And unlike Colbert's jokes about Bush's inflexibility or his tendency to think with his "gut," the jokes told on the network shows rarely transcend the level of pure ad hominem mockery to consider how such personal traits might manifest themselves in terms of policy.

The bottom line of all the jokes about Bush's dumbness, Kerry's dullness, Al Gore's stiffness, Bob Dole's "hey-you-kids-get-outta-my-yard" crankiness, and so on, is that all politicians are created equal—equally unworthy, that is—and that no matter who wins the election, the American people lose. Thus, despite their efforts to play it safe by offending equally (and superficially), the mainstream late-night comics actually present an extremely bleak and cynical view of American democracy.

What, then, is the secret of their appeal? Why do millions of us tune in, night after night, to be told—not overtly, but insinuatingly and consistently—that our cherished system of self-government is a joke? Perhaps because this confirms what we have always suspected: democracy is a nice idea but not, ultimately, a practical one. And if Americans doubt democracy, we hate politics. Politics is treated like an infection, or a tumor. It is to be avoided if possible, and when found lurking—in a sitcom writers' room, in an Oscar acceptance speech, in the funnies (*Doonesbury* has been exiled to the editorial pages of many of the papers that carry it)—it must be excised before it can infect the nation's body non-politic. Politics is *icky*.

Even our politicians disdain politics. A candidate can't go wrong by running against Washington, D.C., and all that it supposedly stands for. George W. "I'm from Texas" Bush successfully campaigned as an anti-establishment "outsider"—and his dad was the president! Ronald Reagan got applause when he proclaimed that government was not the solution but the problem—though he himself had just campaigned for, and achieved, the government's top job.[13]

Most Americans see nothing strange in this; for as much as we like to 25 wave the flag, and pledge our allegiance to the republic for which it stands, as a people we regard our government, its institutions, and its representatives (save those who take care to inoculate themselves with anti-political rhetoric) with contempt. This feeling is reflected not only in our appallingly low voter turnout rates but also in our culture—particularly in our humor.

Which is why most of this country's "political" humor—from Artemus Ward° to Will Rogers,° from Johnny Carson to Jay Leno, from Andy Borowitz to JibJab.com—has in fact been *anti*-political. "All politics is applesauce," Rogers once said, by which he did not mean that it was a tasty side dish with pork chops.[14] He meant that progress was the opposite of Congress, that the Democrats were worse than any other party except for the Republicans, and vice versa, that six of one was half a dozen of the other. Will Rogers was an equal-opportunity offender.

Rogers's observation that "both parties have their good and bad times . . . they are each good when they are out, and . . . bad when they are in" reappears almost seventy years later as Jay Leno's characterization of the 2000 election as a choice between "the lesser of two weasels." It appears again, in an "edgier" guise, when the *South Park* kids are given the opportunity to learn about democracy by nominating and voting for a new school mascot: "We're supposed to vote between a giant douche and a turd sandwich," Stan tells his parents, "I just don't see the point." His parents react with shocked sanctimony: "Stanley," scolds his mother, "do you know how many people died so you could have the right to vote?" Mom just doesn't get it.[15]

Whether the metaphor describes electoral choice as a contest between a pair of rodents or between a feminine hygiene product and a piece of excrement, it's the same old joke. Anti-political humor is everywhere, clean or dirty, hip or square, as told by professionals over the airwaves and amateurs over the cubicle divider. In fact, what I think of as the quintessential anti-political joke is one I heard not from any television show but from my dad—and although this version dates from 1980, all that is necessary to make it work in any other presidential election year is to change the names:

> Q: If Jimmy Carter, Ronald Reagan, and John Anderson [that year's third-party threat] were all in a rowboat in the middle of the ocean, and the boat flipped over, who would be saved?

> A: The United States.

What Is Government For? What Are Jokes For?

The implications of the rowboat riddle are fairly grim: no choice would be better than the choices we have, and anyone who would presume to be worthy of the people's vote deserves to drown like a rat. Yet this nihilistic punch line is no more than a crystallization of the message repeated

Artemis Ward (1834–1867): the pen name of Charles Farrar Browne, a U.S. humor writer beloved by President Lincoln, among others.
Will Rogers: (1879–1935) a world-famous newspaper writer and political wit. He ran a mock campaign to become U.S. president in 1928.

night after night, joke after joke, by Jay, Dave, and Conan. Late-night's anti-political jokes are implicitly anti-democratic. They don't criticize policies for their substance, or leaders for their official actions (as opposed to their personal quirks, which have little to do with politics per se); taken as a whole, they declare the entire system—from voting to legislating to governing—an irredeemable sham.

To understand the appeal of such anti-democratic heresy, it is helpful 30 to start with a couple of fundamental questions. First, what is government for? The answer, according to the framers of the Constitution, is to provide for the common defense, to promote the general welfare, and so on. Or as Abraham Lincoln more succinctly put it, our government is for the people—as well as by and of them. We, the people, choose our government and therefore—indirectly, at least—are the government. The U.S. is "us." Most of us learned this in elementary school.

When we grow up, however, this naïve faith in representative democracy joins Santa Claus and the Easter Bunny on the scrap heap of our childish beliefs. Even if we continue to believe, we tend to be a little bit embarrassed about it. The majority of voters, in most election years, would probably tell anyone who asked that they were holding their noses as they entered the voting booth. We participate in the political process in only the most minimal ways: we ignore local elections; few of us attend caucuses or work as campaign volunteers; and between the first Wednesday of November and the kickoff of the next season of attack ads, we pay little attention to what our representatives do (unless there's a sex scandal, of course). We treat democracy, our civic religion, only about as seriously as what so-called C-and-E Christians (for Christmas and Easter— the only occasions they bother to show up in church) treat theirs. And, of course, the majority of those eligible to vote don't even bother.

Even lapsed voters may still profess faith in the democratic ideal but are likely to consider it lost to some more perfect past—before Watergate, Irangate, or Monicagate; before PACs and lobbyists; back in the days when politicians were statesmen, not these clowns you see running for office nowadays. In just a century and a half, this version of the anti-political argument goes, we've gone from Lincoln versus Douglas to a douche versus a turd.

Of course, this is nostalgic nonsense; American leaders have been failing to live up to their predecessors since Adams succeeded Washington. The problem with the democratic ideal—with any ideal—is that reality will always fall short. Our candidates can never measure up to the Founding Fathers' patriarchal nobility, nor can our day-to-day experience of liberty, equality, and justice live up to the ringing words of the Declaration of Independence. Some years ago, Professor Louis Rubin dubbed the gap between the City on a Hill of our star-spangled dreams and the somewhat less utopian actualities of the nation we actually inhabit "the Great American Joke": "On the one hand there are the ideals of freedom, equality, self-government, the conviction that ordinary people can evince the wisdom to vote wisely, and demonstrate the capacity for understanding and cherishing the highest human values through embodying them in their political and social institutions. On the other hand there is the *Congressional Record*."[16] When you live in a country founded upon ideals—rather than the mere commonalities of tradition, language, and culture that formed the basis of older nations—you are doomed to perpetual disappointment.

But before further considering America's strained relation with its founding principles, let us turn to the second question: what are jokes for? This seemingly trivial query has in fact tested the cognitive powers of some pretty heavy-duty thinkers, from Aristotle to Immanuel Kant, to Thomas Hobbes. Sigmund Freud provided one of the most useful contributions to this body of inquiry a century ago, in a book entitled *Jokes and Their Relation to the Unconscious*.[17] The purpose of joking, he theorized, is to help individuals cope with societal repression. At the core of all of Freud's work lies the assumption that even the most well-adjusted of us are carrying a heavy burden of hostility and sexual aggression. Bottling all that up can make us crazy, but if we allowed ourselves to express these impulses in an open and straightforward way, civilized society would be impossible—day-to-day life would resemble some unholy double feature of *Mad Max* and *Animal House*. So how do we get through the day? Freud identified a number of ways—many of which don't cost a hundred dollars an hour—including telling, and laughing at, jokes. Laughter is a safety valve for our antisocial drives. The rules of polite society (and the need to keep your job) prevent you from acting on your intensely felt desire to punch your boss in the teeth, but you can safely express that hostile impulse by imitating his stupid, jackass laugh for your coworkers during happy hour at the local bar.

Thus, laughter helps the individual cope with society. But might it also 35 help society cope with the individual? According to Freud's contemporary the philosopher Henri Bergson, the principal function of laughter is not so much to keep people sane as to keep them in line. "By laughter," he wrote, "society avenges itself for the liberties taken with it."[18] Whenever we laugh at someone whose comportment or behavior is somehow "wrong"—whether he or she is a nerd, a klutz, a pervert, a ninny, or a fanatic—we reinforce what we consider to be "normal," non-laughable behavior. Laughter enforces conformity; it's the border collie that helps maintain the herd mentality.

How do these turn-of-the-twentieth-century Continental theories apply to contemporary American political comedy? First, and most obvious, laughing at political big shots is satisfying in the same way as laughing at your boss (because you can't punch the president, either). In fact, says Freud, if the target is big and important enough, the joke doesn't even have to be that good, "since we count any rebellion against authority as a merit" (a loophole *Saturday Night Live* has been exploiting for years).[19] Add to this basic truth the fact that America was born in rebellion and celebrates anti-authoritarianism in any form, from the Boston patriots' dumping tea in the harbor to Elvis's hip-swiveling impudence, and it's not hard to see how this point resonates with particular force in our culture.

Bergson's argument about laughter and social conformity speaks to one of the main sources of our democratic skepticism. If we take the idea that "all men are created equal" to be a fundamental American "norm" (and there is no principle we claim to hold dearer), then grasping at political power—seeking, that is, to escape the very equality that allows any one of us to run for office in the first place—is a violation of that norm. A fella (or even a gal) would have to think he's pretty hot stuff to sit in the House or Senate—to say nothing of the White House—and round these parts we don't cotton to° folks what's too big for their britches.° This is the central paradox of American representative democracy: the egalitarian idea anyone can grow up to be president is inseparable from the notion that none of us deserves such an honor. This is why potential leaders of the free world go to such absurd lengths to look like someone you'd like to have a beer with: *I guess it's okay he wants to be president, as long as he doesn't think he's any better than us.*

Oddly enough, our devotion to the principles on which our government is founded—liberty (no one can tell me what I can and cannot do) and egalitarianism (none of us is any better than anyone else)—makes it impossible for us to believe in government itself. Government makes all kinds of demands on our liberty—we must pay our taxes, obey the laws, serve on juries, or even, at various points in our history, serve in the military. Moreover, it derives its authority to do all of this based on the unacceptably contradictory principle that our elected representatives, who supposedly serve at our pleasure, are also somehow the boss of us.

We carry this paradox, and the resentment that goes along with it, in the backs of our minds, even as we cast our ballots, salute the flag, or send our children off to war. It is the shadow side of our patriotism; the doubt at the heart of our devotion; our secular, civic version of original sin. It's the small, insistent voice that grumbles, even as we recite the Pledge of Allegiance or sing "The Star-Spangled Banner," *Yeah, right.* It is

---

cotton to: a North American colloquialism for "have a liking for."
too big for their britches: an idiom that means a person is conceited and has an inflated sense of him- or herself.

the voice of anti-political, anti-democratic heresy, echoing down the centuries, and from all across the political spectrum. It is the common complaint of left-wing anarchists like Abbie Hoffman (author of *Revolution for the Hell of It*), right-wing libertarians like anti-tax crusader Grover Norquist, civilly disobedient dropouts like Henry David Thoreau—even anti-state vigilantes like Timothy McVeigh.[20] In their own lighthearted way, late-night comics are torchbearers in this same anti–political parade. Unlike McVeigh, the damage they do is merely insidious and largely invisible; but unlike Hoffman, Norquist, and Thoreau, they reach tens of millions of Americans each night.

Defending the Faith: A Place for Satire?

In spite of its anti-democratic implications, anti-politics (and anti-political 40 humor) is itself a bedrock American tradition: a contrarian habit as old as the republic itself. Atop this foundation of anti-political disdain, we have in recent decades been building a towering Fortress of Irony, reaching, by the turn of the twenty-first century, a point where it seems as if every communication is enclosed in air quotes. In contemporary America, sincerity is suspect, commitment is lame, and believing in stuff is for suckers.

Late-night comics did not invent the air-quote culture, anymore than they invented our anti-political sentiments, but they have played a leading role in proselytizing this cynical message. Election after election, night after night, joke after joke, they have reinforced the notion that political participation is pointless, parties and candidates are interchangeable, and democracy is futile.

This is not to suggest that comedy that takes politics as its subject matter is inherently destructive. Mocking our elected representatives and our institutions is an American birthright, and exercising that right is worthwhile, if only to maintain it. The problem is not the presence, or even the proliferation, of political comedy per se. The problem is that too little of it is actually "political" in any meaningful way. Genuine political satire, like good investigative journalism, can function as democracy's feedback loop. It can illuminate injustices, point out hypocrisy, and tell us when our government is not living up to its ideals, thereby raising the awareness that is the first step toward alleviating any of these problems. Real satire—such as Colbert's excoriation of the press and the president—sounds the alarm: something is wrong, people must be held to account, things must be made right. Anti-political humor—the far more common kind, practiced by Leno, Letterman, and O'Brien, among others—merely says, resignedly, "Eh, what are you gonna do?"

Yet the public, and especially the press, are so blinded by anti-political disdain and unblinking devotion to the equal-opportunity offender idea that we have difficulty distinguishing genuine satire from the ersatz kind, even when we see it. In a feature on *The Colbert Report* (published several months before the Correspondents Dinner), *Newsweek* stubbornly hangs on to the news media's beloved apolitical paradigm: "[Though his] character is clearly a parody of God-fearing, pro-business, Bush-loving Republicans . . . Colbert guards his personal views closely, and if you watch the show carefully you'll see subtle digs at everyone on the political-media map." With what seems like willful naiveté, the magazine seizes on the host's rote disclaimer that his show is strictly for laughs: "Despite the fact that politics is a primary inspiration and target, Colbert isn't interested in being political."[21]

Whether he's interested or not, though, Colbert's show *is* political, in a way that the more traditional late-night programs—and, even for all their enthusiastic offensiveness, the works of Stone and Parker—are not. *The Colbert Report* is not an equal-opportunity offender. Neither is *The Daily Show*. Nor, for that matter, is Bill Maher, who has definitely met a man (or two) he didn't like. This is not to say that the *Report* is liberal propaganda, nor to deny that Colbert, Stewart, and Maher take satirical shots at "both sides"—though perhaps it is worth considering what would be so terrible about comedy that expresses a consistent point of view. But the important difference between the smallish vanguard of cable comics and the late-night mainstream is not so much a matter of taking political sides as of taking politics seriously. It is the difference between engaging with the subject and merely dismissing it. Satire, at its best, is not just a drive-by dissing but exactly what the *Times* accuses Jon Stewart of presenting: "a sustained argument."[22] Consider the way Colbert deconstructs Bush's fetish for "resolve." Watch how *The Daily Show* analyzes official rhetoric, as when Stewart goes sound bite for sound bite with a videotaped politician, calling attention to every outrage and evasion. Left or right, right or wrong, fair or unfair, this is comedy that engages us in politics, instead of offering us an easy out. It is a form of debate, not just entertainment, and as such, it should be welcomed, not treated as "rude" or inappropriate.

Undoubtedly, many of the guests at the Correspondents Dinner— 45 including the president—would have had a more pleasant evening listening to the inoffensive humor of, say, Jay Leno. There's nothing wrong with innocent laughter, of course. But insofar as our appetite for the dismissive, plague-on-both-their-houses, progress versus Congress, Tweedledum versus Tweedledee, pot-calling-the-kettle-black variety of "political" humor reflects our fundamental doubts about the value of political participation, and the viability of democracy, it is no laughing matter.

Notes

1. The 2006 White House Correspondents Association Dinner was first broadcast on C-SPAN, April 29, 2006.

2. Elisabeth Bumiller, "A New Set of Bush Twins Appear at Annual Correspondents' Dinner," *New York Times*, May 1, 2006. On "followed suit," see Dan Froomkin, "The Colbert Blackout," *Washington Post*, May 2, 2006. See also Josh Kalven and Simon Maloy, "Media Touted Bush's Routine at Correspondents' Dinner, Ignored Colbert's Skewering," *Media Matters*, May 1, 2006; Julie Millican, "For Third Day in a Row, Good Morning America Touted Bush's White House Correspondents Dinner Skit While Ignoring Colbert's Routine," *Media Matters*, May 3, 2006, both available at http://mediamatters.org.

3. Froomkin, "The Colbert Blackout"; "Thank You, Stephen Colbert" web site, http://thankyoustephencolbert.org.

4. Joan Walsh, "Making Colbert Go Away," *Salon*, May 3, 2006, including Grove, Lehman, and Cox quotes; Mike Allen and Chris Matthews, *Hardball with Chris Matthews*, MSNBC, May 1, 2006.

5. Dan Froomkin, "Why So Defensive?" *Washington Post*, May 4, 2006.

6. Richard Cohen, "So Not Funny," *Washington Post*, May 4, 2006.

7. Letterman, retrieved from About.com Political Humor, "Late-Night Jokes about President Bush from 2004," comp. Daniel Kurtzman; Leno and O'Brien, retrieved from About.com Political Humor, "Late-Night Jokes about John Kerry," comp. Daniel Kurtzman.

8. Center for Media and Public Affairs (CMPA), "Joke Archive, through August 24, 2004. President Bush held a commanding lead over Kerry for the year to date, but when Kerry became the presumptive and then official nominee, the numbers started to even out. Unfortunately, data for the months leading up to the election are unavailable, but in examining this and the other years' joke counts, the trend is clear.

9. Alex Strachan, "Maher Targets Left and Right in Comedy Special," *Montreal Gazette*, Nov. 1, 2003; Doug Moore, "Williams' Act Has St. Louis Laughing at Itself," *St. Louis Post-Dispatch Everyday Magazine*, March 21, 2002; Gary Budzak, "Outspoken Honduras Native an Equal-Opportunity Offender," *Columbus Dispatch*, January 6, 2005; Debra Pickett, "Middle East Duo Bets That Misery Loves Comedy," *Chicago Sun-Times*, June 6, 2003; Duane Dudek, "Blinded by the Bite; Silverman Skewers All with a Smile in 'Jesus,'" *Milwaukee Journal Sentinel*, December 16, 2005; Bruce Westbrook, "Provocative Comedy: No Magic in Silverman's 'Jesus,'" *Houston Chronicle*, December 9, 2005, Lexis-Nexis, via Infohawk.

10. Jason Zengerle, "The State of the George W. Bush Joke," and Sharon Waxman, "The Boys from 'South Park' Go to War," *New York Times*, August 22, 2004, national ed., Arts and Leisure, 1.

11. Marshall Sella, "The Stiff Guy vs. the Dumb Guy," *New York Times Magazine*, September 24, 2000, 74.

12. *Tonight Show* viewership 6.4 million viewers, per Toni Fitzgerald, "Sunrise Surprise: The CBS Early Show"; *Colbert Report* viewership approximately 1.2 million, *Daily Show*'s 1.6 million, per Julie Bosman, "Serious Book to

Peddle? Don't Laugh, Try a Comedy Show," *New York Times*, February 25, 2007, Lexis-Nexis, via Infohawk.

13. In his first debate with Al Gore in 2000, Bush said, "I fully recognize I'm not of Washington. I'm from Texas." See Richard L. Berke, "Bush and Gore Stake Out Differences in First Debate," *New York Times*, October 4, 2000. Reagan's "government is the problem" remark is from his First Inaugural speech, as printed under the headline "Let Us Begin an Era of National Renewal," *New York Times*, January 21, 1981, Lexis-Nexis, via Infohawk.

14. Will Rogers, quoted in *Bartlett's Familiar Quotations*, 15th ed., ed. Emily Morrison Beck (Boston: Little, Brown, 1980), 765.

15. Will Rogers, *The Best of Will Rogers*, ed. Bryan B. Sterling (New York: Crown Publishers, 1979), 55; Leno, *Tonight*, Novevmber 6, 2000; *South Park*, episode 808, "Douche and Turd," first aired October 27, 2004.

16. Louis D. Rubin, "The Great American Joke," in *What's So Funny? Humor in American Culture*, ed. Nancy A. Walker (Wilmington, DE: Scholarly Resources, 1998), 109–110.

17. Sigmund Freud, *Jokes and Their Relation to the Unconscious*, trans. James Strachey (New York: W. W. Norton, 1963).

18. Henri Bergson, *Laughter: An Essay on the Meaning of the Comic*, trans. Cloudesley Brereton and Fred Rothwell (Los Angeles: Green Integer Books, 1999), 176.

19. Freud, *Jokes*, 105.

20. Abbie Hoffman (a.k.a. "Free"), *Revolution for the Hell of It* (New York: Dial Books, 1968). For a useful overview of the history of American anti-political sentiment, see Garry Wills, *A Necessary Evil: A History of American Distrust of Government* (New York: Simon & Schuster, 1999).

21. Mare Peyser, "The Truthiness Teller," *Newsweek*, February 13, 2006, Lexis-Nexis via Infohawk.

22. Zengerle, "The State of the George W. Bush Joke," 1.

Understanding the Text

1. What is the function of satire, according to Peterson?

2. What criticisms does Peterson lob at the humor of late-night comedians on network television? For example, why does he have a problem with "the equal-opportunity offender ideal" (par. 19) and "personality jokes" (par. 20)?

3. Peterson attributes part of the problem of anti-political humor to "the central paradox of American representative democracy" (par. 17). What is this paradox and how does it contribute to anti-political humor on late-night television?

Reflection and Response

4. Peterson calls democracy a "Faith" (par. 13) and "our civic religion" (par. 30). Do you agree with his comparison of the American political system to a religious faith? What is revealed and/or concealed in this analogy?

5. Respond to Peterson's overall argument. Do you believe that the political humor of late-night talk-show hosts on network television is cynical while that of fake news hosts on cable television provides genuine satirical commentary and critique? What is your experience with the sort of political humor that Peterson mentions?

6. Peterson begins his conclusion by claiming that "we have in recent decades been building a towering Fortress of Irony, reaching, by the turn of the twenty-first century, a point where it seems as if every communication is enclosed in air quotes" (par. 39). Do you believe that our culture has come to be dominated by irony? Do you and your friends communicate ironically?

Making Connections

7. Peterson — like Rappoport (p. 13), Critchley (p. 79), and Tueth (p. 103) — refers to Sigmund Freud's theories of humor (par. 33). Tueth, for example, mentions Freud's concept of *tendentious jokes* when writing about the "genuinely oppositional" satire found in the transgressive humor of *South Park*. Peterson does not share Tueth's opinion of Matt Stone and Trey Parker's show, citing it as an example of anti-political, equal-opportunity offender comedy. Write an essay about *South Park* or about a comic text, writer, or performer that you believe successfully employs tendentious jokes for political purposes.

8. Peterson's piece is from 2008, and many of the late-night hosts whom he mentions have retired. Notably, Stephen Colbert ended his satirical show on cable television and replaced David Letterman as the host of the *Late Show*. Watch a few opening monologues from Colbert and other contemporary late-night talk-show hosts. Analyze the humor of these shows to determine if it is genuinely satirical or merely anti-political. Then write an essay based on your research that responds to Peterson's claims.

Stooping to Conquer

Elizabeth Kolbert

In the previous selection, Russell Peterson focuses on a stark difference that he perceives between the political humor of satire shows on cable and that performed by late-night comedians on network television. In this piece from 2004, *New Yorker* staff writer Elizabeth Kolbert examines the rise of self-parody humor among politicians, nearly all of whom do their best to get laughs — and votes — on the shows Peterson discusses. Politicians use this form of mass communication to joke about their own campaign gaffes and policy blunders, thus beating their opponents to the punch line. Self-effacing humor makes them appear just like you and me, but what effect does it have on how seriously we take our democratic system?

Kolbert has written a book that profiles acclaimed New Yorkers, *The Prophet of Love: And Other Tales of Power and Deceit* (2004), as well as two books on anthropogenic climate change, *Field Notes from a Catastrophe: Man, Nature, and Climate Change* (2006) and *The Sixth Extinction: An Unnatural History* (2014), which won the Pulitzer Prize for nonfiction in 2015. Her biographical page on newyorker.com includes a video link to her guest appearance on *The Daily Show*. When reading this article, try to recall more recent examples of the kind of preemptive self-mockery Kolbert discusses.

Three days after placing third in the Iowa caucuses and delivering the much replayed "scream," Howard Dean° made a taped appearance on the *Late Show with David Letterman*. His task was to deliver the Top Ten list of "ways I, Howard Dean, can turn things around":

10. Switch to decaf.

9. Unveil new slogan: "Vote for Dean and get one dollar off your next purchase at Blimpie."

8. Marry Rachel on the final episode of *Friends*.

7. Don't change a thing—it's going great.

6. Show a little more skin.

5. Go on *American Idol* and give 'em a taste of these pipes.

4. Start working out and speaking with Austrian accent.

Howard Dean: former governor of Vermont and chairperson of the Democratic National Committee who was a candidate for the Democratic nomination in the 2004 presidential election.

3. I can't give specifics yet, but it involves Ted Danson.

2. Fire the staffer who suggested we do this lousy Top Ten List instead of actually campaigning.

1. Oh, I don't know—maybe fewer crazy, red-faced rants.

Dean followed up the *Letterman* appearance with an interview with Jon Stewart on Comedy Central's *The Daily Show*. When the segment aired, the day before the New Hampshire primary, it consisted mostly of voice-overs of the two men's "thoughts." At one point, Dean was asked his position on gay marriage. As he held forth, his answer was drowned out by Stewart's interior monologue: "Mrs. Jon Dean . . . Mr. Howard Stewart . . . Howard and Jon Dean . . . Dr. and Mr. Jon Dean-Stewart."

Dean's performances on late-night television in no way distinguished him from his rivals. While stumping in Iowa, Representative Dick Gephardt, of Missouri, also showed up on *Letterman*, in his case to enumerate the ten "signs you've been on the campaign trail too long." (No. 6: "You ask yourself, 'What would Schwarzenegger do?'" No. 2: "You agree to appear on a lame late-night talk show.") Right before officially entering the presidential race, last September, Senator John Edwards, of North Carolina, "announced" his candidacy on *The Daily Show*. And, the day after the Missouri primary, Edwards duly recited his list of ten "things never before said by a presidential candidate." (No. 7: "I'd give you my plan for economic recovery if I wasn't ripstinkin' drunk.")

Making fun of politicians is a pastime practically as old as politics itself. Before the Greeks got around to inventing romantic comedy, they amused themselves by lampooning their leaders; in Aristophanes' *The Knights*, for instance, the Athenian despot Cleon is replaced in office by a sausage seller. (Standard garb for actors in the days of "old comedy" was a padded suit and a large red leather phallus.) The Romans, too, loved a witty put-down, like this one, aimed at Caesar and reported by Dio Cassius: "If you behave well, you will be punished; if you behave badly, you will be king."

> "In the new comic order, the most devastating joke is circulated not by an irreverent observer or a sly opponent but by the target himself, who appears on national television solely in order to deliver it."

What sets contemporary political humor apart is its curious—one is tempted to say unprecedented—configuration. In the new comic order, the most devastating joke is circulated not by an irreverent observer or a sly opponent but by the target himself, who appears on national television solely in order to deliver it. There seem to be two ways to look at this trend: as a sign of how seriously we now take light entertainment or as an indication of how lightly we have come to regard politics. Either way, it's an unsettling development. Perhaps Triumph, the Insult Comic Dog, put it best when he was given a better time slot than Senator John Kerry, of Massachusetts, recently on *The Tonight Show*.

"John Kerry, a war veteran, has to follow a freaking dog puppet!" he 5 shrieked. "What's going on in America?"

Not long ago, I went to the Museum of Television and Radio, on West Fifty-second Street, to see episode No. 15 of *Rowan & Martin's Laugh-In*.° When the episode originally aired, on September 16, 1968, *Laugh-In* was just beginning its first full season—it had débuted eight months earlier, as a mid-season replacement—but was about to become the No. 1 show on television. The program begins with all the usual *Laugh-In* mayhem. "It must be 'Sock it to me' time," a youthful Goldie Hawn announces, before hitting herself over the head with a plastic mallet. The mayor of Burbank gets pelted with Ping-Pong balls; Joanne Worley is doused with water; Ruth Buzzi is crushed by a stage set; and Judy Carne is pelted, doused, crushed, and then sprayed by a skunk. Still wet, she answers a phone, and on the other end (ostensibly) is Governor Nelson Rockefeller. "Oh, no, I don't think we could get Mr. Nixon to stand still for a 'Sock it to me,'" she chirps, at which point the show cuts away to Richard Nixon.

Nixon's appearance on *Laugh-In* lasts four seconds. At first, he is looking stage right; then he turns toward the camera. He widens his eyes in what seems to be an effort at feigned surprise but comes off looking more like mock dismay. "Sock it to me?" he asks, drawing out the "me?" in a way that suggests he has perhaps never heard the line before.

Episode No. 15 was broadcast at the height of Nixon's (ultimately successful) campaign against Vice President Hubert Humphrey, and was an immediate sensation. George Schlatter, the creator of *Laugh-In*, now runs a television production company in Los Angeles. He told me that Nixon had been extremely reluctant to be on the show; although the producers had repeatedly entreated him to appear, his campaign aides had even more insistently urged him not to. Eventually, the race brought Nixon out to Los Angeles. He gave a press conference, and Schlatter and one of *Laugh-In*'s writers, Paul Keyes, who happened to be a close friend of the former vice president's, went over to watch it, bringing a TV camera with them.

"While his advisers were telling him not to do it, Paul was telling him how much it would mean to his career," Schlatter recalled. "And we went in, and he said, 'Sock it to me.' It took about six takes, because it sounded

Rowan & Martin's Laugh-In: a sketch comedy show that aired on NBC from 1968 to 1973.

angry: 'Sock-it-to-me!' After that, we grabbed the tape and escaped before his advisers got to him.

"Then, realizing what we had done—because he did come out look- 10
ing like a nice guy—we pursued Humphrey all over the country, trying to get him to say, 'I'll sock it to you, Dick!'" Schlatter went on. "And Humphrey later said that not doing it may have cost him the election. We didn't realize how effective it was going to be. But there were other factors in the election, too—I can't take all the blame."

Nixon on *Laugh-In* is often cited as a watershed moment in the history of television—the unthinking man's version of Nixon in China.° What had once seemed antithetical—parody and power—had proved not to be. Was the joke on Nixon or on his hosts? Who could say? But if the episode announced the new order, many people, including Nixon himself, seemed not to have noticed. As president, he never went near *Laugh-In*, or anything like it. Indeed, according to Schlatter, he became critical of the show and eventually pressured NBC into muffling its politics.

Laugh-In's godchild *Saturday Night Live* [*SNL*] premièred in the fall of 1975. Its approach to political satire was less staccato and more sustained. Week after week, Chevy Chase portrayed Gerald Ford, a former college football star, as an irredeemable klutz. The following spring, Ford's press secretary, Ron Nessen, agreed to appear on *SNL* as a guest host. In one sketch, Nessen, playing himself, looked on indulgently as Chase, playing Ford, lurched around the set, stapling his ear and signing his hand instead of a piece of tax legislation. Nessen's participation in the show was widely criticized—reportedly by the head of NBC, among others—as demeaning to the presidency, even though, in an early example of life imitating parody, Ford himself appeared in the same episode, on tape, to recite a variation of Chase's signature line: "I'm Gerald Ford and you're not." ("There's really nothing you can do in that situation," Ford said years later. "You can't stand up and say. 'I was the best athlete' and all that stuff.")

The next four years were a period of strict separation: Jimmy Carter avoided humor, at least of the purposeful variety, whenever possible. (Jerome Doolittle, a White House speechwriter who sometimes composed funny lines for Carter, likened his role to that of Franklin Roosevelt's tap-dance coach.) "Who do they think they elected?" Carter

---

Nixon in China: a reference to former president Richard Nixon's historic visit to China in 1972. Nixon's anticommunist reputation shielded him from public criticism for meeting with Chairman Mao Zedong, and the trip became a metaphor for a politician with a secure enough reputation to act in a way that would otherwise draw criticism from supporters.

supposedly once asked a staff member who was urging him to be more lighthearted. "Fred Allen?"°

A few days after watching Richard Nixon on *Laugh-In*, I went down to Washington to meet Landon Parvin. Parvin, who is fifty-five, is a slight man with pale-blue eyes, prominent ears, and gray hair that sticks up from the top of his head, like Homer Price's.° He has an earnest manner, which tends to surprise people who have first been introduced to him, as it were, through his work. Depending on how you look at things, Parvin is either the capital's funniest serious speechwriter or its most serious funny one. He is particularly in demand during what is referred to in Washington as the "silly season," when the nation's leaders gather at a series of dinners to listen to the powerful crack jokes. If the program consists of four speeches, it is not uncommon for Parvin to have written three of them, and it is not unheard of for him to have written all four. In January, for instance, for the annual dinner of the Alfalfa Club — an association of political and corporate bigwigs named for the plant whose roots, according to club lore, "will do anything for a drink" — Parvin wrote the speech delivered by President Bush, and the one delivered by Jack Valenti, the Alfalfa nominee for President of the United States, and also the one delivered by the outgoing club president, Vernon Jordan. "As I look around the room, I am reminded that it is a long way from the public-housing projects of Atlanta to the presidency of Alfalfa," Jordan said in his remarks, which, in keeping with capital tradition, were labelled "off the record," then extensively reported anyway. "I only wish my daddy — Strom Thurmond° — could see me tonight!"

I had been urged to visit Parvin by people who remembered or, per- 15 haps more accurately, remembered having heard about a groundbreaking bit he wrote back in 1982, when he was working as a speechwriter in the Reagan White House. That spring, Nancy Reagan had decided to sing a song at the Gridiron Club dinner, and it fell to Parvin to come up with the lyrics. The assignment was an unpromising one. The Gridiron Club, an association made up of assorted members of the Washington media élite, exists solely in order to spoof the even more powerful. Among the numerous public-relations debacles of Mrs. Reagan's first year had been a

---

Fred Allen: (1894–1956) famous American comedian best known for the topical humor of his radio work, which would influence later news satires like *Saturday Night Live*'s "Weekend Update."
Homer Price: protagonist of Robert McCloskey's children's books *Homer Price* (1943) and *Centerburg Tales* (1951).
Vernon Jordan . . . Strom Thurmond: Vernon Jordan is a civil rights activist and Storm Thurmond (1902–2003) was a U.S. Senator from South Carolina who infamously campaigned against civil rights legislation.

trip to England during which she was photographed wearing fifteen different outfits and the purchase, in the midst of a national recession, of a set of china valued at $200,000. The first lyrics that Parvin wrote, to the tune of "Second Hand Rose," Mrs. Reagan rejected as too easy on her, so in the next set he took aim directly at the First Lady's image problems. "Even though they tell me that I'm no longer queen / Did Ronnie have to buy me that new sewing machine?" she asked plaintively. Then she smashed a plate on the floor. The number—entitled "Second Hand Clothes"—was such a hit that Mrs. Reagan had to sing it twice; Parvin hadn't thought to write her an encore. When, in the months that followed, the First Lady began to receive better press coverage, the shift was attributed to her song-and-dance routine.

Mrs. Reagan's success makes sense only by the logic of self-parody, according to which, as in fairy tales, straw is gold. The First Lady didn't answer her critics' charges; she merely repeated them, in the process emptying them of one kind of significance and filling them with another. As Parvin put it to me, if a politician can make fun of his faults, he is, in effect, saying, "I'm not really worried about it; you shouldn't be, either."

"What most people don't realize is there are two kinds of political humor," Parvin went on. "There is the kind satirists do. Then, there's what I do. The easiest thing in the world, I learned in the White House, is to get a zinger on the evening news. The press will pick it up like that. But what I learned over the years is that that doesn't necessarily serve the politician's purpose, because what you want is for him to be better liked. Really, that is the purpose of political humor for a politician: to be better liked."

Parvin left the White House in 1984, and in the years since has written hundreds of speeches, for scores of politicians. He prefers straight speeches, like the inaugural address he composed last fall for Governor Arnold Schwarzenegger, of California, but he is constantly getting calls from people who want him to repeat the trick he performed for Mrs. Reagan.

"A politician will be in some trouble and he'll say, 'Will you do me some lines on it?,' because he's heard that humor can get him out of trouble," Parvin told me. Sometimes he can help, and sometimes the trouble—misuse of public funds, for example—is intractable. "I tell them, depending on the situation, 'No, this is trouble. You should not make fun of this.'"

On March 1, 2000, shortly before the New York presidential primary, 20 George Bush, then the governor of Texas, made the first of his election-year appearances on the *Late Show with David Letterman*. It was an educational experience for him. Bush seems to have only half understood why he was there, and so he came prepared with several jokes about Letterman, who had recently undergone heart bypass surgery. "It's about time you had the heart to invite me," Bush said early in the show, prompting a round of boos. Later, Letterman asked what he meant by his slogan "I'm a uniter, not a divider." Bush replied, "It means when it comes time to sew up your chest cavity, we use stitches," a line that elicited more boos from the audience. At one point, when the conversation grew particularly testy, Letterman said to Bush: "Let me remind you of one thing, Governor: the road to Washington runs through me." Bush at least knew enough not to argue with this. At the end of the interview, he held up a "Dweebs for Bush" T-shirt that he had had specially made for the occasion.

Bush did not make the same mistake again. Later in the campaign, appearing as himself to introduce a special election edition of *Saturday Night Live*, he announced, "When they asked me to help introduce tonight's special, I felt fairly ambilavent. Although I'm a big fan, I've seen things on the show I thought were, in a word, offensible." He also gamely went on *The Tonight Show* to misspeak, pronouncing the word "flammable," for instance, "flammamabababable." And when he went back on *Letterman* he vowed that, if elected, he would "make sure the White House library has lots of books with big print and pictures." Meanwhile, Vice President Al Gore was similarly making the late-night-comedy rounds, poking fun at his woodenness, his pedantry, and his tendency to exaggerate his own achievements. "Remember, America: I gave you the Internet, and I can take it away," he said on *Letterman*. On the election edition of *SNL*, which aired just two days before voters went to the polls, he declared, "I was one of the very first to be offended by material on *Saturday Night Live*." Even after losing, Gore continued to make the comedic rounds, appearing, for example, on *SNL* again, in December 2002, to sit, half naked, in a hot tub.

One frequently offered explanation for what happened between Nixon's going on *Laugh-In* and Bush's and Gore's going on everything is the shift in American viewing habits. In 1968, 35 million Americans tuned in every night to the network news, out of a total TV-owning audience of 56 million households. Although by 1992, when Bill Clinton went on *The Arsenio Hall Show* to play "Heartbreak Hotel" on his sax, network-news viewership had increased slightly to 39 million, the total TV audience had nearly doubled, to 92.1 million. By 2000, network-news viewership had dropped to 29 million, while the total audience continued to increase, to a 101 million households.

A few months ago, the Pew Research Center for the People and the Press set out to quantify how Americans were getting information about the current presidential campaign. In a randomized survey, 1,500 adults were presented with a list of possible sources and asked which ones they were "regularly learning" something from. Among all age groups, the network news shows were cited by 35 percent and daily newspapers by

31 percent. Among respondents under the age of thirty, those figures both drop to 23 percent. Comedy shows, meanwhile, were cited by 21 percent of young people as a source that they regularly "learned" something from. And these numbers, disconcerting as they may be, only begin to tell the story.

Owing to the way that elections operate, the most sought-after voters also tend to be the most indifferent ones—those who, deep into a campaign, still don't have a clear impression of the candidates in contention. "My guess is that 95 percent of the people watching *Meet the Press* already have decided whom they're going to vote for," Jon Macks, a former political consultant who now writes for Jay Leno, told me. "Nothing is going to make them change their mind. But there's a lot of people that watch *The Tonight Show*, or any of the shows like it, who are going to see someone and they are going to connect."

Looked at in these terms, an exercise like delivering the Top Ten list   25 comes to seem just another way of reaching a critical demographic, like touring a senior citizens' center or learning Spanish. The indignity of it is simply the price the candidate pays to achieve his purpose, which is always to "connect." What this account misses, however, is the extent to which indignity *is* the purpose. Consider, for example, President Bush's recent jokes about the U.S.'s failure to find weapons of mass destruction in Iraq. At the annual Radio and Television Correspondents' dinner last month, the president presented a slide show in which he appeared as a hapless dupe, rummaging under the furniture in the Oval Office, as if for a set of lost keys. "Those weapons of mass destruction have got to be somewhere," he said brightly. The sketch, which Landon Parvin helped write, made no sense as an appeal to the youth vote—it was presented to an audience of reporters. But it was entirely consistent with the notion of preëmptive self-mockery. (When the slide show provoked outrage, a White House spokeswoman declared that the president was just "poking fun at himself," as if no further defense were needed.)

As I spoke to people who write political comedy, I kept hearing versions of Parvin's theory. Mark Katz, who recently published a memoir about his experiences writing jokes for the Clinton White House, told me, "Humor is all about acquiring political capital through likability." Al Franken, who has written for, among others, Gore and Hillary Clinton, put it this way: "Americans don't want their president or their senators to be the funniest person in the world. They just want to see that their senator or their president has a sense of humor and is a human being."

As has often been observed, one of the ways in which television has changed politics is by collapsing distinctions—enlarging the trivial and trivializing the large. In this context—the context of no context—any claim to significance is fated to descend into parody. While aspiring to be likable, or just a human being, seems a modest goal for the leader of the free world, it may, at this point, be the best that can be hoped for. When Humphrey declined to say, "I'll sock it to you, Dick!," a reluctance to compromise one's dignity could still be claimed as a political virtue. Now it can be seen for what it is: a liability that needs to be corrected by appearing, say, after a dog puppet.

Understanding the Text

1. Explain the logic of self-parody. How does such humor help political figures?

2. According to speechwriter Landon Parvin, what purpose does political humor hold for a politician?

3. What explanation does Kolbert provide for the increasing rise in self-effacing humor?

Reflection and Response

4. What kinds of evidence does Kolbert use to support her discussion of politicians employing preemptive self-parody? Which one do you find most effective and why?

5. Although Kolbert's purpose appears to be more informational than editorial, there are a couple of moments where she hints at having an opinion on the matter. Can you discern her personal view? What is your opinion of the self-parodic humor of politicians?

6. Kolbert's essay was published over a decade ago. In your view, how has the political logic of self-parody changed since then? Has this "new comic order" subsided, intensified, evolved, been replaced by another type of comedy?

Making Connections

7. What role did the logic of self-parody play during Barack Obama's presidency? What about the 2016 U.S. presidential election? Write an essay that uses Kolbert's article to analyze the appearances of President Obama and / or the 2016 presidential candidates on late-night comedy shows. Do these politicians follow or modify the script of their predecessors' self-parodic performances?

8. Russell L. Peterson observes that political candidates "go to such absurd lengths to look like someone you'd like to have a beer with" because American democracy is premised on egalitarianism (p. 227). Write an essay that synthesizes the selections from Kolbert and Peterson. Discuss how the ideas of these two authors are related. What might each author say about the other's work?

The Joke's on You

Steve Almond

Was critical consensus about the comedy of Jon Stewart and Stephen Colbert wrong by not being critical enough? Did the American public err in its positive assessment of their satire? That is the take of author Steve Almond, who casts a skeptical eye on America's most famous contemporary satirists before they left their award-winning shows on Comedy Central, *The Daily Show with Jon Stewart* (1999–2015) and *The Colbert Report* (2005–2014). Writing in 2012 for *The Baffler*, an art and criticism magazine that specializes in exposing fraudulent counterculture, Almond argues that we may be the ultimate butt of Stewart's and Colbert's satirical jokes rather than those in positions of power.

Almond is an essayist and short story writer with a background in newspaper journalism. He has taught fiction and nonfiction workshops at several universities and writer's conferences, and he is the author of ten books, including *Candyfreak: A Journey through the Chocolate Underbelly of America* (2005) and *Against Football: One Fan's Reluctant Manifesto* (2014). This provocative piece should inspire you to question your own assumptions about two of America's most beloved comedians, and it may even draw your ire.

A mong the hacks who staff our factories of conventional wisdom, evidence abounds that we are living in a golden age of political comedy. The *New York Times* nominates Jon Stewart, beloved host of Comedy Central's *Daily Show*, as the "most trusted man in America." His protégé, Stephen Colbert, enjoys the sort of slavish media coverage reserved for philanthropic rock stars. Bill Maher does double duty as HBO's resident provocateur and a regular on the cable news circuit. *The Onion*, once a satirical broadsheet published by starving college students, is now a mini-empire with its own news channel. Stewart and Colbert, in particular, have assumed the role of secular saints whose nightly shtick restores sanity to a world gone mad.

But their sanctification is not evidence of a world gone mad so much as an audience gone to lard morally, ignorant of the comic impulse's more radical virtues. Over the past decade, political humor has proliferated not as a daring form of social commentary but a reliable profit source. Our high-tech jesters serve as smirking adjuncts to the dysfunctional institutions of modern media and politics, from which all their routines derive. Their net effect is almost entirely therapeutic: they congratulate viewers for their fine habits of thought and feeling while remaining careful never to question the corrupt precepts of the status quo too vigorously.

Our lazy embrace of Stewart and Colbert is a testament to our own impoverished comic standards. We have come to accept coy mockery as genuine subversion and snarky mimesis as originality. It would be more accurate to describe our golden age of political comedy as the peak output of a lucrative corporate plantation whose chief export is a cheap and powerful opiate for progressive angst and rage.

Fans will find this assessment offensive. Stewart and Colbert, they will argue, are comedians, offering late-night entertainment in the vein of David Letterman or Jay Leno, but with a topical twist. To expect them to do anything more than make us laugh is unfair. Besides, Stewart and Colbert do play a vital civic role—they're a dependable news source for their mostly young viewers, and de facto watchdogs against media hype and political hypocrisy.

Michiko Kakutani of the *New York Times* offered a summation of the 5 majority opinion in a 2008 profile of Stewart that doubled as his highbrow coronation. "Mr. Stewart describes his job as 'throwing spitballs' from the back of the room," she wrote. "Still, he and his writers have energetically tackled the big issues of the day . . . in ways that straight news programs cannot: speaking truth to power in blunt, sometimes profane language, while using satire and playful looniness to ensure that their political analysis never becomes solemn or pretentious."

Putting aside the obvious objection that poking fun at the powerful isn't the same as bluntly confronting them, it's important to give Stewart and Colbert their due. They are both superlative comedians with brilliant writing staffs. They represent a quantum improvement over the aphoristic pabulum of the thirties satirist Will Rogers or the musical schmaltz of Beltway balladeer Mark Russell.° Stewart and Colbert have, on occasion, aimed their barbs squarely at the seats of power.

The most famous example is Colbert's turn as the featured speaker at the 2006 White House Correspondents' Association Dinner. Paying tribute to President George W. Bush, seated just a few feet away, Colbert vowed, "I stand by this man. I stand by this man because he stands for things. Not only for things, he stands on things. Things like aircraft carriers and rubble and recently flooded city squares. And that sends a strong message, that no matter what happens to America, she will always rebound—with the most powerfully staged photo ops in the world." He went on to praise, in punishing detail, the media who had served as cheerleaders for the president's factually spurious rush to war in Iraq,

---

Mark Russell: an American stand-up comedian known for his lighthearted political satire, which often takes the form of parody piano tunes.

and his embrace of domestic surveillance and torture. The crowd, composed of A-list cheerleaders, sat in stunned silence.

Stewart has generated a few similar moments of frisson, most notably when he eviscerated Jim Cramer, the frothing former hedge fund manager who hosts the CNBC show *Mad Money*, and Betsy McCaughey, an unctuous lobbyist paid by insurance companies to flog the myth of government-run "death panels" during the debate over health care reform. Stewart also played a vital role in shaming Senate Republicans into supporting a bill to provide medical care for 9/11 first responders.

What's notable about these episodes, though, is how uncharacteristic they are. What Stewart and Colbert do most nights is convert civic villainy into disposable laughs. They prefer Horatian satire to Juvenalian, and thus treat the ills of modern media and politics as matters of folly, not concerted evil. Rather than targeting the obscene cruelties borne of greed and fostered by apathy, they harp on a rogues' gallery of hypocrites familiar to anyone with a TiVo or a functioning memory. Wit, exaggeration, and gentle mockery trump ridicule and invective. The goal is to mollify people, not incite them.

> "What Stewart and Colbert do most nights is convert civic villainy into disposable laughs. They prefer Horatian satire to Juvenalian, and thus treat the ills of modern media and politics as matters of folly, not concerted evil."

In Kakutani's adoring *New York Times* profile, Stewart spoke of his comedic mission as though it were an upscale antidepressant: "It's a wonderful feeling to have this toxin in your body in the morning, that little cup of sadness, and feel by 7 or 7:30 that night, you've released it in sweat equity and can move on to the next day." What's missing from this formulation is the idea that comedy might, you know, change something other than your mood.

Back in October of 2004, Stewart made a now-famous appearance on the CNN debate show *Crossfire*, hosted by the liberal pundit Paul Begala and his conservative counterpart Tucker Carlson. Stewart framed his visit as an act of honor. He had been mocking the contrived combat of *Crossfire* on his program and wanted to face his targets. The segment quickly devolved into a lecture. "Stop, stop, stop, stop hurting America," he told Carlson. "See, the thing is, we need your help. Right now, you're helping the politicians and the corporations. And we're left out there to mow our lawns." The exchange went viral. Stewart was hailed as a hero: here, at last, was a man brave enough to condemn the tyranny of a middling cable shoutfest.

But who, exactly, did Stewart mean by "we"? He's not just some poor schnook who works the assembly line at a factory then goes home to mow his lawn. He's a media celebrity who works for Viacom, one of the largest entertainment corporations in the world. Stewart can score easy points by playing the humble populist. But he's as comfortable on the corporate plantation as any of the buffoons he delights in humiliating.

The queasy irony here is that Stewart and Colbert are parasites of the dysfunction they mock. Without blowhards such as Carlson and shameless politicians, Stewart would be out of a job that pays him a reported $14 million per annum. Without the bigoted bluster of Bill O'Reilly and Rush Limbaugh, *The Colbert Report* would not exist. They aren't just invested in the status quo, but dependent on it.

Consider, in this context, Stewart's coverage of the Occupy Wall Street movement. His initial segment highlighted the hypocrisy of those who portrayed the protestors in Zuccotti Park as lawless and menacing while praising Tea Party rallies as quintessentially patriotic. But Stewart was careful to include a caveat: "I mean, look, if this thing turns into throwing trash cans into Starbucks windows, nobody's gonna be down with that," he said, alluding to vandalism by activists during a 1999 World Trade Organization summit. Stewart then leaned toward the camera and said, in his best guilty-liberal stage whisper, "We all love Starbucks." The audience laughed approvingly. Protests for economic justice are worthy of our praise, just so long as they don't take aim at our luxuries. The show later sent two correspondents down to Zuccotti Park. One highlighted the various "weirdos" on display. The other played up the alleged class divisions within those occupying the park. Both segments trivialized the movement by playing to right-wing stereotypes of protestors as self-indulgent neo-hippies.

Stewart sees himself as a commonsense critic, above the vulgar fray of 15 partisan politics. But in unguarded moments—comparing Steve Jobs to Thomas Edison, say, or crowing over the assassination of Osama bin Laden—he betrays an allegiance to good old American militarism and the free market. In his first show after the attacks of September 11, he delivered a soliloquy that channeled the histrionic patriotism of the moment. "The view from my apartment was the World Trade Center," he said shakily, "and now it's gone, and they attacked it. This symbol of American ingenuity, and strength, and labor, and imagination, and commerce, and it is gone. But you know what the view is now? The Statue of Liberty. The view from the South of Manhattan is now the Statue of Liberty. You can't beat that."

It does not take a particularly supple intellect to discern the subtext here. The twin towers may have symbolized "ingenuity" and "imagination" to Americans such as Stewart and his brother, Larry, the chief operating officer of the New York Stock Exchange's parent company. But to most people in the world, the WTC embodied the global reach of U.S.-backed corporate cartels. It's not the sort of monument that would showcase a pledge to shelter the world's "huddled masses." In fact, it's pretty much the opposite of that. To imply a kinship between the towers and the Statue of Liberty—our nation's most potent symbol of immigrant striving—is to promote a reality crafted by Fox News CEO Roger Ailes. Stewart added this disclaimer: "Tonight's show is not obviously a regular show. We looked through the vault and we found some clips that we thought might make you smile, which is really what's necessary, I think, uh, right about now."

You got that? In times of national crisis, the proper role of the comedian is not to challenge the prevailing jingoistic hysteria, but to induce smiles.

The Daily Show and *The Colbert Report* are not just parodies of news shows. They also include interview segments. And it is here that Stewart, at least occasionally, sheds his greasepaint and red rubber nose. With the help of his research department, he is even capable of exposing lightweight frauds such as Jim Cramer.

More often, though, his interviews are cozy affairs, promotional vehicles for whatever commodity his guest happens to be pimping. He's not interested in visitors who might interrogate the hegemonic dogmas of corporate capitalism. On the contrary, his green room is often stocked with Fox News regulars. Neocon apologist Bill Kristol has appeared on the show a record eleven times since 2003. Mike Huckabee has visited seven times, Newt Gingrich, Chris Wallace, and Ed Gillespie five times, and so on and so forth, on down the dismal demagogic food chain: Lou Dobbs, Ron Paul, Michael Steele, Juan Williams, Ralph Reed, Dick Armey. Stewart, who is nothing if not courteous, allows each of these con men to speak his piece. He pokes fun at the more obvious lines of bullshit. The audience chortles. *Now for a message from our sponsors.*

When Stewart hosts a figure of genuine political power, the discussion 20 usually winds up anodyne. A 2010 visit with former Secretary of State Condoleezza Rice was especially painful to witness. Stewart, a prominent critic of the Bush administration's war in Iraq, seemed starstruck. "What does the burden feel like," he asked Rice, "on a day-to-day basis, agree or disagree with the policy?" It was a textbook illustration of the golden parachute of politics. Having left office, Rice's sins were, if not forgotten, then at least deferred for promotional purposes. His guest had a new memoir to sell, after all. "I'm telling you, you gotta pick up [Rice's book] about a patriotic American who is, if I may, doing the best that . . ." Stewart paused awkwardly, as if suddenly recognizing what a shill he'd become. "We'll have the other conversation a different time."

When Rice returned a year later to promote a book about her years in the Bush White House, what emerged was Stewart's obeisance to figures of authority. "I hate to harp on this," he said at one point, attempting to redirect Rice back to her use of bogus intelligence. He asked her no explicit questions about, for instance, a report by the House Committee on Government Reform citing twenty-nine false or misleading public statements she had made about Iraq's weapons of mass destruction and links to Al Qaeda. While Stewart played the milquetoast, Rice commandeered the conversation, suggesting that without the Iraq war the Arab Spring would never have happened and (by the way) Iraq and Iran would be locked in a nuclear arms race. Once a charming propagandist, always a charming propagandist!

In a sense, Rice owed Stewart an even larger debt. His criticism of the Iraq war—a series of reports under the banner Mess O'Potamia—might have done more to diffuse the antiwar movement than the phone surveillance clauses embedded in the Patriot Act. Why take to the streets when Stewart and Colbert are on the case? It's a lot easier, and more fun, to experience the war as a passive form of entertainment than as a source of moral distress requiring citizen activism.

Colbert's interviews are even more trivializing. While he occasionally welcomes figures from outside the corporate zoo, his brash persona demands that he interrupt and confound them. If they try to match wits with him, they get schooled. If they play it straight, they get steamrolled. The underlying dynamic of Colbert's show, after all, is that he never loses an argument. The only acceptable forms of outrage reside in his smug denial of any narrative that questions American supremacy.

In this sense, Colbert the pundit can be seen as a postmodern incarnation of the country's first comic archetype, the "Yankee" (a designation that was then a national, rather than regional, term). As described by Constance Rourke in her 1931 survey, *American Humor: A Study of the National Character*, the Yankee is a gangly figure, sly and uneducated, who specializes in tall tales and practical jokes. Unlike Stewart, whose humor clearly arises from the Jewish tradition of outsider social commentary, Colbert plays the consummate insider, a cartoon patriot suitable for export. But Colbert's mock punditry reinforces a dismissive view of actual corporate demagogues. Bill "Papa Bear" O'Reilly and his ilk come off as laughable curmudgeons, best mocked rather than rebutted, even as they steer our common discourse away from sensible policy and toward toxic forms of grievance.

And Colbert's own flag-fellating routine often bends toward unin- 25 tended sincerity. His visit to Iraq in June 2009 amounted to a weeklong infomercial for the U.S. military. It kicked off with a segment in which black ops abduct Colbert from his makeup room and transport him to a TV stage set in Baghdad, which turns out to be one of Saddam Hussein's former palaces. Colbert is a brilliant improvisational comedian, adept at puncturing the vanities of his persona in the same way Bob Hope once did. (Colbert even brandished a golf club for his opening monologue in Baghdad, an homage to Hope, a frequent USO entertainer.) Still, there's something unsettling about seeing America's recent legacy of extraordinary rendition mined for laughs.

Colbert's first guest, General Ray Odierno, commander of the multinational forces in Iraq, was treated to questions such as, "What's happening here that's not being reported that you think people back home should know about?" The hulking general then gave the host a buzz cut, as a crowd of several hundred uniformed soldiers roared.

Colbert himself acknowledged his reverence for the troops in interviews leading up to his visit. ("Sometimes my character and I agree.") So it wasn't exactly shocking that the shows themselves were full of reflexive sanctification of the military. Soldiers, by Colbert's reckoning, aren't moral actors who choose to brandish weapons, but paragons of manly virtue whose sole function is to carry out their orders—in this case "bringing democracy" to a hellish Arab backwater. This is an utterly authoritarian mind-set.

Stewart, at least, has displayed the temerity to question American military might on occasion. A few months before Colbert's Iraq adventure, in the midst of a heated debate over torture with yet another neocon guest, Cliff May, Stewart dared to opine that President Harry S. Truman was a war criminal for ordering the bombing of Hiroshima and Nagasaki during World War II. His statement was shocking in its candor: "I think if you dropped an atom bomb fifteen miles offshore and you said, 'The next one's coming and hitting you,' then I would think it's okay. To drop one on a city, and kill a hundred thousand people. Yeah. I think that's criminal."

Two days later, Stewart issued an on-air apology: "The atomic bomb— a very complicated decision in the context of a horrific war, and I walk [my statement] back because it was in my estimation a stupid thing to say. Which, by the way, as it was coming out of your mouth, you ever do that, where you're saying something and as it's coming out you're like, 'What the fuck?' And it just sat in there for a couple of days, just sitting going, 'No, no, he wasn't, and you should really say that out loud on the show.' So I am, right now, and, man, ew. Sorry."

This mea culpa was not spurred by a media uproar or a corporate 30 directive (as far as we know) or any apparent reexamination of Truman's decision, which (for the record) led to the deaths of an estimated

250,000 Japanese, most of them civilians. It was, more revealingly, the result of Stewart's inbred aversion to conflict, to making any statement that might depart too dramatically from the cultural consensus and land him at the center of a controversy.

An even more dramatic example came during his 2010 interview with Rachel Maddow, during which Stewart trotted out one of his favorite canards, that "both sides have their way of shutting down debate."

Maddow asked, "What's the lefty way of shutting down debate?"

"You've said Bush is a war criminal," Stewart replied. "Now that may be technically true. In my world, a war criminal is Pol Pot or the Nuremberg trials. . . . But I think that's such an incendiary charge that when you put it into conversation as, well, technically he is, that may be right, but it feels like a conversation stopper, not a conversation starter." This is the Stewart credo distilled: civility at any cost, even in the face of moral atrocity.

By contrast, consider the late Bill Hicks, a stand-up comedian of the same approximate vintage as Stewart and Colbert. "You never see my attitude in the press," Hicks once observed. "For instance, gays in the military. . . . Gays who want to be in the military. Here's how I feel about it, alright? Anyone dumb enough to want to be in the military should be allowed in. End of fucking story. That should be the only requirement. I don't care how many push-ups you can do. Put on a helmet, go wait in that foxhole, we'll tell you when we need you to kill somebody. . . . I watched these fucking congressional hearings and all these military guys and the pundits, 'Seriously, aww, the esprit de corps will be affected, and we are such a moral'—excuse me! Aren't y'all fucking *hired killers?* Shut up! You are thugs and when we need you to go blow the fuck out of a nation of little brown people, we'll let you know. . . . *I don't want any gay people hanging around me while I'm killing kids!"*

Fellow comics considered Hicks a genius, and he did well in clubs. But 35 he never broke into national television because he violated the cardinal rule of televised comedy—one passed down from Johnny Carson through the ages—which is to flatter and reassure the viewer. David Letterman invited Hicks to perform on his show but cut his routine just before the broadcast. Several years after Hick's death, an apologetic Letterman ran a clip of the spot Hicks had recorded. It was obvious why Letterman—or the network higher-ups—had axed it. The routine openly mocked everyone from pro-lifers to homosexuals.

To hear Hicks rant about the evils of late-model capitalism ("By the way, if anyone here is in advertising or marketing, kill yourself"), or militant Christians, or consumerism, is to encounter the wonder of a voice free of what Marshall McLuhan called the "corporate mask." Hicks understood that comedy's highest calling is to confront the moral complacency of your audience—and the sponsors. This willingness to traffic in radical ideas is what makes comic work endure, from Aristophanes's indictments of Athenian war profiteers to Jonathan Swift's "modest proposal" that Irish parents sell their children as food to rich gourmands, from Lenny Bruce's anguished, anarchic riffs to George Carlin's rants. "There's a reason education sucks, and it's the same reason that it will never, ever, ever, be fixed," Carlin once said, though not on *The Daily Show*. "The owners of this country don't want that. I'm talking about the real owners now. The real owners, the big wealthy business interests that control things and make all the important decisions. Forget the politicians. The politicians are put there to give you the idea that you have freedom of choice. You don't."

In a 1906 address at Carnegie Hall entitled "Taxes and Morals," Mark Twain lambasted plutocrats who advertised their piety while lying about their incomes. "I know all those people," Twain noted. "I have friendly, social, and criminal relations with the whole lot of them." He said that word—*criminal*—knowing that many of these folks were seated in the gallery before him. Twain had this to say about the patriotism of his day: "The Patriot did not know just how or when or where he got his opinions, neither did he care, so long as he was with what seemed the majority— which was the main thing, the safe thing, the comfortable thing." It's this quality of avoiding danger, of seeking the safety of consensus, that characterizes the aesthetic of Stewart and Colbert. They're adept at savaging the safe targets—vacuous talking heads and craven senators. But you will never hear them referring to our soldiers as "uniformed assassins," as Twain did in describing an American attack on a tribal group in the Philippines.

It's worth noting that Twain's scathing indictment of the military initially was redacted from his autobiography by an editor concerned that such comments would tarnish the author's reputation. And it's equally worth pondering the constraints that define Stewart and Colbert's acceptable zone of satire. After all, their shows air on Comedy Central, which is owned by Viacom, the fifth largest media conglomerate in the world.

Apart from bleeped out profanity, there appears to be no censorship, ideological or otherwise, enforced by the suits at Viacom. So long as Stewart and Colbert keep earning ratings (and ad dollars), they can do what they like. This is how the modern comedy plantation functions. It's essentially self-policing. You find yourself out of a job only when your candor costs the bean counters more than it makes them.

Bill Maher learned this in 2001, when, as the host of ABC's *Politically* 40 *Incorrect*, he offered a rebuttal to President Bush's assertion that the

9/11 hijackers were cowards. "We have been the cowards," Maher observed. "Lobbing cruise missiles from two thousand miles away. That's cowardly. Staying in the airplane when it hits the building. Say what you want about it. Not cowardly."

What followed was a textbook case of economic censorship. The right-wing media launched into the expected paroxysms, and the mainstream media fanned the fury. Maher insisted he was making a linguistic argument, not endorsing the terrorists. But it was too late. FedEx and Sears Roebuck pulled their ads, and ABC cancelled *Politically Incorrect* in early 2002. Soon after, the Los Angeles Press Club awarded Maher an award for "championing free speech," and he took his act to HBO, where he didn't have to worry about offending sponsors.

For Viacom chief Sumner Redstone, airing shows with offensive content isn't a problem. Redstone grew up in the entertainment business. After earning a law degree and acquainting himself with the intricacies of tax law, he joined his father's movie theater chain. Redstone's crucial insight was to recognize that, while new means of distribution might evolve, content was the vital commodity. He built his father's business accordingly, eventually acquiring Viacom in a hostile takeover. The corporation now owns 170 media networks and thousands of programs, including *Jersey Shore*, which celebrates binge drinking, brawling, and the vigorous pursuit of venereal disease and melanoma.

In the corporate mind-set, the specifics of "content" are irrelevant. Either you generate the necessary margin, or you cease to exist. "Content is king," as Redstone is famously fond of pointing out. And profit is God.

If there's one program on Comedy Central that affirms this maxim, it's not *The Daily Show* or *The Colbert Report*, but the cartoon satire *South Park*. Over the course of sixteen seasons, the show's creators, Trey Parker and Matt Stone, have pursued taboo topics with abandon. An episode entitled "Trapped in the Closet" not only played off rumors that Tom Cruise is gay but also condemned Scientology as "a big fat global scam" and exposed its various loony secrets. Other *South Park* episodes have used epithets and profanity as a way of confronting our collective neuroses about race, religion, and sexual orientation. The only publicized instances of Comedy Central censoring *South Park* have been in response to episodes in which Parker and Stone used images of the Prophet Muhammad that provoked threats of violence.

South Park indulges in a good deal of bathroom humor—perhaps 45 inevitably, given that its protagonists are ten-year-olds. But the show is far more radical than its polished stablemates for the simple reason that it is willing to confront its viewers. Parker and Stone savage both the defensive bigotry of conservatives and the self-righteous entitlement of the left. They accomplish this not by riffing on the corruption of our media and political cultures, but by creating original dramas that expose the lazy assumptions and shallow gratifications of the viewing audience.

Surveying the defects of American governance more than eight decades ago, H. L. Mencken° issued the following decree: "The only way that democracy can be made bearable is by developing and cherishing a class of men sufficiently honest and disinterested to challenge the prevailing quacks. No such class has ever appeared in strength in the United States. Thus the business of harassing the quacks devolves upon the newspapers. When they fail in their duty, which is usually, we are at the quacks' mercy."

To their millions of fans, Jon Stewart and Stephen Colbert represent the vanguard of just such a class. And hope for their leadership was never more keenly felt than in the weeks leading up to their vaunted Rally to Restore Sanity and/or Fear. The gathering, a hastily conceived send-up of Glenn Beck's Restoring Honor Rally, took place three days before the 2010 midterm elections, with a stated purpose of calling for civility.

But the event itself accomplished nothing beyond revealing the bathos of Stewart and Colbert. It boiled down to a goofy variety show, capped by one of Stewart's mawkish soliloquies. His central point was that Americans are a decent people, capable of making "reasonable compromises." By way of proof he showed a video of cars merging in the Holland Tunnel. "These millions of cars must somehow find a way to squeeze one by one into a mile-long, thirty-foot-wide tunnel carved underneath a mighty river," Stewart said. "And they do it. Concession by concession. 'You go. Then I'll go. You go, then I'll go. . . . Oh my God, is that an NRA [National Rifle Association] sticker on your car, is that an Obama sticker on your car? Well, that's okay. You go and then I'll go.' Sure, at some point there will be a selfish jerk who zips up the shoulder and cuts in at the last minute. But that individual is rare and he is scorned, and not hired as an analyst."

It's hard to know where to begin with a metaphor this misguided. But it might be instructive to contemplate the rise of right-wing radio, an industry borne of commuter rage, which now dominates not just the Republican Party but our national discourse. Stewart would have us believe that selfish jerks never get hired as analysts. But as his sidekick Colbert clearly demonstrates, that's exactly who gets hired at the networks—folks who can excite our primal states of negative feeling: wrath, envy, fear. In Stewart's daffy formulation, pundits and politicians are the ones who prey

---

H. L. Mencken: (1880–1956) an American journalist, satirist, and cultural critic.

on an otherwise noble citizenry. But it's us citizens who watch those pundits and elect those politicians. We've chosen to degrade our discourse. Stewart and Colbert make their nut by catering to those citizens who choose to laugh at the results rather than work to change them.

Having convinced more than 200,000 such folks to get off their butts 50 and crowd the National Mall—not to mention the two and a half million who watched the proceedings on television or online—Stewart's call to action amounted to: "If you want to know why I'm here and what I want from you, I can only assure you this: you have already given it to me. Your presence was what I wanted." Such is the apotheosis of the Stewart-Colbert doctrine: the civic "rally" as televised corporate spectacle, with special merit badges awarded for attendance.

Bill Maher was one of the few prominent voices to call his comrades out. "If you're going to have a rally where hundreds of thousands of people show up, you might as well go ahead and make it about something," he said. He went on to point out the towering naïveté of their nonpartisan approach, with its bogus attempt to equate the insanity of left and right: "Martin Luther King spoke on that mall in the capital and he didn't say, 'Remember folks, those Southern sheriffs with the fire hoses and the German shepherds, they have a point too!' No. He said, 'I have a dream. They have a nightmare!' . . . Liberals like the ones on that field must stand up and be counted and not pretend that we're as mean or greedy or shortsighted or just plain batshit as they are, and if that's too polarizing for you and you still want to reach across the aisle and hold hands and sing with someone on the right, try church."

Maher's dissent, all but lost amid the orgy of liberal self-congratulation, echoed Mencken's exhortation: one must *challenge* the quacks to get rid of them. The reason our discourse has grown vicious, and has drifted away from matters of actual policy and their moral consequence, isn't because of some misunderstanding between cultural factions. It is the desired result of a sustained campaign waged by corporations, lobbyists, politicians, and demagogues who have placed private gain over the common good.

In a sense, these quacks have no more reliable allies than Stewart and Colbert. For the ultimate ethos of their television programs is this: the customer is always right. We need not give in to sorrow, or feel disgust, or take action, because our brave clown princes have the tonic for what ails the national spirit. Their clever brand of pseudo-subversion guarantees a jolt of righteous mirth to the viewer, a feeling that evaporates the moment their shows end. At which point we return to our given role as citizens: consuming whatever the quacks serve up next.

Understanding the Text

1. What criticisms does Almond lob at comedians Jon Stewart and Stephen Colbert? How does he characterize the purpose of their humor?

2. According to Almond, what distinguishes Colbert's humor from Stewart's? How does the purpose of humorists Bill Hicks's and Mark Twain's comedy differ from that of Stewart's and Colbert's comedy?

3. What "constraints" does Almond claim "define Stewart and Colbert's acceptable zone of satire" (par. 38)? What limitations blunt their political satire, making it more Horatian than Juvenalian?

Reflection and Response

4. Almond's powerful diction gives his refutation of Stewart's and Colbert's widespread acclaim a polemical tone. Examine Almond's word choices as well as the general tone he adopts. What assumptions about the purpose of political satire do they reveal? In what ways does Almond's language disclose his own political ideology? Do you agree with his assumptions? Is his assessment fair and accurate?

5. Like any skilled rhetorician, Almond incorporates counterarguments into his essay. What opposing positions does he include, and how does their presence strengthen his own argument? Are there any counterarguments that you feel undermine his position's persuasiveness?

6. Who is your favorite satirist? Does your opinion of this satirist lead you to agree or disagree with Almond's critical assessment of Stewart and Colbert, or do you feel ambivalent about it? Explain.

Making Connections

7. Almond criticizes fake news anchors for the same reason that Peterson (pp. 220–224) finds fault with late-night talk-show comedians. Write an essay that examines how Almond's argument relates to Peterson's. Do you agree with one author more than other? Support your assertions by citing relevant passages from these selections.

8. Almond praises the satirical cartoon *South Park* at the expense of Stewart and Colbert, writing, "But [*South Park*] is far more radical than its polished stablemates for the simple reason that it is willing to confront its viewers" (par. 45). Peterson (p. 222) and Tueth (p. 104) also evaluate this show. Write an essay that synthesizes the views of these authors and offers your own take on the quality of *South Park*'s comedy and satire.

Moving Beyond Critique

Amber Day

Amber Day is Assistant Professor of Media and Performance Studies in the Department of English and Cultural Studies at Bryant University. She has published in several academic journals, including *Social Research, Popular Communication*, and the *International Journal of Communication*.

This excerpt originally served as the concluding chapter of Day's book *Satire and Dissent: Interventions in Contemporary Political Debate*, published by Indiana University Press in 2011. The book examines a common purpose of parody news shows, satiric documentaries, and ironic activist performances: to disrupt, critique, and correct the scripted political discourse of mainstream media. As she writes in this chapter, these three comedic genres share a "desire to reframe political narratives" (par. 3). When reading, consider how "Moving Beyond Critique" relates to Almond's criticisms of Jon Stewart and Stephen Colbert in the previous reading.

Though they are distinctly different genres, parodic news shows, satiric documentaries, and ironic activist groups are all manifestations of similar impulses. There is no question that the three genres are linked to larger cultural trends, of which both viewers and practitioners are cognizant. As one reviewer for the first Yes Men documentary put it in reference to the film's potential appeal, "[T]his is the era of Bush-Kerry, *Jackass: The Movie, The Corporation, Super Size Me*, the *Onion* and of course Michael Moore (who even makes a cameo appearance in *The Yes Men*), which is to say an era in which things once considered commercial anathema—like politics, documentaries, and anti-corporate dissent—are bankable."[1] The popularity of each serves to fuel the momentum of all. It is not a coincidence that Andrew Boyd of Billionaires for Bush explicitly links the sensibility of his group with that of *The Daily Show* and Michael Moore, arguing that each incorporates an "ironic sensibility, which is a deep current in youth culture,"[2] or that Mike Bonanno of ®™ark and the Yes Men argues that, like Michael Moore's, his work is built on communicating information that is otherwise not found in the American press.[3]

The three genres share a cluster of characteristics, the first being a generalized political dissent, as the critic quoted above points to. More specifically, they share a desire to make an end run around the standard conduits of political information and around the standard formulas within the mainstream media. While the parodic news shows critique the substance and tenor of the debates carried on mainstream news programming, a group like the Yes Men mimics the performance of power and expertise in order to draw critical attention to its core. All attempt to reframe the terms of discussion and/or to temporarily hijack the discussion out of the hands of authority. All irreverently question taken-for-granted attributions of rationality and where that rationality resides, claiming alternative forms of expertise. They aim not just to dissent but to shift the topics and terms of the debate, often attempting to undermine the power of the dominant narrative.

In addition to this desire to reframe political narratives, all share a pointedly comedic and improvisational mode. This involves a heightened sense of irony; highlighting contradictions, inconsistencies, and absurdities; mining them for their humor; and even highlighting their own flaws and fakeries. This mode also involves an emphasis on impromptu encounters between individuals. The dynamic, first-person frame not only sets these genres apart from many traditional forms of satire but also allows them to actively impact the world of political deliberation. The performers interact with public officials, draw real political issues into their own satiric frames, and usurp traditional authority. They are always potentially threatening to their targets in that their parodic send-ups, satiric attacks, and ironic impersonations run the risk of becoming definitively real—of actually tripping up, revealing, or sabotaging. As performative satire, these forms have the potential to bring into being precisely that which they name or enact.

That is not to say that the people and groups surveyed here are always equally successful in achieving their goals, that they necessarily share exactly the same goals, or that they all have an analogous effect. As Richard Schechner explains about all forms of performance, including ritual and theater, each individual example involves some combination of both efficacy and entertainment. The two qualities, he writes, "are not so much opposed to each other; rather they form the poles of a continuum,"[4] and no performance is entirely lacking in one or the other. Accordingly, these particular examples embody differing combinations of efficacy and entertainment. The parodic news shows, for example, must position themselves primarily as entertainment, attracting significant numbers of viewers for their networks and advertisers. They do certainly contain political material, serving as spaces for critique of the inadequacies of contemporary political discourse, but they do not necessarily involve an active politics nor an organized call to action. Yet, due to their high profile and topical immediacy, they sometimes end up having a larger impact on the political discussion than do many of the other examples. The documentaries are also objects of mass entertainment designed for market consumption, though they have a more developed mandate to educate, to inspire, and, most important, to create a sustained sense of community in opposition. Finally, the activist groups have political efficacy as their primary goal, but they employ entertaining techniques as a means of attracting notice and maintaining enthusiasm since they are by far the most marginal of the case studies. Since they do not have steady media amplification at their disposal, they seek to momentarily capture the attention of existing sympathetic communities and, in so doing, to turn these discursive communities into actively politicized ones.

Regardless of their respective mixes of efficacy and entertainment, however, these genres and their practitioners have all succeeded to differing degrees in becoming pop culture phenomena, striking resonant chords for numerous fans. Each is able to function as a cultural reference point, becoming the medium through which particular issues are identified and pushed into wider discussion. In the process, they provide audience members with the satisfaction of hearing their own perspectives articulated in a public forum, while functioning as a shared reference for identification.

As widely circulated cultural texts, these entertainers and activists attract strong affective communities, or counterpublics, around them. While much of the sentiment expressed in these genres clearly preexists many of the particular texts themselves, the texts serve to heighten the feeling of community in opposition and to fuel the continued circulation of discourse around the issues in question. Indeed, this community-building function is one of the most significant aspects of their overall effect. I have conceptualized this element of rallying the troops and encouraging community in opposition in terms of building counterpublics, communities of discussion and opinion that are somehow opposed to the dominant. And, indeed, it seems that the ironic mode is particularly adept in this regard. The remaining issue is whether this counterpublic creation can move from simple opposition to a more fleshed-out platform for concrete change.

One of the most damning criticisms leveled at ironic, parodic, and satiric modes of critique is that they are parasitically linked with the society they are critiquing, meaning that these modes are always locked in a negative bind, criticizing but not helping to produce a positive vision for the future. Along these lines, Christine Harold argues that appropriation artists and pranksters, while providing some satisfaction, are always acting in reaction to corporations and brands, meaning they are "not up to the task of providing new material, new ways of responding to or amplifying the legal substrates that make brands and markets work in the first place,"[5] though they can help to call our attention to these substrates. Indeed, much of the time, parody and satire focus on what is wrong with the current situation, but they can sometimes do little toward articulating what an alternative might look like. This would seem to be a serious limitation, particularly for explicitly political material. However, . . . the highly politicized and engaged forms of satire chronicled here tend to gesture beyond the problematic present, often even providing concrete suggestions for alternatives. The parodic news hosts frequently use their interview segments, in particular, as a form of inquiry into what alternatives might look like, actively searching for solutions to problems while modeling some of the qualities they would like to see in journalism. And the documentarians do often provide their audiences with suggestions for what could be done differently. Granted, they do not always succeed in this regard; *Fahrenheit 9/11*, for example, spends a lot of time tracing the links between enormous foreign political contributions and government policy, but it has few suggestions for reforming the system beyond voting George W. Bush out of office, even though he was clearly not the first to be influenced by these factors. However, elsewhere, Moore does offer a number of international examples (from countries like Canada, France, and Cuba) as illustrations of better solutions to a variety of problems. Most important, he attempts to rally his fans to demand change.

As far as activist groups are concerned, it is admittedly more common for them to mount a critique of the way things currently are or, in ironic mode, to poke fun at the flaws of policies, but some of the playful contemporary groups are also experimenting with ways of moving beyond negative critique alone. Most spectacularly, in November 2008, only a few days after the presidential election, a number of diverse activist groups, including the Yes Men, United for Peace & Justice, Code Pink, the Anti-Advertising Agency, Improv Everywhere, and others, came together in a massive collaboration, printing and distributing tens of thousands of copies of a fake edition of the *New York Times*. Rather than critique the state of the news media or a particular topical story, the activists created a vision of the world that they hoped to see in the not-too-distant future. The paper was a spot-on reproduction of the layout of the *Times*, which might have fooled most readers at first glance, but closer examination revealed that the date of publication was listed as July 4, 2009, roughly eight months in the future, and the slogan on the masthead was not "All the News That's Fit to Print" but "All the News We Hope to Print." The content was indeed aspirational. The top headline blared "Iraq War Ends," and the story explained that U.S. troops were all coming home while the

United Nations was moving in to perform peacekeeping duties and to aid in rebuilding the country. Other stories included Congress passing a "maximum wage law," the treasury announcing a "true cost" tax plan which would tax items that are damaging to the environment, and impending national health care. Everything in the 14-page paper conjured an image of what the country could look like, given a progressive tilt in priorities. Even the advertisements were designed as a form of wishful thinking. A full-page fake ad for KBR,° for instance, explained that, though it had supported military operations in Iraq in the quest for its resources, it would now celebrate the outbreak of peace, as it is a "solutions company" that will work toward planning municipal roads, power grids, schools, and hospitals. An advertisement for ExxonMobil declared that the company was committed to meeting the new congressional guidelines for "socially, economically, & environmentally responsible energy" and that it had learned that peace, not just war, can be lucrative.

The scale of the action was impressive, involving the production and printing of thousands of copies of the newspaper, the coordination of hundreds of volunteers handing out copies at subway stations, the creation of an accompanying fake *New York Times* website, and the release of a coordinated series of press releases. It also required the collaboration of a wide variety of existing groups and the amassing of funds in the form of small online donations solicited through the Yes Men's email list (without giving away exactly what they were raising money for). Beyond the logistical triumphs, though, the stunt also represented a significant shift in focus for many of the ironic and parodic activist groups involved. No longer loudly protesting the policies and tone of the Bush administration, as these groups had for eight years, this action was focused on creating a vision for what the upcoming Obama era *should* look like (a deliberately idealized one). As one of the participants explained in a press release, she thought of it as a reminder that they needed to push harder than ever, since "we've got to make sure Obama and all the other Democrats do what we elected them to do. After eight or maybe twenty-eight years of hell, we need to start imagining heaven."[6] Another contributor explained, "It's about what's possible, if we think big and act collectively."[7]

This approach is what [Henry] Jenkins and [Stephen] Duncombe have 10 referred to as "critical utopianism,"[8] which is what happens when satiric, parodic, and ironic activists imagine a world that almost cannot be. Using

---

KBR: an American engineering, procurement, and construction company formerly known as Kellogg Brown & Root that has been involved in a number of controversies, most notably for its lucrative contracts during the Iraq War when it was a subsidiary of Halliburton.

Scott Beiben holds up a copy of the fake *New York Times* at the premiere of *The Yes Men Fix the World* during the 2009 Sundance Film Festival.
WireImage/Getty Images

the Yes Men's Dow Chemical stunt° as an example, the authors explain that the group creates a glimpse of a world in which Dow would actually appear on the BBC and take moral and legal responsibility for its corporate actions, ideally leading viewers to ask the questions, "Why is it so crazy that a corporation would do this? Why is this something that has to be a prank?" The intent is to ultimately pose the larger question of "What if?" Contemplating the "what if?" should then spur people to consider alternatives and to start thinking about what actually needs changing. As Jenkins puts it, "[W]hen we imagine alternatives, we go back to the world we live in and ideally we also begin to think of the steps that will get us from the undesirable present to the much more desired future."[9] While the activists involved in the *New York Times* hoax likely did not believe that all of their policy predictions would come to pass in just a few

Yes Men's Dow Chemical stunt: a reference to a 2004 hoax pulled off by the activist group Yes Men. On the twentieth anniversary of the Bhopal, India disaster, in which thousands died from a hazardous gas leak at a plant owned by Dow Chemical, Andy Bichlbaum appeared on the television program *BBC World*, posing as a spokesperson for Dow and claiming full responsibility for the disaster. Dow's stocks took a hit as a result of the hoax before the BBC issued an on-air apology.

months of a new administration, they were setting up the "what if?" by asking people to imagine alternatives to the present and to inspire them to work toward some of the objectives. One of the articles in the paper, in fact, gives a pointed account of the mass popular pressure that had supposedly resulted in the recent progressive tilt, explaining that a recent (fictional) study reported that there had been "a three-fold increase in the incidence of letters, phone calls, faxes, and email received by congressional offices, 88 percent of which were from people who identified themselves as new members of particular activist organizations."[10] The message is clear: some of this is possible if more of us get involved.

This stunt is particularly notable for its attempt to draw on the power of counterpublics, not just to get everyone angry about the present (which is certainly important in itself, as I have argued), but to further spur them to work toward particular alternatives. I am closing with this anecdote because it is a particularly good example of ironic critique that manages to move beyond criticism toward articulating a vision of what the future might look like. This is another instance of irony used in the service of entirely earnest ends, in this case very concrete ends. And, importantly, as some activists' opening salvo in the new era of the Obama presidency, an era that had been predicted to quash parody and irony, this stunt is both parodic *and* entirely sincere, hopeful, and engaged.

Regardless of technique, all of these examples of irony, satire, and parody are intended as methods of intruding into the public conversation. Rather than engendering cynicism, as their critics charge, they are a calculated shot across the bow of the cynically manufactured elements of public debate. The fact that these hybrid, highly political, and satiric genres are sparking so much interest, innovation, and enthusiasm is particularly significant, especially when seen against the background of what is reported as continued widespread political apathy and disinterest. In an era when political discourse is so often overproduced, stage-managed, and predictably choreographed, these examples of performative satire, parody, and irony offer a way of satisfyingly breaking through the existing script. That these modes are providing a sense of connection and purpose to many in a way that organized politics has often struggled to do should be significant to all those interested in political communication and in the circulation of cultural and political narratives.

> "In an era when political discourse is so often overproduced, stage-managed, and predictably choreographed, these examples of performative satire, parody, and irony offer a way of satisfyingly breaking through the existing script."

Notes

1. Geoff Pevere, "Yes Men: Droll Pranksters," *Toronto Star*, Oct. 1, 2004, D8.

2. Donovan Slack, "Billionaires for Bush? Well, Yes and No," *Boston Globe*, March 26, 2004, A16.

3. Lawrie Zion, "Affirmative Action Men," *Australian*, July 6, 2005, 14.

4. Richard Schechner, *Performance Theory*, London: Routledge, 1988, 120.

5. Christine Harold, *Ourspace: Resisting the Corporate Control of Culture*, Minneapolis: University of Minnesota Press, 2007, 160.

6. New York Times Special Edition Writers, "Newspaper Blankets U.S. Cities," *New York Times*, Nov. 12, 2008.

7. New York Times Special Edition Writers, "Hundreds Claim Credit for *New York Times* Spoof," *New York Times*, Nov. 12, 2008.

8. Henry Jenkins and Stephen Duncombe, "Politics in the Age of YouTube," *Electronic Journal of Communication* 18.2–4, 2008.

9. Ibid.

10. Samuel Fielden, "Popular Pressure Ushers Recent Progressive Tilt," *New York Times Special Edition*, Nov. 12, 2008, A1.

Understanding the Text

1. What characteristics do parody news shows, satiric documentaries, and ironic activist performances share?

2. What does Day mean by the term *counterpublics*?

3. What is "one of the most damning criticisms leveled at ironic, parodic, and satiric modes of critique" (par. 7)? How does Day defend these modes against this criticism?

Reflection and Response

4. What is your opinion on the tension between "efficacy and entertainment" within political comedy (par. 4)? Should performers prioritize their political goals over their commercial ones? Can they? Is it possible to mix efficacy and entertainment successfully?

5. Have you ever come across an example of what Henry Jenkins and Stephen Duncombe call "critical utopianism" (par. 10)? What do you think about humor's ability to challenge the status quo by imagining a better world?

Making Connections

6. Day's argument does not directly respond to Almond's (pp. 242–253), but it could be read as a more optimistic retort to his pessimistic view of the political efficacy of news satire shows. How so? Compare their views and put these authors into conversation with each other.

7. Day's discussion ends with "the new era of the Obama presidency" (par. 11). Now that Obama's two terms as president have concluded, where do we

stand with regard to irony, satire, and parody "as methods of intruding into the public conversation" (par. 12)? Write an essay in which you examine newer forms of these comedic modes. Who is doing cutting edge political comedy currently? What and who are they ironizing, satirizing, and parodying?

8. Day lists a series of ways in which parodists, satirists, and ironists work within a "comedic and improvisational mode" (par. 3). In Burke's dramatistic pentad, these comic rhetorical methods would be categorized as forms of *agency*, which is the topic of the next chapter. They are the means by which these activist comedians try to achieve their goals. Watch one of the comedic texts that Day refers to (e.g., a Michael Moore documentary or Yes Men film), and write an essay that analyzes the comic agency or purpose of its creators. What purpose does the text serve and what humorous methods do its creators employ?

How John Oliver Usurped a Genre

Daniel J. Kenny

The HBO comedy series *Last Week Tonight with John Oliver* premiered on April 27, 2014, to great fanfare. The show follows the general format of the late-night news satire popularized by *The Daily Show*, which is where Oliver worked as a correspondent starting in 2006 and as a guest host for eight weeks in 2013 when the former host Jon Stewart directed the film *Rosewater*. Some cultural commentators have argued, however, that *Last Week Tonight* departs from the genre by pushing the boundaries of political satire. These critics go so far as to categorize the show as investigative journalism, muckraking, agitprop, and activist pranksterism.

Daniel J. Kenny joins the chorus of positive reviewers who believe that Oliver's show marks an evolution in the parodic news genre. Writing for the *Harvard Political Review* (*HPR*) in 2014 before Stewart and Colbert left Comedy Central, Kenny compares Oliver favorably to his satirical predecessors. A New Jersey native, Kenny is a student at Harvard University who writes about politics and comedy for *HPR*.

Before taping the second-ever episode of HBO's *Last Week Tonight*, host John Oliver implored members of the audience not to internalize their laughter like they do when watching comedy programs at home. The studio audience must laugh hard and externally, he explained, or the show will not work.

He began with a quick recap of the previous week's news, including the Ukrainian crisis and the White House Correspondents' Dinner. Then, something different happened. "I know what you're thinking," Oliver said. "You're thinking, 'Wait, you're not going to really do a comic take on the death penalty, right? It's your second episode—I haven't even decided if I like this show yet.'"

He then ranted for 12 minutes about the death penalty, earning two million views on YouTube. And the audience laughed externally.

John Oliver commands a bully pulpit. After more than seven years as a correspondent on Comedy Central's *The Daily Show with Jon Stewart*, Oliver, much like fellow former correspondent Stephen Colbert, now hosts his own late-night news and political satire TV show. Oliver's eight-week, critically praised stint as acting host of *The Daily Show* prepared him to host his own Jon Stewart–style program. But HBO's *Last Week Tonight* is not *The Daily Show*. Oliver has found his voice and his place in political commentary separate from Stewart and—in several respects—better.

"A good satirist is someone who hits a point, cares about something, 5 and wants you to care about it," Jonathan Gray, professor of media and cultural studies at the University of Wisconsin–Madison, told the HPR. A good satirist "makes a statement" about his or her subject and does not simply mock for comedy's sake.

In an interview with the HPR, Amber Day, associate professor of English and cultural studies at Bryant University and author of *Satire and Dissent: Interventions in Contemporary Political Debate*, describes TV news satire as an "evolving genre." According to Day, Stewart made his name by delivering insightful critiques of contemporary political issues, analyzing how the press discussed those issues, and monitoring the mass media pandemonium of the cable news era. Stewart, along with Comedy Central colleague Colbert, defined the genre. But now, Day says, just as Stewart and Colbert separated themselves from the *Saturday Night Live* model of news satire, Oliver has separated himself from the Comedy Central model.

> "A good satirist 'makes a statement' about his or her subject and does not simply mock for comedy's sake."

To make a statement, a TV news satirist must introduce relevant topics, satirize them with the goal of improving conditions, and both analyze and serve as a check on the mass media. Stewart, Colbert, and Oliver all do this—but Oliver does it *better*. He is an outsider who satirizes American politics and news, but he also satirizes international affairs. He satirizes topics that viewers of the genre have never before considered, and his presence on HBO gives him more time, more freedom, and a better schedule to do so. But it is the traits unique to Oliver himself—his format, his style, and his tone—that truly propel him past his peers.

The hosts of satire news programs usually present themselves as outsiders, and Oliver speaks with a unique voice as a British citizen living in America. While Stewart and Colbert are "insider-outsiders," according to Day, Oliver is better positioned to offer a true outsider's perspective. He lives in the United States, but he is a British citizen. He alternates between addressing the audience as "we" and "you," giving himself an advantage in comedic range over Stewart and Colbert. According to Gray, Stewart will "invoke the rest of the world" and speculate about other countries' opinions on American domestic issues. Oliver does not have to speculate.

Oliver offers a global focus previously missing in TV news satire. In his first episode, he lambasted the American media's lacking coverage of the Indian general election.

American television viewers recognize this dance, but Oliver's unique 10 rants simplify and popularize complicated issues like net neutrality, corruption in FIFA, and the American prison system. His net neutrality rant crashed the FCC website when he called upon fans to bombard the site's comments section in support of net neutrality. In his original critique of Oliver's program, *New York Times* TV critic Neil Genzlinger claims that Oliver "dived into a couple of . . . pools already occupied" and delivered "pretty standard stuff." But in an interview with the HPR, Genzlinger praised Oliver's "leaps of faith" to examine rarely discussed issues as unmatched in late-night TV, especially on talk shows like *The Tonight Show Starring Jimmy Fallon*, but even on Stewart's and Colbert's programs.

Last Week Tonight derives from the behind-the-desk format of *The Daily Show* and *The Colbert Report*, but it deviates in length and programming schedule. Stewart and Colbert air Monday through Thursday night for 22 minutes, whereas Oliver airs only on Sundays for a full half-hour on HBO. Those eight minutes make the difference.

According to Day, Oliver's lack of commercial breaks allows him to tackle issues "newsmagazine style," unlike Stewart and Colbert who must cut to commercial two to three times per episode. HBO does not air commercials, so Oliver can discuss student debt or net neutrality at greater length. But he can also better satirize the issues because his writing staff only needs to produce one show per week. To produce four shows per week and remain relevant requires the *Daily Show* and *Colbert Report* writing staffs to sacrifice quality for quantity. "He does only one show a week," HitFix.com TV critic Alan Sepinwall said in an interview with the HPR, "and therefore has depth where his Comedy Central pals have breadth." According to Genzlinger, Stewart can "take the easy way out" and "bash Fox News" four times a week, a format that Oliver is rendering "predictable." Repetition cannot discredit Oliver's criticism of Fox News because he airs once a week and normally comments on issues rather than the media itself.

HBO's liberal censorship policy is no secret. According to Day, although advertisers do not censor Stewart and Colbert, HBO's pay cable system frees Oliver and his writers from ever thinking twice about airing a piece on, for example, General Motors. Gray disputes Oliver's increased freedom, but Oliver clearly has more freedom than if his show aired on Comedy Central. For example, HBO provided Oliver a space to air a piece on Kentucky's U.S. Senate race featuring full-frontal male nudity. Oliver does not exploit his freedom; he used the male nudity once to underscore Democratic candidate Alison Lundergan Grimes's emphasis on her Republican opponent Sen. Mitch McConnell's old age. If Oliver maintains this methodical use of obscenity, he can deliver a truer satire that carries more comedic weight than anything his Comedy Central comrades can produce. Stewart and Colbert can explain Grimes's *ad hominem* attack, but Oliver can show it.

Oliver already has a recognizable format: recap, rant, and crescendo. The recap keeps the show current; it fulfills the show's duty to its title. Then Oliver can rant about whatever issue he wants for however long he wants, although usually between 12 and 16 minutes. Finally, the show reaches a crescendo. Sometimes Oliver will issue a call to action for his audience to tweet with a certain hashtag, leave comments on the FCC's website, or write letters to the Kremlin addressed to Russian President Vladimir Putin. Other times Oliver will invite an unexpected guest such as Steve Buscemi to tap dance or "A Great Big World" to sing a swan song for Russian space geckos. The crescendo engages the audience and plays to the show's viral potential. This points to another advantage over Stewart and Colbert: HBO uploads Oliver's clips to YouTube.

Last Week Tonight has thus far prevented its format from slipping to 15 Stewart's and Colbert's predictability. The audience anticipates Oliver's extended commentary for a week. They wonder what issue Oliver will rant about this week, but they know it will be important and under-the-radar. It will engage the audience and reveal an under-covered and rarely discussed problem. Stewart and Colbert do not command this level of anticipation, not only because they only air four nights a week but also by nature of their material. They rely on their comedic talents rather than their shows' substance. Simply put, viewers tune in to Stewart and Colbert to watch some timely commentary in a familiar style. But they tune in to Oliver's program to learn something new, and new is never predictable.

There are no panelists, no correspondents, and few interviews. After the recap and rant, Oliver says, "And now, this," and the camera cuts to an unrelated segment—such as clips of *60 Minutes* reporters asking leading questions. These segments air where Stewart and Colbert air commercials, and they allow Oliver to squeeze every possible minute of satire out of the show. The brief segments often focus on the media, which helps Oliver analyze and check the big networks while cleansing the audience's palate before the next bit. However, Oliver himself does not contribute to or comment on the segments. A disembodied voice narrates the segments, distancing Oliver from what is normally the show's only media-bashing aspect. Oliver projects a sense of urgency to transition to the next topic, whereas Stewart obsesses over demonstrating Fox News's conservative bias. Colbert does the same: his entire faux-conservative character is a Fox News satire that has spanned the entire nine-year run of his program.

The critics agree that Oliver can do more with his program than Colbert or, especially, Stewart. According to Genzlinger, Oliver's "baffled" persona remains consistent throughout the length of his program, whereas Stewart shifts personas during the three "acts" of his show.

Colbert stays in character for all of his 22 minutes, but he must still pander to a guest every night—and Oliver is just not doing that. Oliver delivers 30 full minutes of material, polished and perfected by a writing staff that has had a week to prepare, unhampered by shameless plugs for Hillary Clinton's new book or promotional movie clips.

Stewart and Colbert cannot control their tones like Oliver can. Oliver, according to Genzlinger, is "incredulous at how stupid and idiotic humanity is on its face." In fact, Oliver's baffled tone allows him to mine humor out of simply presenting news items *without even telling a joke.* Colbert has to tell a joke because his humor depends on his character's verbal reaction, and the insider Stewart cannot appear *as* baffled about American politics as the outsider Oliver.

According to Genzlinger, *Last Week Tonight* "is much better [than *The Daily Show*]. It does more, it goes deeper, the writing is smarter, and the research is smarter." And although *The Colbert Report* delivers a fresher perspective than *The Daily Show* by way of Colbert's character, the reality is that Colbert is leaving. The faux-conservative pundit Stephen Colbert will give way to a network TV, appeal-to-the-masses Stephen Colbert, and only Stewart and Oliver will remain in the genre (until Larry Wilmore,° Colbert's Comedy Central replacement, arrives at 11:30 p.m. on weekdays). Oliver has more time and a better venue to introduce and satirize issues important to the audience. He delivers an outsider's perspective on America's mass media system. He starts each program with a timely recap of the week's news, but then delivers a timeless, in-depth commentary on issues like the death penalty and native advertising.

Success in late-night comedy—and in this niche subcategory of politi- 20 cal and news satire—requires originality. The genre must evolve to satisfy its viewers. It must hold up a mirror to the audience and challenge them to think critically about society. Oliver surpasses Stewart and Colbert in this respect. There is no perfect formula, and thus fans should not fear or reject Oliver's superiority to Stewart. If Oliver better mines for societal hypocrisy through extended commentary, and if the audience invests more credence in that commentary, then he is the better host and the better satirist. His formula is better than Stewart's, and he has demonstrated that a show in this genre can better accomplish its goals by doing what *Last Week Tonight* does. Oliver need not fear compartmentalized laughter; the audience will laugh hard and true for as long as *Last Week Tonight* is on the air—or at least until the genre evolves again.

Larry Wilmore: *The Nightly Show with Larry Wilmore* took over Colbert's time slot on January 19, 2015. Trevor Noah began hosting *The Daily Show* in September of that year.

Understanding the Text

1. How does Kenny summarize the format of *Last Week Tonight with John Oliver*? From Kenny's perspective, in what ways does this format improve on the Comedy Central model of news satire?

2. According to Kenny, what traits does Oliver exhibit that set him apart from other hosts of parody news programs? How does HBO give *Last Week Tonight* an advantage over news satire shows that air on network and cable television?

Reflection and Response

3. What is your opinion of *Last Week Tonight*'s satire? (You can watch clips for free on the show's YouTube page.) Do you agree with Kenny that the show improves on the late-night news satire format? Why or why not?

4. Write a rhetorical analysis of one of *Last Week Tonight*'s long-form, investigative journalistic segments. Analyze the act, scene, agent, and purpose of the segment. Other items you might identify and evaluate include: issue, stasis, thesis, evidence, assumptions, Oliver's point of view, and ethos, pathos, and logos appeals.

5. In August 2014, Oliver told Asawin Suebseing of the *Daily Beast* that *Last Week Tonight* is "not journalism, it's comedy — it's comedy first, and it's comedy second." Why do you think Oliver views his own show as having the sole purpose of making people laugh? Do you believe him? Do you think that authors' intentions matter when it comes to how their work is received?

Making Connections

6. Kenny cites an interview with Amber Day (pp. 265–266) to support his argument. How does *Last Week Tonight* relate to Day's discussion in the previous reading of parody news shows, satiric documentaries, and ironic activist performances? How might Oliver's show be understood as combining these three genres and their comic strategies?

7. According to Kenny, Oliver's show epitomizes Russell Peterson's (pp. 219–220 and 228–229) definition of genuine political satire. Using the criteria of political satire delineated by Peterson, Steve Almond (pp. 242–243 and 250) and Kenny, write an essay that evaluates another work of contemporary political satire, like TBS's *Full Frontal with Samantha Bee*.

8. With a group of your classmates, write, shoot, and produce a video that imitates an episode of *Last Week Tonight*. Like Oliver's, your segments can treat national and international news satirically. Alternatively, you could cover local issues or those affecting your university and the life of college students. To prepare for your imitation episode, read through analyses of *Last Week Tonight* and study the format of the show closely.

FourOaks / Getty Images

5 Agency: How Do You Write a Comic Argument?

Comedy may be more art than science, but comic writing can still be subjected to the rigors of analysis. The online software program Comedy Evaluator Pro, for example, has broken down the elements of a successful stand-up set in order to help amateur comedians improve their craft. According to the company's studies of famous comedians, in a 5-minute set, a stand-up comedian should deliver 20 punch lines in 400 words on one to three topics for an average of at least 18 seconds of "positive audience response" per minute.[1] Such studies demonstrate that humor can be understood quantitatively, but it can also be approached rhetorically, as you have done by entertaining the central questions posed by the first four chapters of this book: What takes place when we laugh? When and where does (and doesn't) humor occur? Who (or what) is a comedian? What is the function of satire in a democratic society?

Your inquiries in the previous chapters have instigated investigations into the act, scene, agent, and purpose of comic rhetoric. In other words, you've explored the what, when, where, who, and why of humor. The time has now come to turn your attention to *how* humor succeeds in making us laugh by looking at the final element of Burke's dramatistic pentad: agency. Burke uses the term *agency* to refer to the means by which agents achieve their purpose. Inquiries into the agency of humor ask how comedians write material that gets them from point A (the drawing board) to point B (a laughing audience). Comedy Evaluator Pro's program provides one formulaic answer to how a stand-up comedian can perform well in a comedy club. The selections in this chapter deal with writing humor that makes readers think as it makes them laugh.

Chapter 5 begins with two selections that discuss specific strategies for writing comedy. Comedian Franklin Ajaye provides tips for discovering,

photo: FourOaks / Getty Images

---

[1]These numbers come from Katy French's infographic report on the program. See "What Do You Need to Perform 5 Minutes of Stand-up Comedy? This Graphic Breaks It Down," Visual News, visualnews.com, March 18, 2015.

developing, and structuring your own comic material. Although he explicitly writes for an audience of amateur stand-up comedians, you will find that his suggestions apply just as well to comedy writing in general. Also useful is what the television comedy writers interviewed by Megh Wright say about their craft. Wright's subjects relate how the collaborative nature of improvisational comedy can help inspire ideas for writing scripted comedy shows. In reading the first two selections, you should glean practical advice for composing your own comic arguments.

The remaining selections provide models of persuasive comedy writing for you to imitate. Political writer Conor Friedersdorf and sociologist Michael Kimmel demonstrate the imitation process in pieces inspired by famous comic essays. Friedersdorf channels Jonathan Swift's "A Modest Proposal" to criticize defenders of government surveillance, while Kimmel satirizes college fraternities in the style of anthropologist Horace Mitchell Miner's ethnography parody, "Body Ritual Among the Nacirema." Graduate student Julia Drake follows with her own parody, imagining the college application essay that the young boy from Steven Spielberg's classic film *Jurassic Park* (1993) would write about his experience of being hunted by velociraptors in his grandfather's failed amusement park. Paul Davidson, a writer and television producer, then tests the limits of corporate person-hood by sending prank letters to a few of the most recognizable corporations in the vein of Don Novello's *The Lazlo Letters* (1977). He includes their responses to his outlandish, but not entirely unreasonable, complaints, questions, and suggestions. Comedian and cultural critic Baratunde Thurston extends Davidson's ribbing of corporate America by writing a satirical survival guide for "The Black Employee." Blogger Christian Lander takes up Thurston's focus on race but casts his critical eye on "Stuff White People Like" (SWPL) by writing sketches on phenomena like irony, vintage clothing, self-aware hip-hop references, Ivy League schools, and unpaid internships for his blog (parts of which were published as a book also titled *Stuff White People Like*). These selections serve two purposes: (1) to familiarize you with different strategies for writing humorous arguments on

You will likely receive plenty of feedback, both positive and not-so-positive, on your early drafts. Just remember: *All* writing requires rewriting. You are not alone.
Jorge Cham © 2011, www.PHDCOMICS.COM

pertinent topics, and (2) to help and guide you as you compose your own comic arguments.

As you craft your own comic arguments, don't forget that writing is a form of thinking out loud. Writing requires you to put your thoughts into words, and because thinking is messy, writing necessitates rewriting. One might even say that *all writing is rewriting*. To find the right words to express your ideas, keep in mind this advice from the late great wordsmith and comedian George Carlin: "The best way I know to clarify my thinking is to hear and see what I think I'm thinking. Because however clear it may seem to you internally, it's never clear exactly what it is, until you speak and hear the words. You are your own first-night audience."[2]

---

[2]George Carlin. *Last Words: A Memoir.* New York: Free Press, 2009, 144.

First Steps to Becoming a Stand-Up Comedian

Franklyn Ajaye

In this excerpt from the book *Comic Insights: The Art of Stand-Up Comedy* (2002), comedian Franklyn Ajaye reveals some tricks of the trade to aspiring comedians. Known as "the jazz comedian," Ajaye is a stand-up performer and actor who was raised in Los Angeles and now resides in Melbourne, Australia. He has five comedy albums, including *I'm a Comedian, Seriously* (1974) and *Vagabond Jazz & the Abstract Truth* (2004), and has written for and appeared on several comedy television shows such as *In Living Color*, *Politically Incorrect*, and *Thank God You're Here*. You may be familiar with him from the HBO show *Deadwood* (2004–2006) or the movie *Bridesmaids* (2011).

Excluding wit and improvisation, all forms of comedy begin with words on the page. Therefore, when reading through Ajaye's advice for budding stand-ups, think about how what he says pertains to comedy writing in general. What pointers might apply to your upcoming writing assignments?

Study the Good Ones

The first and most important step for anybody who wants to be a good stand-up comedian is to make sure that you watch the good ones and study them intently so that you can get a feel for *why* they're funny. You may think that's unnecessary advice, but when I taught my class, on the first day I asked each student to name his or her favorite comedian. They could all answer with no problem. But when I asked them what made that comedian so funny, they didn't have a clue. They'd invariably answer, "I don't know; they're just funny." That's not good enough. You have to be able to coolly appraise a comedian's techniques, strengths, and weaknesses to notice what works and doesn't work so that you can dispel any sense of awe and become more objective. Only then can you understand how they generate laughter and thus apply their expertise to help you develop.

So what should you study in a comedian? You must study their deliveries, their use of their bodies, their timing, and their use of audio and vocal effects. Videotape their routines and play them back to see if you can understand the logic that got them to their punch lines. Even better, write down some of their best lines so that you can see how it [sic] looks on paper. That way your own routines and punch lines won't look so strange to you when you write them. A beneficial current development is that many of the top comedians (Seinfeld, Rock, Reiser, Carlin, Sinbad, DeGeneres) have written humorous books, giving you a great opportunity to see their words and the way they think in print. In addition, many have released performance videos that you can rent and study at leisure, but I strongly suggest that you also listen to comedy CDs to discover how "good comedy" performs on many levels to make you laugh. When listening to a comedy album, you don't have any help from your eyes. Yet a good comedian can verbally paint a picture that taps into your imagination and creates a "visual" in your head. When I was starting out in 1972, I listened to the comedy albums of Woody Allen, George Carlin, Richard Pryor, Robert Klein, Lenny Bruce, and Bill Cosby as they used their comedic skills to create pictures and tap into our imaginations. This is the skill that you want to develop, and you'll find studying their comedy CDs invaluable.

Zero In on Your Sensibility

After you've started looking at comedians more analytically, the next step is to zero in on the comedian or comedians whose sense of humor and style of comedy reminds you of the sense of humor you naturally display around your friends and associates when you are relaxed. When you find the comedian who reminds you of what you do naturally, that particular comedian can serve as a guide or influence. In my case, even though I loved the comedy of Bill Cosby, Jonathan Winters, and Woody Allen, the comedians who seemed to embody what I seemed to be doing naturally among my friends were Richard Pryor, Robert Klein, and George Carlin. So I studied those three giants particularly hard. But I never tried to copy them in any way. Instead, I tried to isolate and incorporate elements of their approach in my own approach to writing and performing stand-up. The incisive truth and honesty of Richard Pryor; the offhand informality, conversational delivery, and restless societal probing of George Carlin; the college-educated vocabulary and iconoclastic viewpoint of Robert Klein—all of these were elements that I strove to have in my comedy. Trying to synthesize these various elements with my own interests and point of view enabled me to create an individual style.

If you've never told a joke or been funny around your friends, but you still want to become a stand-up comedian, you can find your own sense of humor by studying the comedian who consistently makes you laugh the most—that particular comedian is tapping into your comedic sensibility and helping you identify where your own sense of humor lies. This will be a great aid to helping you know the direction that you want to take your comedy material.

The Proper Use of Influences

The greatest gift that I received from my main comedic influences 5 (Richard Pryor, Robert Klein, and George Carlin) was their excellence at their craft. Seeing them always let me know how good I wanted to be and how far I had to go. I remember watching Richard Pryor for a week at The Comedy Store° in 1973 and leaving each night both awed and depressed. My material seemed so trivial compared to his—and I had my own comedy album out at the time. I kept looking at his head and saying to myself, "It's just a normal-sized head. How could all those ideas come out of a normal-sized head?" But seeing him perform at such a high skill level made me work harder to try and add more depth to my material. In fact, after I finished brooding, with vivid memories of his brilliance, I worked the next week in Houston and added physical movement to my act for the first time by walking back and forth along the stage. And more importantly, I started to act out the behavior of the high-school characters that I had previously only talked about, which improved my performance immensely. All because of seeing how Richard Pryor's acting added to his performance. A few years later at The Comedy Store, I watched Richard Pryor build his famous "Mudbone"° routine literally from one line on Tuesday into a long, detailed routine by Saturday, which was the night he added the lines about "the Polar bear with the little tiny feet." What was particularly instructive to me was watching him add a little something to the bit each night, which meant that he was either listening to an audiotape or at least thinking a lot about this routine on a daily basis.

At the time I was starting out, I listened to every good comedy album I could. Though I knew nothing formally about stand-up comedy, I would write down my own observations in my own attempt to gain some insight into their art. The following is a twenty-year-old analysis I did of Bill Cosby after listening to his album *To Russell, My Brother Whom I Slept With*, an album I heartily recommend to anyone who wants to do long autobiographical routines and stories. Keep in mind that this was my own unschooled attempt to analyze what a top-flight comedian was doing. However, I can say unequivocally that this neophyte analysis helped me better understand all the things that a good stand-up comedian is doing when he or she is making you laugh.

The Comedy Store: a renowned Los Angeles comedy club that opened in 1972 and seats 450.
"Mudbone": a recurring character in Richard Pryor's stand-up who is an elderly black man from Mississippi and wino street philosopher.

1. Does sound effects (footsteps, doors, covers, bed crashing).
2. No jokes.
3. Lot of energy and animation.
4. Good voices.
5. Gives his point of view.
6. Does not try to go for absurd or bizarre lines, but lets humor come from situation.
7. Uses pauses and takes his time.
8. Does real-life situations from his life.
9. Gives characters attitudes.

I recently watched Bill Cosby's stand-up video *49* while in Melbourne, Australia, preparing for their comedy festival, and did another analysis of the master comedian to see what I could learn. It went as follows:

1. He gives human qualities (voices, thoughts, pride) to objects and body parts.
2. Lets the audience calm down after a long laugh before starting a new routine.
3. Very close observation of his own behavior during an event, which he re-creates for the audience.

I used to also write down specific lines from George Carlin, Redd Foxx, and Cosby so that I could see them in print. Then I'd write an analysis as well. Here's an example that I did with lines by George Carlin and Redd Foxx.

1. "You can say, 'I pricked my finger,' but you can't say, 'I fingered my prick' in public."

   Analysis: An example of a reversal of a commonly used, everyday saying.

2. "I know that Jesus is black because you can't wear no hat for thirty years in the desert and stay white."

   Analysis: Example of a logical statement as an extension from given facts.

3. "Hire the handicapped. They're fun to watch."

   Analysis: Statement of a politically incorrect truth.

There's a big difference between imitating a comedian and being strongly influenced by one. As long as you have the concept of self-expression at the forefront of your mind, you will never be a carbon copy of your comedic influences. And when you take the various elements of a comedian or comedians that you admire and synthesize them with your individual viewpoint, you will create something new and original. When I went to Melbourne to perform in their comedy festival, I took along the Woody Allen tape *Stand-Up Comic* and Richard Pryor's CD *Craps After Hours* and listened to both of them during the days before the festival — along with watching the aforementioned Bill Cosby videotape — to reinforce in me the things that I wanted to put into my comedy. I found myself once again inspired by Woody Allen's ability to write such plausibly absurd stories with clarity, Richard Pryor's ability to inject a sense of theater and real and distinct-sounding characters into his stand-up, and Bill Cosby's inimitable ability to hold an extremely casual, humorous conversation with a large audience. But most importantly I admired all three's ability to take me into my imagination and create pictures in my head.

You can be influenced by artists other than comedians when it comes 10 to the approach you want to take to your comedy as well. In my opinion, all the arts are related. My creative heroes when I was starting were Miles Davis, Richard Pryor, Marlon Brando, and François Truffaut as well as singer-songwriters like Bill Withers, Curtis Mayfield, Gil-Scott Heron, and Joni Mitchell. I was drawn to their continual creativity, and the fact that there was great depth and truth to their work. The lyrics of the singer-songwriters mentioned, as well as those of Bob Dylan and James Taylor, inspired me to try to add a social-commentary aspect to my material. My goal was to combine an ever-changing, "jazzy," loose feel to my presentation with the verbal incisiveness of the best folk-rock lyrics. Whether I ultimately attained that or not is debatable — but though I had never communicated this goal to anyone, one night as I entered The Improv, I heard Bill Maher refer to me as, "the jazz comedian." So, as often as possible, study other art forms and artists (filmmakers, writers, musicians, painters, playwrights, actors, etc.), read what these top practitioners have to say about their approach to their art, and see if you can relate any of their insights to your own comedy.

Structuring Your Funny (Writing Your Material)

To be able to write funny material for yourself, it's essential that you understand your own particular and natural "comedic essence." You want to write humor that captures the freshness of the humor that you do with friends when you're feeling relaxed and comfortable — it's at those moments when you are displaying your "pure funny." You have to learn how to observe and tap into that because your "pure funny" is what you want to transport to the stage, and tapping into your "pure funny" or comedic essence is the quickest shortcut to writing funny material.

When I first started out as a comedian in 1971, my first impulse was to get a notebook and start to try to be deliberately funny and write some jokes. So I wrote down every half-baked zany thought that came into my head. I thought they were jokes, but the first club audiences I tried them on told me differently. I was devastated. For weeks I was totally lost, trying to figure out where I'd gone wrong. Finally I figured out that it started with the fact that my material wasn't me. I realized that I was trying to write material that went counter to the natural sense of humor that I had when I was with friends and almost effortlessly making them laugh. It was what I thought a comedian's material should be, but it wasn't me. With my friends I wasn't trying to be funny—and I was. But when I started writing material and trying to be funny, I wasn't. So one night over iced tea and french fries (which I considered a treat given my poor student Raskolnikov°-like existence), I threw out my notebook of laugh-free jokes and decided to start from scratch. I had to figure out how to re-create the sense of humor I had when I was relaxed with my friends.

Using the "Third Eye"

So I started using the "third eye" when I was with my friends in an attempt to understand what it was that made me funny with them. The third eye is a strange combination of detachment and heightened awareness that keeps you somewhat removed from a situation so that you can observe and record your thoughts and reactions. It's an instinctive way of remembering specific obscure details for re-creation at a later date. For most artists, it operates on a subconscious level. Actors use it all the time. They remember and use gestures and attitudes from real moments in their lives to make their characters behave in a real fashion. For those of you who don't do this instinctively, you'll have to make a conscious decision to apply this technique. But it can be done quite easily. In the film *All That Jazz*, the Bob Fosse character (played by Roy Scheider) had an emotional argument with his lover (played by Ann Reinking). As he headed for the door, she said something particularly biting. Instead of answering back in kind, he stopped, reflected for a moment, and then went, "I'll have to use that." In the midst of this high-pitched excitement, the character's third eye was

---

Raskolnikov: a former law student who lives in abject poverty, Rodion Romanovich Raskolnikov is the protagonist of Fyodor Dostoyevsky's novel *Crime and Punishment* (1866).

still at work, allowing him to make note of something that he could use in a creative endeavor.

When I was in law school and I'd get together with other students and spontaneously and inadvertently make them laugh, instead of just continuing the conversation, I would immediately stop and write in my ever-present notebook the line that made them laugh. And most importantly, I would put it in quotes so that I would know not to change or tinker with it in any way. Putting the line in quotes meant I had the laugh-producing line or lines in its pure form. Then later, when I had some time to myself, I would think about what it would take to make it funny for a bunch of strangers. The key was deciding if it depended on specific knowledge or had a universal context, which would then enable me to construct the appropriate setup. Through this process, I was able to zero in on my comedic essence and thus start generating funny material. By comparison, the previous jokes that I'd tried to write had been contrived.

If you are going to tap into your true pure funny, you must make lib- 15
eral use of the third-eye concept. It will give you insight and understanding of your true sense of humor and make its voyage from the safety of friends to the stage a relatively pain-free one. Surprise is a big element of comedy in that people are not expecting you to say what you say. When you spontaneously say or do something that makes your friends laugh, you have succeeded in catching them by surprise. Once you've created a setup for your already-proven laugh-getter, your punch line will catch the audience of strangers by surprise as well. Tapping into my pure funny relatively early allowed me to escape the months and sometimes years of bombing that many comedians go through.

Once you've used the third eye and tapped into your pure funny, you are on the right track to writing the right material for yourself. Then all you have to do is start the process of what I call "structuring your funny."

Structuring Your Funny

In 1972, I was working in the men's department at a now-defunct clothing store in Century City in Los Angeles. One day a woman came in and bought a suit from me for her husband's birthday—with him to come in and be fitted the next day. When she handed me her credit card to complete the sale, it read Mrs. Bob Newhart, and the next day the comedian himself came in to be fitted. Seizing my chance as I measured his cuffs, I told him that I was an aspiring comedian and asked him the only burning question I could think of at the time: "How do you write your material?" He was very nice and understanding and told me that the most important thing was to outline the points that I wanted to talk about on the subjects that I chose. It was simple but extremely helpful advice, and having a good public-school education, I was able to immediately put outlining (something I learned in the fifth grade) into practice on those routines that I was creating out of my observations. Outlining a subject that you're interested in is a great way to deal with those routines that you want to consciously create, as opposed to those that spring forth spontaneously when with friends. It's essential for the aspiring comedian because it organizes your thoughts and gives them a spine to hang your humorous observations and embellishments on. When you outline and start to think about what you want to discuss, your subconscious will amaze you with all the things that it will reveal that you weren't aware that you'd noticed. This won't necessarily be a process that will have you laughing (though that's always a possibility). Rather, it's a serious thinking session where you jot down and order the odd or ironic things that have caught your attention. The first routine that I outlined concerned my observations about the old *Frankenstein*, *Dracula*, and *Wolfman* films. It was titled "Monsters in General" and the outline was as follows:

> "When you outline and start to think about what you want to discuss, your subconscious will amaze you with all the things that it will reveal that you weren't aware that you'd noticed."

Monsters in General

A. Wolfman

   1. Won't mess with Wolfman 'cause he's faster than black people.
   2. When Wolfman catches you, he doesn't bullshit. You don't walk away with minor cuts and bruises.

B. Dracula

   1. All you need to deal with him is a cross, which you can get at any church or Klan meeting.
   2. If had a cross, I would torture him and steal his wallet.

C. Frankenstein

   1. So slow he can only catch you if you're with a girl, 'cause women in movies always fall down when chased by monsters.
   2. I would warn girl on a date that if monsters chase us, I would be in the wind, so don't fall down.

"Monsters in General" was the first routine I outlined, and outlining it that way enabled me to think about what I wanted to say about what I had seen. And I never would've done it that way if I hadn't fitted Bob Newhart for a suit.

Choosing Topics

When you look across the spectrum of successful comedians and study their material, you will see a wide variety of subject matter that reflects their interests, and things that they've thought about a great deal. You'll also notice that much of the subject matter on first blush would seem to offer very little potential for humor, but that each comedian's point of view on the subject at hand has pointed out the many incongruities and ironies that make us laugh. Therefore, you should choose to talk about what you are truly interested in and concerned about because that will enable you to bring the full weight of your feelings and thoughts (aka your point of view) to the matter.

Dealing with Creative Block

The best weapon against creative block is to be tuned in to your point of   20
view. Writing material is a journey not a destination. Don't try to force it. You may be dry of any funny observations or thoughts at the moment. Just accept that and get out into life, and live and observe. Your subconscious will be working even when you're not because it knows your true point of view. Many times, I'd start a tour thinking that I didn't have any new ideas. But invariably things would start to come out of me on stage as the tour went on. These were fresh ideas that I didn't know I had yet recognized like old friends because my subconscious had been making notes.

The most frightening time I had with creative block was in 1972 after I'd unexpectedly bombed at a Hoot Night at the Troubadour nightclub in Los Angeles. Not only did my new stuff written specifically for that evening bomb, but my previously successfully material bombed as well. My confidence in my ability to write humorous material was completely shattered, and I was feeling desperate. One night I ran into David Brenner at The Comedy Store in Los Angeles, and I asked him what to do. He said to just relax and not force it. He also told me to not think about being funny for a while. So that's what I did. I put the search for new material on the back burner and concentrated on just living my life. Soon I was getting off some good quips around my friends in conversation, making note of them, and was back on track for writing funny material.

Dealing with creative block effectively requires that you (1) use the third eye to observe and record when you are exhibiting your natural comedic essence, and (2) relax and trust the subconscious to do its job of absorbing images, thoughts, and ironies, and releasing its humorous conclusions into your conscious domain. That approach is best used when striving for a more spontaneous flow of creativity. The third, more-studied approach to attacking creative block is the one advocated by Jerry Seinfeld of just forcing yourself to sit down and wrestle with a premise. This way of dealing with creative block doesn't feel as good as the other way, but once you accept that it's going to feel like drudgery, you'll be amazed at how good some of the material is that you come up with. One of the greatest misconceptions about being an artist is that the creative process is always supposed to feel good. When the muse is in gear, it can be exhilarating. But more often than not, you'll have to consciously think your way through a comedy maze to a successful punch line. Believe it or not, this process can be just as satisfying because it feels so much more difficult. If you can continue fighting mentally on a "drudgery day," you'll go a long way toward making your next creative session flow that much easier. But if you give up with the intention of waiting for the muse, you may find that the next day is a drudgery-filled one was well. Grappling with a "drudgery day" will produce more usable material than you ever thought possible. The next day when you review material that might have come out in bone-breaking drips and drabs, you'll almost always be pleasantly surprised by how good some of it is. Not all of the material will be usable, but even the bad stuff can contain a germ of a good idea that can send you off in a promising direction.

Letting the Subconscious Mind Do Its Job

The subconscious mind is a little-considered but very important ingredient in the creative process. When you're out and about or reading newspapers or watching television, you don't need to conduct a frantic search for material. Instead, just go about your daily business, confident that your subconscious mind is absorbing impressions, attitudes, and details that will crystallize at the appropriate time. Just let the world flow over you with an alert mind, and you'll be amazed what comes out when you sit down to write your material. Ideas will pop out that you didn't even know you had.

Equipment for Creating Material

Always carry a microcassette recorder to record any thoughts and impressions that may occur to you. Don't try to keep the ideas in your head. Without fail, you'll forget them later. If you don't have a microcasette recorder, then carry a notebook. If you don't have either, then grab anything available to write on when you get an idea. When you get home, listen to the recorder, or read the notes you made, and transfer the ideas that you think are viable to a notebook, legal pad, or computer. Remember, don't trust your memory.

Understanding the Text

1. How did Ajaye develop his own style of comedy? How does he suggest that you discover your sense of humor?

2. What does Ajaye mean by *third eye*, and how is this concept related to what he calls *pure funny*?

3. What solutions does Ajaye propose for creative block?

Reflection and Response

4. What do you make of Ajaye's ethos? Which of his personal anecdotes cultivates his ethos and enhances the persuasiveness of his advice to budding comedians? Which anecdotes fell flat for you?

5. "In my opinion," Ajaye writes, "all the arts are related" (par. 10). Have you ever considered comedy as an art form before? Do you agree with Ajaye that comedy is related to the other arts of acting, songwriting, filmmaking, painting, and so on? Which art do you believe is closest to comedy?

6. Which of Ajaye's recommendations struck you as most valuable to writing your own humorous material? What are your major takeaways from this piece?

Making Connections

7. Ajaye recommends reading comedians' humorous books and listening to their comedy albums in order to study how their language "performs on many levels to make you laugh" (par. 2). Take his advice. Read a book or listen to an album from your favorite comedian and jot down what you notice in a notebook. Compile your notes when you finish the book or album, and write a rhetorical analysis of the comedian's humorous language. How *exactly* did the comedian make you laugh? What parts were the strongest and the weakest? What did you learn that you can apply to your own comedy writing?

8. Write a 5-minute stand-up routine to be performed at the conclusion of the semester. Over the next several weeks, follow Ajaye's various steps to discover your pure funny. Reflect on comedians that you find influential, the structure of these comedians' material, and your own sense of humor. You may want to form a small writing group with one or two of your classmates to workshop your material and help each other revise your routines in preparation for the show.

How Improv Helps Television's Best Comedy Writers

Megh Wright

Megh Wright is the deputy editor at *Splitsider*, an online Web site dedicated to "comedy and the people who create it." It also strives "to chronicle the changing landscape that comedy is released into." Originally from Harrisburg, Pennsylvania, Wright moved to Brooklyn to attend the prestigious Pratt Institute, where she earned her BFA in 2009. She has previously worked as a barista, studio manager, and research intern for *Saturday Night Live (SNL)*. You can find links to many of her online articles at meghwright.tumblr .com. This piece originally appeared in *Splitsider* on April 28, 2015. As you read, think about how improvisational comedy strategies could also help improve your academic and comedic writing.

The best comedy lives in the moment, and improvisation is as in-the-moment as it gets. Improv proves you can create great comedy on the spot by listening, taking big chances, and working alongside a team, which is probably why the writing staffs of most television comedies today count at least a few experienced improvisers among their ranks. Similar to stand-ups, writers of scripted comedy are tasked with conceiving, writing, reworking, and redrafting funny moments that, when at their most successful, land so naturally that an audience can't help but wonder: "Was this scripted or improvised?"

But true improvisation, *Whose Line* aside, rarely exists on television. Most of today's shows—even the live format of *SNL*—are meticulously blocked and rehearsed ahead of time, leaving little opportunity to go off-script. "What we do here is so nailed down that there's very little improvisation," Lorne Michaels told *Vulture* last year. "Every line, every bit of dialogue has a camera cut attached to it. If you're not where you're supposed to be, then they're going to miss the shot." So why, then, have improv institutions like the Upright Citizens Brigade [UCB], Second City, iO, Annoyance, and The Groundlings become the predominant training ground for television writers, and what skills from the stage best carry over to the writers' room? We reached out to writers with extensive improv backgrounds from *Saturday Night Live, The Colbert Report, Brooklyn Nine-Nine*, and more to find out.

"In a writers' room, you're part of a team, so you need to know how to be a good teammate," says comedian and UCB alum Dan Klein. In addition to his work as a writer (Funny or Die, *Comedy Bang! Bang!*, Adult Swim's *Infomercials*, Netflix's *Wet Hot American Summer: First Day of*

Camp), Klein has been involved in the improv scene since he took his first class at Boston's Improv Asylum while in college. Whether on the stage or in a writers' room, Klein says the foundations of success are the same: "Listen, react, support, build. All that stuff is important. Also, you gotta know when to slam dunk it, too."

"Improvisation not only taught me how to write comedy, it taught me how to write collaboratively," says former *Colbert Report* writer and soon-to-be *Late Show with Stephen Colbert* writer Ariel Dumas, who studied theater in college before training at Second City, iO, and the Annoyance in Chicago. "In improvisation, you use your relationship with your scene partner to grow the story together. It doesn't matter if one of you has some genius comedic premise about working in a hot dog factory—if the other person immediately shoots it down

> "Similar to stand-ups, writers of scripted comedy are tasked with conceiving, writing, reworking, and redrafting funny moments that, when at their most successful, land so naturally that an audience can't help but wonder: 'Was this scripted or improvised?'"

or won't let go of their competing idea about being at a rodeo, the whole thing falls flat." Fellow iO and Annoyance alum Conner O'Malley, who performs at UCB and writes and frequently appears on *Late Night with Seth Meyers* in New York, agrees: "When I try to sit down and write something it's hard to do it by myself, but if I have another person that I can bounce ideas off, it's really easy to do," he says. "It's kind of like in horror movies when they're about to show a really gruesome scene, and they cut away and the director's always like 'Whatever the audience has in their head is much more terrifying than anything we could show them.' It's similar with improv, where the thing we direct together is much better than anything I could sit down and do by myself."

Even solo writing can reap the benefits from an improv skill set. UCB   5 performer and *SNL* "Weekend Update" writer Josh Patten learned a lot about distilling ideas into punch lines from two of O'Malley's *Late Night* collaborators. "My favorite show back when I was a student and seeing improv every night was *2 Square*, with Peter Grosz and John Lutz," he says. "Those guys blew me away with how damn efficient they were at improv—no line or emotion or movement was ever dropped, and every second mattered and paid off in some way during the show. That sense of efficiency has translated into how I write, and rewrite, and rewrite again to make sure that the final draft is as tight as possible. And as a joke writer, the more economical and efficient I can be, the more it will read as the same idea I had in my brain."

Like Patten's job writing for "Weekend Update," much of the seemingly candid moments over at *Late Night with Seth Meyers* are thanks to the writing staff constantly reworking scripts. "But when we do pre-tapes and stuff like that," O'Malley explains, "we'll have a take or two where we can improvise a little bit, and those are where I'm learning more how to take my improv skills and translate them—where I'm free to do whatever I want. Which is really fun, but it's also challenging because I'm editing the things that I'm about to say in my head before I say them to make sure it's usable and I'm not just going on and on where it's like 'Oh this is 28 minutes—we can't use it,' you know? We did a pre-tape on the show recently where I got to do that, and I was like 'Aw man, I just wanna do that for the rest of my life.'" The segment, called "The Blacklist: Late Night Edition," plays like a warped version of "Laser Cats" complete with intentionally shoddy delivery and camerawork and a cardboard cutout Seth Meyers as O'Malley's trusty sidekick "Sex Addict," and it's just one of many *Late Night* moments that prove there'll always be room for experiments in absurdity from rising writers/performers; as long-time Chicago improv coach Liz Allen's saying goes, "If it feels weird, do it more."

UCB performer and teacher Tricia McAlpin writes for Fox's *Brooklyn Nine-Nine*, where she's found plenty of opportunities to use her improv skills in her work: "In improv we say that you shouldn't 'make jokes,' but I think improv has helped my joke writing tremendously," she says. "Because the funniest jokes are true to characters and don't sell them out, and I think that's something you really learn when you're improvising. What's the game of this character? If this character reacts this way in a certain situation, what might she say in this similar situation? When I started at *Brooklyn Nine-Nine* [in season 2] the creators and writing staff had already developed these amazing, specific characters in the first season. So to write 23 more episodes with the funniest jokes and situations possible, I think those improv rules for character that I learned really helped out in finding new, funny ways to explore their character games." Dumas says that while she used to consider herself more of a performer than a writer, "when you do enough comedy, you start to think 'Oh, this shit is good. We should write this down.' At Second City, especially when you're on a touring company, you learn how to take your improvised bits and turn them into sketches that you can perform again and again." Second City's decades of live revues—where uncensored, anything-goes improvised scenes are developed and condensed into fully realized and rehearsed sketch shows—are a testament to the effectiveness of this transition.

For O'Malley, hanging out backstage with fellow performers at UCB and the Annoyance has been the biggest carryover from improv to his

Original founding members Matt Besser, Amy Poehler, Ian Roberts, and Matt Walsh perform at an Upright Citizens Brigade anniversary. Poehler, now a famous comedian, actress, writer, and producer, got her start doing improv.
WireImage/Getty Images

work as a writer. "Doing bits with people is pretty much our job in the writers' room—to sit there and basically fuck around and try to come up with stuff," he says. "There are other times where it's not so much like that where we have to come up with structured pitches to say to the head writer or Seth, but that free-flowing, no-judgment, having-fun kind of 'bitting around' is the meat of our job." It's similar for McAlpin at *Brooklyn Nine-Nine* and Dumas during her *Colbert* days: "The happiest writing moments I've experienced are when a bunch of writers are crammed into a room, doing bits together," Dumas says. "When everyone supports each others' jokes and has each others' backs, you can really strike comedy gold." McAlpin cites improv's most famous rule as the source of this: "It seems so basic, but truly the improv lesson of 'Yes And' has informed the way I write the most. It opens up so many fun avenues when a character is like 'Fuck it, sure, I'll hop on the boat with you' or whatever. I think audiences like watching a character take big risks because it makes them imagine what it would be like to take a big risk in their life [sic]."

When it comes to Patten's job at "Weekend Update," he says knowing how to feel out the audience has been the most useful improv lesson.

"In improv I always would have a small corner of my thought devoted to what the audience is feeling while watching it—are they peaking at this moment? Then edit. Are they not excited about a particular idea? Then move and explore something else," he says. "It's the same way with joke writing—to understand and feel where the audience is on a particular issue, and try to push them a step or two beyond that to where they can think about something in a new way and laugh, is where we're hitting our sweet spot." Klein echoes the same idea and says active listening is just as important as good writing: "When I first started performing with a sketch group in college, I was a really bad listener. I was 19, so I was kind of a bad person all around. I talked over people and didn't take into account everyone's point of view. Interesting lesson: being a shithead doesn't help make things good." And what better advice is there to give—in comedy or in life—than that? Improvisation, above all, is an open-minded, positive, collaborative exercise, and writers who are tapped into this know that mistakes are only "happy accidents" and "if you treat the audience like poets and geniuses, that's what they will become." The ultra-supportive, comedy nerd-filled audiences at improv theaters might differ greatly from the much larger, tougher, unpredictable masses watching TV, but the lesson is universal: Take chances, be open to ideas, listen to your collaborators, and trust the poet buried in the dude who just wants to laugh.

Understanding the Text

1. What evidence does Wright use to support her claim that improvisational comedy aids television comedy writers? What other information could she have included to defend her thesis?

2. What does Conner O'Malley mean when he says, "When I try to sit down and write something it's hard to do it by myself, but if I have another person that I can bounce ideas off, it's really easy to do" (par. 4)?

Reflection and Response

3. What pieces of advice about comedy writing struck you as pertinent to academic writing? Which ones do you try to follow when you have a writing assignment?

4. How do you feel about the informal language used by the writers cited in this article? Did you find the expletives jarring or appropriate? Would Wright's argument improve if she had censored her quotes, or does their unscripted quality enhance the point she is trying to convey?

5. Comment on the quality and quantity of quotes in Wright's article. Does she incorporate the words of others successfully into her own writing? Would your professor approve of the percentage of words that come from her sources?

Making Connections

6. How do the comedy writers' comments about improv in Wright's piece connect with Franklyn Ajaye's advice on stand-up comedy (p. 275)? Where does their advice overlap? Where does it differ?

7. Research one of the improv groups that Wright references as well as book-length studies on the genre of improvisational comedy. Write an academic essay based on this research. (Professors, you can have your class celebrate completing the assignment by holding your own improv theater performance.)

8. At one point Wright mentions a segment of absurdist humor on *Late Night with Seth Meyers* (par. 6). Research the genre of absurdist comedy, and write an academic essay based on this research. Then, with a small group of classmates, write, perform, and record a short sketch of absurdist comedy for the entire class.

A Modest Proposal: Don't Worry About Government Surveillance at All, Ever

Conor Friedersdorf

In 1729, the famous satirist Jonathan Swift published "A Modest Proposal for Preventing the Children of Poor People from Being a Burthen to Their Parents or Country, and for Making Them Beneficial to the Publick." The essay proposed cannibalizing young Irish children to solve the poverty problems of Ireland, which was under the economically exploitative rule of Protestant England at the time. The ironic distance between Swift's own views and that of the persona he adopted in his essay makes "A Modest Proposal" the most exemplary model of Juvenalian satire in the English language, so much so that it continues to inspire imitators, as evidenced by this 2013 piece by *The Atlantic* staff writer Conor Friedersdorf.

An avowed libertarian in his political beliefs, Friedersdorf writes in the satirical style of Swift to argue, "Relax! When have federal employees or contractors ever violated anyone's rights?" His ironic commentary responds to Edward Snowden's disclosure of classified documents that revealed the global scope of surveillance conducted by the U.S. National Security Agency (NSA) and its partners in Australia, Canada, and the United Kingdom. Friedersdorf writes about political and economic issues for *The Atlantic* and is the founding editor of "The Best of Journalism," an online subscription newsletter of nonfiction.

I t is melancholy to observe how swiftly Americans have been divided by federal surveillance. A new poll° finds that a majority view Edward Snowden as a whistleblower, and a plurality of respondents say "government goes too far in restricting civil liberties in the name of antiterrorism." These worrywarts need to be reminded of all the reasons to trust their government. What reason do any of us have to doubt that President Obama can be fully trusted on this matter?

Numerous Obama administration officials say that they're acting within the law, that they're careful to protect the Fourth Amendment rights of Americans, and that they'd never abuse their power. Would elected officials really break their promises or lie to the public?

---

new poll: Friedersdorf is referring to a 2013 poll from Quinnipiac University, which found that a majority of Americans surveyed believed Edward Snowden is a whistleblower (55%), instead of a traitor (34%).

What precedent is there in U.S. history to suggest that politicians would violate their oath to uphold the Constitution? Would the government really abuse civil liberties to fight terrorism of all things? And what reason had Obama himself given us to think that he'd brazenly break his word? Besides, the NSA, CIA, and FBI wouldn't dare contravene the law while under the supervision of a constitutional law expert with Obama's reputation for investigating and prosecuting lawbreakers. Seeing how he dealt with Bush-era torturers, would you break the law on his watch?

Some Americans worry that the NSA conducts its surveillance in secret, under the supervision of a secret court with secret rules. But as Hendrik Hertzberg writes, "I still don't know of a single instance where the NSA data program has encroached on or repressed any particular person's or group's freedom of expression or association in a tangible way. Nor have I come across a clear explanation of exactly how the program could be put to such a purpose." Yeah. How would you even abuse a vast database detailing the private communications of Americans?

Sure, the program has been conducted in secret for years, but does anyone really think we wouldn't know immediately if there were problems? The president staked *his word* on running the most transparent government in history! He has specifically promised to protect whistleblowers—who would surely emerge to document NSA abuses, confident that they'd be shielded from prosecution, or at least that they'd be able to get asylum somewhere without being vilified in the media. It's true that the Church Committee° documented abuses totally unknown to the public for decades after they happened. But although we call the generation that committed those abuses the "Greatest," there's good reason to believe today's leaders are more morally upright and much more able to resist being corrupted by secrecy and power. Just think about it. Doesn't it intuitively seem like we're better than our elders, and that the kinds of abuses that happened in the past couldn't possibly happen now? Let's go with our gut.

"Even if the program could be misused in that way, for it to happen 5 you would have to have a malevolent government," Hertzberg continues, "or, at least, a government with a malevolent, out-of-control component or powerful official or officials." Indeed, some low-level guy unknown to most Americans could never steal this data and flee to China or Russia. And obviously, all abuses of power are perpetrated by malevolent, out-of-control sociopaths. Well-meaning leaders never perpetrate abuses, and miscarriages of justice are always deliberate and never mistakes.

Church Committee: a 1975 U.S. Senate committee chaired by Idaho senator Frank Church that investigated the legality of intelligence gathering by the CIA, NSA, and FBI.

Institutional arrangements and the degree of public scrutiny to which they're subject aren't even important unless you've got guys like Richard Nixon or J. Edgar Hoover running things. And what are the odds of a pair like that becoming, say, president and FBI director at the same time?

Listening to civil libertarians, you'd swear that America was capable of building torture chambers. What a bunch of alarmist crazies.

"Some low-level guy unknown to most Americans could never steal this data and flee to China or Russia."

What you have to understand is that rules are in place to protect your rights. Sure, the government has the *technical* ability to look at domestic and not just foreign communications, and it has the technical ability to look at the contents of your communications, not just the metadata. But do you really think that NSA personnel would break the rules? Is there any precedent to suggest they'd break the law, or that people who broke surveillance law would be granted retroactive immunity? And if they just focus on metadata, what compromising material on innocent people could they possibly find? How many members of Congress would gladly hand over their metadata to any reporter who asked? Dozens? Hundreds?

After all, even if a malevolent leader was in charge of the surveillance state, it isn't like innocent people would have to worry. Save terrorists and criminals, who has anything to hide? To worry about public officials being blackmailed by a Snowden type who wants to make a dishonest buck rather than a headline is to assume that our senators, governors, and judges have dark secrets—as if a substantial part of our ruling class is out cheating on their taxes or having affairs or ingesting illegal substances or breaking campaign-finance laws. Cynics!

Regular citizens who have nothing to hide needn't worry about the surveillance state at all. Daniel Solove writes:

> . . . [S]uppose government officials learn that a person has bought a number of books on how to manufacture methamphetamine. That information makes them suspect that he's building a meth lab. What is missing from the records is the full story: The person is writing a novel about a character who makes meth. When he bought the books, he didn't consider how suspicious the purchase might appear to government officials, and his records didn't reveal the reason for the purchases. Should he have to worry about government scrutiny of all his purchases and actions? Should he have to be concerned that he'll wind up on a suspicious-persons list?
>
> Even if he isn't doing anything wrong, he may want to keep his records away from government officials who might make faulty inferences from them. He might

not want to have to worry about how everything he does will be perceived by offi-
cials nervously monitoring for criminal activity. He might not want to have a
computer flag him as suspicious because he has an unusual pattern of behavior.

But this assumes that government officials make faulty inferences. We're talking about highly trained surveillance-state professionals who are always fully cognizant of the power they wield and the seriousness of mistakes. Just look at the unparalleled success that is the No-Fly List. In the absence of any hard numbers about how often people are put on it erroneously, it's only fair to assume that it doesn't happen very often, and surely anyone who is wrongly classified is able to easily remedy the mistake, just as surely as it's very easy to correct mistakes made by the IRS or by federal prosecutors whose convictions are called into question by DNA evidence.

Watching the behavior of the parts of the federal government that 10 operate with relative transparency, can anyone doubt the eagerness of huge bureaucracies to promptly acknowledge, address, and remedy mistakes? Just imagine how much more diligent and conscientious employees of a *secret* bureaucracy must be. There's certainly no reason for citizens to avoid using words in private emails or making innocent purchases that might appear suspicious.

Like David Simon said, intrusive surveillance has long been used in the War on Drugs. That should definitely make you less upset about the NSA. After all, if there's any government effort that demonstrates how heavy-handed tactics can achieve important goals without infringing on civil liberties, it's the highly successful eradication of narcotics from our society. If civil libertarians had succeeded in stopping the War on Drugs, there might still be drug gangs running large chunks of Latin American countries and waging war on our streets. With all we've gained, thank goodness the Fourth Amendment was weakened.

In the final analysis of NSA surveillance, blogger Jennifer Rubin of the
Washington Post puts it best. "This is very straight forward. It is therefore
somewhat shocking (maybe we shouldn't expect more) that lawmakers (not to
mention pundits) got themselves riled up, claiming gross constitutional viola-
tions. . . . The administration, which failed to adequately explain the program,
is partly to blame. But there really is no excuse for lawmakers charged with
national security obligations to be so ignorant of both the law and the facts.
They have a serious obligation to conduct oversight and to keep the American
people safe and informed. In running through the halls with their hair on fire,
they show themselves, not the program, to be deficient. If anything this episode
should remind us to exercise some quality control—when it comes to voting."

Yes, as Rubin explains, Congress can only fulfill its oversight responsibilities when its members stop paying so much attention to NSA and the possibility of constitutional violations. And we should make sure to elect a Congress that does much less to challenge these programs.

That's the best way to safeguard our liberty, especially if there's ever another terrorist attack, which the national-security state would never overreact to or use as an excuse to tap into data that it stores but isn't presently allowed to look at. No, these powers will never, ever be abused.

Understanding the Text

1. What is Friedersdorf's sincere take on the U.S. government's surveillance of its citizens? Describe his real position in your own words, without irony.

2. How do you know that Friedersdorf is being ironic? How does he reveal his position on the issue of federal surveillance?

3. The persona Friedersdorf adopts lobs several *ad hominem* attacks at his opponents. What is the effect of these name-calling insults? How do they support Friedersdorf's real take on the issue?

Reflection and Response

4. How do you feel about Friedersdorf's approach to this issue? Do you believe that defenders of government surveillance deserve to be ridiculed with Juvenalian satire? Is Friedersdorf being fair with regard to the complexity of the issue?

5. What do you think is the most rhetorically persuasive moment of Friedersdorf's satirical essay? What is the least successful?

Making Connections

6. Read (or reread) Jonathan Swift's "A Modest Proposal," which is in the public domain and available for free on the Internet. How does Friedersdorf successfully imitate Swift? When does his imitation fall short of the original? What might he have added to strengthen his position on defenders of the NSA's surveillance tactics?

7. Research the rhetorical term *apophasis*. How does Friedersdorf use this rhetorical strategy? Cite specific examples.

8. What positions on social or political issues do you believe warrant a satirical treatment? Write your own "modest proposal" on an issue that you feel passionately about.

Ritualized Sexuality in Nacirema Subculture

Michael Kimmel

In 1954, anthropologist Horace Mitchell Miner (1912–1993) published the essay "Body Ritual Among the Nacirema" in the academic journal *American Anthropologist*. The piece examined the peculiar practices of this little-known North American tribe. If you spell "Nacirema" backward, you get the joke: Miner was having a go at both Americans and anthropologists. Nevertheless, his ability to estrange the modern American lifestyle as well as to defamiliarize social scientific discourse made the essay famous and eminently imitable.

Michael Kimmel returns to the North American tribe to study the sexuality of its "esoteric subculture," the *Tarfs*. Kimmel is a sociology professor at Stony Brook University who specializes in gender studies. He is the founder of the journal *Men and Masculinities*, and is the author of several books on gender, including *Guyland: The Perilous World Where Boys Become Men* (2008), *Manhood in America: A Cultural History* (2012), and *Angry White Men: American Masculinity at the End of an Era* (2014).

Students of anthropology have long been aware of the esoteric customs of the Nacirema, a culture situated in the northern hemisphere in the territory between the Canadian Cree, the Yaqui and Tarahumare of Mexico, and the Carib and the Arawak of the Antilles (see Miner, 1956). According to Horace Miner, the Michigan anthropologist who first discovered them, the Nacirema exhibit a strange and almost perverse preoccupation with the body and its ritual purification, spending enormous amounts of time and exchanging significant amounts of currencies to purify what they believe is an essentially disgusting and fetid physical form.

We have recently become aware of an even more esoteric subculture among the Nacirema, one more curiously preoccupied with body ritual, and especially with ritualized homosexuality. This subculture, known as the *Tarfs*, is the subject of this essay.

I

Ritual homosexual behavior is certainly not unknown to cultural anthropologists. In perhaps the most famous example, Gilbert Herdt described the sexual rituals of the Sambia, a mountain people who live in Papua New Guinea. The Sambia practice ritualized homosexuality as a way to initiate young boys into full adult manhood. Young boys ritually daily fellate the older boys and men so that they (the younger boys) can receive the vital life fluid (semen) from the older men and thus become men. "A boy must be initiated and [orally] inseminated, otherwise the girl betrothed to him will outgrow him and run away to another man," was the way one Sambia elder put it. "If a boy doesn't eat semen, he remains small and weak."

When they reach puberty, these boys are then fellated by a new crop of younger boys. Throughout this initiation, the boys scrupulously avoid girls and have no knowledge of heterosexuality until they are married. Neither the boys nor the older men think of themselves as engaging in homosexual behavior: In fact, when Herdt suggested that this behavior made them homosexual, or at least bisexual, they grew angry and diffident. This had nothing whatever to do with homosexuality, they assured Herdt. The older men are married to women, and the younger men fully expect to be. There is no adult homosexuality among the Sambia. But these young boys must become, as Herdt puts it, "reluctant warriors." How else are the boys to receive the vital life force that will enable them to be real men and warriors (Herdt, 1981: 1, 82, 165)?

A nearby culture, the Keraki, engage in a related practice. There, the ⁵ boys are sodomized by older men because the Keraki believe that without the older men's semen, the boys will not grow to be men. This ritual practice occurs until the boys hit puberty and secondary sex characteristics appear—facial hair, dropped voice—at which point the ritual has accomplished its task. When an anthropologist asked Keraki men if they had been sodomized, many responded by saying "Why, yes! Otherwise how should I have grown?" Other ritualized homosexual practices have been reported from other cultures (Williams, 1936: 159; see also Schiefflin, 1976; Carrier, 1977; Kelly, 1977).

Interestingly, such ritual practices, as among the Sambia and Keraki, are more evident in cultures in which sex segregation is high and women's status is low. This conforms to other ethnographic evidence that suggests that elaborate rituals of male bonding have the effect of excluding women from ritual life and thus correlate with women's lower status (Davenport, 1977; see also Herdt, 1984: 66).

Herdt's book was greeted with significant academic acclaim and equally significant shock and disbelief among undergraduate students. When this writer has asked students what they think they would do if they were brought up among the Sambia, the male students invariably declare that they would be the first Sambian youth to refuse to ingest the life force. They may end up sterile outcasts, but better that than to be gay.

II

Among the Nacirema, there is ample evidence of homosexual activity, especially among males, that is neither experienced nor understood to be homosexual in nature. A researcher named Prok, who studied sexual behavior among Nacirema males, found that fully two in five had at least one homosexual experience to orgasm. In the largest villages, for example, there is often a group of young males, many of whom are married and virtually all of whom consider themselves to be heterosexual, who have sex with other men for money. The *"reltshu"* (pronounced relt-suh), as he is known, will typically only perform certain acts (anal penetration) or will only allow certain acts (permitting themselves to be fellated but not reciprocating). By remaining the "insertor" in homosexual acts, these males maintain a heterosexual identity, and identify as "men." Men are insertors—whether with women or with men; so as long as they remain insertors, they believe their masculinity is not compromised.

A casual observer may believe that if two males are engaging in sex, it is, by definition, "gay sex," but these particular Nacirema males do not see it that way. They believe that the meaning of sexual acts does not inhere in the gender identity of the actor, but rather either in the sexual orientation of the actor or in the acts themselves. Thus, they believe, if two heterosexual males engage in sex, it may be heterosexual sex; conjointly, if one of the males performs as heterosexual males perform—that is, remains the penetrator and scrupulously avoids being penetrated—he is still a male, i.e., heterosexual.[1]

However, these relatively exotic denizens of the Nacirema demimonde° are only the tip of the ritualized homosexual iceberg. It turns out that there is a large subculture of Nacirema males who engage in ritualized homosexual activities quite openly. They are the *"Tarf"* subculture. 10

The *Tarf* subculture has developed in villages where the youth of the culture gather for education and entertainment. The youth of the culture who gather in these villages are called *"dentstuds"* (pronounced dent-stoods). While most of the village's youth are *dentstuds*, not all are *Tarfs*. *Tarfs* are a special group of *dentstuds*.

Dentstuds congregate within these villages in an enclosed area called the *"supmac"* (prounced sup-mack). Supmacs encompass many buildings for ceremonial inductions, Nacirema instruction, and often also have a special type of building called an *"mrod"* (pronounced em-rod). Mrods

---

demimonde: an outsider group to mainstream society, typically with a poor reputation; comes from the nineteenth-century French term for women with questionable morality and social standing.

are long houses where the members of the village, *dentstuds*, live and socialize. They eat in special dining huts, and are often expected to eat inferior food.

Tarfs, however, most often live apart in ceremonial men's huts that abut or are adjacent to the *supmac*. These men's huts are ritually forbidden to women; indeed, *Tarfs* celebrate sex segregation as a necessary ingredient in their main activity: exclusionary bonding. It is the defining feature of the *Tarf* subculture that they develop hyper-extended kinship networks, appropriating kinship terms like "brother" to denote the specialness of their relationship. However, as we shall see, this further complicates the ritualized homosexuality among the *Tarf* subculture, lending also an element of incest to its mix.

Tarf huts are residential huts, in which the *Tarfs* live, eat, and socialize. *Tarfs* are apparently exempt from most of the formal educational activities that occupy the time of the majority of *dentstuds* in the village, for they spend virtually no time in formal training, and most would have a hard time finding the *"yrarbil"* (pronounced y-ar-bill), which is where the sacred texts of the village are housed. Ceremonial activities occupy most of the *Tarfs'* time.

Some of these ceremonies include bacchanalian festivals, at which there is a significant amount of ingestion of alcoholic libations and copious feigned heterosexual contact. Their substance abuse rivals that of the Yanomamo and Jibaro. During their festivals, *Tarfs* frequently become intoxicated and attempt to perform heterosexual activities. They call these attempts at heterosexual coupling *pukooh* (pronounced pook-oo). Obviously, heterosexual activity is so distasteful to the *Tarfs* that they need to be sufficiently drunk in order to accomplish it. 15

When a *Tarf* is successful in a *pukooh*, he immediately tells the other *Tarfs*, and they then credit him with successful heterosexual accomplishment. Tallies may be kept of these *pukoohs*, and the names and physical descriptions of the heterosexual women with whom the *Tarfs* have *"pukooh-ed"* are written down in a sacred book, to be consulted only by other members of the *Tarf* subculture.

However, it is clear that the purpose of the *pukooh* is not the sexual satisfaction that might accompany sexual relations among typical heterosexuals in Nacirema culture, or, indeed, among non-*Tarfs* in the same *supmac*. It is clear that the main purpose of these feigned heterosexual events is to win the praise of the other *Tarfs*. Even in *Tarf* heterosexual behavior, there is a strong undercurrent of homosocial validation.

Tarfs live for the validation of other *Tarfs*. They are willing to undergo extreme punishment and degradations in order to do so. *Tarfs* begin their career not as full-fledged *Tarfs* but must undergo an arduous initiation period, during which time they are probationary *Tarfs*. When a *Tarf* is in this probationary stage he is called a *"Jelp."*

Like many cultures, *Tarfs* have developed elaborate rituals of initiation (see, for example, Gilmore, 1990). These initiation rituals demand that the young novice prove his worth to enter the society as a full-fledged member, often after undergoing some severe test or hardship. For example, in some East African cultures the 12-year-old boys live alone and isolated for four years. When they return, they are circumcised without anesthesia by a stone knife. They must not flinch. Mende boys, a West African culture, are scarified by a "monster" (an elder in disguise). Pueblo Indian (Hopi, Zuni) kachinas whip the boys with yucca whips until they bleed (kachinas are animal-human hybrids, also elders in disguise). Others use nasal incision to stimulate bleeding. But, as several of these examples illustrate, these rituals are supervised and conducted by elders who prepare the initiation ritual, preside over the events, and confer *their* validation of masculinity on the successful initiates.

Tarf subcultural norms are slightly different. For one thing, the 20 "elders" who supervise the ritual initiations are elders only in a symbolic sense; they are usually no more than one or two years older than the *Jelps*. *Tarf* initiation rituals are, in fact, organized to take place away from any and all adult supervision by the elders who administer the life of the *supmac*. In this way, the administrators can maintain a façade of "plausible deniability" in case any legal challenges are made to the homosexual excesses of the *Tarf* rituals. Administrators routinely feign surprise and shock when the structure and content of *Tarf* rituals are disclosed.

And for this reason, *Tarf* rituals are shrouded in the deepest of secrecy. *Tarfs* and also the *Jelps* swear oaths to maintain the strictest of secrecy about their activities, perhaps because there is some shame about their overtly homosexual content. (Nacirema society is among the least permissive of the advanced cultures we have studied when it comes to homosexual behavior.)

It is during his apprenticeship as a *Jelp* that the true homosexual nature of *Tarf* life is revealed. To prove himself worthy to be a *Tarf*, he must engage in a variety of homosexual practices with the other *Jelps*. Although, as we have noted, these are often veiled in secrecy, we have been able to describe several of them here. These are by no means universal among all *Tarfs*, nor does every *Tarf* hut require these. However, they are well-known among most *Tarfs*, either in practice or as a reference point for other, more inventive, local variations.

Bagging Tea

In Nacirema culture, the small pouch employed to concoct morning libations, drunk hot, is believed to resemble the male scrotum. In the "Bagging Tea" ritual, the *Tarf* removes his trousers and loin cloth, and squats over a sleeping *Jelp*. The *Jelp* is then awakened to find a dangling scrotum directly over his face. While this is intended to be humiliating to the *Jelp*, it is not clear if he then is expected to engage with the other man's scrotum orally.

The Walk of the Elephants

In this ritual, all the *Jelps* are stripped naked and stand in a straight line, one behind the other. Each *Jelp* reaches through the legs of the *Jelp* standing in from of him, and grabs that man's penis. The entire effect resembles a line of elephants walking in a single line, in which each holds the other's tail in his trunk. By performing the Walk of the Elephants, the *Jelps* learn the homosexual behavior that is expected of them by other *Tarfs*. Apparently, it is not typical for *Tarfs* to walk around their secret men's hut in this way during nonritual periods, or secular time. Only during ritual events are they permitted to do so.

Anal Egg Transport

In this collective ritual, each *Jelp* is asked to place a peeled hard-boiled 25 egg in his rectum and then all proceed to walk a certain distance, either inside the ceremonial men's hut or in a secluded place. While this ritual clearly signifies anal intercourse, it is unclear whether *Tarfs* themselves insert the eggs into the *Jelp*'s rectum, or if the *Jelp* is required to do this himself.

Block Party

In this ritual, *Tarfs* and *Jelps* stand on a balcony or ledge of a building. The *Tarfs* measure a rope, with a cinderblock tied to one end, so that it reaches almost, but not quite, to the ground. Then the *Tarfs* tie the other end of the rope to the *Jelp*'s penis. They tell him that only if his penis is large enough will the cinderblock reach the ground; otherwise, the weight of the block falling will likely rip the *Jelp*'s penis off. While the manifest function, according to *Tarfs*, of this ritual is to test how much trust the *Jelp* has in his future brothers, it also reveals *Tarf* and *Jelp* anxiety about penis size. Since *Tarf* culture revolves so centrally around ritualized homosexuality, anxiety about penis size—whether they measure up—is heightened for the *Jelps*.

Ookie Cookie

As if in imitation of the Sambia, this ritual is one of the most overtly homosexual of the entire *Tarf* subculture. *Tarfs* masturbate together (although they are prohibited from masturbating each other) and ejaculate on a cookie. *Jelps* are then required to eat the cookie. In this homosexual form of communion, bonds of solidarity are forged, and the *Jelps* can ingest the *Tarf* life force from their elders. Among all *dentstuds* within a particular *supmac, Tarfs* are the most closely allied with their Sambia cousins.

Gnag Gnab

This is a particularly odious variation of the *oookie cookie*, in which the shared semen is located in the genitals of a drugged female, who is often unconscious or at least incapable of consenting to heterosexual sex. The unconscious or unconsenting woman is then said to "have sex" with several *Tarfs* or *Jelps*. This homosexual activity is a most cleverly disguised homosexual ritual, since it involves many different male *Tarfs* seemingly having heterosexual sex with the same woman. However, as Sanday and others have observed, participants in *gnag gnabs* often say that the best part was feeling the semen of the other *Tarfs* inside the unconscious woman. While technically illegal, the absence of any *supmac* administrators, and the veneer of "plausible deniability" that such activities are taking place, ensure that the illegal activities often go unpunished.

Of course, like Herdt's Sambia, the *Tarfs* vigorously deny the obvious homosexual elements in their rituals. Indeed, when pointed out to them by the naïve researcher, several threatened physical harm to the researcher for suggesting it. This reaction leads us to the obvious psychoanalytic conclusion: *the vigorousness of the denial is directly related to the obviousness of the behavior being denied.*

There is one other ritual that we must consider: *"norp."* Norp consists of 30 images and pictures, and also movies, of naked people engaged in sexual relations. Originally we suspect that these films were created for physicians and other health professionals because they use extreme close-ups of the genitals to reveal the various methods people use to engage in sexual intercourse. The actors in the movies possess enormous penises, so as to enable the viewer to observe all facets of erection, coitus, and ejaculation. Concerns for birth control are evident, as well, because the male in the *norp* movie ejaculates outside the female, to ensure that she will not conceive. (We can only briefly comment here that such a method of birth control is obviously ineffective, judging from the high rates of unwanted pregnancies among the Nacirema. However, it should be noted that other cultures whose territories abut that of the Nacirema are far more adept at providing adequate contraception and therefore have lower rates of unwanted pregnancy.) These clinical depictions of sex are interesting to the anthropologist because we can only conclude from watching them that the Nacirema do not like sex very much at all.

Yet *norp* is everywhere in Nacirema society. It is especially prevalent in educational villages, where it may appear on the information boxes that all the *dentstuds* use to record information. And it is omnipresent in the *Tarf* subculture. We understand from our informants that they enjoy *norp* because it facilitates masturbation. Its function is to arouse the viewer sexually, and he then proceeds to masturbate. (Virtually all Nacirema males of this age cohort, regardless of *Tarf* status, engage in masturbation, although few actually discuss it publicly.) Only a small fraction of the Nacirema—and an even smaller percentage of *Tarfs*—employ *norp* in their heterosexual unions; its use is mostly a solitary experience.

Naïve readers may assume that since the depictions of sexual congress contained in *norp* are images of heterosexual couples, then the viewing experience would hardly qualify as ritualized homosexuality. However, in our field research we noticed that within the *Tarf* subculture, even the most evidently heterosexual experiences can be transformed into ritualized homosexuality. Indeed, it may be that the *Tarf* subculture feels a bit ashamed about its evident rampant homosexuality, and so they attempt to conceal it under a veil of surface hetero-

> *"It may be that the Tarf subculture feels a bit ashamed about its evident rampant homosexuality, and so they attempt to conceal it under a veil of surface heterosexuality."*

sexuality. If *norp* is manifestly heterosexual, its latent function may be to provide an outlet for ritualized homosexuality.

Tarfs tend to view *norp* collectively. They will gather together, drink alcoholic libations, and sit very close to one another on the sofa. As they watch the *norp* together, they will, of course, begin to become sexually aroused, but there are strict prohibitions against acknowledgment of that arousal, let alone permission to masturbate in the presence of the other *Tarfs*. Thus, *Tarfs* are frustrated in the gratification of their arousal, and we can only conclude that this frustration is intentional: they want to have their heterosexual impulses (heterosexual fantasies tend to accompany their masturbation) frustrated in order to facilitate their ritualized homosexual arousal.

However, *Tarfs* also feel so guilty about their homosexual arousal that their frustration becomes aggression, as would be predicted by social psychologists. Again, however, this aggression is often directed not at the other males but at the images of the women depicted in *norp*. The *Tarfs* will yell at the image of the woman, hoping that the male actor will hurt her, hit her or "nail her." (We assume that this bears some relationship to Nacirema spiritual beliefs.) In this way, the *Tarfs* reaffirm their secret homosexual identities, as they repudiate their interest in women so that they can remain together.

III

Many of the most overtly homosexual rituals occur following ceremonial   35
sporting events known as *"toofball."* In this athletic contest, the contes-
tants dress in gladiatorial costumes that exaggerate masculine muscula-
ture in the shoulders and thighs, while ensuring that any observer can
view the entire buttocks without obstruction. Armored helmets conceal
their faces. This is no doubt to enable them to engage in overtly homoerotic behavior anonymously, as adult homosexuals among the Nacrimea
often do.

The object of this athletic contest, as Berkeley folklorist Alan Dundes
has eloquently pointed out, is itself ritually homosexual (Dundes, 1985).
"The object of the game, simply stated, is to get into the opponent's endzone while preventing the opponent from getting into one's own endzone," Dundes writes (1985: 81). This helps explain the "bottom patting"
that is often observed among players. "A good offensive or defensive play
deserves a pat on the rear end. The recipient has held up his end and has
thereby helped protect the collective 'end' of the entire team. One pats
one's teammates' ends, but one seeks to violate the endzone of one's
opponents!" (p. 81).

In one particularly homoerotic display, the largest of the *toofball* players
make themselves vulnerable to anal penetration by their teammates, facing
their opponents. The largest and heaviest men bend over into an untenable
stooped position, leaning forward so far (to expose their buttocks to their
teammates) that they need to rest their heavy frame on one hand as well.
This three-point stance is simultaneously more impervious to one's opponents and exceptionally vulnerable to one's trusted teammates.

When arrayed for competition, the most handsome of these warriors
is required to place his hands on the buttocks of the largest and least
mobile of the other combatants. (Only he may do so; all others are
enjoined from this display.) He recites a ceremonial incantation as he
moves his hands rhythmically. The larger man does not move, nor does
he indicate sexual gratification from this simulation of masturbation. At
a specified point, he passes the oblong projectile through his legs, and

the handsome warrior either gives it away to another combatant, or he throws it in the air. Regardless, as soon as the initial homosexual rubbing is over and the *toofball* is passed, all the combatants in both colored costumes fall on top of each other, grabbing each other's bodies, until they lie together in a big undulating pile. Adults, wearing costumes like zebras, run to the pile and blow a whistle to ensure that all the combatants are stimulated fairly. (The zebra-men are dressed this way to make sure that the experience is as natural as the jungle which their costumes signify.)

Observing such a spectacle of public homosexuality is obviously arousing for the many spectators. Many wear strange costumes themselves to the spectacle, perhaps to indicate their fanatic allegiance to the combatants from one side or the other. After the large piles are dispersed, strangers often hug each other, and show other forms of affection such as holding hands for a fraction of a second, or slapping a neighbor's hand or buttocks. Many drink ceremonial libations from paper bags.

Tarfs are regular spectators; indeed, they are the most consistent   40 attendees at these *toofball* spectacles. Perhaps it is their heightened state of sexual arousal that leads to the *Tarfs'* ritualized homosexual behavior; their rituals often take place in the evenings following these *toofball* events.

IV

That *Tarfs* routinely engage in such ritualized homosexuality need not concern citizens of open and tolerant societies. Indeed, the only concerns we raise here about ritualized homosexuality in *Tarf* culture are the layers of homophobic denial that so often accompany it and the ways in which women become a vehicle by which the ritualized homosexuality is simultaneously enacted and denied.

Attitude surveys have consistently found high levels of homophobia among the *Tarf* subculture—which is ironic when one considers that the *Tarfs* spend virtually all their time together in their men's hut engaging in ritualized homosexual activity. Since the *Tarf* males so evidently want to be with each other, and have sex with each other, we can only hope that they become active campaigners for more tolerant attitudes and laws regarding homosexuality. Surely that is in their interests as *Tarfs*.

Second, we must register concern for the ways in which *Tarf* denial of the obvious homoeroticism in their rituals leads to certain compensatory efforts to demonstrate heterosexuality. Male heterosexual predatory sexual behavior has been consistently remarked upon by observers of

Nacirema life, especially in its *supmacs*. While it is no doubt the case that an overall decline in cultural homophobia among the Nacirema in general might reduce such behavior, we also hope that the acknowledgment of the manifest homosexual content of *Tarf* rituals will enable *Tarfs*, particularly, to relax their obsession with proving what they are unable to prove.

Further, the specific forms of ritualized homosexuality known as *gnag gnabs* must be vigorously prosecuted as crimes against the women whose sole function is to provide a vessel by which the ritualized homosexuality can take place. This requires the active intervention of administrators and other elders in the *supmac*.

Surely, now that the ritualized homosexuality of the *Tarf* subculture 45 has been described, future researchers will be able to better understand the activities of this strange and esoteric tribe.

Notes

While I intend this essay to be provocative, it should also be clear that in no way do I assume that all members of the *Tarf* subculture engage in these practices. For research on the subculture, I am grateful to Lauren Joseph and Tyson Smith for their insights and explanations. Denny Gilmore helped to situate the *Tarf* subculture in a wider cross-cultural literature. Three anonymous reviewers helped me sharpen the analysis and restrain potential excesses.

1. While these particular *reltsuhs* may believe the meaning of acts do not inhere in the gender of the actors, their view is not widely shared. Generally, Nacirema believe in the "one drop rule"—in which one sexual experience with a member of the same sex brands the person indelibly as gay.

References

Carrier, J. (1977). "Sex Role Preference as an Explanatory Variable in Homosexual Behavior," *Archives of Sexual Behavior* 6.

Davenport, W. (1977). "Sex in Cross-Cultural Perspective," in F. Beach and M. Diamond (eds.). *Human Sexuality in Four Perspectives*. Baltimore, MD: Johns Hopkins University Press.

Dundes, A. (1985). "The American Game of 'Smear the Queer' and the Homosexual Component of Male Competitive Sport and Warfare," *Journal of Psychoanalytic Anthropology* 8: 115–29.

Gilmore, D. (1990). *Manhood in the Making*. New Haven, CT: Yale University Press.

Herdt, G. (1981). *Guardians of the Flutes*. Chicago, IL: University of Chicago Press.

Herdt, G. (ed.) (1984). *Ritualized Homosexuality in Melanesia*. Berkeley: University of California Press.

Joseph, Lauren J. (2003). "Masculinity in the Greek System: Race, Sexuality, and the Stratification of Fraternity Men." Unpublished master's thesis, University of California, Irvine.

Kelly, R. (1977). *Etero Social Structure*. Ann Arbor: University of Michigan Press.

Miner, H. (1956). "Body Ritual among the Nacirema," *American Anthropologist* 58(3).

Schiefflin, E. L. (1976). *The Sorrow of the Lonely and the Burning of the Dancers*. New York: St Martin's Press.

Williams, F. (1936). *Papuans of the Trans-Fly*. Oxford: Oxford University Press.

Understanding the Text

1. What ritualized practices of the *Tarf* subculture does Kimmel observe? Why does he choose these practices to focus on?

2. What serious point is Kimmel making with his satirical anthropological study? In other words, what is his thesis?

3. How does Kimmel create an ironic tone? What aspects of his essay are ironic? How can you tell?

Reflection and Response

4. Would you classify Kimmel's satire as Horatian, Juvenalian, or both? Explain your answer with specific examples.

5. How do you feel about Kimmel's qualification that the practices of the *Tarfs* are not universal? Why do you think Kimmel includes this remark more than once (in par. 22 and the Notes)? What effect does it have on his overall argument?

6. What was your response to Kimmel's discussion of the sport *toofball*? Are there other aspects of the game that can be satirized in Kimmel's style?

Making Connections

7. Read Horace Mitchell Miner's "Body Ritual Among the Nacirema," which is in the public domain and available for free on the Internet. How does Miner do a sendup of Americans and anthropology? What satirical aspects of Miner's essay does Kimmel imitate successfully?

8. Write your own mock ethnographic study of a ritualized practice of the Nacirema tribe or one of its subcultures. What aspects of American life, or your life as a student, need to be studied by the satirical anthropologist?

The Boy from *Jurassic Park*'s College Application Essay

Julia Drake

McSweeney's Internet Tendency (www.mcsweeneys.net /tendency) is a literature and humor Web site that is part of McSweeney's nonprofit publishing house, founded and edited by writer Dave Eggers in 1998. *McSweeney's Internet Tendency* features shorter pieces that demonstrate dry wit, wordplay, and an absurdist sense of humor, and they assume that readers possess a degree of familiarity with literature and popular culture. The site frequently publishes brief works of incongruous humor that trade in comic juxtapositions, such as parodies that mix high- and low-brow culture.

Julia Drake's piece fits the bill of traditional *McSweeney's* fare because she writes a parodic college application essay in the persona of Tim Murphy, the boy (played by Joseph Mazzello) from Steven Spielberg's 1993 film *Jurassic Park*. At the time of publication, Drake, a graduate of Williams College, was an MFA fiction student at Columbia University School of the Arts, where she teaches university writing. When reading her piece, think about the conventions of the college application essay that you followed in applying to universities. How does Drake's essay compare to your own college application essays?

Claws scrabbled at the door, each scratch a shock of fear to my heart. Inside the kitchen, my sister and I hid behind a stainless steel table, slick as the sweat that dripped from my brow. A creak of the door handle; a clicking of prehistoric toenails across the tile floor, and I looked at my sister, panic searing through me: the raptors had made it inside.

I never thought I would find myself in such a situation when I went to visit my grandfather on his remote island where he'd created a paradise of living dinosaurs. In fact, my face lit up with childlike joy upon seeing the place, my intellectual curiosity instantly piqued. I got my first taste of fieldwork examining an ailing triceratops with seasoned paleontologists, which instilled in me a passion for hands-on learning. That passion for learning is certainly something I would bring with me to a college classroom; it is also a feeling I have tried to impart to my fellow students in my work as French Peer Tutor.

However, my experience in the park was more than a simple voyage of academic discovery. It was also a complicated and profound transition into adulthood. I overcame copious obstacles such as surviving a Tyrannosaurus

309

rex attack, escaping from a treed car, and being electrocuted by a high-voltage fence. Overcoming these obstacles required great courage and also newfound maturity. Indeed, the adult traits I acquired surviving dinosaurs will make me an enthusiastic and passionate member of a college community, whether I brave a Friday night dance or experiment in a new discipline, such as figure drawing.

> "The adult traits I acquired surviving dinosaurs will make me an enthusiastic and passionate member of a college community, whether I brave a Friday night dance or experiment in a new discipline, such as figure drawing."

My experience there in many ways marked my transition into adulthood. However, perhaps the most important thing I learned was not one of reptilian past but of human present. My grandfather taught me that summer about the ongoing process of learning. Though some critics may read failure in his attempt to safely clone dinosaur embryos, his experience helped me to realize that no matter the age, learning never stops. My grandfather's learning experience with terrible lizards mirrors my personal experience in my position as Senior Class Co-Treasurer, which required me to learn how to share leadership and how to manage a budget.

In addition, my time at the park marked an intellectual transition into adulthood because it sparked a new interest in history. Though the park itself centered on prehistoric history, I credit my visit there with a lifelong interest in history in general, in particular the French Revolution. My senior capstone project on the Tennis Court Oaths demonstrates my dedication to academics, and I can easily foresee myself continuing this project in a rigorous academic environment. Though the raptors were the guillotine—nay, the *Robespierre*—of my childhood, they helped me realize the importance of intellectual curiosity.

Pliny the Elder once said, "From sad experiences spring new beginnings." Rather than give into sadness and mourn my lost childhood, I escaped the kitchen, the raptors, and the park. My childhood stayed behind in the jungle, crystallized like amber. Thus I was able to move forward into the world as an adult.

Thanks to my experiences on Isla Nublar, I am comfortable tackling the plethora of challenges that await me on campus, be they academic or physical, modern or prehistoric, quotidian or genetically engineered.

The boy from *Jurassic Park*, learning some valuable life lessons during his "complicated and profound transition into adulthood."
Everett Collection, Inc.

Understanding the Text

1. How does Drake create humor through incongruities? Provide examples of incongruous humor in her faux college application essay.

2. Analyze the structure of Drake's essay. How does it begin? What points does she make to support Tim's case for being admitted? How does the essay conclude? It may be helpful to construct an outline of the piece.

Reflection and Response

3. A thought experiment: ignore the patent absurdity of a fictional character writing about his escape from an imaginary island of biogenetically resurrected dinosaurs. If you were a university admissions officer, would you accept Tim to your school? Does he (through Drake) make a convincing case for being a prospective student? Why or why not?

4. What is your favorite part of Drake's application essay? What part did you find the most humorous? Do you think the seriousness of tone helps or hurts the humor of Drake's piece? Why?

Making Connections

5. Write your own parody college application essay in which you adopt the persona of a fictional or real-life character. How would this persona fulfill the conventions of such an essay? What experiences would she or he cite as evidence of her or his college preparedness?

6. Choose another genre of writing to parody. For example, you could write a farcical newspaper article in the style of *The Onion*, or a parodic movie review, commercial, pop song, travel brochure, and so on.

7. Surf the *McSweeney's* Web site for another type of humorous piece to imitate, and then write a version of it with different content.

Consumer Joe

Paul Davidson

The customer is always right, or so we've been told. In *Consumer Joe: Harassing Corporate America, One Letter at a Time* (2003), Paul Davidson adopts the persona of a patronizing customer to test whether some of today's largest companies still abide by this best-business practice. In the letters reprinted below, which were originally published in *Consumer Joe*, Davidson confronts Starbucks about its desire for "world domination," quibbles with Procter & Gamble over its Charmin brand toilet paper, and asks FedEx CEO Frederick Smith whether his employees would treat packages like the fictional FedEx worker Chuck Noland (Tom Hanks) does in the film *Cast Away* (2000).

Davidson is a Los Angeles–based screenwriter and journalist who also works in the television industry as a producer. He is the author of *The Lost Blogs* (2006), a book of imaginary weblogs penned by famous historical figures, and has contributed to *Wired*, *Mental_Floss*, and NPR's *All Things Considered*.

Starbucks

December 12, 2001

Starbucks Customer Relations
P.O. Box 3717
Seattle, WA 98124-3717

Dear Sir or Madam:

Well, congratulations! You did it. According to your "Year 2000 Fiscal Report," your company has over 3,500 locations worldwide, serving more than 12 million customers per week. And your current goal to have more than 20,000 locations, is now "well within your reach." Apparently, the conspiracy theories about your company seeking "world domination" are more than conspiracy theories.

My question is simply, where will it all end? At what point will the leaders of your company decide that enough is enough? A Starbucks in every city, on every corner, perhaps in every apartment complex throughout the world? On the moon? I mean, c'mon, there is such a thing as overdoing it, don't you think?

I personally don't drink coffee. Never have, never will. But for me, it's a personal reason, stemming from a strange incident in a cotton-field that befell me in my early teens. Because of my refusals to imbibe your product, my life is safe from any meddling that Starbucks seeks to inflict upon me. But what of the helpless ones? Those who cannot fight back against your soy-milk drenched lies?

Aaah, but what is the real truth? Why is Starbucks so hell bent on conquest? Why do they grow each year like an infection that cannot be stopped? This is the question I would like the answer to. Sooner than later, please.

Holiday wishes to you and yours,

David Paulson

December 19, 2001

David Paulson
264 Doheny Drive #8
Beverly Hills, CA 90211

Dear Mr. Paulson,

Thank you for contacting Starbucks Coffee Company. I was disappointed to hear that you do not want Starbucks to continue growing.

Starbucks goal is to provide customers with the world's finest coffee in a friendly environment and convenient neighborhood locations. Starbucks prides itself on being good citizens locally and globally by giving back to its communities in many ways.

The stores employ local people and serve pastries made by local bakeries. In addition, Starbucks contributes to food banks and sponsors community programs that support children, the arts, the environment, and AIDS research. For example, Starbucks stores consistently donate coffee beans that are more than seven days old, as well as any leftover pastries to its local food banks. Also, many of our store managers are actively involved with their local Chamber of Commerce.

I hope this letter adequately demonstrates Starbucks aim as a company. If you have any further questions, I invite you to call the Customer Relations department at 1-800-23-LATTE.

Warm Regards,

Casey E.
Customer relations representative

Procter & Gamble

September 21, 2001

President
Procter & Gamble
1 Procter & Gamble Plz.
Cincinnati, OH 45202

Dear Sir or Madam:

As I often read while taking a bathroom pit stop, I recently found myself looking at the text on the back of one of your CHARMIN packages. Quite honestly, it so confused me, I couldn't finish doing my business. If you know what I mean.

There's a chart on the back of your package that says CHARMIN is soft, strong, and thick. At the same time, it says that CHARMIN ULTRA is softer, stronger, and thicker. On top of that, it tells me that CHARMIN PLUS has aloe. I know the United States is a country of democracy and choices, but this is ridiculous!!

Why would I purchase CHARMIN now that I know that CHARMIN ULTRA is better in every single way? And why would I purchase CHARMIN ULTRA if I knew that CHARMIN PLUS has aloe? And since I'm one of those white, pasty guys, and I'm always getting burnt by the sun, if I can get a product with aloe, you bet your bottom I'm going to!

> "Why would I purchase CHARMIN now that I know that CHARMIN ULTRA is better in every single way?"

What's your thought process here? Why so much confusion? Why not just make it easy for everyone and make *one* CHARMIN product that includes all the best elements?

Just so you know, I called your 1-800 number to ask this question, and was met with confusion as well. Your operators eventually told me to "just buy whichever one you want, we've got other calls to take care of." I thought it was a little insensitive, especially since we're talking about my quest for a "quality-wiping experience."

Can someone please clear this all up? Until you do, I'm going to have a really hard time deciding in which way to wipe my butt.

Sincere, Sincerely, and Ultra Sincerely!

David Paulson

Mr David Paulson
264 South Doheny Drive #8
Beverly Hills CA 90211

Dear Mr. Paulson:

Thanks for contacting us with your creative suggestions for Charmin.

We appreciate your loyalty and are glad you let us know of your interest in another version of Charmin. Making products people want and like is what we're all about. I'm sharing your feedback with the rest of our Charmin Team.

Please bear in mind that we try to satisfy the diverse wants of the public. "To each his own" as they say.

Thanks again for getting in touch with us.

Sincerely,

Consumer Relations – PT

[Letter included a Charmin coupon for "One 4, 6, 9 or 12 Roll Pack Any Version"]

FedEx

September 27, 2001

Mr. Frederick W. Smith
Chairman, President, & CEO
Federal Express Corporation
3610 Hacks Cross
Building A
Memphis, TN 38132

Dear Mr. Smith:

First of all, I must say that I'm quite impressed with the variety of jobs you currently hold. Chairman, President, and Chief Executive Officer! I bet you can hardly find the time to watch *Friends* and eat TV dinners!! (I do . . . that's why I mention that. And, on a totally unrelated note, is it me or has Matthew Perry gained like twenty pounds lately?)

The reason I'm writing, however, is in regard to a set of packages I plan on sending through your company to my Aunt Beatrice and Uncle Howie in Paris, France. They've been a loving set of family members for years, excluding the years 1993–94, when they believed that someone in a black car was out to get them, and weren't too cheery when you'd call them on the phone. Nonetheless, I'm planning on sending them a family heirloom that, if lost in the Atlantic, could never be replaced (even if I paid for insurance).

As you may or may not remember, a FedEx cargo plane crashed into the water in last year's film *Cast Away*. And of course, I know it's a movie, but the main character opened some of the packages, and kept some sealed — eventually returning them to their rightful owners at the end of the film. I simply had to ask — if such a scenario really happened, and my family heirloom ended up on an island in the middle of nowhere, would your employees open my package and use them to stay alive? Or would they treat them with the respect that I'm sure you'd like them to treat them with, and return them to my aunt and uncle upon being rescued and returned to the mainland?

You may think it's an unreal scenario, or something you'd rather not address, but it's a valid concern when contemplating sending a valuable family heirloom across choppy Atlantic waters, in a plane owned by you.

Kindest regards,

David Paulson

P.S. — I've already contacted UPS on this scenario, and they seem to think that their employees would NOT open the package, and would be sure to return them to the rightful owner upon their rescue. Their only caveat was if the package included food that may be able to save their life (like coconuts, dried fruit, or See's Candies); then in that scenario it may have to be consumed. And you know what, I buy that explanation.

October 25, 2001

Mr. David Paulson
264 South Doheny Dr., #8
Beverly Hills, CA 90211

Dear Mr. Paulson:

Thank you for your letter bringing Mr. Smith's attention to your reflections on what real FedEx employees would do if they found themselves in a situation such as the one Tom Hanks' character faced in *Cast Away*.

Most of us at FedEx were very proud of the character's actions and devotion to duty as expressed in that film, and felt it reflected positively on our best traditions. As you suggest, the chance of a similar scenario occurring in real life is quite remote, but, as we all know, especially since September 11, anything is possible and nothing is more important that the lives saved in a critical situation.

FedEx is committed to a *People • Service • Profit* philosophy. We make money by providing the best service in the industry while showing the highest level of respect and loyalty to the people involved, that means to our employees as well as the customers. So, in the simplest terms, I think we would want any employee in that situation to do everything they possibly could to preserve their life until they could make it home safely to the arms of their family. And if they brought customers' packages back with them, all the better.

We value the trust our customers place in us to handle their priority package needs. I hope this answer gives you all the confidence in us you need.

Sincerely,

Oran Quintrell
Executive Management Assistant

Understanding the Text

1. Analyze the language of Davidson's prank letters. How would you characterize his comic rhetoric? What humorous strategies and styles does he employ?

2. Analyze the language in the responses from the corporate representatives. What parts of these three letters use corporate jargon? What purpose does such "business speak" serve, and how do the conventions of this boilerplate genre try to achieve that goal?

3. What kind of comic ethos does Davidson develop in these letters? How does he build this ethos and why?

Reflection and Response

4. Did you find any parts of the corporate representatives' letters unintentionally humorous? Which ones, and how so?

5. How would you classify the satire of Davidson's letters? What serious motives may underlie his comic rhetoric? In answering these questions, consider the power dynamics between an individual consumer and a multinational corporation.

6. Have you been a customer of Starbucks, Procter &Gamble, FedEx, or a similar corporation? Did your consumer experience ever resemble Davidson's? What other kinds of corporate behavior do you find worthy of satirical treatment?

Making Connections

7. In the book in which these letters appear, Davidson has a second and even third correspondence with some company representatives. Adopting Davidson's persona, write a letter that replies to one of the three response letters.

8. Write your own letter to a company that draws your ire. Wrap your serious argument in humor. (Your answer to question 6 should prove helpful in coming up with an idea.)

How to Be the Black Employee

Baratunde Thurston

Baratunde Thurston is a stand-up comedian, cultural critic, and author of the *New York Times* best-selling satirical memoir, *How to Be Black* (2012), from which the following excerpt is taken. A Harvard graduate with a degree in philosophy, Thurston works in the intersections between comedy and technology. He served for five years as the Director of Digital for *The Onion*; wrote a monthly column for *Fast Company*; and co-founded Cultivated Wit, a business that brings together developers and comedians to build funny apps during the company's Comedy Hack Day. Thurston is also interested in race issues: He is the cohost of the podcast *Our National Conversation about Conversations about Race* and the cofounder of the blog *Jack & Jill Politics*, which provides "a black bourgeoisie perspective on U.S. politics."

In this excerpt from *How to Be Black*, Thurston delivers hilarious advice on what to do and what not do to be successful as The Black Employee in a corporate environment. As with the comic rhetoric of Davidson's letters, Thurston's parody guide includes commentary on serious issues about race and economics in the United States. Look for those serious points as you laugh at what it takes to navigate corporate America as a black person.

So you got a job in an office; you're one of the few minorities and possibly the only black person. First of all, congratulations on having obtained a job. In this economy, that is amazing and makes you a superhero. Protect the job at all costs! Second, I'm so sorry for the awkwardness you have endured or will endure in this environment. Hopefully this guide will help you weather the scenarios ahead or give you a different perspective on those you've already managed.

The truth is, you have two jobs.

The first is the explicit job for which you were hired. This is the job you saw posted on the Web or heard about through a friend. It's the job title printed on your business card and in the company directory. It's what you put on your LinkedIn profile.

For the sake of argument, let's say the job was research associate at Optimus Research Group.[1] When you heard about this position, you were excited. Why? Because you love research, and you're good at it. You prepared yourself. You updated your résumé. You boosted your past research experience and added personal details that connect you to the type of research this job requires. You read the company's Web site thoroughly. You Googled the business and its customers. You may even have done your own research on particular employees, especially management. You are prepared to be an excellent research associate, and when you get the job, and sign the papers, and show up for your first day, that's a role you are excited to play.

The thing is, you were also hired for another job: your blackness. 5 That's not to say you were merely accepted due to some affirmative action quota. If that were the case, nothing more would be expected of you than simply being black and doing Job #1 above. That would make you a research associate who happens to be black. No, you have another job with specific responsibilities far beyond inhabiting your skin. The people who hired you likely weren't even conscious of this extra job. It's not as if they had one meeting about your research skills and another about your blackness talents. Nevertheless, they expect great things from you, even if subconsciously. In Job #2, you will be expected to:

- Part A: Represent the black community.
- Part B: Defend the company against charges of racism or lack of diversity.
- Part C: Increase the coolness of the office environment by enthusiastically participating in company events.

If you interpret this job description a certain way, you might conclude that you have two, three, or even four jobs because your blackness duty combines the roles of politician, lawyer, and entertainer. Now you're Jamaican! For the sake of simplicity and sanity, however, we will keep these jobs consolidated under the umbrella of Job #2.

Also of note, it is not a requirement that you fully embrace all parts of the second job. I'm merely informing you of the expectations. It's up to you to decide how good of a Black Employee you really want to be.

During your first days on the job, before diving into Parts A, B, and C of Job #2, there's something urgent you must do: *Spot the Negro.*

Like vampires and extremely rich people, black folk can sense one another. Use your Spidey Sense (Blacky Sense?[2]). Use your blackdar to inspect the workplace for signs of Other Negroes. They may be working security for the building. They may be in administrative support. They may be among the associate pool, or they may even be in upper management. Black folk can be anywhere. After all, *you're* here. But one of the biggest mistakes you can make as The Black Employee is to assume you are the only one. You were hired as a research associate, remember? So do some research!

If you find that there is another Black Employee, do not panic. Employ 10 the CARS system, as in *Collect* information, *Analyze* the data, *Review* your

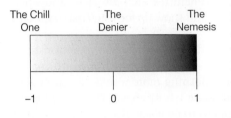

The Inter-Negro Spectrum of Hostility

options, and *Set* your strategy. Like dogs sniffing each other's butts, you will need to figure out what your relationship to this other black person will be. How black do you expect him or her to be, and vice versa? Is this the type of person who feels threatened by your presence? Does this person even acknowledge that he or she is black? You must find answers to all of these questions. Your career may depend on it. For example, if you sit in the middle of the corporate ladder and the other black person is a blue-collar employee, the last thing you want to do is alienate this person. He or she probably knows lots of office secrets, has read discarded memos, and can either make your life easier or make sure your office always smells like rotten fish. On the other hand, if The Other Negro is above you and older, she may see you as a small version of herself and offer mentorship, advance warning on promotions, or just good information about what to avoid in the cafeteria. These and all other black-on-black intra-office interactions can be plotted on the Inter-Negro Spectrum of Hostility.[3] Whether you gain or lose in these relationships depends heavily on where the other black employee falls on the INSH.

On one end, you have **The Chill One.**

This other black employee takes everything in stride. She acknowledges you in subtle ways, occasionally offers advice, and is overall an easygoing presence in the office and in your professional life. At a company meeting, when there's a mildly embarrassing racial moment, the two of you subtly smile at each other, connect eyes briefly, knowingly, and then return to business. Sometimes The Chill One will display light hints of subversion, but it's nothing over-the-top. For example, when the two of you are in the coffee room, she might say to you, "Hey, we should just take all these white people's shit and burn it." But then she laughs, and you laugh, and another coworker enters the room, asking, "What's so funny?" and without missing a beat you both say, "Tina Fey!"

My advice: if you encounter someone on the Chill end of the spectrum, be natural. This is the best type of other black employee to have.

At the other extreme of the Inter-Negro Spectrum of Hostility, you have **The Nemesis.**

This other black employee feels threatened by you. Everything is a competition. If you sign up for the community service committee, he brags about how much they got done last year. If you stay an hour late, he stays ninety minutes. He probably brandishes his education more than necessary, and he laughs too loud. He is naturally insecure, and your presence there serves to elevate his self-doubt further.

Do not respond directly to the competitive energy from The Nemesis. The best defense in this case is simply to do your job. You will probably find many opportunities to publicly undermine him, but don't. That's cruel. He's probably just scared because he's never not been the only black person before, and he's afraid you'll take his place. Take the high road. Be inclusive. Hopefully, with time, he will learn that there is room enough for two, maybe even three black people at this company.

At the very center of the spectrum you may encounter a type of black employee known as **The Denier**. This person simply does not acknowledge her race at all, perhaps hoping that by ignoring it, she'll never have to deal with any negativity associated with her race. While not explicitly combative with you, she's also unlikely to be a useful ally, especially if she ranks above you. It's not that she feels threatened by you. It's that she feels nothing. So she won't act to improve the situation at the company, either. Your best bet here is to accrue as much power in the company as you can so you can use your position for good and undo some of the damage caused by The Denier's apathy.

There's no guarantee you will be the only black employee, so I hope these descriptions help you orient yourself accordingly. Now, let's get into the details of your second job's requirements.

What Do You Think?

Your biggest Job #2 responsibility is to represent the black community (Part A). . . . . Representing the race spans many roles, but representing all of blackness as The Black Employee is unique. When you're vying for the spokesperson role on cable news, that's a conscious act and desire. You know what you're signing up for. When you entertain the questions and assumptions of your white friends, you have the mutual love and respect of your relationship with them to keep you motivated and temper your frustration. As The Black Employee, though, the potential upside is far more limited. There's no media exposure. There's no friendship. You just get irritated. You didn't sign up for this. You don't want to do this. You think, understandably, that *this is not your job*. My goal here is to gently remind you that *yes, this is your other job.*

So when you're in the elevator and a coworker asks, "Hey, Tiffany, Jim and I were wondering, are you disappointed with Obama?" you have some choices to make. The Black Friend would be honest and might go back and forth with your coworker on the substance of the question, relishing the opportunity to learn and enlighten. The Black Spokesperson 20 would check his teeth for leftover food, adjust his blazer, and present a nuanced theory on the effectiveness of President Obama versus early expectations of his term, then attempt to get on MSNBC that night to say the same thing.

What you need to realize before opening your mouth is that, although this appears to be a question for you to answer, it is, in fact, a setup for your coworkers to share their own ideas on the subject and passively seek validation of their opinions from you.

In this situation, The Black Employee has three basic options:

1. **Avoidance:** "You know, that's a really interesting question. I haven't spent much time thinking about it, honestly. These quarterly reports have been kicking my ass!"

2. **Confrontation:** "What? Are you asking me because I'm black?? You know we don't all think alike, right?"

3. **Answer the question:** "Honestly, I am a bit disappointed with President Obama. I'd still vote for him, but I feel let down in a number of ways and think he hasn't been a strong enough advocate for working people."

Which option did you choose?

Let's review the possibilities.

Option 1 (avoidance) is a passive and polite way of telling someone to fuck off. You preserve a cordial and professional work environment and also manage to avoid getting any deeper into the subject. By pivoting the conversation back to work matters, you've effectively dodged the bullet. If you chose Option 1, you did well. This is an acceptable choice. If you're feeling generous that day, you could use the same deflective response but then add, "What do *you* think?" This will give your white colleagues the opening to express themselves they were hoping for. Whether you choose to listen to what he or she has to say is completely discretionary.

Option 2 (confrontation) is a risky move because it puts your coworkers on the defensive, and no one wants to be in that place. You're one step short of calling someone a racist, which is a far worse crime than actual racism. However, it's also a guaranteed method of drawing a clear boundary, and it discourages any similar inquiries in the future. If you choose the path of confrontation and rejection, you won't be the most liked employee, but being left alone leaves you time to focus on Job #1. Remember, you love research. If you chose Option 2, you did well. People will be less likely to engage you in office small talk of any kind, but that's likely a benefit when you consider the fact that every ten minutes of office small talk takes one year off of your life. If you are overly concerned about your coworkers' feelings, Option 2 is still available to you. Just make sure you deliver your response with a smile, maybe even a little laugh. Folks love happy black people, even when those black people are dissing them.

Option 3 (honesty) is a classic mistake. If you chose this, you have failed the exercise. Read carefully to understand why. You probably thought that by being honest, you were giving your coworker the benefit of the doubt. You're a good person, and that's a lovely way to live, on occasion, but under no circumstances should you tell your white coworkers what you actually think about a race-related matter! This leads to them sharing their own ideas, which leads to you getting upset, which leads to them wanting to talk about it even more, which leads to you getting even more upset. It's a vicious cycle, which likely ends in you storming out in the middle of a conference call, singing the Black National Anthem at the top of your lungs, and boarding the next flight to South Africa.

> *"You probably thought that by being honest, you were giving your coworker the benefit of the doubt. You're a good person . . . but under no circumstances should you tell your white coworkers what you actually think about a race-related matter!"*

Even if your honesty in this case doesn't lead you to start roommate-hunting on Craigslist Johannesburg, answering the question with your true thoughts sends a signal to your white coworkers that you're down to play this game. Before long, you'll be on the receiving end of every black-related thought in the office, no matter how tenuous the connection:

"So, I was thinking of checking out this Ethiopian restaurant on Saturday. Have you heard anything about it?"

"I think it's so tragic the way the kids at that pool were discriminated against. Can you believe some people still think that way? I mean, it's the twenty-first century!"

"How do you get your hair to do that?? It's so cute! Can I touch it?"

By being too accommodating in some aspects of the implicit Job #2, you leave no time to do the explicit Job #1 and risk your position at the company. It's much less costly to avoid saying anything that commits you to a position (Option 1) or risk mildly hurting people's feelings but protecting your sanity (Option 2).

Notes

1. At the time of this writing, I could find no business named Optimus Research Group. In the event that such a company is formed by the time you read this, I sincerely apologize for unintentionally besmirching that organization's reputation in the name of this teachable moment. Any similarities between this thought exercise—this includes names, company activities, job positions, and the number of minority employees—and the actual work environment at Optimus Research Group are purely coincidental. Also, if Optimus does have a job opening for research associate, hook a brother up!

2. No, don't call it a Blacky Sense. I regret typing that.

3. The INSH is a proprietary scale developed by scholars at the Blackness Advanced Research Projects Agency (BARPA).

Understanding the Text

1. What are the two jobs that The Black Employee is hired to do? Provide specific examples of the duties required for Job #2.

2. How does Thurston parody the conventions of business self-help and motivational books? How does he imitate and undermine this genre?

Reflection and Response

3. Do you have any familiarity with the situations that Thurston addresses? Have you been or known the only person of color in a work or school setting? Reflect on what that experience was like.

4. What did you learn about the significance of being the Black Employee? Were there any points raised that you hadn't thought about before, at least not in the way that Thurston presented them?

5. How does Thurston use comedy effectively to address the sensitive subject matter of race in America? What does comedy allow him to do that a formal criticism could not achieve? Identify at least two places in the selection where his humor makes a point in a more convincing manner than if he had argued straightforwardly.

Making Connections

6. How does Thurston's commentary on corporate behavior relate to Davidson's (p. 313)? What similarities and differences exist in their ridiculing of corporations? What other institutions could likewise be criticized?

7. Write your own satirical self-help or survival guide. You need not address such a political issue as Thurston does, but you should write with a particular audience in mind. What problems are these potential readers trying to overcome? How do you suggest they ameliorate their situation?

Stuff White People Like

Christian Lander

A self-proclaimed "asshole with a blog," Christian Lander is the creator of the web site stuffwhitepeoplelike.com, which became such an Internet phenomenon in 2008 that Random House published a book version, *Stuff White People Like: A Definitive Guide to the Unique Taste of Millions*, as well as a sequel, *Whiter Shades of Pale: The Stuff White People Like, Coast to Coast, from Seattle's Sweaters to Maine's Microbrews* (2010). Lander's Horatian satire lampoons a particular group of white people that Lander admits to being a member of himself: the affluent, left-leaning set that consumes hipster-bohemian culture. An alumnus of McGill University in Montreal, he was Indiana University's 2006 public speaking instructor of the year before dropping out of their Ph.D. program in film and media studies. He currently lives in Los Angeles with his photographer wife, Jess.

Irony

White people hate a lot of stuff (white people who vote Republican, television, Vin Diesel movies, SUVs, fast food) but every once in a while they turn that hate into sweet irony.

Often times, white people will make a joke about how hard it is to define irony. It's not that funny, and back in the 1990s people got all upset at Alanis Morrisette for using the term improperly in her song "Isn't It Ironic?"

But the reason that white people love irony is that it lets them have some fun and feel better about themselves.

The most horrific recent example is Trucker hats that shockingly went from mainstream in the eighties to ironic in the early 2000s back to mainstream, at which point they are no longer rare or unique. Once something reaches this stage, irony cannot be restored for 10 years.

Other examples would include white people getting together to have a 5 "white trash" night where they would eat Kentucky Fried Chicken, drink Bud Light, and watch Larry the Cable Guy or *The Marine*. Maybe listen to Kid Rock or P.O.D. These events allow white people to experience things they are supposed to hate, all while feeling better about their own lives, decisions, and cultured tastes. Occasionally, white people will put an ironic knick knack in their home or apartment such as a "Support our Troops" magnet or a bottle of Mickey's.

This can be used to your advantage. If you need to appear cool to white people, you just need to pick something that was popular 10+ years ago and put it in a prominent place at your desk or in your home.

*"*The reason that white people love irony is that it lets them have some fun and feel better about themselves.*"*

A C+C Music Factory Cassette, or a "2 Legit 2 Quit" T-shirt would both be acceptable examples.

Also, you might find yourself in conversation where you mention that you like something and there is an awkward silence indicating that it is not cool. In this situation, you must say, "Oh yeah, I also like [insert similar things]" and smile, the white people will laugh and all will be well.

The Ivy League

The Ivy League is expensive, exclusive, located in the Northeast, and features beautiful old buildings. All of these things are beloved by white people, so logically it would seem that they all love the Ivy League. But this is not true!

White people have a tortured relationship with the Ivy League, and if you broach the subject in the wrong way, you can offend and even anger a white person.But before getting into the more nuanced aspects of the subject, it's important to know that all white people believe they have the intelligence and work ethic required to attend an Ivy League school. The only reason they did not actually go to one is that they chose not to participate in the "dog and pony show" required to gain acceptance. White people also like to believe that they were not born into a privileged (enough) family to get legacy admission. This should always be at the back of your mind as you talk to a white person about the Ivy League.

Once you have determined that a white person did not attend an Ivy 10 League school, you should try to give them the opportunity to explain why their school was actually a superior educational experience.

Some easy ways to do this are to mention grade inflation, professors who value research over teaching, or high tuition costs. Any one of these will set a white person off on a multi-minute rant.

When they have finally run out of arguments about why they chose the right school, you should say, "I knew a whole bunch of people who went to Harvard and none of them work as hard or are as smart as you." This is a very effective technique for gaining acceptance since white people need constant reassurance that they are smart and that they made the right choice with their life.

If you actually went to an Ivy League school, you will be seen as a threat so prepare for a lot of questions from white people. They will constantly ask questions about how much work you had, the type of students at the school, the professors, your dorm room, your reading lists, and they will try so hard to figure out your SAT score. They desperately need a source of comparison so that they need to figure out if you are actually smarter than them. In fact, the only way to stop this line of questioning is to imply that you only got in because of your minority status. Once you say that, white people will stop feeling threatened since they can now believe they too would have been accepted to an Ivy League school if they were a minority. It also gives them a personal story about the effectiveness of Affirmative Action.

White people also like to call their school "The Harvard of the <insert region or conference>." Do not challenge this, it will ruin their confidence.

Self-Aware Hip Hop References

Among the wrong kind of white people, there are few more hated than 15 the *wigger* or *whitethug*. Though it is very acceptable and common for the right kind of white people to dress and act as though they were Japanese, Chinese, or European, it is completely unacceptable for them to act like rappers.

This distaste caused a dilemma for white people who had to show both that they loved hip hop but also that they were aware they were white. The brilliant solution they came up with was to appropriate hip hop words and mannerisms and filter them through a white appropriateness system.

For example, white people find it particularly hilarious to take slang and enunciate every word perfectly.

"Homey, that béarnaise sauce you made is wack. Do you know what I am saying? For real."

"Well, I used a different type of butter. I switched the style up, so let the haters hate and I'll watch the deliciousness pile up."

Since the above exchange involves people who are very aware of their 20 whiteness, it is hilarious, but if it were to be said by wiggers, it would be tragic. The difference is subtle but essential.

This is also an excellent way to make white people like you. If you can recite rap lyrics with perfect enunciation, they will always find it funny. As a rule of thumb, the more popular the rapper, the funnier it gets. Best options: 50 Cent, Tupac, Biggie Smalls, or Jay Z. Note: avoid Kanye West as the irony of reciting his lyrics with perfect English is not as great.

In terms of physical actions, there are few things white people enjoy more than throwing up fake gang signs in photos. Again, the same rules apply: if it is done by wiggers, it is tragic; if it's done by the right kind of white people, it's hilarious. It's not a good idea to mention how these signs have often resulted in awful, senseless deaths—that will ruin the joke.

In both cases, the actions are done in hopes that a white person will be recognized as "one of the good ones," who love hip hop, but don't try to appropriate it in any nonhilarious ways.

In both cases, your best response is to say, "Did you go to the last Dead Prez/Roots/Mos Def/Twaleb Kwali/Michael Franti concert? It was incredible. I smoked weed and kept this one finger up for almost an hour!"

Though this information has very little use in and of itself, it could be 25 the final piece in the puzzle of cementing your white friendship. At the very least, it is a guaranteed way to help your progress.

Unpaid Internships

In most of the world when a person works long hours without pay, it is referred to as "slavery" or "forced labor." For white people this process is referred to as an internship and is considered an essential stage in white development.

The concept of working for little or no money underneath a superior has been around for centuries in the form of apprenticeship programs. Young people eager to learn a trade would spend time working under a master craftsman to learn a skill that would eventually lead to an increase in material wealth.

Using this logic you would assume that the most sought after internships would be in areas that lead to the greatest financial reward. Young White people, however, prefer internships that put them on the path for careers that will generally result in a DECREASE of the material wealth accumulated by their parents.

For example, if you were to present a white 19-year-old with the choice of spending the summer earning $15 an hour as a plumber's apprentice or making $0 answering phones at Production Company, they will always choose the latter. In fact, the only way to get the white person to choose the plumbing option would be to convince them that it was leading toward an end-of-summer pipe art installation.

White people view the internship as their foot into the door to such 30 high-profile low-paying career fields as journalism, film, politics, art, nonprofits, and anything associated with a museum. Any white person who takes an internship outside of these industries is either the wrong type of white person or a law student. There are no exceptions.

If all goes according to plan, an internship will end with an offer of a job that pays $24,000 per year and will consist entirely of the same tasks they were recently doing for free. In fact, the transition to full-time status results in the addition of only one new responsibility: feeling superior to the new interns.

When all is said and done, the internship process serves the white community in many ways. First, it helps to train the next generation of freelance writers, museum curators, and director's assistants. But more importantly, internships teach white children how to complain about being poor.

So when a white person tells you about their unpaid internship at the *New Yorker*, it's not a good idea to point out how the cost of rent and food will essentially mean that they are PAYING their employer for the right to make photocopies. Instead it's best to say: "You earned it." They will not get the joke.

Vintage

The love affair between white people and old stuff literally goes back for hundreds of years. In the older days, it was almost exclusively contained within the realm of furniture. While white people still love antiques, they don't always fit so well with a modern lifestyle and kitchen.

Beginning in their late teens, white people begin an obsession with 35 finding cool vintage clothing at local thrift shops and Goodwills. Making purchases at these locations address[es] a number of white person needs.

First, it allows them to say, "Oh, this? I got this shirt at Goodwill for $3." This statement focuses the attention on the shirt, taking attention away from the $350 jeans and $200 shoes. The white person can then retain that precious "indie" cred.

Secondly, it allows a white person to have something that other white people don't. This is an important consideration when trying to determine the worth and ranking of white people.

As white people get older, and the opportunities to wear a "Pittsburgh Special Olympics '76" T-shirt diminish, they must move their vintage fetish from clothes to furniture and knick knacks. For a post-thirty white person, the mention of a "vintage stove" or "vintage card catalog" can send their imaginations racing about how to incorporate it into their current home decor.

By having at least one vintage, unique piece of furniture in a room full of IKEA, white people can still tell themselves that they are unique and cooler than their friends.

When you enter a white person's home, you should immediately 40
search for anything not made by IKEA, Crate and Barrel, or Athropologie.
Upon finding such an item, you should ask, "Where did you get that? It's
really cool." The white person will then tell you a story about how they
acquired it, allowing them to feel cool and giving them a reminder about
their fantastic taste.

Understanding the Text

1. Why is *irony* a favorite thing among white people? Cite examples from more than one blog entry to support your answer.
2. What sorts of contradictory beliefs and actions does Lander unearth about white people? Reference the "Self-Aware Hip Hop References" and "Unpaid Internships" in your answer.
3. In what ways is *Stuff White People Like* about social class as much as race? Reference the entries for "Vintage" and "The Ivy League" in your answer.

Reflection and Response

4. Which piece of "stuff" from these five entries do you like most? Do you like it for the reasons that Lander mentions, or do you have other justifications for your enjoyment? Explain.
5. When Lander's web site gained fame in 2008, it drew controversy. While some people heralded the site for making fun of a new generation of yuppies, others argued that it traded in offensive stereotypes. Now that you have read a sampling of the blog entries, what is your opinion of Lander's humor? Do you find the humor offensive? If you do, to whom and to what degree is it offensive? If you find the humor inoffensive, what effect do you believe it intends to have on its readers?

Making Connections

6. How does Lander's treatment of race relate to Thurston's (p. 320)? What similarities and differences exist in their racial satire?
7. Lander's bohemian yuppies have been skewered by others, such as Fred Armisen and Carrie Brownstein's sketch comedy TV show *Portlandia* and David Brooks's oxymoronic concept of the *bobo* (bourgeois bohemian). Write a research essay that examines the humor surrounding white, wealthy liberals. Alternatively, write a research essay that examines the humor about another stereotypical subculture of white people.
8. Lander's web site has spawned several imitators. Write a handful of entries for your own imitation piece titled "Stuff ____ People ____" in which you fill in the blanks.

Acknowledgments (continued from page iv)

Franklin Ajaye. "First Steps to Becoming a Stand-Up Comedian" (pp. 3–9) and "Structuring Your Funny (Writing Your Material)" (pp. 22–29) from *Comic Insights: The Art of Stand-up Comedy*. Copyright © 2002 by Franklin Ajaye. Reprinted by permission of Silman-James Press.

Steve Almond. "The Joke's on You" by Steve Almond from *The Baffler* (No. 20, 2012). Copyright © 2012 by Steve Almond. Reprinted by permission of the author.

Chris Bachelder. "The Dead Chipmunk" from *The Believer*, February 2011. Copyright © 2011 by Chris Bachelder. Reprinted by permission of the author.

Matt Buchanan. "Why Twitter Parody Accounts Should Stay Anonymous" from *The New Yorker*, July 22, 2013. Copyright © 2013 by Matt Buchanan. Reprinted by permission of the author.

Simon Critchley. "Foreigners Are Funny–the Ethicity and Ethnicity of Humour" from *On Humour*. Copyright © 2002 by Simon Critchley. Reproduced by permission of Taylor & Francis Books UK.

Ian Crouch. "Is Social Media Ruining Comedy?" by Ian Crouch from *The New Yorker*, December 30, 2014. Copyright © 2014 by Condé Nast. All rights reserved. Reprinted by permission.

Paul Davidson. "Starbucks," "Proctor and Gamble," and "FedEx" from *Consumer Joe: Harassing Corporate America, One Letter at a Time* by Paul Davidson. Copyright © 2003 by Paul Davidson. Reprinted by permission.

Amber Day. "Moving Beyond Critique" from *Satire and Dissent*. Copyright © 2011 by Amber Day. Reprinted with permission of Indiana University Press.

Julia Drake. "The Boy from *Jurassic Park*'s College Application Essay" by Julia Drake from *McSweeney's*, originally published November 12, 2014. Copyright © 2014 by Julia Drake. Reprinted by permission of the author.

Caitlin Flanagan. "That's Not Funny!" from *The Atlantic Magazine*, September 2015 issue. Copyright © 2015 by The Atlantic Media Co. as first published in The Atlantic Magazine. All rights reserved. Distributed by Tribune Content Agency, LLC.

Signund Freud. "Humor" by Sigmund Freud. Reprinted by permission from *The Philosophy of Laughter and Humor*, edited by John Morreall, the State University of New York Press © 1986, State University of New York. All rights reserved.

Conor Friedersdorf. "A Modest Proposal: Don't Worry About Government Surveillance At All, Ever" from *The Atlantic Magazine*, July 5, 2013. Copyright © 2013 by The Atlantic Media Co. as first published in The Atlantic Magazine. All rights reserved. Distributed by Tribune Content Agency, LLC.

Daniel Harris. "How Many Light-Bulb Jokes Does It Take to Chart an Era?" from *The New York Times Magazine*, March 23, 1997. Copyright © 1997 by Daniel Harris. Reprinted by permission of the author.

Daniel J. Kenny. "How John Oliver Usurped a Genre" originally written by Daniel J. Kenny from *Harvard Political Review*, October 31, 2014. Copyright © 2014 by Harvard Political Review. Reprinted by permission of Harvard Political Review.

Michael Kimmel. "Ritualized Homosexuality in Nacirema Subculture" from *Sexualities*, February 2006, Vol. 9, No. 1. Copyright © 2006 by Michael Kimmel. Reprinted by permission of the author.

Jeffery Klassen. "He Looked Into the Grim Reaper's Eyes and Nervously Laughed–Bergsonian Comedy Theory, *Office Space*, and the Fear of Losing Reality" from *Offscreen*, December 2012, Vol. 16, Issue 11–12. Copyright © 2012 by Jeffery Klassen. Reprinted by permission of the author.

Elizabeth Kolbert. "Stooping to Conquer: Why Candidates Need to Make Fun of Themselves" from *The New Yorker*, April 19, 2004. Copyright © 2004 by Elizabeth Kolbert. Reprinted by permission of the author.

Index of Authors and Titles